Jesus Christ Our Lord

Jesus Christ Our Lord

By John F. Walvoord

MOODY PRESS

CHICAGO

Library of Congress Catalog Card Number: 70-80941

ISBN: 0-8024-4325-7 (cloth edition)
ISBN: 0-8024-4326-5 (paper edition)

23 24 25 26 27 28 Printing/LC/Year 95 94 93 92 91

Printed in the United States of America

CONTENTS

CHAPTER   PAGE

Preface   7

1. Christ in Contemporary Theology   11

2. Christ in Eternity Past   22

3. Christ in Old Testament History   36

4. Christ in Old Testament Typology   62

5. Christ in Old Testament Prophecy   79

6. The Incarnation of the Son of God   96

7. The Person of the Incarnate Christ   106

8. The Life of Christ on Earth   123

9. Christ in His Suffering and Death   153

10. Christ in His Resurrection   191

11. The Present Work of Christ   219

12. The Future Work of Christ   258

Bibliography   291

Subject Index   298

Selective Scripture Index   305

PREFACE

EIGHT HUNDRED YEARS AGO Bernard of Clairvaux penned the beautiful hymn:

> Jesus, the very thought of Thee
> With sweetness fills my breast;
> But sweeter far Thy face to see,
> And in Thy presence rest.

Ever since the holy Babe was laid in the manger in Bethlehem of Judea, devout souls have found in Jesus Christ One who is the worthy object of their worship, whose ineffable person compels their love and obedience. As the Word of God expressed in human form, Jesus Christ has drawn all believing souls to Himself. Although no other person is the object of more scriptural revelation, human pens falter when attempting to describe Him.

The poet, biographer, theologian and orator alike confess their inability to delineate the glories and perfections of our blessed Saviour. Charles Wesley expressed the aspiration of those conscious of their limitations when he composed this great hymn:

> O for a thousand tongues to sing
> My great Redeemer's praise,
> The glories of my God and King,
> The triumphs of His grace.

Lewis Sperry Chafer in introducing his *Christology* expressed this same sense of inadequacy when he wrote,

> In attempting to write of His adorable Person and His incomprehensible achievements—which achievements when completed will have perfected redemption, exercised to infinite satisfaction the divine attribute of grace, manifested the invisible God to His creatures, and subdued a rebellious universe in which sin had been permitted to demonstrate its exceeding sinfulness—the limitations of a finite mind which is weakened by a faulty perception are all too apparent.[1]

[1]Lewis S. Chafer, *Systematic Theology*, V, 3.

7

The impossible task of circumscribing the glories of our Lord and Saviour Jesus Christ stems from the infinity of His person and the omnipotence and omniscience of all His works. From Genesis to Revelation Jesus Christ is the most important theme of the Bible and almost every page is related in some way to either His person or work. Christianity is Jesus Christ. No other subject is given more complete revelation and yet the half has not been told. No other theme is more intimately related to the creation of the natural world. For "all things were made by him; and without him was not any thing made that was made" (John 1:3). The glories of the natural world therefore declare the power and Godhead of Jesus Christ as the Son of God.

No other person is given more biographical attention than Jesus Christ, whose life is portrayed in the four Gospels with supplementary theological revelation in other books of the Bible. The four portraits afforded in the four Gospels give depth and perspective to the incomparable One who lived among men. Yet it is still true, as John states, "that even the world itself could not contain the books that should be written" (John 21:25) concerning what He said and did.

The story of redemption, anticipated in the protevangelium of Genesis 3:15, is foreshadowed in every sacrifice of the Old Testament as well as detailed in anticipatory prophecy. It had its supreme revelation in those dark hours when Jesus Christ hung upon a cross on Calvary. No other man lived as Christ lived and no other man died as Christ died. Here supremely revealed was the love and righteousness of God and His redemptive purpose for man. The power of His resurrection added a new dimension to the omnipotence of God, and His ascension in glory was prophetic of His ultimate subjugation of the universe, when every knee would bow and every tongue confess that Jesus Christ is Lord.

The riches of divine revelation embodied in Jesus Christ are as measureless as the ocean and His perfections as numberless as the stars. To attempt to state in complete theological form all that should be said about Jesus Christ leaves the writer with a sense of futility. He has dipped but a cup from the ocean of infinite glory and perfections of his Lord and Saviour.

With the confession of inadequacy, however, comes the practical necessity of setting forth in systematic form, insofar as words can do, the many truths relating to the person and work of Christ. Upon this systematization the whole structure of Christian preaching and teaching must be erected, and by this means the individual faith and devotion of a believer in Christ can be immeasurably enriched by enlarging as far as possible his understanding of the scriptural revelation concerning his Saviour.

The theological presentation of the person and work of Christ must necessarily be in the form of an extended outline. Any division of Christology is capable of almost indefinite extension whether viewed biblically, historically or philosophically. In the main, the present study is concentrated on the question What saith the Scripture? with attention to the writings of men only as they cast light upon particular subjects. A student of Christology needs to be constantly reminded that while there is progress in doctrine, there is no increase in scriptural revelation. In the last analysis contemporary Christology has in many respects confused rather than clarified the extended revelation of the Word of God. It is, therefore, more important to discover what Paul or John says about Jesus Christ than to follow the latest learned theological pronouncement. When the Word of God has spoken clearly and plainly, the unbelief of men, the reasonings of the natural mind and the wisdom of the world can be safely disregarded.

The author desires to express sincere appreciation to those who have helped in the production of this work. In particular, he is indebted to Dr. S. Lewis Johnson, Jr., Professor of New Testament Literature and Exegesis at Dallas Theological Seminary, for his critical reading of the manuscript, and Dr. John A. Witmer, Librarian of Mosher Library, Dallas Seminary, for his bibliographical and other suggestions. The editors of Moody Press have also been most cooperative. Acknowledgment is made to publishers of works that have been quoted.

In attempting to set forth the biblical revelation concerning Jesus Christ the author has sought to glorify his Saviour by providing enrichment of the life and faith of all who read. With Edward Perronet he would say,

> All hail the power of Jesus' name!
> Let angels prostrate fall;
> Bring forth the royal diadem,
> And crown Him Lord of all.

1

CHRIST IN CONTEMPORARY THEOLOGY

CHRISTIANITY by its very name has always honored Jesus Christ as its historical and theological center. No other person has been more essential to its origination and subsequent history and no set of doctrines has been more determinative than the doctrines of the person and work of Christ. In approaching a study of Christology, one is therefore concerned with central rather than peripheral theological matters. One's faith in and understanding of Jesus Christ involve the most important theological issues anyone can face.

DOCTRINE OF THE TRINITY

In the history of theological thought concerning Christ until modern times there was always a solid core of doctrine which can be equated with biblical orthodoxy. The early church Fathers, struggling with the obvious problem of the doctrine of the Trinity and how could God be Three and yet One, stated in enduring terms that while God is One numerically, He subsists in three Persons, God the Father, God the Son and God the Holy Spirit who are equal in eternity, power and glory, Each possessing all the divine attributes and yet having properties which distinguish Them within the unity of the Trinity. A milestone in the statement of this important doctrine of the Trinity was reached in the Nicene Council in 325 and was matured and restated by the Protestant Reformers.

ORTHODOX DOCTRINE OF THE PERSON AND WORK OF CHRIST

Following the delineation of the doctrine of the Trinity, the subject of the person of Christ incarnate also received major at-

11

tention in the early church. Discussions concerning the relationship of the human and divine natures finally achieved a standard of orthodoxy when the person of Christ was defined as having a complete human nature and a complete divine nature united in one Person without moral complication (e.g., in the Chalcedonian Creed, 451). Although Calvinistic and Lutheran definitions of the human nature of Christ differ in some details in their doctrine of the person of Christ, a well-defined pattern emerged which can be described as orthodox.

Discussions of the person of Christ inevitably led to study of His work, especially His work in death on the cross. Here again, though definitions varied, the objective fact that Christ died for our sins and by this act of redemption achieved reconciliation of man to God forms the mainstream of orthodox conviction. Generally speaking, within orthodoxy the bodily resurrection of Christ and His bodily second coming to the earth have not been questioned.

EARLY DISSENT FROM ORTHODOXY

From the early days of the church, however, some have dissented from what might be described as the main thrust of orthodoxy. During the third century, the Alexandrian School of Theology with its attempted harmonization of Plato and Christianity tended to regard all Scripture as a revelation in symbolic or allegorical rather than literal and historical terms. An important fourth century event was the challenge by Arius to the eternity of Christ which ended in his condemnation at the Council of Nicaea. The allegorical approach to biblical revelation, which characterized the Alexandrian school, had its counterpart in the later philosophy of Hegel who regarded the biblical record as presenting concepts which belong to the Christian faith in symbolic terms. In various forms this point of view has persisted to the present day and has influenced many diverse systems of theology both conservative and liberal.

RISE OF MODERN LIBERALISM

Another major movement in the history of the doctrine of Christ can be observed in the introduction by Ritschl and Schleiermacher of the concept that the language of Scripture should be studied for its spiritual intent, namely, the ethical and theological implications rather than the explicit statements of the Bible.[1] This led to contemporary liberalism of the twentieth century which assumes that the Bible cannot be taken seriously in its historical or factual content, but considers Scripture only a means of gaining spiritual insights. Obviously this point of view often resulted in the rejection of the full deity of Christ, the doctrine of the Trinity, and substitutionary atonement as well as questions concerning the bodily resurrection of Christ and His bodily second coming.

The conflict between orthodoxy and modern liberalism had many causes. John S. Lawton traces it first to a shift from a priori to a posteriori method, that is, a change of acquiring and interpreting knowledge from consideration of principles to formulating knowledge by an induction based upon all the facts which could be obtained, an approach in keeping with the modern emphasis on science. A second major factor was the rise of evolution as a means of explaining complex modern life with an emphasis on God's being in the natural process. Hence God is knowable by experience in a way that a transcendent God could never be understood. This in turn laid the groundwork for the third major factor, the so-called historical approach to the Scriptures, and a naturalistic explanation of life as a whole. These approaches undermined the whole superstructure of orthodoxy including traditional approaches to Christology. An attempt to explain God and His world inductively and by a process of natural evolution left no real basis for worship of a supernatural Deity, and this opened the way for the reaction to liberalism which has been called neoorthodoxy.[2]

RISE OF NEOORTHODOXY

The religious insights of liberalism were so anemic and subjective that they did not provide a living faith for people and nations in crisis. Out of World War I came the new movement known as neoorthodoxy sparked by Karl Barth's *The Epistle to the Romans* which challenged the naturalism of liberalism and

---

[1]Albrecht Ritschl, for instance, refers to orthodox interpretation depending on "its mechanical use of Bible authority for its theological system" and agrees with Schleiermacher in regarding terms like "prophet, priest, and king" in reference to Christ as *"metaphorical expressions"* and as "typical notions" (cf. *A Critical History of the Christian Doctrine of Justification and Reconciliation,* pp. 3-4).

[2]Cf. John S. Lawton, *Conflict in Christology,* pp. 1-23.

its doctrine that God is immanent or in the world, but not transcendent or greater than the world. Barthianism restored revelation to a supernatural communication of the infinite God to finite man, communication in which Jesus Christ is the principal medium.

Although Barth tended to reestablish Jesus Christ as the virginborn Son of Mary who was in fact God and Man at the same time, his failure to be clear on the role of history in revelation and his tendency to regard real communication as suprahistorical has tended to make the main facts concerning Christ experiential. Hence, the Christ of the Scriptures is to some extent supplanted by the Christ of experience, and the resulting doctrines become subjective in contemporary theology rather than historical and revelatory in absolute terms in the Scripture.

Karl Barth is sometimes charged with Christomonism, the reduction of all theology to Christology.[3] Although the charge is only partially true, Barth has emphasized the incarnation as the major act of God's self-revelation to man. The major question of theology is how to understand God's communication in the incarnation of Christ. It is through the incarnation that God speaks to man and reconciles man to Himself.

Introducing the subject of "Jesus Christ" in his *Dogmatics in Outline*, Barth writes,

> The heart of the object of Christian faith is the word of the act in which God from all eternity willed to become man in Jesus Christ for our good, did become man in time for our good, and will be and remain man in eternity for our good. This work of the Son of God includes in itself the work of the Father as its presupposition and the work of the Holy Spirit as its consequence.[4]

A discussion of Barthian Christology is a major field of contemporary theology. While agreeing with most orthodox doctrines relating to Christ as illustrated in his treatment of the Apostles' Creed in *Dogmatics in Outline*, Barth's approach is more philosophic and experiential in that the Bible is considered a channel of experiencing Christ theologically, but Barth does not hold with orthodoxy that the Bible is factual revelation. He is, however, closer to orthodoxy than most in the neoorthodox

---

[3]Cf. Arnold B. Come, *An Introduction to Barth's "Dogmatics" for Preachers*, pp. 133 ff.
[4]Karl Barth, *Dogmatics in Outline*, p. 65.

school, and unquestionably believes in the deity of Jesus Christ, His virgin birth, and His death and resurrection, in contrast to Reinhold Niebuhr, who seems to question all of these important doctrines.[5] All theologians classified as neoorthodox tend to emphasize contemporary experience rather than historic revelation as embodied in Scripture. The work of Emil Brunner *Revelation and Reason* is a classic expression of the neoorthodox concept of revelation.

RISE OF BULTMANNISM

The swing to a more supernatural God with its resulting effect upon the subject of the person and work of Christ in the period following World War II was followed by a movement back to a more liberal concept crystallized in the writings of Rudolf Bultmann. Seeking to establish the viewpoint of the early church, Bultmann adopted the approach of demythologizing Scripture and with it *Formgeschichte* as the main means of determining the real meaning of the New Testament and the viewpoint of the early church. Bultmann holds that "the so-called social gospel" as well as "eschatological preaching"—the idea that the kingdom of God is wholly future—are both unsatisfactory.[6] He prefers *"de-mythologizing,"* an attempt to get behind "the mythological conceptions" of Scriptures to their "deeper meaning."[7] In his attempt to eliminate the supernatural and arrive at a nonmiraculous interpretation of the New Testament, Bultmann tended to dilute the facts concerning the historical Jesus in the Bible with emphasis on what he believed the early church held rather than what the Bible itself actually teaches.

Bultmann's concept of demythologization is based on a technical definition of a myth, not as a fantasy, or a mere fiction, but the sense in which it is used in comparative religion where it is a statement of man's experience. Jesus, according to Bultmann, spoke in the terms of His day, and thus taught that He had descended from heaven, that He was contending against Satan, and used the concept of a three-story universe, that is, the heavens above, the earth, and that which is below the earth. This was coupled with reference to miracles and other supernatural events.

[5]Cf. Hans Hofmann, *The Theology of Reinhold Niebuhr,* or any of Niebuhr's many works.
[6]Cf. Rudolf K. Bultmann, *Jesus Christ and Mythology,* pp. 11-18.
[7]*Ibid.,* p. 18.

According to Bultmann, all these are ideas clothed in language which now must be stripped of its superficialities and invested with the true intent of the teaching. We must get away from the pictures to the event itself.

The return to the historical Jesus is complicated by the fact that Bultmann considers the Gospels merely a record of what the early church believed Jesus thought and did. Actually, according to Bultmann, all the facts presented in the Bible were filtered through the mind and faith of the church, and probably Jesus did not do the things and say the things which the Scripture ascribes to Him. The process of demythologizing is to get back to the experience of the early church which prompted scriptural accounts. Their experiential encounter with Christ is the *kerygma,* or the message which must be repeated today, even though the precise details of the Bible may be uncertain.

Bultmann opens his treatment of *Theology of the New Testament* with the statement

> The message of Jesus is a presupposition for the theology of the New Testament rather than a part of that theology itself. . . . But Christian faith did not exist until there was a Christian kerygma; i.e., a kerygma proclaiming Jesus Christ— specifically Jesus Christ the Crucified and Risen One—to be God's eschatological act of salvation. He was first so proclaimed in the kerygma of the earliest Church, not in the message of the historical Jesus. . . . Thus, theological thinking— the theology of the New Testament—begins with the *kerygma* of the earliest Church and not before.[8]

Bultmann, however, acknowledges that Paul's theology shows frequent use of primitive Christian tradition. Vincent Taylor, for instance, cites numerous passages in Bultmann's *Theology of the New Testament* where Paul is said to rely upon earlier traditions of the church.[9] Significantly, Bultmann by this confession relates Paul more intimately with the early church than would otherwise be the case.[10]

[8]Bultmann, *Theology of the New Testament,* I, 3. For a summary of Bultmann, cf. John Lawson, *Comprehensive Handbook of Christian Doctrine,* pp. 35-38.
[9]Vincent Taylor, *The Person of Christ,* p. 36. Taylor cites Bultmann, *Theology of . . .,* I, 46-47, 50-52, 81, 98, 125, 129, 131-32.
[10]For a broad discussion of influences leading from Schleiermacher to Bultmann and the contemporary revolt against Bultmann, see Carl E. Braaten, *History and Hermeneutics,* pp. 130-59.

CONTEMPORARY CONFUSION

When Bultmann was overtaken by age and infirmity, his disciples tended to return to the search for the so-called historical Jesus with the implication that the Bible is not an accurate presentation of the actual Jesus of history. All varieties of divergent opinion can be observed from the relatively conservative point of view of Oscar Cullmann, who considers as fact that Jesus regarded Himself as the Messiah, to the more radical disciples of Bultmann such as Herbert Braun and Manfred Mezger, who have reduced revelation almost entirely to personal communication between God and man with corresponding neglect of Scripture.[11] At the beginning of the final third of the twentieth century, the pendulum seems to be swinging back again to a position more friendly to Barth, but still far from historical orthodoxy.

EMERGING FACTORS IN CONTEMPORARY CHRISTOLOGY

In surveying contemporary Christology, certain major factors emerge. First and probably most important is the fact that any Christological system can be no better than the view of Scripture on which it rests. Orthodoxy historically has assumed the accuracy, authority and the inerrancy of the Scripture record. Hence, the search for the historical Jesus as well as the theological facts concerning Him are determined under this point of view by what the Scriptures actually teach. It is significant that aside from a few cults, whose teachings are quite contradictory, students of Christology who have accepted the Bible as the inerrant and authoritative Word of God have invariably also accepted the deity of Jesus Christ and the historical accuracy of His virgin birth, sinless life, substitutionary death and bodily resurrection. Variations on these major aspects of Christology almost always stem from a denial in some form of the accuracy and authority of the Scriptures.

A second major fact in Christology has been the hermeneutics or principles of interpretation of Scripture. Those who, like the ancient school of theology at Alexandria, deny that the Bible is normally to be considered in its grammatical and historical sense and who substitute a symbolic interpretation, have also tended to question the major facts concerning Jesus Christ. If the Bible is

[11]Cf. Carl F. H. Henry (ed.), *Jesus of Nazareth: Saviour and Lord,* p. 7.

not to be taken literally, then the virgin birth, the miracles of Christ, His death on the cross and His resurrection as well as the theological explanation of these historical facts are all left in question. The search for a true Christology which is not linked to the authoritative Scriptures is therefore endless and almost fruitless.

Modern confusion and the multiplied divergent views concerning Christ which have arisen in the twentieth century are the product of this uncertainty as to whether the Bible speaks authoritatively and in factual terms. The pendulum will, therefore, continue to swing erratically between those who take the Bible more seriously than others such as Barth and those who attempt to rewrite the Scriptures completely as does Bultmann. The fact that these theoretical interpretations have their rise and fall often within the same generation is a testimony to their lack of objective connection with the Bible and with any norm of truth which endures the scrutiny of succeeding generations.

MAJOR TRENDS IN CONTEMPORARY CHRISTOLOGY

Unquestionably, the modern world does not accept the orthodox definition of the person and work of Christ. As John Baillie wrote in the context of liberalism following World War I, "In most of our communities there is to be found a surprisingly large number of men and women who are prevented from a wholehearted sympathy with the Christian teaching and a whole-hearted participation in the life of the Christian Church by the necessity of making some kind of reservation."[12] He goes on to state that the modern mind has no problem with the doctrine of God the Father, and its human need can be met by divine love and acceptance of many Christian ideals. But he states, "The doctrines of the Trinity and the Incarnation and the Atonement have never been anything else to them than a stone of stumbling and a rock of offence."[13] The attitude of a friendly interest in Jesus Christ, but an unwillingness to accept the theological statements of the Bible concerning Him as a Member of the Trinity, as virgin-born and incarnate, and His death as a real redemption from sin, continues to grip a major section of the church today.

[12]John Baillie, *The Place of Jesus Christ in Modern Christianity*, p. 1.
[13]*Ibid.*, pp. 1-2.

Baillie goes on to restate in simplest form basic Christian doctrine almost totally rejected by the modern mind.[14]

Carl Henry has summarized the major trends of the past century in these words:

> The rationalistic liberalism of Schleiermacher, Ritschl, and Troeltsch was the dominant religious force in the forepart of our century. Classic modernism, a theology of intensified divine immanence, so neglected God's transcendence in relationship to man and His universe that it left no room for miracle, special revelation, or special redemption. The Christian religion was viewed as a variety of religion in general—even if it had certain unique features, and could in some respects be viewed as "higher" than the others. Compatible with this basic outlook, Christian religious experience was viewed as a variety of universal religious experience. Against this speculative immanentism, Karl Barth reasserted God's transcendence and special divine initiative, His wrath against man as sinner, and the reality of miraculous revelation and miraculous redemption. So contagious was this "theology of crisis" that by 1930 most German theologians conceded the death of rationalistic modernism, or classic liberalism, which Barth had deplored as heresy. They proclaimed the triumph of dialectical theology over immanental philosophy.[15]

Although Bultmann overtook Barth in many areas and to some extent supplanted him, his supposed victory is now seen to be transitory and fading. As Henry says,

> The central problem of New Testament studies today is to delineate Jesus of Nazareth without dissolving Him as the Bultmannians did, without demeaning Him as many dialectical theologians did, and without reconstructing Him as nineteenth-century historicism did, so that it becomes clear why and how He is decisive for Christian faith.[16]

The revolt against Bultmann is described by Henry as the *Heilsgeschichte* school, with more emphasis on the historical and factual character of the Bible than was allowed by Bultmann. Henry summarizes it,

> The *Heilsgeschichte* school reflects important points of agreement with evangelical positions. First, divine revelation and redemption are acknowledged as objective historical realities. Second, the sacred events are considered as know-

[14]*Ibid.*, pp. 5-10.
[15]Henry, p. 4.
[16]*Ibid.*, p. 16.

able to historians by the methods of historical research. Third, the Old Testament is interpreted as the history of God which was fulfilled in Jesus Christ, and the New Testament is interpreted as the fulfillment of the Old Testament. Fourth, the meaning of these events is held to be divinely given, not humanly postulated.[17]

Henry may be overly optimistic in considering this a partial return to an evangelical position, but the rising and falling of opinions concerning Christ in the Scriptures illustrates the dilemma of the modern mind attempting to avoid commitment to the factual accuracy of divinely inspired and authoritative Scripture and at the same time trying to achieve normative truth concerning Christ and the Christian faith in general.

PRINCIPLES GOVERNING A BIBLICAL CHRISTOLOGY

In the study of the person and work of Christ, the theological and hermeneutical principles assumed will dictate to some extent the resulting interpretation. A student of Christology must necessarily decide in preliminary study such important questions as to whether the Bible is an infallible and authoritative revelation concerning the facts of Jesus Christ. Historically, the view of Scripture assumed by any interpreter is almost determinative, and those who assume the infallibility and verbal inerrancy of the Bible, generally speaking, support the orthodox view of Christ.

Important in basic principle is the dictum that the Bible is factual and propositional in its presentation of truth. Neoorthodox theologians such as Barth, Brunner and Niebuhr regard Scripture as a channel of revelation rather than an objective factual record and, while attributing some authority to Scripture, do not regard it as inerrant or infallible. Bultmann and his school of thought regard Scripture as a much edited and amended record of first century teaching which cannot be taken at face value. Liberal theologians in general deny an authoritative character to the Bible and, to varying degrees, question both the facts and presentation of Scripture as truth. Obviously a Christology can be no better than the scriptural premises upon which it stands.

Within orthodoxy there are a number of problems of interpretation. The four Gospels presenting four different treatments of

[17]*Ibid.*

the life, death and resurrection of Christ are an area of specialized study. Generally orthodox scholars adopt the principle that theological and factual harmonization of these accounts can be achieved, although solutions to some problems are obscure. Although the four Gospels present four different portraits of Christ, orthodoxy assumes that the variations do not constitute contradictions, but rather different pictures of the same Person.

Any system of Christological interpretation must also rely not only on the gospel narratives but on the interpretation of facts about Christ given in Acts and the Epistles as well as the book of Revelation.

The task of the Christology student is to take the facts presented in Scripture and organize them into theological statement. Contemporary theology has erred because of premises which do not recognize the accuracy of scriptural revelation, unwillingness to take as factual scriptural pronouncements concerning the person and work of Jesus Christ, and emphasis upon experiential contemporary revelation rather than the Scriptures. The Christ of contemporary experience provides no norms, and a variety of Christological concepts resulting from this approach characterizes modern Christology. The biblical approach, while accounting for all genuine spiritual experience, relies upon the historic and theological record of Scriptures, and upon this a biblical Christology must be built.

2

CHRIST IN ETERNITY PAST

ONE OF THE MOST CRUCIAL PROBLEMS in approaching the study of the person and work of Christ is the question of His existence from all eternity past as the second Person of the Trinity. It was this issue which aroused the immediate antagonism of the Jews when Christ said, "Before Abraham was, I am" (John 8:58). His listeners immediately understood that Christ was claiming to be eternal and thereby was asserting Himself to be God. As Stauffer points out, this "I am" is the climax of a series of affirmations in John 8 beginning with "I am the light of the world" (John 8:12).[1] The Jews accordingly took up stones to stone Him, which was the prescribed penalty for blasphemy.

In the history of the church this controversy came to a head at Nicaea in A.D. 325 when the Arian heresy, which taught that Christ was the first of created spirits but not eternal, was denounced, and the eternity of the Son of God was plainly stated. In much of the religious literature of the twentieth century, while terms like "deity" and the "Son of God" are recognized as belonging to Christ, there is often lacking the solid note that He is eternal. The study of Christ in eternity past becomes therefore the key to understanding the total scriptural revelation, and the definition of His person in eternity past is for all practical purposes a statement and proof of His eternal deity.

ETERNITY OF THE SON OF GOD

The doctrine of the eternity of the Son of God is the most important doctrine of Christology as a whole because if Christ is not eternal then He is a creature who came into existence in time and lacks the quality of eternity and infinity which characterizes God Himself. If on the other hand it is held that Christ is eternal, it is immediately affirmed that He is not dependent upon another

[1]Ethelbert Stauffer, *Jesus and His Story*, pp. 91-92.

for His existence, but is in fact self-existent. To say that Christ is eternal is to affirm more than to say that He is preexistent. Arius, for instance, believed in the preexistence of Christ but, because he held that Christ was the first of created spirits, he did not believe that Christ was eternal. If Christ is eternal, of course He is also preexistent, that is, existed before His birth in Bethlehem. The arguments for His eternity and for His deity are therefore inseparable.

In general, those who accept the scriptural testimony as inerrant find ample evidence to support the conclusion that Christ is not only eternal but that He possesses all the attributes of God. The works of Christ, His titles, His majesty, and promises that are related to Him are all those of God Himself. His appearances in the Old Testament referred to as theophanies also provide historical evidence of His existence in the Old Testament period prior to His birth in Bethlehem.

The Old Testament evidence for the eternity of Christ is both direct and indirect. In Messianic prophecy Christ is spoken of as the Child to be born in Bethlehem "whose goings forth have been from of old, from everlasting" (Micah 5:2). This is one of many passages which state in effect His eternity. As A. R. Fausset has said, "The terms convey the strongest assertion of infinite duration of which the Hebrew language is capable (cf. Ps. 90:2; Prov. 8:22, 23; John 1:1)."[2]

Keil in a long discussion defends the concept of the eternity and deity of the promised Child. He states,

> The announcement of the origin of this Ruler as being before all worlds unquestionably presupposes His divine nature; but this thought was not strange to the prophetic mind in Micah's time, but is expressed without ambiguity by Isaiah, when he gives the Messiah the name of "the mighty God."[3]

Even those who do not affirm biblical inerrancy, but who accept the general reliability of the Scriptures, find ample evidence to support the doctrine of the eternity of Christ. Scholars such as Westcott and Lightfoot, and more modern scholars such as J. S. Stewart, A. M. Hunter and D. M. Baillie, would fall into this classification. Baillie, for instance, cites Barth with approval as

[2]Robert Jamieson, A. R. Fausset and David Brown, *A Commentary, Critical, Experimental and Practical on the Old and New Testaments*, IV, 600.
[3]C. F. Keil and Franz Delitzsch, *Biblical Commentary on the Old Testament: The Twelve Minor Prophets*, I, 480-81.

affirming the eternity of the Trinity which involves eternity of Christ.[4]

All of the Old Testament predictions of the coming of Christ which assert His deity are also evidence for His eternity. For instance in Isaiah 9:6 Christ is declared to be not only "mighty God" but also "everlasting Father" or, better translated, "Father of eternity." The name Jehovah frequently given to Christ as well as to God the Father and the Holy Spirit is another assertion of eternity, for this title is defined as referring to the eternal I AM (cf. Exodus 3:14).

The eternity of Christ is frequently asserted also in the New Testament in even more definite terms than in the Old Testament. The introduction to the gospel of John is generally considered an affirmation of the eternity of Christ in the statement "In the beginning was the Word . . . and the Word was God" (John 1:1). The phrase "in the beginning" (Greek, *en archēi*) seems to refer to a point in time in eternity past beyond which it is impossible for us to go, as I. A. Dorner interprets it.[5] The verb is also chosen to state eternity as the word "was" (Greek, *ēn*) implies continued existence. As Marcus Dods states, "The Logos did not then begin to be, but at that point at which all else began to be He already *was*."[6]

As previously noted, the statement in John 8:58 is another express proof of eternity recognized as such even by the enemies of Christ. When Christ said, "Before Abraham came to be [Greek, *genesthai*], I am [Greek, *eimi*]" (literal trans.) He was not only claiming to have existed before Abraham, but He was claiming to be the eternal I AM, that is, the Jehovah of the Old Testament.

Evidence for the eternity of Christ is also found in the Pauline Epistles as in Colossians 1:16-17 where both His eternity and work as Creator are affirmed: "For by him were all things created, that are in heaven, and that are in earth, visible and invisible, whether they be thrones, or dominions, or principalities, or powers: all things were created by him, and for him: and he is before all things, and by him all things consist." The two statements found in these verses declare not only that Christ was before all creation,

---

[4]D. M. Baillie, *God Was in Christ*, p. 141.
[5]I. A. Dorner as cited by A. H. Strong, *Systematic Theology*, pp. 309-10.
[6]Marcus Dods, "The Gospel of St. John," in W. Robertson Nicoll (ed.), *The Expositor's Greek Testament*, I, 683.

but that all creation stemmed from His creative activity. If Christ was before all creation, it is obvious that He Himself could not have been created.

Additional proof of the eternity of Christ is found in statements concerning the eternal promises of God (Eph. 1:4) and in the declaration by Christ Himself: "I am Alpha and Omega, the first and the last" (Rev. 1:8). In the New Testament as in the Old, there are many contributing arguments to support the assertions of His deity and eternity such as His titles, His works, His divine attributes, His eternal promises, and almost any other aspect of His person and work which would imply His deity. If Christ is truly God, He is also truly eternal. In the history of the church it is significant that no denial of the eternity of Christ has endured which has not also denied the Scriptures as the very Word of God and ultimately lowered the person of Christ to something less than God Himself. Within orthodoxy there never has been any effective denial of the eternity of Christ, and orthodox creeds throughout the history of the church have either stated or implied His eternity.

PREEXISTENCE OF THE SON OF GOD

Although technically the affirmation that Christ was preexistent, that is, existed before His birth in Bethlehem, is not precisely the same as to state that He is eternal, for all practical purposes proof of His preexistence has been accepted by theologians as evidence of His eternity. Since the Arian controversy in the fourth century there has been no successful denial of His eternity which has not also denied His preexistence. Evidence that Christ existed in the Old Testament is therefore supporting evidence for His eternity.

The doctrine that Christ existed from all eternity past has been the orthodox theology of the church clearly annunciated as such ever since the Council of Nicaea. The eternity of Christ is not only essential to the deity of the second Person, but also intrinsic in any proper doctrine of the Trinity. The dogma of the eternity of Christ is the only proper basis on which to begin a biblical Christology and there is a growing tendency even among liberal scholarship to recognize that this is the teaching of the Bible. The Christ of the Scriptures is God, and a God who is not eternal is not God. The evidence for the eternity of Christ is therefore linked intrinsically with His deity and constitutes an essential concept for all study of Christology.

Evidences which support the concept of the preexistence of Christ are so many that it is impossible to deny them without denying the accuracy of both the Old and New Testaments. Such a common text as John 3:17, which states, "God sent not his Son into the world to condemn the world; but that the world through him might be saved," implies that the Son of God existed before the incarnation. John 3:31 is more specific: "He that cometh from above is above all: he that is of the earth is earthly, and speaketh of the earth: he that cometh from heaven is above all." Christ Himself said, "For I came down from heaven, not to do mine own will, but the will of him that sent me" (John 6:38). In John 17:5, 24 Christ speaks of His memory of the glory of heaven prior to His incarnation as an evidence for His preexistence. Other Scriptures too numerous to quote speak of His heavenly origin (John 1:15, 18, 30; 3:13, 16; 6:33, 42, 50-51, 58, 62; 7:29; 8:23, 42; 9:39; Eph. 1:3-5; I Peter 1:18-20). While references to the preexistence of Christ are found throughout the Bible, it is significant that most of the references are in the gospel of John in connection with the proof of His deity.

The doctrine of the preexistence of Christ is substantiated by so many other lines of evidence (cf. Heb. 1:5-14, etc.) that the subsequent discussion of various aspects of His person and His work may be taken in themselves as proof of this. His preincarnate works of creation, providence, preservation and His promises in eternity past, the appearances of Christ in the Old Testament, and the many other intimations of preexistence combine to form a massive proof that Christ existed before His birth in Bethlehem. The total testimony leaves no possibility of doubt as to the preexistence and eternity of Christ for anyone who accepts the testimony and accuracy of Scripture. The attribute of eternity is supported also by all the other divine attributes.

Even a neoorthodox scholar such as Oscar Cullmann recognizes the preexistence of Christ. He writes,

> We must recognize the special significance the evangelist attaches to the pre-existent being of Christ. The Incarnate One, the Son of Man as he appeared in the flesh, is the centre of *all* history. Therefore the question of his pre-existent work arises too. The one who is the centre of the whole *Heilsges-*

chichte cannot simply have appeared from nowhere. Therefore the Gospel of John emphasizes very strongly the participation of the pre-existent Christ in creation—even more
strongly than the other New Testament writings in which we
have found the same idea.[7]

DIVINE ATTRIBUTES OF THE SON OF GOD

The divine attributes ascribed to Christ present a clear revelation that in Him "the whole fulness of deity dwells bodily"
(Col. 2:9, RSV). Every attribute related to Deity or ascribed
to the Father or the Holy Spirit can also be attributed to Christ.
Only in Their personal properties is it possible to distihguish the
Members of the Trinity and in no case are these properties, such
as the term Father, any reflection on the deity of Christ. Since
the Council of Nicaea in 325 there has been no denial of the
deity and eternity of Christ which did not also deny the infallibility of Scripture.

Although the incarnation introduced many additional factors
in the person of Christ which relate to His humanity, it may be
safely assumed from the testimony of Scripture that the deity of
Christ in His preincarnate state is the same as that which is
found in the person of Christ after His birth in Bethlehem. For
all practical purposes, therefore, the revelation of His divine
attributes found in either the Old or New Testament can apply
equally to the subject of the person of Christ. Within orthodoxy
it has been held that the kenosis or self-emptying of Christ did
not constitutionally affect His divine nature (see later discussion
of the *kenosis*).

The scriptural revelations of the divine attributes of Christ
are so interrelated that the proof of one divine attribute naturally
leads to evidence for the other divine attributes. Hence, if Christ
is eternal, He is also preexistent, omniscient, omnipotent and so
on. The explicit statements, however, are so complete that it is
hardly necessary to appeal to this self-evident conclusion.

Eternity and Preexistence

As previously discussed, it is evident that Christ is declared by
the Scriptures to be eternal (Micah 5:2; John 8:58; Col. 1:16-17;
Rev. 1:8). All of the Scriptures which point to His preexistence

[7]Oscar Cullmann, *The Christology of the New Testament*, p. 250.

and activity in the Old Testament also sustain the conclusion that He is eternal and if so, therefore, God.

Self-existence

If Christ is eternal, it also is obvious that He is the uncaused cause, the self-existent One. As the Creator of all things, He Himself must be uncreated (John 1:1-3; Col. 1:16-17).

Omnipresence

The fact that God in His infinity is everywhere present in the total of His deity is clearly stated in many scriptures. The psalmist for instance writes eloquently, "Whither shall I go from thy spirit? Or whither shall I flee from thy presence? If I ascend up into heaven, thou art there: if I make my bed in hell, behold, thou art there. If I take the wings of the morning, and dwell in the uttermost parts of the sea; even there shall thy hand lead me, and thy right hand shall hold me" (Ps. 139:7-10). The fact that God is everywhere present is supported by other scriptures (Deut. 4:39; Prov. 15:3; Isa. 66:1; Jer. 23:24; Acts 17:27). The omnipresence of God is especially ascribed to Jesus Christ in promises to His disciples that He will abide with them forever (Matt. 28:20), His promise of indwelling the believer (John 14:18, 20, 23) which would be impossible if Christ were not omnipresent. It is confirmed by His experience with Nathaniel (John 1:48). If the disputed translation of John 3:13 be allowed to stand, the clause "which is in heaven" is an explicit statement of this doctrine. If Christ is God, then He is omnipresent; and if He is omnipresent, He is God.

The fact that Christ is omnipresent does not contradict the concept that He also has locality. While living on earth, He also was omnipresent in His deity. At the present time, Christ is at the right hand of the Father (Mark 16:19; I Peter 3:22) although at the same time omnipresent and indwelling the believer. With the exception of Lutheran theologians, most interpreters regard Christ as omnipresent in His deity and local in His humanity.

Omniscience

Frequently in the Scriptures Christ is portrayed as having omniscience. As a Child of twelve in the temple, He astounded the teachers of His day with His wisdom. In John 2:25 (RSV) it is stated that Christ "knew all men" and again, "he . . . knew what was in man." In John 16:30 (RSV) the disciples bear witness, "Now we know that you know all things" and again in John 21:17 (RSV) Peter declares, "Lord, you know everything." Perhaps Acts 1:24 refers to Christ when it states, "Lord, which knowest the hearts of all men. . . ." In keeping with His omniscience, Christ was said to have foreknown those who would believe not and betray Him (John 6:64). In a similar way Christ's foreknowledge is affirmed in other passages (John 13:1, 11; 18:4; 19:28). In keeping with His omniscience, He is declared to have the wisdom of God (I Cor. 1:30). Such qualities could not be ascribed to even the wisest of prophets, and they constitute another proof that He possessed all of the divine attributes.

Omnipotence

The evidence for the omnipotence of Christ is as decisive as proof for other attributes. Sometimes it takes the form of physical power, but more often it refers to authority over creation. Christ has the power to forgive sins (Matt. 9:6), all power in heaven and in earth (Matt. 28:18), power over nature (Luke 8:25), power over His own life (John 10:18), power to give eternal life to others (John 17:2), power to heal physically, as witnessed by His many miracles, as well as power to cast out demons (Mark 1:29-34), and power to transform the body (Phil. 3:21). By virtue of His resurrection "he is able also to save them to the uttermost that come unto God by him" (Heb. 7:25). He is "able to keep that which I have committed unto him against that day" (II Tim. 1:12). He is "able to keep you from falling, and to present you faultless before the presence of his glory with exceeding joy" (Jude 24; cf. Eph. 5:27). The Greek text of Jude 25 seems to imply that this is "through Jesus Christ our Lord," that is, by God the Father; but in any case the power of Christ is needed. It will be observed that the incarnation, death and resurrection of Christ permitted Christ to act in regard to sin and salvation. His omnipotence in any case is restricted to that which is holy, wise and good.

Immutability

The attribute of immutability, that Christ never changes, as stated in the classic passage of Hebrews 13:8, affirms that Christ is "the same yesterday, and to day, and for ever." In the incarnation Christ added a complete human nature, but orthodox scholars have always held that the divine nature of Christ remains unchanged and is, therefore, immutable. In Hebrews 1:10-12 a quotation is given of Psalm 102:25-27 and it is stated of Christ, "Thou art the same, and thy years shall not fail." If it is true that Christ has never changed, it also follows that the same Person who existed from eternity past is the One seen on earth during the period of the Gospels and the One who is now the glorified Son of God in heaven. The unchangeableness applies to all of the divine attributes as well as to His divine nature.

The Fullness of the Godhead in Him

As a confirmation of specific attributes it is also revealed in Scripture that in Christ is all the fullness of the Godhead: "For in him the whole fulness of deity dwells bodily" (Col. 2:9, RSV). The passage is very emphatic in the original. The expression "in him" (Greek, en autōi) stands first and is thereby emphasized. The word "dwells" (Greek, katoikei) means "permanently dwells."[8] The phrase "the whole fulness of deity dwells bodily" is obviously intended to convey the thought that in Christ is all that is in Deity. As A. S. Peake puts it, "It is vain to seek it [the Godhead] wholly or partially outside of Him."[9] The statement constitutes a blanket endorsement of all that is taught, in particular concerning the divine attributes of Christ.

Sovereignty

In keeping with the concept of His omnipotence, the Scriptures also assign sovereignty or authority to Christ. According to Matthew 28:18 (RSV), Christ declared, "All authority in heaven and on earth has been given to me." Again in I Peter 3:22 (RSV), Christ in heaven is declared to be at the right hand of God, "with angels, authorities, and powers subject to him." Other passages bear out the same concept of absolute sovereignty (John 5:27; Acts 2:36; I Cor. 12:3; Phil. 2:9-10; Col. 1:18). He is indeed "KING OF KINGS, AND LORD OF LORDS" (Rev. 19:16).

[8]A. S. Peake, "The Epistle to the Colossians" in W. Robertson Nicoll (ed.), *The Expositor's Greek Testament*, III, 523.
[9]*Ibid.*

Other Qualities of Deity

Christ is constantly represented in Scripture as having qualities which could be possessed only by God. His divine glory is mentioned in John 17:5 and seen in the vision of Revelation 1:12-18. Christ refers to Himself as "the way, the truth, and the life" (John 14:6), qualities which inhere only in God. He is the "righteous Branch . . . Jehovah our righteousness" (Jer. 23:5-6, ASV), He is the holy Son of God of Luke 1:35. Above all, Christ is the manifestation of grace—divine love and righteousness combined (John 1:17). There is not an attribute of Deity which is not directly or indirectly ascribed to Christ.

Charles Hodge presents the following summary of the scriptural evidence for the divine attributes of Christ:

> All divine names and titles are applied to Him. He is called God, the mighty God, the great God, God over all; Jehovah; Lord; the Lord of lords and King of kings. All divine attributes are ascribed to Him. He is declared to be omnipresent, omniscient, almighty, and immutable, the same yesterday, today, and forever. He is set forth as the creator and upholder and ruler of the universe. All things were created by Him and for Him; and by Him all things consist. He is the object of worship to all intelligent creatures, even the highest; all the angels (*i.e.*, all creatures between man and God) are commanded to prostrate themselves before Him. He is the object of all the religious sentiments; of reverence, love, faith, and devotion. To Him men and angels are responsible for their character and conduct. He required that man should honour Him as they honoured the Father; that they should exercise the same faith in Him that they do in God. He declares that He and the Father are one; that those who had seen Him had seen the Father also. He calls all men unto Him; promises to forgive their sins; to send them the Holy Spirit; to give them rest and peace; to raise them up at the last day; and to give them eternal life. God is not more, and cannot promise more, or do more than Christ is said to be, to promise, and to do. He has, therefore, been the Christian's God from the beginning, in all ages and in all places.[10]

The total picture of the person of Christ in eternity past is enhanced by a study of His titles given in the Old and New Testament which are considered in the next chapter. Further evidence is found in the theophanies of Christ and in His work as Creator, Preserver and Director of the providence of God.

[10]Charles Hodge, *Systematic Theology*, II, 382.

The eternal Son of God who always existed with God the Father and God the Holy Spirit is the same Person who is found to be active in the Old Testament scene and who became incarnate in Jesus Christ born in Bethlehem.

THE SON OF GOD IN THE TRINITY

The evidence which has already been considered testifying to the deity and eternity of Christ also contributes to the concept of God existing in three Persons. Historically, the trinitarian doctrine turns largely on the question of whether the Son of God is eternal, whether He has the attribute of personality and the very nature of God. The problems of the doctrine of the Trinity largely arise in the studies of Christ in His incarnate state. The Old Testament, while it assumes the doctrine of the Trinity, does not actually define the relationships of the Father, the Son and the Holy Spirit except to indicate subordination of the Son to the Father and of the Holy Spirit to the Son as brought out more clearly in the New Testament.

If Christ is God and as such is distinguished from the Father and the Spirit, preliminary evidence is provided to support the doctrine of the Trinity as normally stated in orthodoxy. It is safe to say that no attack on the doctrine of the Trinity can be made without attacking the person of Christ. It is also true that no attack on the person of Christ can be made without attacking the doctrine of the Trinity, as they stand and fall together. It is for this reason that current liberalism is usually Unitarian, that is, denies the three Persons of the Godhead, or is modalistic, that is, affirming simply that the Persons are modes of existence of the one Person and not actual entities. From our preliminary study it is fair to conclude that the doctrine of the eternity of Christ tends to support the orthodox doctrine of the Trinity, and the subsequent study of the person and work of Christ in the Old and New Testaments will amplify and support this preliminary conclusion.

WORK OF THE SON OF GOD IN
ETERNITY PAST

In the popular study of the person and work of Christ, many have assumed that His ministry began with His life on earth.

There is abundant evidence that Christ ministered not only to men in the Old Testament, but that He also participated in the work of God in eternity past. Long before the world was created or Adam and Eve were placed in the garden God had established His sovereign purpose described by the theological term "decree" or by more common words such as the "purpose," "promise" or "covenant" of God. In attempting to establish precisely what this work of Christ in eternity past is, one must of course submit completely to the Scriptures, as there are no human sources of information apart from that which the Bible itself gives.

In attempting to understand what is meant by the eternal decree of God, it may be well to begin with the concise definition given by the Westminster Shorter Catechism: "The decrees of God are his eternal purpose, according to the counsel of his will, whereby, for his own glory, he hath foreordained whatsoever comes to pass."[11] If this concept of the decree of God is correct, Christ must have had an important part in this eternal decree and therefore is involved in all aspects of the total purpose and work of God. It would have been impossible for God as a Trinity to have decreed without Christ being involved in the act.

In attempting to understand what is meant by the decree of God, students of theology have recognized that this area of theology is most difficult to comprehend inasmuch as it affects the whole concept of man's will and responsibility in relationship to the sovereignty of God. In the study of the decree of God, attention has been particularly directed to the work of God in salvation and such expressions as the covenant of redemption or the covenant of grace have been used to describe the eternal promises of God relating to salvation. Without questioning the importance of salvation in the eternal purpose of God, it must nevertheless be held that the decree of God relates to all of God's work, not simply His work in saving the elect. The decree therefore includes creation, providence, preservation, the permission of sin, the provision of salvation, the judgment of all men, and the sovereign will of God as it is related to all events of time and eternity. The participation of Christ in the eternal decree of God is therefore the most comprehensive concept which the theologian can face.

Although Calvin and Luther did not develop the idea of an

[11]*Constitution of the Presbyterian Church in the U.S.A.*, p. 209.

eternal covenant with God to any great extent, their successors in the Reformed churches introduced what is known as covenant theology which holds that in eternity past God made a covenant of grace between Himself and the elect and a covenant of redemption between the Father, Son and Holy Spirit in regard to the work of salvation. The work of God in saving the elect is therefore made the major undertaking of God in time and eternity.[12] The neoorthodox attempt to begin Christ's preexistence with creation and to ignore His existence prior to creation falls short of the biblical revelation.[13]

The plan of redemption is clearly a part of God's eternal purpose and therefore is included in the decree of God. To this concept the Scriptures give specific testimony (Rom. 8:28-30; Eph. 1:4-11; 3:11; II Thess. 2:13; II Tim. 1:9; James 2:5; I Peter 1:1-2). A careful reading of the Bible will reveal that the plan of salvation was not an emergency device conceived after the fall of man as a plan of rescue, but rather that it was the solemn decision of God in eternity past in contemplating the whole of creation. It is a matter of great significance that it was decreed from eternity past that Christ should become incarnate, that He should suffer the death on the cross for the sin of the world, and that He should triumph in His resurrection, in the salvation of all who believe, and in the ultimate consummation of God's plan. All this was as certain and clear to God from eternity past as it will be from the viewpoint of eternity future.

It is most important, however, in having a proper approach to the Scriptures to recognize that not only the work of Christ in salvation, but also His work in creation, preservation, providence and revelation, His part in the church in the New Testament and the program of Israel in the Old Testament as well as His future fulfillment of the promises given to David of a King who will sit on the throne of David are all embodied in the eternal decree and purpose of God. Although no single passage of Scripture spells out in detail all of these conclusions, it is a reasonable conclusion from the Scriptures as a whole that the events of history in all their magnitude stem from the original decree of God (cf. Eph. 1:11). The decree includes His sovereign

[12]A concise summary of the covenant idea in salvation is found in Louis Berkhof, *Systematic Theology*, pp. 265-71.
[13]Cf. Cullmann, *ibid.*

CHRIST IN ETERNITY PAST

choice in creation in establishing natural and spiritual laws which have characterized the history of the world to this point as well as its final judgment and consummation. The all-inclusive character of the decree is usually recognized by covenant theologians. Important for our consideration here is the fact that Christ actively participated in this decree as God and as the future Saviour. It was determined long before the world was created that Christ would go to the cross and that He would ultimately triumph over death and sin. Although much of this is inscrutable and difficult for man in his limitations to comprehend, the qualities which inhere in a God who existed from eternity past are also found completely in Jesus Christ.

3

CHRIST IN OLD TESTAMENT HISTORY

THE REVELATION OF JESUS CHRIST in the Old Testament forms a most important background to the New Testament narratives. In general, the major lines of divine revelation relating to Jesus Christ in the Old Testament include His titles, His work as Creator, His work as the Preserver and Executor of the providence of God, His activity especially in relation to the people of Israel, and the many theophanies of Christ in the Old Testament. To these can be added one of the major themes of the Old Testament, namely, the Messianic prophecies largely fulfilled after His incarnation which are treated in chapter 4. In presenting the Old Testament record, some New Testament material immediately pertinent to the discussion is included.

TITLES OF THE SON OF GOD IN THE OLD TESTAMENT

The titles given to Christ in both the Old and New Testaments constitute an important aspect of the total revelation of His person. A distinction should be observed between those titles which apply to His preincarnate person and those which refer to His incarnate person. Such designations as "Jesus Christ," "Son of man," "prophet," "priest," "king," etc., have primary reference to Christ in the incarnate state, even though they are found in the Old as well as the New Testaments. Their meaning and contribution falls properly under the discussion of Christ incarnate. To be considered here are the titles which refer to His deity and preincarnate person.

Jehovah

A comparison of the Old Testament and New Testament passages proves beyond doubt that the Christ of the New Testament bears the title Jehovah or Lord in the Old Testament. This fact has long been recognized by conservative theologians. This does not deny that the Father and the Spirit bear the title Jehovah, but affirms that it also belongs to Christ. The name is used both of the Persons of the Trinity severally and of the Trinity as a whole.

Many passages link Christ with the name Jehovah. In Zechariah 12:10b (ASV), where Jehovah is speaking, the description is to be applied clearly to Christ: "They shall look unto me whom they have pierced." Revelation 1:7 describes Christ in the same language. Again in Jeremiah 23:5-6 (ASV), Christ is declared to be "Jehovah our righteousness" (cf. I Cor. 1:30). Similar comparisons are found in other passages (Ps. 68:18, cf. Eph. 4:8-10; Ps. 102:12, 25-27, cf. Heb. 1:10-12; Isa. 6:5, cf. John 12:41). Christ is the Jehovah of the temple (Mal. 3:1; Matt. 12:6; 21:12-13) and the Jehovah of the Sabbath (Matt. 12:8).[1]

The fact that the term Jehovah was used of Jesus Christ is most significant as it affirms that Jesus Christ is worthy of the most ineffable name of God used in Scripture. This is confirmed by the New Testament use of *Kyrios* for Christ, the word used in the LXX as equivalent to Jehovah (cf. Acts 2:36). So holy was this name regarded that Jews reading the Old Testament would substitute some other name for Deity rather than to express vocally what the text actually said when it used the word Jehovah. The use of this term alone affirms beyond any question the deity of Jesus Christ and with this all the attributes of God.

Elohim

It is easily demonstrated that Christ is identified also with the Elohim of the Old Testament. In Isaiah 40:3, Christ is spoken of as both Jehovah and Elohim (cf. Luke 3:4). In Isaiah 9:6-7 Christ is called "the mighty God [Elohim]." It is apparent that Elohim in the Old Testament is God in the New Testament (Greek, *theos*). Hence all passages in the New Testament referring to Christ by this title link Him with the Elohim of the Old

[1]Cf. L. S. Chafer, *Systematic Theology*, I, 332-34.

Testament (cf. Rom. 15:6; Eph. 1:3; 5:5, 20; II Peter 1:1).[2]

If Christ is the Elohim of the Old Testament, it also follows that He is the One introduced in Genesis 1:1 as the God of creation and in the hundreds of other instances of Elohim in the Old Testament. Unless the context explicitly limits the usage to the Father or the Spirit, the conclusion should be reached that the triune God, including Christ, is meant. Although Elohim also was used of heathen gods, as the general and common word for Deity in the Old Testament it implies all that is indicated in the term God in English and is another line of evidence for the deity of Jesus Christ.

In a few isolated instances in the Old Testament, Elohim is used for men as God's representatives. Christ quoted such an instance in John 10:32-36, citing Psalm 82:6. Similar instances are found in Exodus 22:8-9 where Elohim is translated "judges." Such occasions are rare, however. Quoting Psalm 82:6, Christ introduces in John 10:32-36 the argument from the less to the greater. If men as representatives of God can be called Elohim, how much more Christ, "whom the Father hath sanctified and sent into the world." Obviously Christ is claiming to be more than a mere representative and is asserting that He is God in the fullest sense.

Adonai

This common title of God in the Old Testament, meaning Lord, is often used of Deity as well as human masters. Although not a specific title of Christ in the Old Testament, it is used in Psalm 110:1 (ASV) in a clear reference to the second Person: "Jehovah saith unto my Lord, Sit thou at my right hand, until I make thine enemies thy footstool." This prediction refers to the ultimate triumph of Christ over His enemies and is quoted frequently as fulfilled in Christ in the New Testament (Matt. 22:44; Mark 12:36; Luke 20:43; Acts 2:34-35; Heb. 1:13; 10:13). The New Testament equivalent is Lord (Greek, *kyrios*). The title emphasizes that Jesus Christ is properly Lord and Master over men and angels.

Son of God

This title, used in the Scriptures of both angels and men, when used of Christ is designed to express His eternal relationship to

2*Ibid.*, p. 392.

the Father. Although various concepts have been advanced in theological discussion relative to the meaning of this term, in the main the doctrine of the church, since the Council of Nicaea in 325, is that the title refers to an eternal relationship of the Son to the Father.

A number of other views are often discussed in theological literature, of which several may be mentioned:

The theory of sonship by means of incarnation. This view has been expounded at length by Wardlaw and others and holds that Christ was not properly a Son before His birth. As Wardlaw defines it, sonship is inseparably linked with the incarnation and, while Christ existed from eternity past, He was not a Son until the incarnation.[3] This view has the advantage of being simple in concept. The question remains whether it is adequate. If Christ became a Son by means of the incarnation and was not a Son before that event, then the Father was not a Father of the Lord Jesus before the incarnation. It leaves unexplained the mystery of the relation of the first Person to the second Person—indeed, why the titles and order are justified. While it is clear that the first Person became the Father of the humanity of Christ in time, the relation of the Persons of the Trinity as such must be from eternity and require some definition. While many problems remain, and it is not possible here to discuss them all, the consensus of the great theologians of the church and the great church councils is to the effect that Christ has been a Son from eternity; and the theory that He became a Son by incarnation is inadequate to account for the usage of the term, as is shown later.

The theory of sonship by means of baptism. This view has been held on the basis of the scriptural accounts of the baptism of Christ. On that occasion Christ was declared the Son of God: "This is my beloved Son, in whom I am well pleased" (Matt. 3:17, ASV). This cannot be taken as evidence that He was not the Son of God before this event. In fact, the baptism of Christ is totally inadequate to account for the Father and Son relationship. This theory must be excluded as trivial.

The theory of sonship by means of resurrection. Here again is a viewpoint based upon misapplication of Scripture. According to Romans 1:4 (RSV), it is revealed of Christ that He is "designated Son of God in power according to the Spirit of holiness by

[3]Ralph Wardlaw, *Systematic Theology*, II, 32-60.

his resurrection from the dead, Jesus Christ our Lord." It is clear to all that the resurrection is an outstanding proof of the deity and of the divine sonship of Christ, but this is not to say that He was not the Son of God before this event. Such interpretation is definitely ruled out by the fact that He is called the Son of God repeatedly before His death and resurrection, and used the term Father in relation to the first Person.

Another passage which bears on the issue is Acts 13:32-33 (RSV) : "And we bring you the good news that what God promised to the fathers, this he has fulfilled to us their children by raising Jesus: as also it is written in the second psalm, 'Thou art my Son, today I have begotten thee.' " Here the reference is to Psalm 2:7, in which the decree of God is revealed concerning the generation of the Son. At first glance, the application in Acts seems to be to the resurrection, but the expression "raising Jesus" as here used does not refer to the resurrection at all, but to the simple fact that God gave His Son to the world in the incarnation. The word "raise" (Greek, *anastēsas*) is used in the same sense as "arise" (cf. Matt. 22:24; Acts 7:18; 20:30) , that is, to come on the scene of life. The common expression that "a prophet arose" is the same idea. Acts 13:34 (RSV) introduces the resurrection as a new idea to the context: "And as for the fact that he raised him from the dead, no more to return to corruption, he spoke in this way, 'I will give you the holy and sure blessings of David.' " In other words, the thought of resurrection is not introduced until verse 34. It is true, of course, that the resurrection brought the humanity of Christ into the new victory of resurrection in which the deity of His person and His victory over sin, death and the grave are demonstrated. It is not true that His divine sonship began with the resurrection.

The theory of sonship by means of exaltation to the right hand of God. Based on Hebrews 1:3, it is held that Christ was made a Son when He was exalted at the ascension. It can be objected to this view as to others that He is clearly a Son from eternity and is declared to be a Son before His exaltation. There are constant references to Jesus Christ as Son throughout His earthly life and in His death and resurrection. To begin His sonship at the ascension is an artificial and unwarranted teaching. This exaltation is a declaration of His divine sonship and of His victory over sin and death.

The theory of sonship by means of title or office. This theory, based on Philippians 2:9, holds that Christ was a Son in the sense only of bearing this title and that He was not actually a generated Son. Against this it may be objected that such a concept of sonship destroys most of its meaning. Unless there is corresponding reality which justifies the term, sonship becomes merely a compliment. The Scriptures speak of Christ as a begotten and generated Son and, while His generation is not the same in kind as human generation, being different and unique, it is nevertheless a constitutional aspect of the second Person rather than an acquired title.

The theory of sonship by means of covenant relation. This view which is based on the concept of the eternal covenant between Members of the Godhead holds that the sonship of Christ is an assumed office, beginning with the covenant in eternity past and ending when the covenant relationship and work is completed. Again this view is inadequate to explain the scriptural terminology. It would give to the term Son merely the significance of a title or office which has no real connection with the ordinary human connotations of the word.

The eternal sonship of Christ. The Scriptures represent Christ as eternally the Son of God by eternal generation. While it must be admitted that the nature of the sonship and the nature of the generation are unique, being eternal, sonship has been used in the Bible to represent the relationship between the first Person and the second Person. Clear evidence for eternal sonship is found in the fact that Christ is represented as already the Son of God and given to the world (John 3:16-17; Gal. 4:4). The same idea is found in Isaiah 9:6, "A son is given."

Further evidence is found in the doctrine of the eternal decree as it relates to Christ as a Son. In Psalm 2:7 (ASV) Jehovah speaks, "I will tell of the decree: Jehovah said unto me, Thou art my son; this day have I begotten thee." According to this passage, Christ is declared to be the Son of God and begotten in the day of the eternal decree. This is, in effect, a statement that Christ is eternally the Son of God as the decree itself is eternal. He is not only declared a Son from eternity but begotten from eternity.

Some have interpreted this passage as prophetically future on the ground that the context is prophetic. It is rather that the prophesied victory is on the ground of His sonship. The passage in Psalm 2:7 is quoted three times in the New Testament (Acts 13:33; Heb. 1:5; 5:5). The Acts passage deals with the fact of Christ being raised up to be the incarnate Saviour. In Hebrews 1:5, the appeal is made to the majesty of Christ as that above the angels because He is the Son of God. The appointment of Christ to the priesthood by the Father is said to be added to His sonship in Hebrews 5:5. All three of the citations in the New Testament draw on Psalm 2:7 for proof of the unique status of Christ and confirm rather than deny His eternal sonship.

Joseph Klausner, in discussing Psalm 2:7: "Thou art my Son; this day have I begotten thee," states, "For Jews this was a common poetic-figurative expression." He defines the Christian concept as

> Jesus is "son of God" in the sense of a "heavenly man" not susceptible to sin nor even to death . . . in his resurrection for eternity he ascended into heaven and sits at the right hand of God because he is closer to God than are the angels. This was the first step toward deification.[4]

Klausner, presenting the Jewish point of view, holds that the Gentiles to whom Paul brought Christianity took the final step in making Jesus God. For him, therefore, the expression "Son of God" merely implies nearness to God rather than essential Deity.

The scriptural view of the sonship of Christ, as recognized in many of the great creeds of the church, is that Christ was always the Son of God by eternal generation, and that He took upon Himself humanity through generation of the Holy Spirit. The human birth was not in order to become a Son of God, but because He was the Son of God. Principal scriptures bearing on the doctrine in addition to those discussed are numerous (Matt. 16:13-16; 26:63-64; Luke 2:11, 26, 38; John 1:49; 3:16, 18, 35, 36; 11:27; Acts 9:20; Heb. 1:2, 8; I John 2:23; 5:9-12). As God, Christ addresses the first Person as His Father, while as Man, Christ addresses Him as His God (John 20:17).

The First Begotten

This New Testament term (Greek, *prōtotokos*), while not occurring in the Old Testament, is introduced in effect in declarations that Christ is begotten, as in Psalm 2:7, and as such is another support for the concept of Christ as the Son of God.

*Joseph Klausner, *The Messianic Idea in Israel*, pp. 527-28.

Seven times in the New Testament the term "the first begotten" (or "firstborn") is used of Christ (Matt. 1:25; Luke 2:7; Rom. 8:29; Col. 1:15, 18; Heb. 1:6; Rev. 1:5). It occurs twice in reference to others (Heb. 11:28; 12:23). As a descriptive name of Christ, it appears with three distinct meanings:

1. As the "firstborn among many brethren" (Rom. 8:29), and as "the firstborn of all creation" (Col. 1:15, ASV), it is used clearly in reference to the eternal existence of the divine Son of God and helps to confirm the doctrine of eternal generation.

2. As the Firstborn of Mary (Matt. 1:25; Luke 2:7) the title is given to Christ as Mary's firstborn Son. It is used clearly in reference to His incarnate person. As Mary's Firstborn, Christ was not only first in time but also in rank and position. Under the law, the firstborn received a double inheritance and was regarded as the prime descendant of his father.

3. A third usage is found in the description of Christ as "firstborn from the dead" (Col. 1:18, RSV), and "the first-born of the dead" (Rev. 1:5, RSV). Here the meaning is that Christ is the first to be raised from the dead in resurrection. There had been a number of restorations, as in the case of Lazarus, but no one before had received resurrection life and an immortal, resurrection body. Christ is the first of this order.

As Alford writes in connection with Colossians 1:15,

> The safe method of interpretation therefore will be, to take into account the two ideas manifestly included in the word [first begotten], and here distinctly referred to—priority, and dignity, and to regard the technical term . . . [*prōtotokos*] as used rather with reference to both these, than in strict construction where it stands. "First-born of every creature" will then imply, that Christ was not only first-born of His mother in the world, but first-begotten of His Father, before the worlds,—and that He holds the rank, as compared with every created thing, of first-born in dignity.[5]

The concept of priority in time is used by Alford to support the idea that other children were also born to Mary.[6] Alford, however, refutes the Arian and Socinian view that this implies that Christ is the first of created beings and hence not eternal.[7] The aspect of dignity, carried over from the idea that the firstborn was

[5]Henry Alford, *The Greek Testament*, III, 203.
[6]*Ibid.*, I, 457.
[7]*Ibid.*, III, 203.

given a more important place than later children, has the resultant idea of sovereignty or place of authority and tends to
support the deity of Christ.

The Only Begotten

This is another title (Greek, *monogenēs*) related to the sonship of Christ as introduced in the Old Testament, but expounded
in the New Testament where it is used of Christ five times (John
1:14, 18; 3:16, 18; I John 4:9), all in the writings of John. The
Revised Standard Version translates the expression by "only Son,"
which, although not actually incorrect, seems to be an oversim-
plification of the real meaning which leaves the concept of "begotten" implied but not explicitly stated. The Authorized Version is more literal here. The thought is clearly that Christ is the
Begotten of God in the sense that no other is. This is illustrated
in the use of the same word in regard to Isaac (Heb. 11:17), who
was not literally the only begotten of Abraham but was the only
begotten of Abraham in the sense that he was the promised seed.
It is used in the ordinary sense also in Scripture (Luke 7:12; 8:42,
the only other references in the New Testament). The term is
again a confirmation of the idea of eternal generation, though
Christ was also the only Begotten in reference to His humanity.
The thought of John 3:16 seems to be that the Son who was the
only Begotten from eternity past was given by the Father.

The Angel of Jehovah

One of the significant and important titles is that given Him
in the Old Testament when He appeared as the Angel of Jehovah.
As one of the principal theophanies, it is important for many
reasons, confirming the preexistence of Christ, and revealing the
ministry of God to men in the Old Testament period. It is the
teaching of Scripture that the Angel of Jehovah is specifically the
second Person of the Trinity. At least three lines of evidence substantiate this claim:

1. Christ as the Angel of Jehovah is identified as Jehovah in
numerous Old Testament passages. When the Angel of Jehovah
spoke to Hagar (Gen. 16:7-13, ASV), He was identified as Jehovah
(v. 13, ASV). The account of the sacrifice of Isaac (Gen. 22:15-
18, ASV) affords the same identification. In some instances the
expression "Angel of God" is used as a synonym for Jehovah. The

Hebrew for God in these instances is Elohim. In either case the deity of the Angel is confirmed by many passages ("angel of God," Gen. 31:11-13; "God . . . the Angel," 48:15-16; cf. 45:5; "angel of Jehovah," "God" and "Jehovah" used interchangeably, Exodus 3:1 ff., ASV; cf. Acts 7:30-35; "Jehovah," Exodus 13:21, ASV; "angel of God," Exodus 14:19; both "angel of Jehovah," and "angel of God," Judges 6:11-23, ASV; both "angel of God" and "angel of Jehovah," Judges 13:9-20, ASV).

2. The Angel of Jehovah is also revealed to be a distinct Person from Jehovah, that is, a Person of the Trinity. In Genesis 24:7 (ASV), for instance, Jehovah is described as sending "his angel." The servant of Abraham testifies to the reality of this in Genesis 24:40 (ASV). Moses speaks of Jehovah sending an angel to lead Israel (Num. 20:16, ASV). An instance which is clear is that found in Zechariah 1:12-13 (ASV), where the Angel of Jehovah addressed Jehovah: "Then the angel of Jehovah answered and said, O Jehovah of hosts, how long wilt thou not have mercy on Jerusalem and on the cities of Judah, against which thou hast had indignation these threescore and ten years? And Jehovah answered the angel that talked with me with good words, even comfortable words." Many other similar passages occur (Exodus 23:20; 32:34; I Chron. 21:15-18; Isa. 63:9; Dan. 3:25-28). Still other passages affirm the deity of the Angel of Jehovah without trinitarian personal distinctions (Judges 2:1-5; II Kings 19:35).

3. The Angel of Jehovah is the second Person of the Trinity. Having determined the deity of the Angel of Jehovah and that He is a Person of the Trinity, it remains to demonstrate that He is the second Person. That is, in fact, the only solution of an otherwise confused picture. How can a Person be God and at the same time address God? The answer lies in the personal distinctions of the Trinity. There are at least four lines of evidence which identify the Angel of Jehovah as the second Person:

a. The second Person is the visible God of the New Testament. Neither the Father nor the Spirit is characteristically revealed in bodily and visible form. While the Father's voice is heard from heaven, and the Holy Spirit is seen descending in the form of a dove, Christ, the second Person, is the full manifestation of God in visible form. It is logical that the same Person of the Trinity should appear in bodily form in both Testaments.

b. Confirming this induction is the fact that the Angel of Jehovah of the Old Testament no longer appears after the incarnation. References to angels in the New Testament seem to refer to either angelic or human messengers. It is a natural inference that the Angel of Jehovah is now the incarnate Christ.

c. The similarity of function between the Angel of Jehovah and Christ can be observed in the fact that Both are sent by the Father. In the Old Testament, the Angel of Jehovah is sent by Jehovah to reveal truth, to lead Israel and to defend and judge them. In the New Testament, Christ is sent by God the Father to reveal God in the flesh, to reveal truth and to become the Saviour. It is characteristic for the Father to send and the Son to be the sent One. These facts again point to the identification of the Angel of Jehovah with Christ.

d. By the process of elimination, it can be demonstrated that the Angel of Jehovah could not be either the first Person or the third Person. According to John 1:18 (RSV): "No one has ever seen God; the only Son, who is in the bosom of the Father, he has made him known." This passage seems to imply that only Christ could be visible to man and that the first Person and the third Person did not reveal Themselves in visible fashion. As the Angel of Jehovah is the sent One, He could not be the Father for the Father is the Sender. As the Angel of Jehovah characteristically appears in bodily, usually human form, He could not be the Holy Spirit who does not appear bodily, except in the rare instance of appearing in the form of a dove at the baptism of Christ. It may, therefore, be concluded that the Angel of Jehovah is the second Person of the Trinity. The other theophanies of the Old Testament tend to confirm this judgment.

In the New Testament many of the Old Testament titles are confirmed and enriched such as the word Jesus embodying the entire anticipation of Christ as the Saviour in the Old Testament, the word Christ including all the Messianic prophecies of the Old Testament, the word Logos referring to Christ as the revelation or declaration of God, the word Lord (Greek, *kyrios*) with its Old Testament counterpart (Hebrew, *Adonai*) and the term Son of Man. The titles of Christ in both the Old and New Testament are another line of evidence in support of His deity and in confirmation of His attributes.

CHRIST AS THE CREATOR

The doctrine of creation *ex nihilo* as the free act of God has been the generally accepted doctrine of the historic Christian church. It is opposed on the one hand to ancient theories of the eternity of matter and the theory that matter emanated from God and is of His substance. It is also opposed to modern theories of evolution as the means or process of creation. If philosophy cannot deal, in the last analysis, with ultimates, as is commonly admitted, then it cannot solve this problem of the truth or error of the doctrine of creation. It is a doctrine which can be made known only by a revelation of the Creator Himself. Concerning creation, the Scriptures give an adequate testimony for all who are prepared to receive it. From Genesis 1 to the book of Revelation, the universe is presented in the Bible as that which God created.

Creation is commonly considered a work of the Father rather than of the Son and the Holy Spirit. The Scriptures, however, in the work of creation attribute it to all three Persons of the Trinity. The use of Elohim and Jehovah for the triune God gives clear intimation of this even in the Old Testament. It is the Elohim who creates in Genesis 1, and already in Genesis 1:2 the Spirit of God is acting creatively. The Holy Spirit is mentioned frequently in the Old Testament as the Creator (Job 26:13; 33:4; Ps. 104:30; Isa. 40:12-13). The Father is also mentioned specifically in the New Testament (I Cor. 8:6). It is therefore to be expected that a similar revelation will be given concerning the Son of God.

The Son of God is revealed to be the eternal Word of God of whom it is said: "All things were made by him; and without him was not any thing made that was made" (John 1:3). In I Corinthians 8:6 similar revelation is given: "But to us there is but one God, the Father, of whom are all things, and we in him; and one Lord Jesus Christ, by whom are all things, and we by him." The doctrine is given its fullest statement in Colossians 1:15-17 (RSV): "He is the image of the invisible God, the first-born of all creation; for in him all things were created, in heaven and on earth, visible and invisible, whether thrones or dominions or principalities or authorities—all things were created through him

and for him. He is before all things, and in him all things hold
together."

Many attempts have been made to explain these citations as
teaching something less than that the Son of God is the Creator.
All such attempts fail before the plain intent of these passages. It
can be seen at once that the name of no man or angel could be in-
serted in these descriptions without blasphemy. The work revealed is the work of God. There is no excuse either for Unitarian interpretations which make Christ merely a manifestation
of God. The passages at once distinguish the Son of God from
the other Persons of the Trinity and at the same time link the
work of creation to all of Them. It may be that we can concede
with Berkhof that there is a distinction in the form of Their
work: "All things are at once *out of* the Father, *through* the Son,
and *in* the Holy Spirit. In general it may be said that *being* is out
of the Father, *thought* or *idea* out of the Son, and *life* out of the
Holy Spirit."[8] The Scripture does seem to make distinctions
which are in keeping with the order of the Trinity, but even the
distinctions do not carry through in all passages. Life is said to
be in Christ (John 1:4), which seems to be the function of the
Holy Spirit. Again it is said of Christ that all things are "in him"
(Col. 1:16, RSV), which is ordinarily said of the Spirit. Again,
"in him all things hold together" (Col. 1:17, RSV). These distinctions do not divide the work of creation or make Christ or the
Spirit mere agents. In all the work of creation there are manifest
the power and activity of the triune God.

The significance of the work of creation as ascribed to Christ is
that it reveals His eternity, power, wisdom and omnipresence. As
the Creator He is specifically "before all things" (Col. 1:17), and
therefore eternal. The nature of creation reveals His power, wisdom and presence in creation. The telescopic wonder of the
heavens as well as the microscopic wonders of the world too small
for human eyes to see combine in their witness to His power. It is
such a God who became the Saviour.

CHRIST IN PRESERVATION AND PROVIDENCE

The doctrine of providence has always formed an essential part
of the Christian faith. The fact that God preserves His creation,
guides it into intelligent and wise consummation of His purposes,

---

[8]Louis Berkhof, *Systematic Theology*, p. 129.

and governs it as sovereign God is by its very character essential to a true theism. Even the liberal scholar Millar Burrows states emphatically: "The basic issue for religious faith in this connection is whether the universe is governed by a personal God. . . . If it is not, biblical religion is basically false."[9] Conservative theologians have agreed with one voice concerning the fact of providence though struggling somewhat in its definition. It is usually held that providence includes (1) preservation, (2) concurrence or cooperation with creatures, and (3) government.[10] In regard to the study of the work of the preincarnate Son of God, the question may be raised concerning His part in this undertaking of God.

Scriptural evidence for providence in its various phases, which involves hundreds of passages, usually uses the names of God which are not specifically related to one Person of the Trinity. Hence, Jehovah or Elohim is frequently used in the Old Testament (cf. Gen. 28:16; Exodus 14:29-31; Deut. 1:30-31; II Chron. 20:17; Ps. 31:1-3, 20-21). As work of the triune God, then, providence is a work also of Christ, and all that is said of Jehovah or Elohim may be said of Christ.

There are reasons to believe, however, that the Son of God is specifically active in the work of God in providence. First, the work of the Angel of Jehovah, which is considered later, presents monumental proof that the Son of God preserved and guided Israel. Second, the various references to Jehovah as the Shepherd of Israel may be taken as specific references to Christ (cf. Gen. 49:24; Ps. 23:1; 80:1; Isa. 40:11; Jer. 31:10; Ezek. 34:11-12, 23; 37:24). Although these references contextually could refer to God as a Trinity, the fact that Christ is specifically the good Shepherd in John 10 would give some justification for this identification. As the good Shepherd, He died for His sheep as prophesied in Psalm 22; as the great Shepherd (Heb. 13:20), He fulfills Psalm 23; as the chief Shepherd (I Peter 5:4), He will come to reign as the King of glory (Ps. 24). Third, the language of Isaiah 63:9 specifically refers to the Son of God under the title "the angel of his presence": "The angel of his presence saved them: in his love

[9]Millar Burrows, *An Outline of Biblical Theology*, p. 132.
[10]Cf. John T. Mueller, *Christian Dogmatics*, pp. 189 ff.; Berkhof, pp. 165 ff. G. C. Berkouwer's *The Providence of God* is an excellent contemporary treatment.

and in his pity he redeemed them; and he bare them, and carried
them all the days of old." This is clearly the work of providence
and preservation in the Old Testament period.

In the New Testament a fourth line of evidence is revealed
which is also specific: "He is before all things, and in him all
things hold together" (Col. 1:17, RSV). Here again is a comprehensive statement—the universe "holds together" because of the
immediate agency of Christ. Alford comments, "And in Him (as
its conditional element of existence, see above on . . . [en autōi]
ver. 16) the universe subsists ('keeps together,' 'is held together
in its present state') ."[11] In view of modern discoveries concerning the atomic structure of all matter—in which each atom is a
miniature solar system—this work of Christ becomes especially
significant. The immaterial bonds which hold together the atom
as well as the starry heavens are traced in this passage to the
power and activity of the Son of God.

The same doctrine as revealed in Colossians 1:17 is found again
in Hebrews 1:3 (RSV), "He reflects the glory of God and bears
the very stamp of his nature, upholding the universe by his word
of power." In other words, without denying the validity and use
of second causes, the universe is said to be upheld by the *word* of
the power of the Son of God. The clause "by the word" refers to
the expression of the power of Christ in the universe (cf. Rev.
3:10, "the word of my patience"). Westcott comments, "As the
world was called into being by an utterance . . . [Hrema] of God
(c. xi. 3) , so it is sustained by a like expression of the divine will.
The choice of the term as distinguished from . . . [logos] marks,
so to speak, the particular action of Providence."[12] While the
context of Hebrews 1:3 bears on the incarnate person of Christ, its
reference is clearly to His deity and eternal power and authority.

Another important aspect of providence is the scriptural revelation concerning divine government and its relation to Christ.
Without attempting to solve here the problems of the relation of
this aspect of divine sovereignty to human will and the permission
of sin, it is important to note that God has not turned from His
purpose to bring every creature under the immediate authority
of Christ. This is true in regard to God's purpose for the *earth*.
The Son of God "shall have dominion also from sea to sea, and

---

[11]Alford, III, 204.
[12]B. F. Westcott, *The Epistle to the Hebrews*, p. 14.

from the River unto the ends of the earth. Yea, all kings shall fall down before him; all nations shall serve him" (Ps. 72:8, 11, ASV). It is also the will of God that creatures in heaven acknowledge the Son as supreme Lord: "Therefore God has highly exalted him and bestowed on him the name which is above every name, that at the name of Jesus every knee should bow, in heaven and on earth and under the earth, and every tongue confess that Jesus Christ is Lord, to the glory of God the Father" (Phil. 2:9-11, RSV).

To a large extent the fulfillment of these prophecies is yet future. Throughout the period before the incarnation, human will and sin were permitted to go on in accomplishing the ultimate purpose of God. The theocracy in the Old Testament is to be related to this place of Christ in the government of God. In the millennium Christ will reign as the Son of David in fulfillment of many prophecies.

One of the major revelations in the Old Testament in connection with the providential work of the Son of God is His ministry to Israel which is discussed in connection with the theophanies. A careful study will reveal that Christ was very active in the Old Testament and an integral factor in every page of Israel's history. The work of the Son of God did not begin when He died on the cross or when He ministered to men in His public ministry as recorded in the Gospels, but is an essential ingredient in all the work of God throughout the pages of human history. Taken as a whole, the work of the preincarnate Christ in providence includes all the major features of the doctrine, and the Son of God is seen preserving, guiding, delivering and governing His creatures. The aspects of the work of Christ yet to be considered, the theophanies and their revelation of God, the work of Christ in salvation in the Old Testament, and the types of Christ, combine to confirm and enlarge the doctrine of providence.

OLD TESTAMENT THEOPHANIES

The word "theophany," coming from the Greek words for God (*theos*) and "to appear" (*phainō*), has historically been taken to refer to appearances of Christ in the Old Testament. Another term often used is epiphany ("appearance" to someone). In the Bible, theophanies have reference specifically to Christ.[13] Usually

[13]The words are also used in Greek mythology of appearances of the gods.

they are limited to appearances of Christ in the form of man or
angel while other forms of appearance, such as the Shekinah, are
not considered as formal theophanies. The principal theophany
of the Old Testament is the Angel of Jehovah who has been
shown in previous discussions to be the Son of God appearing in
the form of an angel.

The Angel of Jehovah

As the most frequent form of theophany in the Old Testament,
the Angel of Jehovah affords a rich study in revelation of the
person and work of Christ in His preincarnate state. Reference
to the Angel of Jehovah or the Angel of the presence is found
throughout the entire Old Testament (Gen. 16:7-13; 21:17; 22:11-
18; 24:7, 40; 31:11; 32:24-32; cf. Hosea 12:4; Gen. 48:15-16; Exodus 3:2; cf. Acts 7:30-35; Exodus 13:21; cf. 14:19; 23:20-23; 32:34;
33:2; Num. 20:16; 22:22-35; Judges 2:1-4; 5:23; 6:11-24; 13:3-
23; II Sam. 14:17-20; 19:27; 24:14-17; I Kings 19:5-7; II Kings 1:3,
15; 19:35; I Chron. 21:11-30; Ps. 34:7; 35:5-6; Eccles. 5:6; Isa.
37:36; 63:9; Zech. 1:9-21; 2:3; 3:1-10; 4:1-7; 5:5-10; 6:4-5; 12:8).
In some passages reference is merely to "the angel" or to "the
angel of God." In general, the context determines whether this
is specifically a reference to the Angel of Jehovah. There are
some passages in which it is not clear (see Dan. 3:28; 6:22). In
other references the context leaves little doubt as to the meaning
of the term.

A study of the many passages dealing with the Angel of Jehovah
will reveal a most remarkable breadth to the preincarnate work
of Christ for His people. At the same time, His person is revealed
in all its grace and righteousness. In the first instance (Gen. 16:7-
13), Christ is seeking the fleeing and disheartened Hagar. To her
He gives comfort and assurance. Again in Genesis 21:17-19 Christ
as the Angel comes to her aid. It is certainly a revelation of the
gracious care of God that in the first two theophanies of Scripture
in which the Angel appears, it is on behalf of a friendless and
comfortless person who is not even included in major features of
the Abrahamic covenant.

In Genesis 22:11-18 the Angel stays the hand of Abraham about
to sacrifice Isaac, and a substitute is provided—a beautiful type
of the substitution of Christ on behalf of those under the curse of
death. The Angel goes before the servant of Abraham seeking a

wife for Isaac and prospering his way (Gen. 24:7, 40). The Angel ministers to Jacob (Gen. 31:11; 48:15-16). He appears to Moses in the burning bush to call him to his work as leader (Exodus 3:2). The Angel of God is in the pillar of a cloud and the pillar of fire and leads Israel through the wilderness to the promised land (Exodus 13:21; 14:19; 23:20-23; 32:34; 33:2; Num. 20:16; Isa. 63:9). He warns Balaam (Num. 22:22-35). He warns and judges Israel (Judges 2:1-4). Gideon is called and commissioned as a leader and judge by the Angel (Judges 6:11-24). An entire chapter of Scripture is devoted to the Angel of Jehovah and His dealings with the parents of Samson (Judges 13:3-23). The common belief in the Angel of Jehovah as God Himself is shown in the conversation of various people in the Old Testament: the woman who appears before David (II Sam. 14:4-20); Mephibosheth (II Sam. 19:27); and Nebuchadnezzar (Dan. 3:28).

The Angel of Jehovah as the righteous Judge is revealed also in His judgment upon sin, as in the case of David's sin in numbering Israel (II Sam. 24:14-17; I Chron. 21:11-30), and the slaying of 185,000 Assyrians (II Kings 19:35; Isa. 37:36). The thoughtful care of the Angel of Jehovah is shown in His treatment of Elijah (I Kings 19:5-7). He instructs Elijah in his controversy with Ahaziah and the judgment on the messengers (II Kings 1:1-16). He is the Protector of Daniel (Dan. 3:28; 6:22), if these passages are correctly applied to the Angel of Jehovah. He is the Revealer of secrets to Zechariah in his prophecy (Zech. 1:9).

The combined testimony of these passages portrays the Son of God as exceedingly active in the Old Testament, dealing with sin, providing for those in need, guiding in the path of the will of God, protecting His people from their enemies and, in general, executing the providence of God. The references make plain that this ministry is not occasional or exceptional but rather the common and continual ministry of God to His people. The revelation of the person of the Son of God thus afforded is in complete harmony with the New Testament revelation. The testimony of Scripture has been so complete on this point that in general scholars who accept the inspiration and infallibility of Scripture are agreed that the Angel of Jehovah is the Christ of the Old Testament. Not only Christian theologians but Jewish scholars as well have come to the conclusion that the Angel of Jehovah is more than an angel.[14] It is at once a revelation of the person and preincarnate work of Christ and an evidence for His preexistence and deity.

Other Theophanies

While fewer in number, other forms of theophany are afforded in the Old Testament. In Genesis 18:1-33 (ASV), Jehovah appears in the form of a man, accompanied by two other men who were probably angels. In view of the revelation in other theophanies, there can be little doubt that this theophany is also an appearance of Christ. Jacob's experience of wrestling with God (Gen. 32:24-32) is identified in Hosea 12:4 as the time when Jacob "had power over the angel, and prevailed." The appearance of God to the elders of Israel is probably another theophany of Christ (Exodus 24:9-11). The cloud of the Lord, the glory of the Lord (Exodus 40:38) and the cloudy pillar (Exodus 33:9-23) are all to be taken as appearances of Christ in the Old Testament, even though in somewhat different character than a formal theophany like the Angel of Jehovah. It is safe to assume that every visible manifestation of God in bodily form in the Old Testament is to be identified with the Lord Jesus Christ. The "prince of the host of Jehovah" (Joshua 5:13-15, ASV), "the appearance of the likeness of the glory of Jehovah" of Ezekiel (Ezek. 1:1-28, ASV), and other similar appearances are best explained as theophanies of Christ. Some passages must, however, remain in dispute, as the appearance of an angel to Daniel (Dan. 10:1-21).[15] The number of theophanies which are without question furnish one of the major forms of Old Testament revelation of God. Their identification with the Son of God refutes at once the Arian heresy that Christ was a created being and the Socinian and Unitarian perversions of the person of Christ. For anyone who

[14]A. C. Gaebelein, *The Angels of God*, p. 20, says, "It is noteworthy and of great interest that the ancient Jews in their traditions regarded the Angel of the Lord, in every instance, not as an ordinary angel, but as the only mediator between God and the world, the author of all revelations, to whom they gave the name *Metatron.*" Richard Watson, *Theological Institutes*, I, 501, also affirms the support of ancient Jews to this interpretation.

[15]H. A. Ironside views this passage as a reference to an angel, based on the angel's need of the help of Michael. William Kelly considers it a theophany. Cf. Ironside, *Lectures on Daniel the Prophet*, pp. 174-75; Dan. 10:1-21; Rev. 1:12-16.

will accept the Scriptures in their plain intent, there is a clear portrayal of Christ in these Old Testament theophanies.[16]

CHRIST AS THE SAVIOUR IN THE OLD TESTAMENT

The revelation of the plan of God in salvation in the Old Testament has occasioned no little dispute as to its exact character. Modernists in theology have attempted to conform the revelation of the Old Testament to an evolutionary pattern which tends to eliminate any revelation of the love and mercy of God until late in the Old Testament. On the other hand conservative theologians have pointed out the evident mercies of God from Genesis to Malachi. Confusion also has arisen on a number of other important points. The problem of interpreting the Old Testament without undue influence from later revelation in the New Testament continues to plague the student of Old Testament theology. Others have been confused concerning the relation of the plan of salvation to the different Old Testament dispensations. Without attempting to discuss in full all these important aspects, certain facts stand out as constituting the elements of salvation in the Old Testament.

[16]The testimony of the early Fathers on the theophanies of Christ in the Old Testament is full and conclusive. Justin Martyr declared: "Permit me, further, to show you from the book of Exodus how this same One, who is both Angel, and God, and Lord, and man, and who had appeared in human form to Abraham and Isaac, appeared in a flame of fire from the bush and conversed with Moses" ("Dialogue with Trypho," 59).

Irenaeus wrote, ". . . because the Son of God is implanted everywhere throughout his writings: at one time, indeed, speaking with Abraham, when about to eat with him; at another time with Noah, giving to him the dimensions [of the ark]; at another, inquiring after Adam; at another bringing down judgment upon the Sodomites; and again, when He becomes visible, and directs Jacob on his journey, and speaks with Moses from the bush" ("Against Heresies," IV. 10. 1).

Tertullian stated, "It is the Son, therefore, who has been from the beginning administering judgment, throwing down the haughty tower, and dividing the tongues, punishing the whole world by the violence of waters, raining upon Sodom and Gomorrah fire and brimstone, as the LORD from the LORD. For He is who was at all times came down to hold converse with men, from Adam on to the patriarchs and the prophets, in vision, in dream, in mirror, in dark saying; ever from the beginning laying the foundation of the course [of His dispensations], which He meant to follow out to the very last. Thus was He ever learning even as God to converse with men upon earth, being no other than the Word which was to be made flesh ("Against Praxeas," 16). A similar statement is found in Tertullian, "Against Marcion," II. 27. See also Watson, I, 501-2. Watson also cites Clement of Alexandria, Origen, Theophilus of Antioch, the Synod of Antioch, Cyprian, Hilary, St. Basil and others as holding the same viewpoint of theophanies of Christ in the Old Testament.

In the Old Testament, salvation is often presented as a collective deliverance rather than an individual matter. In many instances, God intervened to deliver His people from danger or oppression, and this is considered a phase of salvation. Salvation was also viewed eschatologically as contemplating a future deliverance when Christ returned. The contemporary element, however, is not lacking, and individuals in the Old Testament could testify to their personal salvation. The prophesied coming Redeemer was the object of hope of Old Testament saints as illustrated in Job's statement "I know that my redeemer liveth, and that he shall stand at the latter day upon the earth" (Job 19:25). Many scriptures tie together the Saviour of the Old Testament and the Saviour of the New.[17]

One of the major difficulties in the discussion of the Old Testament doctrine of salvation is that modernism and evolution have relentlessly invaded Old Testament teachings. If the primary religion of early man was polytheistic, animistic or reduced to a fetishism and totemism, obviously we shall look in vain for any true revelation of salvation. On the contrary, the Scriptures are explicit that from Adam and Eve down there was a definite primary revelation of true salvation of God. Only by denying the accuracy of Scripture can any other view be supported. It is rather curious that the modernist after declaring as spurious or interpolated the portions of early Scripture which oppose the evolutionary theory then turns to what is left of the Scripture for evidence of his own view. In the doctrine of Old Testament salvation, if the Scriptures are accepted as infallible, the revelation of salvation is not a late development of prophetic writers but a primary and basic revelation of God to the first man and succeeding generations.

The Revelation of Universal Sin and Condemnation

In the account of the fall in Genesis 3 nothing is made clearer to man than the fact that through his sin he had come under condemnation. This was manifest in hiding from God and in con-

[17]For helpful studies in this field consult William D. Kerswill, *The Old Testament Doctrine of Salvation*; F. Michaeli, "Salvation, O.T.," *A Companion to the Bible*, J. J. Von Allmen (ed.), pp. 382-84; Edward M. B. Green, *The Meaning of Salvation*, pp. 15-25, 29-32. As these discussions demonstrate, there is considerable confusion on the precise nature of salvation in the Old Testament.

fessions to God. The need for salvation was patent. In the Garden of Eden began the two contradictory systems—the serpent's suggestion of the possibility of self-improvement and development of natural man, and the revelation by God of sin and depravity and the hopelessness of man's estate apart from God's salvation. Here is the fundamental conflict between biblical Christianity and pagan humanism as reflected in human thought down to the present. As God plainly told Adam and Eve, the penalty of sin is death, both spiritual and physical. There was evident need of salvation, and Adam and Eve knew it.

The Revelation of a Coming Saviour

It is a wonderful revelation of the mercy and love of God that in the Garden of Eden, before He pronounced judgment on Adam and Eve, God—it may have been the Son of God Himself—promised that the seed of the woman should bruise the head of the serpent (Gen. 3:15). Here was the ray of hope in the darkness of human sin and failure. God had a way of salvation. The reference to the seed of the woman is a prophecy of the birth of the Son of God. This is the point of Luke's genealogy (cf. Gal. 4:4). The coming Saviour was to be the seed of the woman—human; and yet in the fact that He is not called the seed of man, we have the foreshadowing of the virgin birth (Isa. 7:14; Matt. 1:21-22). To Adam it was made very plain that his hope lay in this future Child of the woman, that through this Child salvation would come from God. God confirmed His mercy to Adam and Eve by driving them out of the garden—a judgment for sin to be sure, but an act of mercy as well, lest they eat of the tree of life and live forever in bodies of sin.

The Revelation of the Way of Salvation

It must remain for the most part a matter of speculation how much God revealed to Adam beyond what is recorded in the Scriptures. The extent of pre-Scripture revelation has been greatly underestimated. A study of Job, which many believe was among the first books of Scripture to be written and deals with a period long before the Exodus, reveals a most advanced system of theology based on direct revelation of God. It is remarkable how extensive is the knowledge of theology proper, anthropology and hamartiology, soteriology and even eschatology in Job. We must believe that God did not leave the world in complete darkness of knowledge essential to the way of salvation.

In the immediate facts of the Genesis narrative of the lives of Adam and Eve and their children, there is a clear testimony to their knowledge of the way of salvation. Immediately after the account of the fall, the incidence of the offerings of Cain and Abel serves to illustrate the extent of their knowledge. Cain's offering of a bloodless sacrifice is refused by God, and Cain is told that a sin offering lay at the door (for a literal rendering of "sin" see Gen. 4:7). Cain is plainly told that the way of forgiveness is through offering a bloody sacrifice. Abel's offering of the firstlings of his flock and the fat thereof (Gen. 4:4) is accepted. No doubt the offerings reflect the spiritual condition of the offerer, but the illuminating point is that God appeals to Cain on the basis of revelation previously given. Abel and Cain both knew that the sacrifice for sin should be a particular animal, a lamb; a particular lamb, the firstling; and a particular part of the lamb, the fat. Such knowledge could come only from revelation.

The question has often been discussed concerning the condition of salvation in the Old Testament. If the present offer of the grace of God is secure to those who believe in Christ, what was the specific condition of salvation in the Old Testament? The problem has assumed undue proportions as a result of the unwarranted zeal of scholars who emphasize the unity of God's plan without regard for biblical dispensational distinctions. It is clear that Old Testament saints did not believe in Christ in the same way and with the same comprehension that believers with the New Testament do for the simple reason that they were not in possession of the same information. In the nature of the case the issue of faith is to believe in the revelation given.

On the other hand there are not two ways of salvation. All salvation of God stems from the Saviour, the Son of God, and His work on the cross. It is also clear that the salvation of individual souls requires faith. Even a merciful and gracious God cannot save a soul who passes into eternity in unbelief. The two great essentials of salvation remain the same from the salvation of Adam to the last soul which God takes to Himself in the future. Faith is the condition and the death of Christ is the ground.

The chief difficulty, however, rests in the precise definition of these two elements. Faith in what? What is the nature of the object of faith? The gospel of grace was given to Paul as *new* revelation (Rom. 1:2-4). God does not hold the Old Testament saints to account for revelation given in the New Testament. Faith as a condition of salvation is obviously faith in the promises of God insofar as they were revealed. For Adam and Eve this was faith in the promise that the seed of the woman would bruise the head of the serpent—would bring salvation to fallen man and defeat the tempter. As the exact character and work of the Deliverer is only gradually unfolded in the Old Testament, faith took the form of trust in Jehovah Himself without necessarily specific knowledge of the way by which Jehovah was to .provide an adequate salvation.

The remaining principal element is the relation of faith to the system of sacrifices immediately instituted under the patriarchal system from Adam to Moses and of faith to the Mosaic system which followed. In what sense were the sacrifices a necessary condition of salvation? Does this constitute a salvation by works?

Even the New Testament emphasizes, "Faith by itself, if it has no works, is dead" (James 2:17, RSV). In other words, mere belief which does not issue in works is not real faith at all. There is no fundamental antithesis between James 2 and Paul in Romans 4. James is presenting the issue of whether a person has living faith. Paul is dealing with the issue of justification before God. The principle involved is that salvation is by faith, but that faith if real will have certain manifestations. This same principle can be carried into the Old Testament.

Under the system of sacrifices, God provided an outward means of manifesting inward faith. But the sacrifices in themselves could not save because an unbeliever who offered sacrifices was still lost. A believer who really trusted in Jehovah would, on the other hand, be sure to offer his sacrifices. The sacrifices, although not work which was acceptable as a ground of salvation before God, were nevertheless work which demonstrated faith. Faith in the Old Testament therefore took a definite outward form of manifestation. In offering the sacrifice, the offerer was assured that he was performing an act of recognition of God as his Saviour and in particular a recognition of the promise of the coming seed of the woman, the Son of God Himself. The institution of the Mosaic covenant did not alter the way of salvation but specified more particularly the way of sacrifice. Moreover, it provided a detailed rule of life, the means for maintenance of fellowship and communion with God, and the obligation to obey as a condition for blessing in this life. Salvation was still a work of God for man, not a work of man for God.

The Work of the Son of God in Salvation

The unfolding of the plan of God in salvation after Adam is the story of progressive revelation. The mass of humanity moved away from the revelation given and was plunged in darkness and sin. Through succeeding generations a remnant continued to believe in God, to receive further light. Noah and his family were delivered from destruction and after the flood Noah immediately offered his sacrifices. Abraham "believed in Jehovah; and he reckoned it to him for righteousness" (Gen. 15:6, ASV). While Abraham's justification was somewhat different from the Christian's justification *in Christ* by baptism of the Spirit, he nevertheless was counted righteous before God because of faith in Jehovah and His promises regarding Abraham's seed. Sarah was declared in the New Testament to have "considered him faithful who had promised" (Heb. 11:11, RSV). Moses was declared to have had a personal faith in Christ on the basis of which he forsook Egypt: "He considered abuse suffered for the Christ greater wealth than the treasures of Egypt" (Heb. 11:26, RSV). The psalmists are replete with ascriptions of trust in Jehovah for their salvation. It is often presented as taking refuge in Jehovah: "How precious is thy lovingkindness, O God! And the children of men take refuge under the shadow of thy wings" (Ps. 36:7, ASV). "Oh taste and see that Jehovah is good: blessed is the man that taketh refuge in him" (Ps. 34:8, ASV). Of particular interest is the passage in Psalm 2:12b (ASV): "Blessed are all they that take refuge in him." The context indicates that "him" is a specific reference to the Son. To the Son of God is attributed that same confidence and trust that is given to Jehovah.

The work of the Son of God in salvation was not only a matter of salvation from the guilt and condemnation of sin. In many cases the salvation of Jehovah is described in its present application—deliverance from ungodly and wicked men. Again the psalmists can be taken as illustrative of this point: "The salvation of the righteous is of Jehovah; he is their stronghold in the time of trouble. And Jehovah helpeth them, and rescueth them: he rescueth them from the wicked, and saveth them, because they have taken refuge in him" (Ps. 37:39-40, ASV). The familiar Twenty-third Psalm is an expression of this same reality in the experience of David. In declaring, "Jehovah is my shepherd" (Ps. 23:1, ASV), David was declaring his confidence in the pre-incarnate Son of God, the good Shepherd, to care for him as a shepherd cares for his sheep. David believed that the present mercies of God would be crowned by his dwelling "in the house of Jehovah for ever" (Ps. 23:6b, ASV).

The full story of salvation of the Son of God in the Old Testament is too large to be compressed into a limited discussion. Suffice it to say, the salvation provided through the Son of God was a complete salvation. It gave eternal life, assurance, and rest of heart to the believer. It transformed his life even though some of the spiritual enablement provided for the believer today was lacking. Salvation included forgiveness, justification as in the case of Abraham, deliverance from evil, and the full-orbed work of God in providence toward His own. The important fact which stands out above all others is that the Saviour of the Old Testament is the Saviour of the New Testament. He was actively engaged in bringing salvation in its widest sense to those who trusted Him. The full picture of the Son of God in His preincarnate state usually includes the rich field of typology as well as a discussion of Messianic prophecies as found in the Old Testament. Studies of these two fields follow.

4

CHRIST IN OLD TESTAMENT TYPOLOGY

LATENT IN THE OLD TESTAMENT is a rich treasury of Christological truth in the form of biblical types. Typology has always suffered certain disabilities and unbelief which other branches of theological instruction have been spared. For this reason and others it has been unjustly neglected in theological discussion. As Patrick Fairbairn states in opening his classic work on the subject,

> The Typology of Scripture has been one of the most neglected departments of theological science. It has never altogether escaped from the region of doubt and uncertainty; and some still regard it as a field incapable, from its very nature, of being satisfactorily explored, or cultivated so as to yield any sure and appreciable results.[1]

The difficulty has been that typology by its nature is more subject to personal opinion of the interpreter than ordinary exegesis. It is often confused with allegorical interpretation and is not as subject to the corroborating teachings of other Scripture. Typology is primarily concerned with application of an historical fact as an illustration of a spiritual truth. As Webster puts it, a type is "a figure or representation of something to come."[2] It is therefore prophetic by its character, and we may expect a considerable contribution from it to the doctrine of Christ. A study of Christological typology includes about fifty important types of Christ— about half of the recognized total in the entire field of typology.[3]

In the New Testament two Greek words are used to express the thought of a type: *typos* and *hypodeigma*. As Lewis Sperry Chafer has stated:

[1]Patrick Fairbairn, *The Typology of Scripture*, I, 1.
[2]*Webster's New International Dictionary of the English Language*, 2d ed.
[3]See Lewis S. Chafer, *Systematic Theology*, I, xxx.

[*Typos*] means an imprint which may serve as a mold or pattern, and that which is typical in the Old Testament is a mold or pattern of that which is antitypical in the New Testament. The root . . . [*typos*] is translated by five English words ('ensample,' 1 Cor. 10:11; Phil. 3:17; 1 Thess. 1:7; 2 Thess. 3:9; 1 Pet. 5:3; 'example,' 1 Tim. 4:12; Heb. 8:5; 'figure,' Acts 7:43; Rom. 5:14; 'pattern,' Titus 2:7; 'print of the nails,' John 20:25). . . . [*Deigma*] means a 'specimen' or 'example,' and when combined with . . . [*hupo*] indicates that which is shown plainly under the eyes of men. . . . [*Hypodeigma*] is translated by two English words ('example,' John 13:15; Heb. 4:11; 8:5; James 5:10; and 'pattern,' Heb. 9:23).[4]

Typology as a branch of biblical revelation is well established in the Scriptures themselves as evidenced by the frequent use made of it in the New Testament. The problem to be considered here is not the larger discussion of typology as a whole, but its contribution to Christology.

Two extremes in the study of typology should be avoided. A tendency on the part of some is to limit typology to instances clearly authorized in the New Testament. The instances cited in the New Testament, however, clearly are representative. That is, some cases (viz., the two sons of Abraham, Gal. 4:22-31) would probably be labeled as extreme if they did not have New Testament authority behind them. On the other hand, some have found typology in almost every situation in the Old Testament to the neglect of primary exegesis. Typical interpretation may vary greatly from that which seems directly typical to that which is merely a parallelism. It cannot be emphasized too strongly that types which do not have express scriptural authority are illustrative rather than proof for doctrinal points.

As many writers have pointed out, typology is concerned with (1) typical persons; (2) typical events; (3) typical things; (4) typical institutions; and (5) typical ceremonies.[5] It is manifestly impossible to gather into a brief discussion the wealth of revelation afforded in the types which concern Christ in the Old Testament; but rather than omit this important contribution, an attempt is made to summarize the important types and their prophetic contribution.

[4]*Ibid.*, I, xxxi.
[5]Cf. *ibid.*

TYPICAL PERSONS

Aaron

The Scriptures, particularly Hebrews, give a firm basis for believing that Aaron is a true type of Christ. As a priest, Aaron was appointed to his sacred office (Heb. 5:4) as was Christ to His priesthood (Heb. 5:5-6). Aaron was appointed to minister in the earthly sphere as Christ was appointed to the heavenly (Heb. 8:1-5). Aaron administered the old Mosaic covenant while Christ ministered the new covenant (Heb. 8:6). Aaron was appointed to offer sacrifices daily while Christ offered Himself once for all (Heb. 7:27). The Aaronic type reveals Christ in His true humanity and in His priestly work. As Aaron remained a part of Israel even as he served as mediator, so Christ remains genuinely human, on earth knowing weakness, certain limitations, suffering and struggle, as did Aaron, and even in heaven continues in His true humanity. While Hebrews brings out the contrast between Aaron and Christ, there is obviously a typical foreshadowing of Christ in the Aaronic priesthood in the person of Aaron. The intercession of Aaron is a picture of the intercession of Christ.

Abel

In this type we have Christ presented as the true Shepherd who made an acceptable bloody sacrifice to God in obedience to the command of God. As Abel was slain by Cain, representing the world, so Christ was slain. As Abel's offering was accepted by God, so Christ in His offering is accepted. The fact that Abel's offering was accepted because offered by faith (Heb. 11:4) does not take away its essential character. It was because Abel believed revelation concerning sacrifices that he offered his lamb in contrast to Cain's bloodless offering. He is therefore a type of Christ in life as shepherd, in his offering, and in his death.

Adam

One of the important types recognized by Scripture is that of Adam. Adam is the head of the old creation as Christ is the Head of the new creation. This is plainly implied in Romans 5:14 (RSV), "Yet death reigned from Adam to Moses, even over those whose sins were not like the transgression of Adam, who was a type of the one who was to come." Both Adam and Christ entered the world through a special act of God. Both entered the world sinless; both acted on behalf of those whom God considered in them representatively. The sin of Adam is contrasted to the act of obedience of Christ. The Scripture discussion of the subject leaves no room for doubt on the main elements of this type (Rom. 5:12-21). The very terms "first Adam" and "last Adam" and similar expressions are applied respectively to Adam and Christ (I Cor. 15:45-47). Adam as the husband of Eve is also a type of the Bridegroom in relation to the church as the bride.

Benjamin

In the contrast of the two names of Benjamin there was foreshadowed the two aspects of the person of Christ—His sufferings and the glory to follow. With her dying breath, Rachel named her newborn son Ben-oni, meaning "son of sorrow." Jacob, however, named him Benjamin, meaning "son of my right hand." As Ben-oni, Christ was the Son of sorrow to His mother (Luke 2:35) and the One who knew suffering as the Man of sorrows and death. As Benjamin, Christ is "the son of my right hand" to God the Father, victorious in the battle with sin as Benjamin was victorious as the warrior tribe.

David

The historic and prophetic connection between David and Christ is commonly recognized, but the typical significance of David is often overlooked. David is a type of Christ as the one who is first shepherd, then king. David experienced the call of God, rejection by his brethren, was in constant danger of his life because he was anointed king, and during the years of his rejection took a Gentile wife, typical of the church. Later he ruled over Israel in complete power and sovereignty. The typical significance of these events, as well as many minor incidents in his life, are foreshadowings of Christ.

Isaac

In the New Testament Isaac is regarded as a type of the church, composed of the spiritual children of Abraham (Gal. 4:28) and as a type of the new nature which is born of the Spirit in contrast to the old nature typified by Ishmael (Gal. 4:29). It is interesting to note that Isaac is taken to be a type of two distinct things in two successive verses of the New Testament.

In the person of Isaac are many typical truths relating to Christ which are not mentioned in the New Testament. The births of Isaac and of Christ were genuinely miraculous. Both are involved in the promised deliverance first announced to Eve. Their births were anticipated and involved in the promises of God long before fulfillment. Both are the beloved of their fathers and both are declared to be "only begotten" (John 3:16; Heb. 11:17) although Ishmael was born before Isaac, and all believers in Christ call God their Father. In Genesis 22 the sacrifice of Isaac on Moriah is a foreshadowing of the death of Christ. In the type, Isaac is saved at the last moment and a substitute is provided. In the antitype, just as truly offered by the Father, there could be no substitute. Truly, Isaac lived because Christ died. In the beautiful story of Genesis 24 the securing of the bride for Isaac is again a prophetic picture, in type, of the Holy Spirit securing a bride for Christ, and complete in all its details.[6] The entire life of Isaac affords a more complete typical picture of the person and work of Christ than any previous character in Scripture.[7]

Joseph

While the New Testament nowhere authorizes the interpretation that Joseph is a type of Christ, the numerous factors of his life which point to this conclusion indicate in fact that Joseph is the most complete type of Christ in the Old Testament. Both Joseph and Christ were born by special intervention of God (Gen. 30:22-24; Luke 1:35). Both were objects of special love by their fathers (Gen. 37:3; Matt. 3:17; John 3:35); both were hated by brethren (Gen. 37:4; John 15:24-25); both were rejected as rulers over their brethren (Gen. 37:8; Matt. 21:37-39; John 15:24-25); both were robbed of their robes (Gen. 37:23; Matt. 27:35); both were conspired against and placed in the pit of death (Gen. 37:18, 24; Matt. 26:3-4; 27:35-37); both were sold for silver (Gen. 37:28; Matt. 26:14-15); both became servants (Gen. 39:4; Phil. 2:7); both were condemned though innocent (Gen. 39:11-20; Isa. 53:9; Matt. 27:19, 24). As Joseph is a type of Christ in humili-

[6]Cf. the beautiful exposition of this by George E. Guille, *Isaac and Rebekah.*
[7]The New Scofield Reference Bible provides much help on all the types of Christ in the Old Testament and should be consulted.

ation, so is he also in exaltation. Both were raised from humiliation to glory by the power of God. Even Pharaoh saw in Joseph one in whom was the Spirit of God (Gen. 41:38), and Christ is manifested in resurrection power as the very Son of God. Both during the time of exaltation but continued rejection by brethren take a Gentile bride and are a blessing to Gentiles (Gen. 41:1-45; Acts 15:14; Rom. 11:11-12; Eph. 5:25-32). After the time of Gentile blessing begins to wane, both are received finally by their brethren and recognized as a savior and deliverer (Gen. 45:1-15; Rom. 11:1-27). Both exalt their brethren to places of honor and safety (Gen. 45:16-18; Isa. 65:17-25).

Joshua

Attention is directed to Joshua first because of his name, which means "Jehovah saves." It is the Old Testament equivalent of the Greek name Jesus. As a type of Christ, Joshua is significant first because he is the successor of Moses just as Christ succeeded Moses and the law (John 1:17; Rom. 8:2-4; Heb. 7:18-19; Gal. 3:23-25). Joshua like Christ won a victory where Moses had failed (Rom. 8:3-4). In the time of conflict and defeat both Joshua and Christ interceded for their own (Joshua 7:5-9; Luke 22:32; I John 2:1). The portions of Israel were allotted by Joshua even as Christ gives gifts and rewards to His own (Joshua 13 ff.).

Kinsman-redeemer

Throughout the Old Testament there is constant reference to the kinsman-redeemer (Hebrew, *gaal*). It is evident that these instances are typical foreshadowings of Christ as our Redeemer. The general law of redemption in the Old Testament is clear. The redeemer had to be a kinsman, one related to the person or inheritance to be redeemed (Lev. 25:48-49; Ruth 3:12-13; Heb. 2:14-15). Christ fulfilled this by becoming Man and by having the sins of the world imputed to Him. The Old Testament redeemer had to be able to redeem even as Christ did in the New Testament (Ruth 4:4-6; John 10:11, 18; I Peter 1:18). The redemption was accomplished by the payment of the price (Lev. 25:27; Rom. 3:24-26; I Peter 1:18-19; Gal. 3:13). The entire Old Testament order of redemption is a prophetic picture of Christ who would come to redeem through the sacrifice of Himself.

Melchizedek

In Genesis 14 Melchizedek as king of Salem brought forth bread and wine as the priest of the most high God and blessed Abraham after his return from the conquest of the kings. The Scriptures record that Abraham gave to Melchizedek tithes of all. Later in Psalm 110:4, it is predicted that Christ should be a Priest forever after the order of Melchizedek. These two passages are the occasion for the discussion in Hebrews 5-7 in which Christ is declared a Priest according to the prophecy of the psalm. Combining the various elements presented in these passages, it becomes clear upon scriptural warrant that Melchizedek is a type of Christ.

His name is significant for, as many have noted, Melchizedek is a combination of two words meaning "king" and "righteous" which combined as it is with the word Salem, meaning "peace," presents Christ as a type of the righteous king-priest who is king of Salem, with the resultant meaning that Christ is the King of peace. As one who brings forth bread and wine some have suggested that the type refers particularly to the resurrected Christ. In the New Testament Melchizedek is interpreted as proving the eternity of the priesthood of Christ and its superiority to the Levitical priesthood, based on the argument that Levi paid tithes to Melchizedek through Abraham his forefather (cf. Heb. 5:6, 10; 6:20; 7:17, 21).

Moses

As one of the great prophets and leaders of the Old Testament, it is not surprising that Moses should also be a type of Christ. Moses predicted to the children of Israel on the basis of the revelation given to him by Jehovah that a Prophet would come like unto himself to whom they should give ear (Deut. 18:15-19). The typology of Moses is, however, based primarily on the evident significance of events in his life foreshadowing the coming of Christ. Like Christ, Moses as a child was in danger of death, being born in a period during which Israel was under oppression. By sovereign choice of God, both were chosen to be saviors and deliverers (Exodus 3:7-10; Acts 7:25). Both were rejected by their brethren (Exodus 2:11-15; John 1:11; Acts 7:23-28; 18:5-6). During the period of rejection both minister to Gentiles and secure a

Gentile bride, typical of the church (Exodus 2:16-21; II Cor. 11:2; Eph. 5:25-32). Moses, after the period of separation was concluded, returned to deliver Israel, even as Christ is predicted to return to deliver Israel. Both are received by Israel at their second comings (Exodus 4:19-31; Rom. 11:24-26; Acts 15:14, 17). Like Christ, Moses is prophet (Num. 34:1-2; John 12:29; Matt. 13:57;. 21:11; Acts 3:22-23); priest as advocate (Exodus 32:31-35; I John 2:1-2) and intercessor (Exodus 17:1-6; Heb. 7:25); and king or ruler (Deut. 33:4-5; John 1:49). Like Christ, Moses had to die before the children of Israel could enter the land, typical of a Christian's possessions. As Isaac and Joseph, Moses is an outstanding illustration of typical truth valuable for its foreshadowing of the life and ministry of Christ.

Taken as a whole the typology of persons manifests that the Old Testament is Christ-centered, having its main purpose in foreshadowing the person and work of Christ. It is a rich field for devotional study and unfortunately one that has been greatly neglected.

TYPICAL EVENTS

So many events in the Old Testament can be viewed from a typical point of view that it is impossible to provide a comprehensive study of this area of Christological typology. A few suggestions, however, can be made as to the character of this field of revelation.

Clothing of Adam and Eve

In the midst of the ruin of sin and judgment which followed the fall of Adam and Eve, the Scriptures record a gracious thing which God did for fallen humanity. In Genesis 3:21 (ASV) it is written: "And Jehovah God made for Adam and for his wife coats of skins, and clothed them." It was, of course, a supply of a physical need for clothing which God recognized, but it seems evident that the meaning is deeper than this. God was representing to them the fact that He would supply that which would cover the nakedness of sin and provide a righteous covering through the death of Christ, a thought which is given frequent utterance in Scripture (Job 29:14; Ps. 132:9; Isa. 61:10; 64:6; Rom. 3:22; Rev. 19:8).

Preservation in the Ark

Another dramatic event in the early history of the race is the preservation of Noah and his family in the ark. In the midst of almost universal judgment, God singled out the righteous and preserved them. It represents in general God's deliverance of the righteous from judgment, a major aspect of the work of the Saviour. Just as God saved Noah while "bringing in the flood upon the world of the ungodly" (II Peter 2:5) and as God "delivered just Lot" (2:7) from Sodom, Peter concludes: "The Lord knoweth how to deliver the godly out of temptations, and to reserve the unjust unto the day of judgment to be punished" (2:9). This deliverance, however, does not exclude the possibility of martyrdom as indicated in Paul's experience (II Tim. 4:18).

Deliverance from Egypt

The entire picture of Israel being delivered out of Egypt and brought through the wilderness experiences into the promised land is a major field of typology and one which illustrates the work of Christ in salvation. The major elements of the deliverance, the plagues, the institution of the Passover, and the salvation of Israel at the Red Sea all speak of Christ. The plagues represent the judgment upon the wicked world and in type speak of the future deliverance of Israel in the great tribulation. The Passover is an eloquent type of the death of Christ as the believer's only place of safety from the judgment and death which overtake the world. At the Red Sea Israel is delivered through the same waters which destroyed the Egyptians, a type of the death of Christ in its power to deliver from the world. The wilderness experiences with the manna from heaven (Exodus 16:4), speak of Christ as the bread of life, while the water out of the rock (Exodus 17:6), speaks of Christ smitten that we might have life, and many of the other incidents speak of the work of Christ for His own.

Entrance into the Land

The crossing of the Jordan River and the subsequent conquest of Canaan has been recognized as typical truth, although the interpretations have differed. It is preferable to consider Canaan not as a type of heaven but as the believer's present sphere of conflict and possession in Christ. Crossing the Jordan with its piled-up waters, speaking of the death of Christ as the means of victory, is entrance into the enjoyment of our possessions in Christ in the land. The Angel of Jehovah, which is Christ, went before the Israelites, and it was through His power that they achieved the conquest. The experiences of Joshua have their parallel in Ephesians in the New Testament. The believer gains spiritual possessions by faith in Christ, by crucifixion with Christ and by the mighty power of God.

TYPICAL THINGS

It is an essential postulate of theism that creation reveals the Creator. The material world was evidently designed by God to illustrate spiritual things. Such elements as life and death, light and dark, the sun, moon and stars—in a word both the macroscopic and the microscopic—speak of corresponding ideas in the spiritual world. If the study is confined to the more obvious types, two fields of typology stand out—the sacrifices of the Old Testament and the tabernacle. Both were designed and revealed by God Himself and were unquestionably intended to be types and illustrations of spiritual truth. In addition to these, there are a few other outstanding typical things in the Old Testament such as the rod of Aaron, the brazen serpent and the smitten rock.

The Old Testament Sacrifices

The sacrifices of the Old Testament are clearly intended to be a typical foreshadowing of the sacrifice of Christ. Almost every aspect of the meaning of the death of Christ is anticipated. Central in the sacrifices is the feature of shed blood, looking forward to the sacrifice of Christ. The explanation given in the Old Testament is that the blood was shed to make an atonement: "For the life of the flesh is in the blood; and I have given it to you upon the altar to make atonement for your souls: for it is the blood that maketh atonement by reason of the life" (Lev. 17:11, ASV). This central truth demonstrates the typology of the sacrifices.

Among the sacrifices, the offering of a lamb was most common. This was practiced even before the Mosaic law (cf. Gen. 4:4; 22:7). At the institution of the Passover, the lamb was used by Israel for its observance. Under the Levitical ritual, a lamb was offered morning and evening as a sacrifice and two lambs were offered on the Sabbath. Without exception the lamb was to be without blemish and its blood was shed. The New Testament makes plain that in all these sacrifices the lamb prefigured "the Lamb of God, which taketh away the sin of the world" (John 1:29). The lamb speaks of the purity of Christ (I Peter 1:19), of the gentleness and submission of Christ to the will of God (Acts 8:32; I Peter 2:21-23) and of substitution—bearing sin which was not His own. In Revelation, Christ is given repeatedly the title "the Lamb."

Other animals were, of course, used and sometimes prescribed: the ox or bullock in the burnt offerings (Lev. 1:5; Num. 7:87-88; II Sam. 24:22; II Chron. 5:6; 7:5), and in the sin offering (Lev. 4:3, 14). The sacrificed bullock typifies Christ as the one "obedient unto death" and bearing the burdens and sins of others.

Another animal frequently used in sacrifices was the goat. Like the lamb it was used before the Mosaic law (Gen. 15:9), was permitted for use in the Passover (Exodus 12:5), was used as a burnt offering (Lev. 1:10), as a sin offering (Lev. 4:24; Num. 15:27), and as a peace offering (Num. 7:17). A special case is the use of two goats on the Day of Atonement, one of which was killed and the other allowed to escape as a scapegoat (Lev. 16:5-10). In all the instances the use of the goat seems to emphasize the thought of substitution, as in the common English the word "goat" means a scapegoat or one bearing blame for others. It anticipates that Christ would become the sin Bearer for the sins of the whole world. The live goat of Leviticus 16 illustrates Christ bearing away our sins from before God—His present work as Advocate in contrast to His finished work on the cross. The special offering of the red heifer was designed as a means of cleansing from defilement (Num. 19:17). The sacrifice speaks of Christ as cleansing the believer from the defilement of sin through His sacrifice.

Other sacrifices only enlarge the typical truth already mentioned. The turtledove or pigeon was the offering of the poor, and refers especially to the fact that Christ became poor that we might be rich (II Cor. 8:9). The pigeon was acceptable for burnt offerings (Lev. 1:14), sin offerings (Lev. 5:7), trespass offerings (Lev. 5:7), and for various rites of cleansing (Lev. 12:6, 8; 14:22-23, 30-31; 15:13-14, 29-30). The usual pattern was to offer one dove as a sin offering and the other as a burnt offering. Of special interest is the fact that Mary, when offering for her cleansing according to commandment of Leviticus 12:6, 8, brought the offering of the poor (Luke 2:24). Two birds were also used in the ceremony of the cleansing of the leper (Lev. 14:4-7) in which one bird is slain and the other dipped in blood and released, somewhat after the pattern of the two goats on the Day of Atonement. In this sacrifice we have again the two aspects of the work of Christ for sinners—His death and His present work.

Taken as a whole the sacrifices point to the one sacrifice of Christ as forever putting away sin. They make the death of Christ essential to God's plan of salvation and speak of the most profound truths of biblical revelation.

The Tabernacle

Of all typical things in the Old Testament, undoubtedly the tabernacle was the most complete typical presentation of spiritual truth. It was expressly designed by God to provide not only a temporary place of worship for the children of Israel in their wanderings but also to prefigure the person and work of Christ to an extent not provided by any other thing.[8]

Taken as a whole, the tabernacle speaks of Christ in every part. In it is prefigured the person, sacrifice, intercession and provision of the Saviour for those who trust Him. It is the gospel in illustration and undoubtedly is more rich in its meaning to the believer of this dispensation than to the Old Testament saint who only dimly understood all the typical representation. The tabernacle remains an almost exhaustless source of illustration of spiritual things relating to the Son of God.

Other Typical Things

Several other typical things in the Old Testament could be mentioned. Aaron's rod that budded is typical of Christ's resurrection (cf. Num. 17; Heb. 9:4). The brazen serpent of Numbers 21:5-9 bears the testimony of Christ Himself that it is an important type (John 3:14-16). The smitten rock of Exodus 17:5-7 is typical of Christ (I Cor. 10:4). It represents the fact that Christ smitten and crucified provided the water of salvation which completely satisfies. Noah's ark has represented to the people of God of all ages the work of God in delivering His own from judgment.

---

[8]For a résumé of the more important aspects of the tabernacle, see Merrill F. Unger, "The Temple Vision of Ezekiel," *Bibliotheca Sacra*, cv (Oct.-Dec., 1948), 407-13.

It is frequently mentioned in the New Testament in various con-
nections (Matt. 24:37-38; Luke 17:26-27; Heb. 11:7; I Peter 3:20;
II Peter 2:5-9). These types are illustrative of many others which
could be cited.

TYPICAL INSTITUTIONS AND CEREMONIES

In addition to the many typical persons, events and things
which foreshadow the person and work of Christ in the Old Testament, there are typical institutions and ceremonies. As Jesus
Christ is the central theme of revelation, it is not strange that
most types should speak expressly of Him and this is true in the
'types under consideration. Many of the types previously considered are also related to typical institutions and ceremonies.

The important typical institutions and ceremonies include the
Old Testament priesthoods, sacrifices, feasts of Jehovah, cities of
refuge and the Sabbath. These are representative of this field, at
least, and will provide another glimpse of the beauties of the
person and work of Christ.

The Sacrifices

It is necessary only to mention here that the sacrifices previously
considered under typical things are in themselves typical institutions. The sin offering, trespass offering, meal offering, peace
offering and burnt offering occupy a central place. These and
other offerings are an integral part of the Levitical ritual which
was revealed and required by God. All the sacrifices point to the
person and work of Christ as the New Testament makes clear.
They make the essential requirement of shed blood to stand out
boldly in the divine pattern of salvation for lost man and erring
saints.

The Old Testament Priesthoods

Both the Aaronic and Melchizedek priesthoods are types of the
priesthood of Christ. The earliest kind of priesthood in the Old
Testament followed the pattern of the patriarchs. In this system
the father or head of the family was also its priest. In a general
way even this priesthood anticipated Christ, but in Aaron and
Melchizedek there is a full and detailed revelation.

As to order of priesthood, Melchizedek in type brings out the
fact that Christ is supreme over all other priesthoods, introducing

a new order entirely; that His priesthood is eternal, that is, that it had no successors, no beginning or ending; that the priesthood of Christ is untransmitted and untransmissible (Heb. 7:24) ; and that it is based on resurrection anticipated in the elements of memorial, bread and wine. The importance of this revelation is brought out in later consideration of the priesthood of Christ.

In its detail the Aaronic priesthood provides light on the work of Christ as Priest and His spiritual qualifications for the office. Aaron anticipates the priesthood of Christ both by similarity and contrast. As Aaron ministers in the earthly sphere, Christ ministers in the heavenly (Heb. 8:1-5) . Christ served realities rather than shadows (Heb. 8:5) and administered a new covenant rather than the Mosaic covenant (Heb. 8:6) . Christ in His sacrifice offered a final sacrifice for sin once for all instead of a daily sacrifice (Heb. 7:27) . In all these things Christ fulfilled what Aaron anticipated. There are also many similarities. Like Aaron, Christ ministered in sacred things (Heb. 5:1) , was made a Priest by God Himself (Heb. 5:4-10) , was a true Mediator (I Tim. 2:5) , was a part of humanity as the second Adam as Aaron was a part of Israel, offered sacrifice to God and, on the basis of sacrifice, offered intercession (Heb. 7:25) . There can be no question that the Aaronic priesthood not only was an *ad interim* dealing of God but that it was also designed to portray in type what Christ was as Priest and what He did.

Feasts of Jehovah

The importance of the feasts of Jehovah in Israel's religious life cannot be overestimated. These seven feasts, as outlined in Leviticus 23 and given further treatment elsewhere, were the backbone of the Levitical system. Most of them have a definite typical meaning in relation to Christology.

The Passover was the first and in some respects the most important feast. It was celebrated in the first month and signified deliverance from the judgment which overtook the Egyptians. The lamb which was sacrificed clearly was a type of Christ. In the New Testament Christ is declared to fulfill the spiritual meaning of the Passover and those who come into the safety of His shed blood are called to a holy life (I Cor. 5:7; I Peter 1:15-19) .

The second feast, the Feast of Unleavened Bread, which immediately followed the Passover, speaks of Christ as the bread of life, the holy walk of the believer after redemption, and the communion with Christ. The absence of leaven typically represents the sinlessness of Christ and the believer's fellowship in that holiness. The prohibition of work during the feast brings out the fact that the holy walk of the believer, like his redemption, is not a result of human effort, but is a divine provision.

The Feast of Firstfruits celebrated for Israel the new harvest in the land and their deliverance from Egypt. The typical truth is that of the resurrection of Christ: "But now is Christ risen from the dead, and become the firstfruits of them that slept. But every man in his own order: Christ the firstfruits; afterward they that are Christ's at his coming" (I Cor. 15:20, 23). The feast occurred on the "morrow after the sabbath" (Lev. 23:11), that is, on the first day of the week, even as Christ was raised on the first day of the week. Like the Feast of Firstfruits, the resurrection of Christ anticipates the harvest which is to follow, the resurrection of the saints.

The Feast of the Wave Loaves, coming exactly fifty days after the Feast of Firstfruits, without question foreshadowed the day of Pentecost at which time the two loaves, typical of Gentiles and Israel, are united into one body, the church (Eph. 2:14). It does not have special Christological significance, however, except as a result of the work of Christ. The Feast of Trumpets, likewise speaking of the regathering of Israel to the land, does not refer specifically to Christ.

The feast of the Day of Atonement represents in large measure the work of Christ on the cross. The sacrifices and preparation of the high priest, of course, were not necessary for Christ, but the sacrifices and ceremonies for the people are foreshadowings of the work of Christ. The Day of Atonement centered on the work of the high priest, even as the work of salvation centers in Christ. The high priest properly prepared and clothed would perform the ceremonies required on behalf of the people. The sin offering of the goat was presented first, the goat killed, and the blood was brought into the holy of holies and sprinkled upon the mercy seat (Lev. 16:15). Then the live goat was allowed to escape in the wilderness after the sins of the people of Israel were confessed with the hands of the high priest on the head of the goat. The whole transaction speaks of Christ as our Substitute, dying and cleansing by shed blood, and putting away our sins from before God, as represented by the scapegoat. The blood of Christ opens the way into the holiest of all, and the seat of the ark of the covenant—representing God's holiness—becomes a mercy seat. This thought is clearly indicated in the New Testament (Rom. 3:25; Heb. 9:7-8, 23-28). Other aspects of the Day of Atonement speak also of the work of Christ. The goat of the sin offering was carried outside the camp and burned, even as Christ was sacrificed outside Jerusalem (Heb. 13:11-13). In addition to the sin offering, a burnt offering was provided (Lev. 16:24), speaking of the obedience and devotion of Christ in His death and constituting a ground for merit for the believer—justification. Most significant is the contrast between the Aaronic high priest entering the holy of holies once a year and the open access afforded every believer-priest in this age to the very presence of God in heaven. The Day of Atonement provides, then, not only a temporary form of worship for Israel, but is a beautiful and suggestive type foreshadowing the wonders of the work of Christ on the cross.

The Feast of Tabernacles seems to have a double meaning. It referred to Israel's deliverance from Egypt but was also prophetic of the future regathering of Israel and will be observed in the millennium (Zech. 14:16-19). In contrast to the other feasts which speak of the finished work of Christ, this feast represents the unfinished work of Christ and the plan of God for the future regathering of dispersed Israel and their blessing in the land of Palestine.

Cities of Refuge

In the Mosaic law provision was made for the protection of those who innocently had taken the life of another. Six cities of refuge were established, three on either side of Jordan, and placed in the hands of the Levites (Num. 35; Deut. 19:1-13; Joshua 20). If judged innocent of willful murder, the party responsible could have deliverance from the avenger of blood as long as he remained in the city of refuge. It was provided that at the death of the high priest he could return to his home, but not before. The cities of refuge are obviously a type of refuge in Christ where the sinner finds refuge from judgment for sin and is made free by the death of the High Priest. God is frequently spoken of as a refuge in the Old Testament (Ps. 46:1; 142:5; Isa.

4:6) and also in the New Testament (Rom. 8:33-34; Heb. 6:18-19) . While God has always been the refuge of His saints, it was not until the death of the High Priest, fulfilled in Christ, that complete freedom was provided.

Taken as a whole, the typical ceremonies and institutions of the Old Testament have as their main theme the person and work of the Lord Jesus Christ. Thus, imbedded in the religious life of saints before Christ are found the principal elements of the New Testament revelation concerning Christ. Beautiful as are the types, they are exceeded by the antitype; and devout souls can long for that future complete revelation when we shall see Him face to face.

5

CHRIST IN OLD TESTAMENT
PROPHECY

FROM GENESIS TO MALACHI the Old Testament abounds with anticipations of the coming Messiah of Israel. Numerous predictions, fulfilled in the New Testament, relate to His birth, life, death and resurrection. Other prophecies speak of His ultimate glory. Although treated here in outline form only, no other prophetic theme of the Old Testament approaches in magnitude and significance the abundant revelation devoted to the subject of Jesus Christ.

The study of Messianic prophecy in contemporary theology has been largely forfeited in favor of attention to the New Testament. As Wilbur M. Smith has commented,

> During the nineteenth century, the Christian Church was blessed with a number of great works on Messianic prophecies of the Old Testament, by such scholars as Delitzsch, Hengstenberg, Kurtz, and Riehm, in Germany, and R. Payne Smith, David Baron, Edersheim, and Saphir, in England, the last three of whom were Christian Jews. In the twentieth century, however, at least until the last few years, the literature on Messianic prophecy, outside of strictly academic circles, has been very thin—ephemeral contributions which were but inadequate, disconnected collections of extracts from the writers of the preceding century, with expository comments of no particular importance.[1]

When the risen Lord conversed with the two disciples on the road to Emmaus, Luke states that Christ "beginning from Moses and from all the prophets . . . interpreted to them in all the scriptures the things concerning himself" (Luke 24:27, ASV). It is implicit in this discourse of several hours that the life, death and

[1]Wilbur M. Smith, Introduction, in Aaron J. Kligerman, *Messianic Prophecy in the Old Testament.*

resurrection of Christ were major themes of prophecy in the Old Testament.

The existence on such a wide scale of prophecy concerning Christ before He was born is of great significance as no other person in all the world ever was predicted in this way nor had such detailed prophecies ascribing to him the power and attributes of God. Such prophecy in itself was a miracle and bore testimony to a supernatural Person whose claims demand that we worship and obey Him.

William H. Thomson brings this out when he writes,

> A real prophecy, on the other hand, is nothing less than a miracle, for it needs but a short train of reasoning to show that it differs so essentially from mere human prediction that a single unmistakable example of the kind would unsettle the very foundation of modern unbelief. A human prediction is never anything more than a guess of results or consequences to something in the present or in the past. It grows entirely out of experience, and can rest on no other basis for its premises, because men are as much bound to the present in time as they are to the earth's surface in space. But prophecy has no necessary connection with experience, nor is it conditioned by it, for it involves a foreknowledge of that which no man may know unaided, any more than unaided he can step off the earth. . . . Now the Apostles appealed to just this miracle of prophecy when proclaiming that God had prepared the world for the advent of Jesus Christ, because to him all the prophets gave witness, foretelling in many ways not only the Coming, but also its manner, time, and object, until not a fact about him which had relations to that object was without its corresponding prophecy. But if the life of Christ, in all its singular fulness of event, purpose, and results, was really written beforehand in the Hebrew Scriptures, then the conclusions as to the truth of the Gospel are too clear to be withstood by the mind of this or any other age. For his was not a life which could have been thought of by human invention.[2]

The term Messiah is derived from the Greek *Messias* which in turn is a transliteration of the Aramaic form of the Hebrew *Mashach*, meaning "to anoint." The equivalent in New Testament terminology is *Christos* or Christ, meaning "the anointed one."

The Old Testament contains frequent references to anointing of priests where the adjective form is used (Lev. 4:3, 5, 16; 6:22),

[2]William H. Thomson, *Christ in the Old Testament*, pp. v-vi.

and of the anointing of kings where the noun form is used (Saul, I Sam. 24:6, 10; David, II Sam. 19:21; 23:1; an unnamed king, probably Zedekiah, Lam. 4:20). The term "the anointed one" translated Messiah in Daniel 9:25-26 was used as a designation of the coming of Jesus Christ as Saviour and Deliverer and was in common use by the Jews at the time of the incarnation to express this general prophetic idea (John 1:41; 4:25). The hope of Israel centered in the coming of this Person who was to be anointed as King and Priest and to whom Israel looked for deliverance from sin as well as from oppression of the Gentiles. Therefore, the Messianic hope for Israel became the center of eschatological expectation.

PRINCIPAL TYPES OF MESSIANIC PROPHECY

Two principal types of Messianic prophecy are found in the Old Testament. First, *general* Messianic prophecy, that is, prophecy expressed in language which only a Messiah could fulfill, may be observed. An illustration of this is afforded in I Samuel 2:35: "I will raise me up a faithful priest, that shall do according to that which is in mine heart and in my mind: and I will build him a sure house; and he shall walk before mine anointed for ever." Although the immediate fulfillment of this prophecy may be found in Samuel, it goes beyond the fulfillment in Samuel and anticipates the ultimate fulfillment in Christ. Both the priesthood of Samuel and his lineage terminated, but the perpetual priesthood anticipated in this prophecy would be completely fulfilled in Christ.

Second, *personal* Messianic prophecy is often found in the Old Testament and can be identified by some specific term. In Isaiah 7:14, for instance, the Messiah is identified by the unusual term Immanuel or "God with us." The passage deals only and specifically with the future Messiah.

GENERAL CHARACTERISTICS OF MESSIANIC PROPHECY

Many of the prophecies relating to Jesus Christ are quite clear, especially when viewed from the New Testament revelation where fulfillment gives added light concerning the intent of the prophecy in the Old Testament. Messianic prophecy, however, has these certain inherent problems:

1. The language of Messianic prophecy is often obscure. The divine intent in this obscurity is to render the prophecy understandable only by true believers in God who are taught by the Holy Spirit and who therefore are able to discern passages belonging to genuine Messianic prediction. Many of these passages cannot be interpreted except in the light of the entire content of the Word of God.

2. Figurative language is frequently used in Messianic prophecy. The meaning is not necessarily uncertain, for often the figure gives a very clear idea even though the passage may require interpretation. For instance, when the Scriptures utter a prophecy such as, "There shall come forth a rod out of the stem of Jesse, and a Branch shall grow out of his roots" (Isa. 11:1), it clearly refers to the Messiah as One who will descend from Jesse. Although figurative language is used, the truth conveyed is quite clear.

3. In Messianic prediction the future is often regarded as past or present and the Hebrew frequently uses the perfect tense in making predictions. The great prophecies of Isaiah 53, for instance, are largely in this prophetic perfect tense. As A. B. Davidson points out, "This usage is very common in the elevated language of the Prophets, whose faith and imagination so vividly project before them the event or scene which they predict that it appears already realized. It is part of the purpose of God, and therefore, to the clear eyes of the prophet, already as good as accomplished (*prophetic perfect*)."[3] The perfect tense used in this way in the Old Testament signifies then that the event predicted is certain of completion even though it is future and not past. Messianic prediction in the perfect tense is an emphatic future.

4. Messianic prophecy, like other forms of prophecy, is often seen horizontally rather than vertically. In other words, while the order of prophetic events is generally revealed in Scripture, prophecy does not necessarily include all the intermediate steps between the great events in view. As has been commonly expressed, the great mountain peaks of prophecy are revealed without consideration of the valleys between the peaks. Hence, Old Testament prophecy may leap from the sufferings of Christ to His glory without consideration of the time which history has proved elapses between these two aspects.

[3]A. B. Davidson, *An Introductory Hebrew Grammar*, pp. 156-57.

The fact that Messianic prophecy does not always take into consideration the passage of time between events is illustrated in the quotation by Christ of Isaiah 61:1-2 in Luke 4:18-19. The Isaiah passage links the first and second comings of Christ without any indication of an intervening period of time. History has shown already that more than nineteen hundred years must elapse between these two events. Christ in His quotation includes the aspects relating to His first coming, but stops abruptly without including the reference to "the day of vengeance of our God" which refers to the judgment at the second coming. When properly understood, this problem in the interpretation of Messianic prophecy does not present too many difficulties, but does warn the interpreter not to form hasty conclusions. Any one prophecy is necessarily incomplete and care must be exercised to understand precisely what the author intended to convey.

THE MESSIANIC LINE: HIS LINEAGE

A well-defined line of prediction is provided in the Old Testament predictions concerning the coming of the Saviour. The line begins with Adam and Eve and is traced through a constantly narrowing focus until all the important factors are revealed. The coming Saviour will be the seed of the woman (Gen. 3:15) ; in the line of Seth (Gen. 4:25) ; through Noah (Gen. 6-9) ; a Descendant of Abraham (Gen. 12:1-3) . Subsequent revelation traces the lineage through Isaac (Gen. 17:19), Jacob (Gen. 28:14), Judah (Gen. 49:10), through Boaz, Obed, Jesse and David (II Sam. 7:12-13) . From here on appeal is necessary to the New Testament genealogies of Matthew 1:2-16 and Luke 3:23-38.

The story of the lineage of the coming Saviour is on the one hand a demonstration of the sovereign purpose and certainty of God's will. On the other hand, the corrupting work of Satan is everywhere present throughout the history of the lineage of Christ. Satan begins corrupting the newly created race by leading Adam and Eve into temptation and the fall (Gen. 3:6) . To fallen Adam and Eve God gave the protevangelium, the first indication of His plan of giving His Son as the Saviour. The seed of the woman would bruise the head of the serpent (Gen. 3:15) . Satan's continued work is manifest in the murder of Abel and the corruption by the act of Cain (Gen. 4:8) . God raises up a new seed in the birth of Seth (Gen. 4:25) .

The lineage of the Messiah in the Old Testament must be taken as a whole. The broad generalization that the "seed of the woman" would bruise or crush the head of the serpent is not clear unless it is interpreted by subsequent prophecy. As J. Barton Payne has said,

> Though the individuality of the Messiah is not yet clearly revealed, neither is it ruled out. Progressive revelation does not invalidate or correct the earlier revelations, as though they were any less inspired; its purpose is rather to clarify them. The wording of Genesis 3:15 was thus providentially designed by the Holy Spirit: the verse is simple, but it is at the same time true, and congruous with its future fulfillment in the one person of Christ.[4]

The corruption of the human race and with it the line of the Messiah continues until the time of Noah. Here in the destruction of all except Noah's family God purifies the race and preserves the godly seed (Gen. 6-9). Defection of the race soon follows and God begins again in the selection of Abraham (Gen. 12:1-3) through whom His purpose in regard to the Messiah is continued. The book of Genesis traces the narrowing line through Abraham's descendants: Isaac (Gen. 17:19), Jacob (Gen. 28:14) and Judah (Gen. 49:10). The continued satanic opposition to the godly line is manifest in the delayed birth of Isaac, the disinterest of Esau and the selection of Jacob in his place, and in the immorality that corrupted Judah. In sovereign grace, God nevertheless declares, "The sceptre shall not depart from Judah" (Gen. 49:10). The prophecy of Jacob, while in language which is somewhat obscure, is nevertheless clear in its main import—the Messiah will come through Judah.

Hengstenberg begins his classic work on Christology with the statement "In the Messianic prophecies contained in Genesis we cannot fail to perceive a remarkable progress in clearness and definiteness. The first Messianic prediction, which was uttered immediately after the fall of Adam, is also the most indefinite."[5] That which was obscure in its introduction is rendered increasingly specific as the Old Testament unfolds.

The story of Ruth and Boaz is another illustration of sovereign design in the lineage of the Messiah. With evident divine preparation, the line of David the king is linked with Judah. In few

---

[4]J. Barton Payne, *The Theology of the Older Testament*, p. 259.
[5]E. W. Hengstenberg, *Christology in the Old Testament*, I, 1.

books of the Bible is the doctrine of providence illustrated more abundantly than in the book of Ruth.

The Old Testament picture of the lineage from David to Christ is by no means complete. This deficiency is more than met by the New Testament genealogies. Of particular interest are the dual lines of Joseph and Mary which connect with David. The genealogies are best explained by referring the genealogy of Matthew to Joseph and the genealogy of Luke to Mary. Thus interpreted, Joseph is seen to descend from David through Solomon and the line of the kings of Judah. Mary is found in the line from David through David's son Nathan. This detail is a striking fulfillment of Old Testament prophecy. To David God had promised both the continuance of his seed and his throne forever (II Sam. 7:12-16). To Solomon, David's son, God promised that his throne and kingdom would continue forever, but the record is silent in the prediction concerning Solomon's seed. This is given further light in the apostasy of the kings of Judah. Jehoiakim, king of Judah, is solemnly cursed because of his sin and the Scriptures declare: "He shall have none to sit upon the throne of David: and his dead body shall be cast out in the day to the heat, and in the night to the frost. And I will punish him and his seed and his servants for their iniquity" (Jer. 36:30-31). Coniah, his son (also known as Jehoiachin and Jeconiah), was carried off captive when Jerusalem fell and the line of the kings of Judah ends in him (cf. Jer. 22:30). The problem is immediately apparent: How can God fulfill His promise to David if this line is cut off? The answer is that the kingly line of the Messiah is preserved through Nathan rather than through Solomon and his descendants. Hence, in the New Testament the legal right to the throne of David is passed through Solomon and Jehoiakim to Joseph and to Joseph's legal son, Christ. The physical seed, however, is passed through Nathan and Mary to Christ. Thus the promises to both David and Solomon are literally fulfilled in and through Jesus Christ. It is at once a striking illustration of the accuracy of the prophetic Word, God anticipating the defection of the kings of Judah and their curse, and at the same time a confirmation of the virgin birth. If Jesus had been the physical son of Joseph, He would have been disqualified by the curse upon Jehoiakim.

The records of Scripture provide then an accurate and indis-

putable record of the qualifications of Christ as the Inheritor of
the promises to David. Conservative scholars are agreed that
Christ fulfills the anticipation of these prophecies, and even un-
believing Jews anticipate that the coming Messiah will fulfill these
prophecies. The genealogies of the Jews were, of course, destroyed in the destruction of Jerusalem in A.D 70. The New Testament records are the only ones extant which provide authentic
genealogies to identify the Messiah.

PROPHECIES OF THE BIRTH OF CHRIST

The prophecies in regard to the birth of Jesus Christ are among
the more transparent of the Old Testament predictions. The
prophecies regarding the lineage of the predicted Saviour in themselves anticipated His birth. The place of His birth was plainly
revealed in Micah 5:2, and the passage is so clear that it was
commonly known that Bethlehem was destined to be the birth-
place of the Messiah. The scribes and the chief priests quickly
informed Herod of this fact when the Magi came for direction to
the King of the Jews.

Other aspects of the birth of Christ are also revealed in the Old
Testament. Isaiah prophesied that His birth would be a sign:
"Therefore the Lord himself shall give you a sign; Behold, a
virgin shall conceive, and bear a son, and shall call his name
Immanuel" (Isa. 7:14). Here both the human aspect of the incarnation, conception and birth, and the divine are clearly revealed—"Immanuel" or "God with us."

The date of birth of the coming Messiah seems also to be revealed within certain limits. According to Genesis 49:10, the
Messiah was to come before the destruction of the Jewish government. This would seem to be identified with the destruction of
Jerusalem at A.D. 70 and the complete end of all Jewish rule in
Palestine for many centuries. The prophecy of Daniel 9:25—that
sixty-nine weeks of seven years each would elapse before the
Messiah should be cut off—has been shown to culminate in the
death of Christ. While the interpretation of the Daniel passage
has occasioned much dispute, it is agreed by many scholars
that a literal interpretation would bring us to the approximate
time of the lifetime of Jesus Christ. Although this revelation was
not comprehended beforehand, there was widespread expectation

among the generation in which Christ was born that the Messiah would come soon.

The prophecies of the Old Testament, then, outline with precision the main elements involved in His birth: the place, time, lineage and supernatural character of His conception and birth.

PROPHECIES CONCERNING THE PERSON OF CHRIST

From the Old Testament predictions certain conclusions can be drawn relative to the person of Christ. In a word, there is an entirely adequate testimony concerning both His humanity and His deity. The revelation is not with the same clarity or force as the presentation in the New Testament, but it is nevertheless clear in its main elements.

The humanity of the coming Saviour is involved in practically all the Messianic passages. From Genesis 3:15, where the Messiah is described as the seed of the woman, to the predictions of the later Old Testament prophets, the Messiah is declared to be human. The testimony concerning His lineage, His connection with Israel, His predicted birth in Bethlehem and His title as a Son leave no room to doubt the intention of the revelation of His humanity. It was the uniform expectation of the Jews that the coming Deliverer would be a Man, born of a Jewish mother.

The remarkable aspect of the predictions, however, is the recurring testimony to His deity. According to Isaiah 7:14, He was to be born of a virgin. Although critics have challenged this prophecy, its denial involves the assumption of error in the accounts of Matthew and Luke as well as rationalization in regard to Isaiah 7:14.

Payne, after a full discussion of the interpretation of Isaiah 7:14,[6] summarizes the proper interpretation of Isaiah 7:14:

> The birth of Immanuel was expressly defined as an *oth*, a miraculous sign (7:14); and with this miracle no contemporary event is known adequately to coincide. Furthermore, King Ahaz had been guilty of pious hypocrisy and had wearied God; so the demonstrative *oth*, or sign, was intended, not as a promise but as a threat. This threat, moreover, was directed not simply against Ahaz, but against the whole house of David (v. 13). That is, when the Messiah should be born, He would eat "butter and honey," which was the sign of an

[6]Payne, pp. 266-68.

> afflicted land (the affliction, as it worked out, was caused by
> the Romans), and which therefore meant that the house of
> David would have been reduced to impotency. The Sign
> would then Himself replace once and for all the merely hu-
> man Jewish kings of Ahaz' house and character.[7]

The clear intent is to state that He was to be supernaturally
conceived without a human father. Why should it be a sensa-
tional prophecy for a man to be born of a woman unless it was
miraculous, that is, the woman was actually a virgin?

The Messiah is declared in Isaiah 7:14 to be worthy of the title
Immanuel—"God with us." In Isaiah 9:6-7, the Child born, the
Son given, is described as "The mighty God, The everlasting
Father, The Prince of Peace." The prediction of His birth in
Micah 5:2 goes on to describe the Child to be born as One "whose
goings forth have been of old, from everlasting." The expression
is the strongest possible statement of His eternal existence before
His birth. The combined testimony of these passages as well as
many others leave no doubt that the Messiah when He came was
to be both God and Man in one Person.

PROPHECIES CONCERNING THE LIFE OF CHRIST

A remarkable foreview of the life of Christ is afforded in many
Messianic prophecies which portray the character of His life. His
important public ministry was to be preceded by a messenger,
"Behold, I send my messenger, and he shall prepare the way before me: and the Lord, whom ye seek, will suddenly come to his
temple; and the messenger of the covenant, whom ye desire, behold, he cometh, saith Jehovah of hosts" (Mal. 3:1, ASV). Previously Isaiah had spoken of the "voice of one that crieth, Prepare
ye in the wilderness the way of Jehovah" (Isa. 40:3, ASV). There
can be no doubt that the reference in both cases is to John the
Baptist (cf. Matt. 3:3; 11:10; Mark 1:2; Luke 7:27), and all the
Gospels record the fulfillment of these prophecies.

The coming Messiah was in His life to fulfill the offices of
Prophet, Priest and King. Moses had predicted the coming of
such a Prophet (Deut. 18:15-18), and the New Testament points
specifically to its fulfillment in Christ (John 1:21; 4:29; 5:46;
6:14; 8:28; 14:24; Acts 3:20-23). The priesthood of Christ was
anticipated in the whole priestly system given by revelation, first

[7]*Ibid.*, p. 269.

the patriarchal and later the Levitical orders. The prophecy given in I Samuel 2:35 can be fulfilled completely only by Christ, even if partially fulfilled by Samuel. The prediction of Psalm 110:4, quoted in Hebrews 5:6, and discussed at length in Hebrews, is clearly fulfilled in Christ. Zechariah combines the priestly and kingly offices in his prophecy "He shall be a priest upon his throne" (Zech. 6:13). The context indicates that the reference is to Christ.

The kingly office of Christ is the first to be mentioned in prophecy and the most prominent in Old Testament prediction. As early as the time of Abraham, God revealed that kings should be among Abraham's descendants. The kingly line is narrowed to Judah's descendants in Genesis 49:10. The hint of a particular King in Genesis 49:10 is made more definite in Numbers 24:17. A major revelation is found in the foreview given David in the classic passage II Samuel 7:12-16. Here it is revealed that David's house will be perpetuated in the coming Messiah whose throne and kingdom will continue forever. Conservative scholarship is agreed that the fulfillment of these prophecies is found in Christ alone. This interpretation is, of course, confirmed by the New Testament (Luke 1:31-33), and the theme is continued throughout the rest of the Old Testament as well.

In Psalm 2, Jehovah declares that He will set His Son on the throne in Zion. The dominion and rule of the King is foretold in Psalm 110. The prophecy of His rule on earth is integral in Messianic prediction (Isa. 2:1-4; 4:1-6; 49:7; 52:15). In Isaiah 9:6-7 (ASV) it is explicit:

> For unto us a child is born, unto us a son is given; and the government shall be upon his shoulder: and his name shall be called Wonderful, Counsellor, Mighty God, Everlasting Father, Prince of Peace. Of the increase of his government and of peace there shall be no end, upon the throne of David, and upon his kingdom, to establish it, and to uphold it with justice and with righteousness from henceforth even for ever.

The passage gathers in one statement the predictions of the incarnation, the deity and eternality of the Messiah, the future government of peace on earth, the righteousness and justice of His kingdom, and the fact that the kingdom will fulfill the promises to David. The promises to David and the prediction of the earthly kingdom of the Messiah are one and the same. The entire chapter 11 of Isaiah is a picture of the rule of the King.

Jeremiah repeats these same major aspects of the future kingship of the Messiah:

> Behold, the days come, saith Jehovah, that I will raise unto David a righteous Branch, and he shall reign as king and deal wisely, and shall execute justice and righteousness in the land. In his days Judah shall be saved, and Israel shall dwell safely; and this is his name whereby he shall be called: Jehovah our righteousness (Jer. 23:5-6, ASV).

The prophecy is turned to its particular effect on Israel. Zechariah speaks of the King coming as the Saviour and Deliverer of His people: "Rejoice greatly, O daughter of Zion; shout, O daughter of Jerusalem: behold, thy king cometh unto thee; he is just, and having salvation; lowly, and riding upon an ass, even upon a colt the foal of an ass" (Zech. 9:9, ASV). Here we have Christ in His character as King in His first coming, in contrast to previous passages quoted which referred to the kingdom after the second advent. The Zechariah passage has its fulfillment in the New Testament (Matt. 21:4-9; Mark 11:9-10; Luke 19:37-38). The Old Testament foreview of Christ as King includes then both His first advent and the kingdom to follow the second advent.

That the Messiah was to be a Saviour and Deliverer had been anticipated in many Old Testament passages beginning with the protevangelium of Genesis 3:15. Even Job, who probably lived before the day of written Scripture, knew of the hope of a coming Redeemer (Job 19:25). Almost all the passages which are Messianic speak of it. The classic passage predicting the saving work of Christ is, of course, Isaiah 53.

One of the important lines of prediction concerning the coming Messiah is embraced in the figure of Christ as a cornerstone and foundation. The principal Old Testament passage is Isaiah 28:14-18. Numerous passages contribute to the total revelation (Gen. 49:24; I Kings 7:10-11; Ps 118:22; Isa. 8:14; Zech. 4:7. Cf. New Testament passages, Acts 4:11; Rom. 9:33; 11:11; Eph. 2:20; I Peter 2:6-8). The thought in these passages is that Christ will bring security to Israel.

Considerable attention is given in the Old Testament to the Messiah as the Servant of Jehovah. Important passages dealing with this line of truth are found in Isaiah 42:1-7; 49:1-7; 52:13—

53:12. The New Testament alludes to these predictions in regard to the Messiah frequently (Matt. 8:17; 12:17-21; Luke 22:37; John 12:38; Acts 3:13, 26; 4:27, 30; 8:32; Rom. 10:13; 15:21; I Peter 2:22-24). The term "Servant of Jehovah" as found in the Old Testament sometimes has reference to Israel, sometimes to the obedient remnant of Israel, sometimes specifically to the Messiah, and in Isaiah 37:35 it refers to David. The principal idea in these predictions is that of Christ as the obedient Servant who through His sufferings and death redeems His people.

In connection with the prophecies of the coming Messianic kingdom, it is revealed that the Messiah will perform many great miracles. The testimony to this is not always related specifically to the Messiah, but is given as a description of the period. Hence in Isaiah 35:5-6, it is written, "Then the eyes of the blind shall be opened, and the ears of the deaf shall be unstopped. Then shall the lame man leap as an hart, and the tongue of the dumb sing: for in the wilderness shall waters break out, and streams in the desert." While the immediate context deals with the Messianic kingdom, it is at once a description of the credentials of the Messiah. Christ called attention to the significance of His miraculous works as a testimony to Himself (John 5:36).

Taken as a whole, the Old Testament provides a remarkable picture of the coming Messiah. He is to be preceded by a messenger, to be a Saviour and Deliverer, to execute the offices of Prophet, Priest and King, to be a cornerstone and foundation, to fulfill the expectation of an obedient Servant of Jehovah who would redeem His people, and is to perform good and miraculous works. His works and teachings were to manifest the power of the Spirit of Jehovah (Isa. 11:2-3).

PROPHECIES CONCERNING THE DEATH
OF CHRIST

The Old Testament preview of the death of Christ is given principally in Psalm 22 and Isaiah 53, though many other passages contribute to the doctrine. Isaiah 53, presenting the suffering of the Servant of Jehovah, reveals most of/the major details of the death of Christ. He is to be brutally beaten (Isa. 52:14), "wounded for our transgressions" and "bruised for our iniquities" (Isa. 53:5); His sufferings provide peace and healing (Isa. 53:5). He is to be silent before His persecutors as a lamb led to the slaughter (Isa. 53:7). His soul will be an offering for sin (Isa. 53:10). He will die with the wicked, but will be buried with the rich (Isa. 53:9). His sufferings arise not from His own sin, for "he had done no violence, neither was any deceit in his mouth" (Isa. 53:9b, ASV). To say the least, we have in Isaiah an accurate and detailed account of the sufferings and death of Christ together with a theological reason for His death—He was dying for the sins of others, as a satisfaction to God. Even a casual examination of the New Testament record reveals a fulfillment of all the details of this prophecy.

While on the cross, Christ Himself quoted from Psalm 22, thereby calling attention to the predictions afforded in this psalm. The Messiah is to be forsaken of God (Ps. 22:1), ridiculed and taunted (vv. 6-8); to suffer unspeakable agony (vv. 14-16); His bones were to be pulled out of joint (v. 14); He was to suffer thirst (v. 15); His hands and feet were to be pierced—an anticipation of His crucifixion (v. 16); His garments were to be divided with the exception of His vesture, for which they would cast lots (v. 18); He was to be brought to death (v. 15). This psalm accordingly presents a graphic picture of the sufferings of Christ on the cross fulfilled in every detail by the events recorded in the Gospels.

Many other scattered references to the death of Christ complete the picture of prophecy. He was to be betrayed by a friend (Ps. 41:9), falsely accused (Ps. 35:11) and spit upon (Isa. 50:6); His bones were not to be broken (Ps. 34:20).

Not only does the New Testament record the fulfillment, but Christ Himself completes the picture of prophecy regarding His death. Again and again He predicts His coming crucifixion (Matt. 12:38-42; 16:21; 17:22-23; 20:18-19; 26:31; Mark 8:31; 9:31; 10:32-34; Luke 9:22, 44; 18:31-33; John 12:32-33). There have been few events which have been given such a complete and detailed prophetic picture in the Scriptures. It is safe to say that the whole prophetic Word has as its central point the sufferings and death of Christ.

PROPHECIES CONCERNING THE RESURRECTION OF CHRIST

While many passages in the Old Testament anticipate the resurrection of Christ, only a few are specific. Of these, the most important is Psalm 16:10 (ASV) : "For thou wilt not leave my soul to Sheol; neither wilt thou suffer thy holy one to see corruption." It is, of course, the fashion among some scholars to minimize and eliminate the Messianic element from Old Testament prophecy wherever possible. Oehler, for instance, finds no Messianic reference in Psalm 16:10.[8] A. B. Davidson does not bother to discuss it in his work on Old Testament prophecy. The New Testament makes clear, however, to all who accept the infallibility of the Scriptures that Psalm 16:10 is specifically a reference to Christ. Peter, after quoting this passage in his sermon at Pentecost, states plainly that the reference is not to David but to Christ (Acts 2:25-31). Paul in his sermon at Antioch in Pisidia expressed the same interpretation (Acts 13:34-37). We have here, then, an interpretation with the double attestation of the inspired teaching of Peter and Paul. While David died and saw corruption, Christ died and was raised again.

The resurrection of Christ is, of course, anticipated in every prophecy which pictures Christ as victorious over sin and the powers of evil. A few passages imply the resurrection. Psalm 22:22 (ASV), where it is predicted of Christ, "I will declare thy name unto my brethren: in the midst of the assembly will I praise thee" is quoted in Hebrews 2:12. The context of both Psalm 22 and Hebrews 2:12 speaks of victory over death. Psalm 118:22-24 speaks of the stone which the builders rejected becoming the head of the corner. Again, the passage implies resurrection after rejection. Isaiah 53:10 (ASV) seems also to imply the resurrection. After referring to the death of the Servant of Jehovah, the passage goes on, "He shall prolong his days, and the pleasure of Jehovah shall prosper in his hands." It is difficult to see how this passage could have any literal fulfillment after the death of Christ except by resurrection.

While the testimony of the Old Testament is, with the exception of Psalm 16:10, somewhat indirect, the New Testament repeatedly predicts the resurrection of Christ. These passages spoken by Christ Himself demonstrate the completeness of the prophetic preparation: Matthew 12:38-40; 16:21; 17:9, 23; 20:19; 26:32; 27:63; Mark 8:31; 9:9, 31; 10:33-34; 14:58; Luke 9:22; 18:33; John 2:19-21. The resurrection of Christ, like His suffer-

[8]G. F. Oehler, *Theology of the Old Testament*, pp. 150, 169, 559.

ings and death, is in its fulfillment of prophecy a majestic unfolding of the sovereign purposes of God.

PROPHECIES CONCERNING HIS GLORY

The Old Testament abounds with references to the glory of God. Many of these are applicable to the Trinity, but others are predictions related to the Messiah. The great sweeps of Old Testament prophecy concerning the coming glorious kingdom in themselves are testimonies to the glory of the King. One of the central purposes of the millennial kingdom is the manifestation of the glory of God and the glory of the Son of God. Psalm 24, for instance, anticipates the coming of the King of glory, and the context indicates that it refers specifically to the Son of God. Psalm 72 (ASV), which affords a general view of the coming kingdom, closes with a benediction, "And blessed be his glorious name for ever; and let the whole earth be filled with his glory." Isaiah predicts, "In that day shall the branch of Jehovah be beautiful and glorious" (Isa. 4:2a, ASV). The reference to the "branch" seems clearly a reference to Christ. Isaiah asks the question "Who is this that cometh from Edom, with dyed garments from Bozrah? This that is glorious in his apparel, marching in the greatness of his strength?" (Isa. 63:1, ASV). The context makes the reference to the Messiah evident. Daniel gives a comprehensive picture: "And there was given him dominion, and glory, and a kingdom, that all the peoples, nations, and languages should serve him: his dominion is an everlasting dominion, which shall not pass away, and his kingdom that which shall not be destroyed" (Dan. 7:14, ASV).

These numerous references to the glory of the Messiah in contrast to His sufferings gave occasion to Peter's mention of this problem: "The prophets who prophesied of the grace that was to be yours searched and inquired about this salvation; they inquired what person or time was indicated by the Spirit of Christ within them when predicting the sufferings of Christ and the subsequent glory" (I Peter 1:10-11, RSV). In other words, the Old Testament prophets themselves while recognizing the dual prophecies of suffering and glory of the Messiah were not able to harmonize this apparent contradiction.

The New Testament confirms this anticipation of glory to follow suffering. Christ at His ascension returned to glory. His glorious present session in heaven is mentioned often in Scripture (Mark 16:19; Luke 24:51; Heb. 4:14; 9:24; I Peter 3:22). From this present glorious state He will return for the church (John 14:1-3; I Cor. 15:51-52; I Thess. 4:13-18). After the church is taken up to glory, it will be judged by Christ (I Cor. 3:12-15; 9:16-27; II Cor. 5:8-10; Rev. 3:11). The glorious return of Christ follows (Matt. 26:64; Luke 21:27; Acts 1:11). After the reign on earth the eternal state is ushered in (I Cor. 15:24-28). From the moment of the ascension, however, Christ is in His glorious estate and all His works and appearances are in keeping with His glory. The New Testament adds many of the details to the outline of prophecy, but the fact of His glory is as well attested by the Old Testament.

6

THE INCARNATION OF THE SON OF GOD

THE INCARNATION OF THE LORD JESUS CHRIST is the central fact of Christianity. Upon it the whole superstructure of Christian theology depends. In one sense, the remaining discussion of Christology as a whole is an amplification of the incarnation. In this chapter, however, attention is directed mostly to the fact of the incarnation rather than theological and critical problems related to it. Of particular concern is the presentation afforded in the Gospels. Probably no portion of Scripture has received more intense examination, and has been the object of more theological debate than the four Gospels because they unfold the birth and life of the Lord Jesus Christ. The interpretation of the biblical revelation of the Gospels inevitably lays down the guiding lines for all other interpretation.

The central character of the scriptural presentation of the incarnation of the Son of God has been recognized by all branches of theology. Those attempting to sustain the thesis that Jesus was only a man have lost no time in questioning the facts as presented in the Bible and in denying the virgin birth of Christ. A few have gone so far as to deny the historicity of Jesus of Nazareth because of the scarcity of extrascriptural literature dealing with the facts of His birth.

As B. B. Warfield points out, there is comparatively little reference to Christ in ancient literature outside the Scriptures:

> The rise of Christianity was a phenomenon of too little apparent significance to attract the attention of the great world. It was only when it had refused to be quenched in the blood of its founder, and, breaking out of the narrow bounds of the obscure province in which it had its origin, was making itself felt in the centers of population, that it drew to itself

a somewhat irritated notice. The interest of such heathen writers as mention it was in the movement, not in its author. But in speaking of the movement they tell something of its author, and what they tell is far from being of little moment. He was, it seems, a certain "Christ," who had lived in Judea in the reign of Tiberius (14-37 A.D.), and had been brought to capital punishment by the procurator, Pontius Pilate (q.v.; cf. Tacitus, "Annals," xv. 44). The significance of His personality to the movement inaugurated by Him is already suggested by the fact that He, and no other, had impressed His name upon it. But the name itself by which He was known particularly attracts notice. This is uniformly, in these heathen writers, "Christ," not "Jesus."[1]

Warfield mentions but questions the authenticity of the reference in Josephus[2] to "Jesus," but cites as authentic the references to Christ by Suetonius[3] and that of Tacitus and Pliny.[4] As Warfield concludes, "Beyond these great facts the heathen historians give little information about the founder of Christianity."[5]

The theological significance of the facts of the incarnation has undoubtedly been the main cause both of faith and unbelief. It is important therefore for the student of the incarnation to examine with care what the Bible actually teaches on this subject and then to ascertain whether that teaching is self-consistent and justifies the belief of orthodox scholars that this is indeed inspired and infallible Scripture. Though none of the four Gospels is especially written as an apologetic for the Christian faith, the gospel of Matthew and that of Luke present the historical facts according to the theme of each gospel. Matthew is especially concerned with the explanation that Jesus is indeed the King of Israel and the promised Messiah. Luke is concerned with the historical narrative, and the facts are presented with the purpose of establishing the certainty of the historical background of Christianity. For purposes of the present study (which is not apologetic in nature), it is assumed that the Gospels are factual history as normally accepted in orthodox theology. Accordingly, opposing views of higher criticism which tend to question the accuracy of the scriptural narrative are not debated.

---

[1]B. B. Warfield, *The Person and Work of Christ*, p. 5.
[2]Josephus, "Antiquities." XVIII. iii. 3; XX. ix. 1.
[3]Suetonius, "Claudius," xxv.
[4]Warfield, pp. 5-6.
[5]*Ibid.*, p. 6.

THE PROPHETIC FORERUNNER OF CHRIST

John the Baptist occupies the peculiar role of being a prophetic bridge from the Old Testament prophets to the New. Luke gives in detail the account of his birth as subject to special revelation to Zacharias his father. In the chronologies in Luke 1 the annunciation to Mary occurs three months before the birth of John the Baptist. The subsequent birth of Christ is therefore presented in the context of prophetic divine preparation for a great work of God about to be consummated. Later in his public ministry John the Baptist was also to be a forerunner of Christ in the sense of providing a spiritual preparation and warning to 'the people of Israel. John's preparatory ministry culminated in his baptism of Christ and the transfer of his disciples to the Lord Jesus. Apart from the denial of the supernatural, there is no bona fide reason for questioning the account given by Luke, substantiated as it is by the historical events which followed.

THE ANNUNCIATION TO MARY

In the gospel narratives only Luke records the annunciation to Mary. With fitting restraint and simplicity Luke unfolds this dramatic incident which he may have heard from the lips of Mary herself.

The annunciation is given the background of a similar announcement to Zacharias by the angel Gabriel. In the account of the annunciation to Mary, Gabriel is once again mentioned. He had also been sent earlier with special revelations to Daniel the prophet. His tidings to Mary were introduced by the fact that she was highly favored and had been chosen by the Lord for an unusual honor: to bring forth a Son whom she should call Jesus. This Son would be called the Son of the Most High and to Him the Lord God would give the throne of His father David. Over the house of Jacob He would reign forever as there would be no end to His kingdom.

In answer to the natural question raised by Mary concerning how this should come about, since she was an unmarried woman, the angel replied: "The Holy Spirit shall come upon thee, and the power of the Most High shall overshadow thee: wherefore also the holy thing which is begotten shall be called the Son of God" (Luke 1:35, ASV). In these unmistakable terms Mary was informed that her Son would have no human father, and that He should be indeed the Son of God who would fulfill the promises given to David of a Son to reign over His house forever. In confirmation of this unusual promise and evidence of the supernatural power of God, Mary was informed that her kinswoman Elizabeth had also conceived a son in her old age as a demonstration of the power of God.

To these tidings Mary replied in devout submission: "Behold the handmaid of the Lord; be it unto me according to thy word" (Luke 1:38). The simplicity of this narrative, the avoidance of all extravagant details, and the very natural movement of the conversation between Mary and the angel testify to the genuineness of this portion of Scripture and lead to the theological conclusion that Jesus Christ was born of a virgin. The Magnificat of Mary[6] recorded in Luke 1:46-55 gives eloquent expression to the godly faith of Mary and provides some indication as to why God chose her for this unique honor.

THE ANNUNCIATION TO JOSEPH

It is in keeping with the purposes of the gospel of Matthew that it, rather than Luke, should record the annunciation to Joseph. Matthew's narrative deals with the legal right of Christ to the throne of David. The annunciation to Joseph apparently was subsequent to that of Mary, and the time interval between the two annunciations was undoubtedly a test of faith both to Mary and Joseph. When Joseph became aware of the fact that Mary to whom he was betrothed was with child, though he was a righteous man as the gospel of Matthew indicates, he was not willing to make his problem public, but intended to break the betrothal privately. As he contemplated this action an angel of the Lord appeared to him in a dream, saying: "Joseph, thou son of David, fear not to take unto thee Mary thy wife: for that which is conceived in her is of the Holy Spirit" (Matt. 1:20, ASV). The angel went on to explain: "And she shall bring forth a son; and thou shalt call his name JESUS; for it is he that shall save his people from their sins" (v. 21, ASV). Then the angel pointed out to Joseph that this was a fulfillment of the prediction recorded in Isaiah 7:14: "Behold, a virgin shall conceive, and bear a son,

[6]Cf. John V. Koontz, "Mary's Magnificat," *Bibliotheca Sacra*, CXVI (Oct.-Dec., 1959), 336-49.

and shall call his name Immanuel." In keeping with this instruction Joseph took to himself his wife, thereby avoiding any scandal that might attach to Mary and at the same time giving to the Son that was born the legal right to the throne of David.

THE BIRTH OF JESUS CHRIST

Though the Apostle Paul gives frequent indication of knowing the fact of the birth of Jesus Christ (Acts 13:23; Rom. 1:3; Gal. 4:4; Phil. 2:6-7; I Tim. 1:15), only Matthew and Luke give the precise account, Matthew dwelling upon the fact that Christ was born in Bethlehem and Luke tracing many of the lesser details. Here again, as in other aspects of the narrative, the simplicity of the account is one of the important testimonies to its authenticity.

Luke goes to great detail to date the birth of Christ, linking it with a decree that went out from Caesar Augustus when Quirinius was governor of Syria (cf. Luke 2:1-2, ASV). Because of this decree Joseph was required to go to Bethlehem to register and Mary accompanied him.

The account of the birth of Christ is given in only two sentences. Luke records: "And it came to pass, while they were there, the days were fulfilled that she should be delivered. And she brought forth her firstborn son; and she wrapped him in swaddling clothes, and laid him in a manger, because there was no room for them in the inn" (Luke 2:6-7, ASV). In utter contrast to the dignity of the Son of God and His ultimate glorification as King of kings and Lord of lords, the birth of Christ was in the rudest circumstances. Some have pictured it as being in one of the outer buildings of the inn used for cattle. Others have favored a cave nearby, also used as a stable.[7] The Scriptures indicate that He was laid in a manger, a rude improvised crib by the loving hands of Mary herself.[8] His obscurity, however, was soon ended by the visitation of the angels to the shepherds in nearby fields. According to Luke's account, "And an angel of the Lord stood by them, and the glory of the Lord shone round about them: and they were sore afraid" (2:9, ASV). Unto the shepherds the angel said: "Be not afraid; for behold, I bring you good

[7]Robert Jamieson, A. R. Fausset and David Brown, *A Commentary, Critical, Experimental, and Practical on the Old and New Testament*, V, 225; Henry Alford, *The Greek Testament*, I, 457.

[8]Alexander Bruce, "The Synoptic Gospels" in W. R. Nicoll (ed.), *The Expositor's Greek Testament*, I, 472.

tidings of great joy which shall be to all the people: for there is
born to you this day in the city of David a Saviour, who is Christ
the Lord. And this is the sign unto you: Ye shall find a babe
wrapped in swaddling clothes, and lying in a manger" (vv. 10-12,
ASV). As the angel delivered his message, suddenly, according
to Luke's account, a multitude of angels appeared in the heavens
chanting: "Glory to God in the highest, and on earth peace
among men in whom he is well pleased" (v. 14, ASV). Under the
stimulus of this dramatic experience the shepherds lost no time
in coming to Bethlehem and found Mary and Joseph and the
Babe lying in the manger.

THE INFANCY OF CHRIST

Both Luke and Matthew record details of the early days of the
incarnate Son of God upon earth. The first event recorded after
the visit of the angels was the observance of the rite of circumcision (Luke 2:21) when He was named Jesus in keeping with the
instruction of the angel to Mary and Joseph before Christ was
born (Matt. 1:21). At that time directives in the law concerning
the offering to accompany circumcision were duly followed (Lev.
12:6). While the holy family was in the temple, the testimony of
Simeon was given as he blessed God and said: "Now lettest thou
thy servant depart, Lord, according to thy word, in peace; for
mine eyes have seen thy salvation, which thou hast prepared
before the face of all peoples; a light for revelation to the Gentiles, and the glory of thy people Israel" (Luke 2:29-32, ASV).
On that occasion Simeon also predicted to Mary: "Behold, this
child is set for the falling and the rising of many in Israel; and
for a sign which is spoken against; yea and a sword shall pierce
through thine own soul; that thoughts out of many hearts may be
revealed" (Luke 2:34-35, ASV). To Simeon's testimony was
added that of Anna the prophetess who gave her word of thanks-
giving to God concerning this provision for the redemption of
His people.

It is probable that the visit of the Magi from the East (Matt.
2:1-12) occurred sometime later and not immediately after the
birth of Christ as is commonly believed. The time interval required for the trip of the Magi after they had seen the star would
point to the passage of at least a few weeks. Alford, in an extended
discussion concerning the star and the chronology involved, thinks

the time was only forty days instead of two years as others have
suggested.[9] Matthew records the dramatic appearance of the Magi
in Jerusalem demanding where the King of the Jews was to be
born. When Herod inquired of the chief priests and the scribes,
he was told that the King of the Jews would be born in Bethlehem. Herod therefore told the Magi to find the child and to return to bring him word that he might come and worship Him.
Herod intended of course to kill the Child as soon as he could
identify Him. The star, reappearing according to Matthew 2:9,
led the Magi to Bethlehem where they found the Child with Mary
His mother now in a house. This was apparently on a subsequent
visit to Bethlehem from Nazareth a number of months after the
birth of Christ. To the Child they offered their gifts of gold,
frankincense and myrrh and worshiped Him in recognition of
His deity. Meanwhile, warned by a dream, the Magi returned to
their land without reporting to Herod, and Joseph also following
instructions from the Lord, fled to Egypt to avoid the destroying
hatred of Herod. The prophecy of Hosea 11:1, partially fulfilled
by the redemption of Israel out of Egypt, is cited by Matthew as
having its complete fulfillment in Christ. Later when it was safe
after the death of Herod, Joseph and Mary and young Jesus returned to Nazareth where He spent His childhood.

CRITICAL PROBLEMS

Though there have been many attempts to weaken the credibility of the accounts of the birth of Christ, there has been little
documentary evidence to support this attitude popular in various
forms of higher criticism. The biblical accounts themselves, presented in a straightforward manner, without the embellishment
that would have occurred in a fictitious account, give the simple
and historical facts pertaining to the birth of Christ. Those who
received the Gospels when they were first written had little ground
to question the approach of Luke as a careful investigator, and
the meticulous precision of his presentation is its own assurance
that the records are true.

The accounts of the birth of Christ of course do not stand
simply on their own credibility, but are supported by the miraculous life, death and resurrection of the Lord Jesus Christ. The
fact of the New Testament church, the spiritual transformation

9Alford, I, 9-15.

of those who are believers, and the evident acceptance of these facts by thousands who were contemporary with Jesus and who had the best opportunity to investigate, combine to substantiate these solid conclusions. An attitude of unbelief too often is linked with an unwillingness to bow before Jesus Christ as divine Lord and Saviour, not from attested facts which contradict the Gospels.

Some problems, however, do exist in the narrative, particularly in the genealogies.[10] Matthew opens his account with a presentation of the book of the generation of Jesus Christ and, beginning with Abraham, traces the lineage to Joseph the husband of Mary. The purpose of this genealogy was apparent to any Jew, for the Messiah must be of the seed of David, and without documentary proof to this end no one could hope to claim recognition that was due a son of David. A careful examination of the genealogies will reveal that the lineage is selective, not necessarily presenting every name that is properly in the line.[11] As itemized by Matthew, fourteen generations are mentioned from Abraham to David, fourteen generations from David to the captivity, and fourteen from the captivity to Christ. Notable omissions are the names of three kings mentioned in I Chronicles 3:11-12, that is, Ahaziah, Joash and Amaziah. The reason for the omission seems to be to maintain the unity of fourteen generations in each section. The names recorded in Matthew 1:13-15 are New Testament additions and are not found in the Old Testament. These names may have been taken from available registers of the families at the time of Christ.

A comparison of the genealogy of Matthew with that of Luke 3:23-38 has occasioned no little discussion. In contrast to Matthew, Luke traces the genealogy to Adam. Many believe there are omissions in the line from Adam to Abraham. There is the problem of variation in Luke as compared to Matthew and the Old Testament. In Genesis 11:12 there is an omission of Cainan, recorded in Luke 3:36. Omissions in genealogy are common, however, as illustrated in the Old Testament omissions found in Ezra 7:1-5 where six generations of the priesthood are left out. It should be clear that genealogies are not necessarily complete, the main point being legitimate descent rather than inclusion of all the links in the genealogy.

[10]See Jamieson, Fausset and Brown, V, 2-3, Remarks 1 and 2.
[11]Cf. Alford, I, 4.

The principal problem of Luke's genealogy, however, is that an entirely different lineage is presented from David to Joseph, the descent coming from Nathan, the son of David, rather than through Solomon as in Matthew's account. The most common explanation of this seems to be the best, that is, that Joseph as the son-in-law of Eli was considered in the descent from Eli through his marriage with Mary and that the lineage therefore is that of Mary rather than of Joseph.[12]

This at least fits in beautifully with the Old Testament predictions given through Jeremiah (cf. Jer. 22:30; 36:30) to the effect that the line of Coniah would never have a man to sit upon the throne. Though the legal right to the throne passed to Christ through Joseph as His legal father, the actual physical lineage could not come through Joseph because of this curse upon his line. The account of Luke therefore seeks to trace the physical lineage of Christ through Mary back to Adam the first man, connecting Christ to the predicted seed of the woman. Though there has been opposition to this interpretation, the arguments for it far outweigh those against it and give a reasonable explanation why there should be two lineages from David to Christ.

One of the most important controversies relative to the birth of Christ has centered on scriptures that declare He was born of a virgin. This claim has been opposed as both unnatural and unlikely, and therefore an invention rather than a solid historical fact. It might be granted that if predictions of the person and work of Christ had been those of an ordinary prophet there might be good grounds for questioning His virgin birth. The whole tenor of Scripture as presented in both the Old Testament prophecies that He was to be God and Man and the New Testament fulfillment makes the virgin birth a divine explanation, insofar as it can be explained, of an otherwise insuperable problem. How could One who was both God and Man have perfectly human parents? The account of the virgin birth therefore, instead of being an unreasonable invention, becomes a fitting explanation of how in the supernatural power of God the incarnation was made a reality.[13]

---

[12]Jamieson, Fausset and Brown, V, 235-36. Alford, however, holds that Luke's genealogy is that of Joseph, leaving the problem unexplained (Alford, I, 473).
[13]Cf. the excellent and comprehensive treatment by J. Gresham Machen, *The Virgin Birth of Christ*.

Much of the discussion on the virgin birth takes for granted that it is possible to ignore the carefully worded record of Scripture. Helmut Thielicke, in response to a question concerning the indispensability of the virgin birth, offered the opinion that the fact of Christ's miraculous birth and His miraculous conception is essential to Christian faith, but that the virgin birth itself may be simply a human explanation.[14] Thielicke's view, arising from form criticism, denies the accurate historicity of the birth narratives. It should be noted that not only does Luke give a very specific account which states in plain language that Christ was born of a virgin, but the account of Matthew written by a different author and from a different point of view confirms this explanation. Throughout the rest of the New Testament there is constant assumption that Christ is indeed the very Son of God and that He was born of a woman but not a man. This is the teaching of Paul in Galatians 4:4 as well as the prophetic record of the book of Revelation 12:1-2. The sign promised through Isaiah 7:14 of a virgin bearing a Son to be called Immanuel and the description of this Child as One who bears the title Mighty God in Isaiah 9:6 add confirming evidence. If the supernatural power of God to perform such an act as this be admitted, there is no logical reason for not accepting the plain intent of the scriptural portions bearing on this great theme. The wisest of scholars as well as the most simple of humble believers have bowed alike to the manger in Bethlehem and acknowledged that the Infant, born of the virgin and laid in swaddling clothes, is their Lord and Saviour in whom is resident all the attributes of the infinite God.

[14]Cf. Helmut Thielicke, *Between Heaven and Earth*, pp. 59-87.

7

THE PERSON OF THE INCARNATE CHRIST

THE STUDY OF THE PERSON of Christ is one of the most complicated and intricate studies that can be undertaken by a biblical theologian. The many single volumes which have been produced, such as B. B. Warfield's excellent book *The Person and Work of Christ*, as well as such massive works as the five-volume set by J. A. Dorner on *The Doctrine of the Person of Christ*, are evidence of the importance of the subject. Contemplation on the person of Christ is an exhaustless mine of theology and vital preaching as well as the heart of any true devotion to the Saviour. Every systematic theology worthy of the name gives considerable attention to the person of the incarnate Christ.

THE PREINCARNATE PERSON OF CHRIST

The person of Christ incarnate is best understood in comparison to the person of Christ before He became incarnate. In any orthodox statement of the doctrine of the Trinity, the second Person is described as possessing all the attributes of the Godhead, being distinguished as the second Person in contrast to the first or third Persons of the Trinity and as the eternal Son in contrast to the Father or the Holy Spirit. In such utterances as Hebrews 13:8 it is made clear that these attributes are the eternal possession of Christ continuing even in His incarnate state. Even before His incarnation, however, Christ had certain properties and ministries which distinguished Him from God the Father and God the Holy Spirit. In the plan of God He was designated as the coming Redeemer. In the Old Testament He appeared frequently in the character of the Angel of Jehovah and other theophanies. His person, however, prior to the incarnation did not include any human or angelic attributes, and the theophanies did not involve any change or addition in His nature. In general the preincarnate person of Christ was not complicated, and does not present the theological problems which originate in the incarnation.

THE DEITY OF THE INCARNATE CHRIST

When the second Person of the Godhead became incarnate there was immediately introduced the seemingly insuperable problem of uniting God with man and combining an infinite and eternal Person with one that is finite and temporal. Orthodox Christianity, however, has been united in the opinion that the incarnation did not diminish the deity of the second Person of the Trinity even during the period of humiliation and suffering while Christ was on earth. Such limitations as may have been involved in the kenosis did not subtract one attribute or in any sense make Christ less than God. The central importance of the continued deity of Christ has been recognized by theologians from early centuries until the present, and any attack on the deity of Christ is justly recognized as an assault upon a central aspect of Christian faith.

Generally speaking, those who accept the inspiration and infallibility of Scripture do not question the deity of the incarnate Christ. Among the early church Fathers a major defection on the deity of Christ was led by Arius; this resulted in his rejection by the orthodox Fathers and the formulation of the Nicene Creed in the fourth century. Earlier the deity of Christ had been denied by sects such as the Ebionites, the Alogi and others. The defection from the biblical doctrine of the deity of Christ was continued by Socinus, the sixteenth century Reformer, and was perpetuated by Schleiermacher and Ritschl in the nineteenth century. Though the denial of the deity of Christ was not embraced by the majority of the Christian church prior to the twentieth century, the biblical doctrine has been openly questioned in many contemporary works, where Jesus Christ is considered the natural son of Joseph and Mary.

Liberal alternatives to the orthodox doctrine of the person of Christ fall into three categories as suggested by William A. Spurrier. Christ may be viewed simply as a great teacher, a great man entirely human but to be respected like other great men of history. Hence, Christ is not to be worshiped but to be followed. Scriptural stories about Him such as His resurrection, miracles and other evidences of supernatural power are denied as human inventions.

A second view emphasizes the goodness of Christ who was sincere to the end and had the courage to die for His convictions. This view tends to minimize His greatness and makes Christ one of many good and sincere men.

A third view sees Christ as an example or model of other men, who although human and not divine, set a new standard for nobility in man, and to some extent was ahead of His time in the evolutionary process. While the majority of mankind follows one or more of these liberal views of Christ, they stand in sharp contrast to the orthodox position that Christ is both God and Man and is in fact the incarnation of the eternal God.[1]

Representative of modern scholarship is the work of Millar Burrows, *An Outline of Biblical Theology*. Burrows doubts the validity of the birth accounts in Matthew and Luke which testify to the miraculous conception of Christ. He approves the poorly supported Sinaitic Syriac rendering of Matthew 1:16: "Joseph . . . begat Jesus."[2] He holds there is no support for the birth narrative elsewhere in the Bible.[3] Though the gospel of John frequently refers to the preexistence of Christ, Burrows nevertheless says: "There is no indication that he ever thought of himself in that way."[4]

The evidence of Scripture is so complete that one who denies the deity of Christ must necessarily reject the accuracy of the Scriptures. Berkhof summarizes the evidence for the deity of Christ in these words:

> We find that Scripture (1) *explicitly asserts the deity of the Son* in such passages as John 1:1; 20:28; Rom. 9:5; Phil. 2:6; Tit. 2:13; I John 5:20; (2) *applies divine names to Him,* Isa. 9:6; 40:3; Jer. 23:5, 6; Joel 2:32 (comp. Acts 2:21); I Tim. 3:16; (3) *ascribes to Him divine attributes,* such as eternal existence, Isa. 9:6; John 1:1, 2; Rev. 1:8; 22:13, omnipresence, Matt. 18:20; 28:20; John 3:13, omniscience, John 2:24, 25; 21:17; Rev. 2:23, omnipotence, Isa. 9:6; Phil. 3:21; Rev. 1:8, immutability, Heb. 1:10-12; 13:8, and in general every attribute belonging to the Father, Col. 2:9; (4) *speaks of Him as doing divine works,* as creation, John

[1]William A. Spurrier, *Guide to the Christian Faith*, pp. 115-18.
[2]Millar Burrows, *An Outline of Biblical Theology*, p. 101.
[3]*Ibid.*
[4]*Ibid.*, p. 102.

1:3, 10; Col. 1:16; Heb. 1:2, 10, providence, Luke 10:22; John 3:35; 17:2; Eph. 1:22; Col. 1:17; Heb. 1:3, the forgiveness of sins, Matt. 9:2-7; Mark 2:7-10; Col. 3:13, resurrection and judgment, Matt. 25:31, 32; John 5:19-29; Acts 10:42; 17:31; Phil. 3:21; II Tim. 4:1, the final dissolution and renewal of all things, Heb. 1:10-12; Phil. 3:21; Rev. 21:5, and (5) *accords Him divine honour,* John 5:22, 23; 14:1; I Cor. 15:19; II Cor. 13:13; Heb. 1:6; Matt. 28:19.[5]

Charles Hodge has provided another summary of scriptural evidence for the deity of Christ (see chap. 2).[6]

All modern defections from the doctrine of the deity of Christ assume that the Bible is not authoritative or final in its revelation of this doctrine. If scholars are free to question the explicit statement of Scriptures on the basis of higher criticism, there can be no remaining norm for the theological doctrine of the deity of Christ. Though a denial of scriptural infallibility does not necessarily result in a denial of the deity of Christ, it is impossible to evade the mass of scriptures representing Jesus Christ as the eternal God without questioning the scriptural record. Even modern liberals pay lip service to this in their recognition of the term "the Son of God" and their recognition of the term "Lord and Saviour" as applying to Christ. Without question the crucial issue in biblical theology is the deity of Christ, and disregard or question of this central doctrine of the Bible leads to inevitable chaos in theology as a whole.

THE HUMANITY OF THE INCARNATE CHRIST

Though the doctrine of the deity of Christ is generally recognized as the indispensable fundamental of Christology, the doctrine of His true humanity is equally important. On the fact of His humanity depends the reality of His death on the cross, His claim to be Israel's Messiah, His fulfillment of the promise to David of a Descendant to sit on his throne, and His offices of Prophet and Priest. Those who deny the true humanity of Christ, such as modern Christian Science, are just as effective at destroying the Christian faith as those who deny the deity of Christ. As in the case of the doctrine of the deity of Christ, the Scriptures bear full testimony to His humanity; and a denial of these aspects of His incarnate person would necessitate a denial of the Scrip-

[5]Louis Berkhof, *Systematic Theology,* pp. 94-95.
[6]See Charles Hodge, *Systematic Theology,* II, 382.

tures themselves. For this reason the doctrine of the true humanity of Christ has always been a part of orthodox Christian faith.

The humanity of Christ is evident first of all in the fact that He possessed a true human body composed of flesh and blood. It was like the bodies of other men except for those qualities which have resulted from human sin and failure. The evidence for His human body in the Scriptures is seemingly even more compelling than the evidence for His deity.

According to the Scriptures, Christ was born of the virgin Mary, fulfilling in this notable historical event of His incarnation all that would normally be expected of a human birth and fulfilling the many Old Testament prophecies which anticipated His genuine humanity.

The life of Christ subsequent to His birth in Bethlehem reveals the same normal human development and growth. According to Luke 2:52 (ASV), "Jesus advanced in wisdom and stature, and in favor with God and men." His bodily growth was normal like that of other children. More difficult to understand, however, is the statement that He advanced in wisdom or knowledge. This is commonly interpreted to refer to His humanity rather than to His divine consciousness. Other aspects of His experience correspond to that of ordinary human beings. He experienced in His life similar feelings and limitations as other human beings, and His physical movements were such as corresponded to a genuine human nature and human body. He, according to the Scriptures, was able to suffer pain, thirst, hunger, fatigue, pleasure, rest, death and resurrection. Both before and after His resurrection He could be seen and felt, and His human body was tangible to human touch just as other human beings. No one seems to have ever doubted that He possessed a true human body prior to His death, and even after His resurrection He went out of His way to demonstrate the genuineness of His human body. The elements of the supernatural evident in miracles such as walking on the water, though admittedly beyond human powers, did not change the essential character of His body any more than in the case of Peter who also walked on the water.

The true humanity of the incarnate Christ is also recognized in Scripture in the human titles which were given to Him such as "Son of man," "the man Christ Jesus," "Jesus," "the Son of

David," "man of sorrows," etc. The Scriptures also testify specifically to the fact that His body possessed flesh and blood (Heb.
2:14; I John 4:2-3). A denial of His humanity, therefore, must
also carry with it a denial of these important scriptures which are
essential to the New Testament revelation of the person of the
incarnate Christ.

The Scriptures not only bear testimony to the physical characteristics of the human body of the incarnate Christ, but also speak
specifically of the fact that He possessed a human rational soul
and spirit. According to Matthew 26:38 Christ said to His disciples: "My soul is exceeding sorrowful, even unto death." This
could hardly be attributed to His divine nature and therefore is
a reference to the fact that He possessed a human soul. A similar
statement is given in John 13:21 in regard to His human spirit
where it is recorded: "When Jesus had thus said, he was troubled
in the spirit." From these and other scriptures it is evident that
Christ possessed a true humanity not only in its material aspects
as indicated in His human body, but in the immaterial aspect
specified in Scripture as being His soul and spirit. It is therefore
not sufficient to recognize that Jesus Christ as the Son of God
possessed a human body, but it is necessary to view Him as having
a complete human nature including body, soul and spirit.

Contemporary theology has largely admitted the true humanity
of Christ though sometimes qualifying or denying His deity.
Neoliberalism as well as neoorthodoxy has raised no serious question about the genuine humanity of Christ. Modern Christian
Science has been the major movement questioning a true humanity, but this is seldom taken seriously by contemporary theologians. For those who accept the Bible as authoritative, there
can be no question that Jesus Christ was in all reality a genuine
Man.

The controversy concerning whether Christ had a genuine
human as well as a genuine divine nature continues to be a central problem in contemporary theology. G. C. Berkouwer introduces his discussion on the person of Christ by a long chapter on
the subject "The Crisis in the Doctrine of the Two Natures." He
finds a serious defection from the early church doctrine of the
person of Christ in the nineteenth century at the hands of Schleiermacher and Ritschl.[7] This arose out of a background of So-

[7]G. C. Berkouwer, *The Person of Christ*, pp. 21-25.

cinianism. The defection was furthered by Harnack, Nitzschl, Hegel, Strausz and the kenosis theory of Thomasius.[8]

This decline from orthodoxy ultimately led to the theories of Bultmann who is evaluated by Berkouwer in these words:

> What in the dogma of the church are regarded as God's acts in history are devaluated by Bultmann to the status of a religious fancy. Theology can sink no farther. The witness of the Scriptures and the dogma found on them are pushed aside and the cross is made into the irrational fact of a decision in which man comes to know himself.[9]

Berkouwer's conclusion to his long chapter is most significant,

> But it has become clearer than ever that the orthodox believer in Christ, in the midst of all the dangers that continually beset him, is called upon to witness in this hour of confusion: to witness to the personal relevancy of the question asked at Caesarea Philippi: to testify that the crisis of the doctrine of the two natures is not merely a theoretical matter but a religious crisis.[10]

THE UNION OF THE DIVINE AND HUMAN NATURES

The overwhelming proof for both the deity and true humanity of Christ makes it self-evident that in His person these natures so widely differing as to their attributes are nevertheless brought together into a personal union which will continue forever. Though Christ sometimes operated in the sphere of His humanity and in other cases in the sphere of His deity, in all cases what He did and what He was could be attributed to His one person. Even though it is evident that there were two natures in Christ, He is never considered a dual personality. The normal pronouns such as I, Thou and He are used of Him frequently.

The hypostatic or personal union of the human and divine natures in Christ is given explicit divine revelation in at least seven major passages of Scripture (Phil. 2:6-11; John 1:1-14; Rom. 1:2-5; 9:5; I Tim. 3:16; Heb. 2:14; I John 1:1-3). These passages which are studied in connection with other doctrines make it evident that the eternal Son of God took upon Himself a complete human nature and became Man. The act of incarnation was not

[8]*Ibid.*, pp. 25-28.
[9]*Ibid.*, pp. 41-42.
[10]*Ibid.*, p. 56.

a temporary arrangement which ended with His death and resurrection but, as the Scriptures make evident, His human nature continues forever, His earthly body which died on the cross being transformed into a resurrection body suited for His glorious presence in heaven. The continuance of His humanity is reflected in such passages as Matthew 26:64 (ASV) where it is stated that Christ will sit on the throne of His glory and return to earth as the Son of man: "Henceforth ye shall see the Son of man sitting at the right hand of Power, and coming on the clouds of heaven." (Cf. Mark 14:62; Luke 22:69-70). The appearances of Christ after His resurrection also substantiate the continuity of His true humanity. When the worshiping women met Christ in Matthew 28:9b (ASV) it is recorded: "They came and took hold of his feet, and worshipped him." Mary Magdalene, according to John 20:17, actually clung to Christ in her joy at seeing Him after His resurrection.

Further evidence is found in the other appearances in the post-resurrection ministry as well as in the fact of His bodily ascension into heaven (Mark 16:19; Luke 24:30-31, 39-43, 50-53; John 20:22, 27-28; Acts 1:1-11; 7:56). According to Philippians 2:10, the human name Jesus is continued in connection with the final judgment. His humanity seems also to be essential to His work of mediation. According to I Timothy 2:5 (ASV), "There is one God, one mediator also between God and men, himself man, Christ Jesus." The term "Son of man" which Christ uses Himself in Matthew 26:64 as describing His reign in heaven is mentioned also in Revelation 1:13; 14:14.

Though certain aspects of His mediatorial work will terminate according to I Corinthians 15:25-28, there is no indication anywhere in the Bible that His humanity will ever be terminated. By its very nature a human personality once brought into existence never ceases to exist, and what is true of ordinary human experience is also true of Christ who became Man. His continuance as a human being in eternity seems to involve also the continuance of a human body. This is demonstrated, first, in the resurrection of Christ where His body was raised and prepared for heaven; second, in the fact of His ascension which was a bodily ascension into heaven; third, in the fact that He will return bodily to the earth; and fourth, that His body is a pattern of the body of believers who are raised or translated. There is every reason, therefore, to believe that the humanity of Christ will continue throughout all eternity to come.

Among conservative theologians the fact of the hypostatic union of the divine and human natures in Christ is well established. The problem does not lie in the fact of the union, but rather in the relationship of the two natures of Christ, the nature of the self-consciousness of Christ and how the two natures relate to the will of Christ. These items form the burden of subsequent discussions.

THE RELATION OF THE TWO NATURES

Few subjects in the realm of theology are more difficult than the definition of the relation of the two natures in the incarnate Christ. Theologians are faced with the problem of definition. The English word "nature" is derived from the Latin *natura* and is the equivalent of the Greek *physis* (cf. Rom. 2:14; Gal. 2:15; 4:8; Eph. 2:3; II Peter 1:4). In the history of Christian doctrine the usage of the term "nature" has varied, but the word is now commonly used to designate the divine or human elements in the person of Christ. In theology the expression "substance" from the Latin *substantia* is also used, corresponding to the Greek *ousia*. All of these terms are used to define the real essence, the inward properties which underlie all outward manifestation. As this refers to the person of Christ, nature is seen to be the sum of all the attributes and their relationship to each other. Necessarily, such attributes must be compatible to the nature to which they correspond and cannot be transferred to another substance or nature. As applied to the problem of defining the humanity and deity of Christ, nature as used of the humanity of Christ includes all that belongs to His humanity. As applied to the deity of Christ, it includes all that belongs to His deity. Hence, theologians speak of two natures, the human and the divine, each with its respective attributes.

Much confusion arose in the early history of the church on the problem of how such incompatible natures could be joined in one Person without one or the other losing some of its essential characteristics. The resulting discussion, however, led to the orthodox statement that the two natures are united without loss of any essential attributes and that the two natures maintain their separate identity. Through the incarnation of Christ, the two natures were inseparably united in such a way that there was no mixture or loss of their separate identity and without loss or transfer of any property or attribute of one nature to the other. The union thus consummated is a personal or hypostatic union in that Christ is one Person, not two, and is everlasting in keeping with the everlasting character of both the human and divine natures.

The proof that the two natures maintain their complete identity, though joined in a personal union, is based on a comparison of the attributes of the human nature and the divine nature. It should be clear that divine attributes must necessarily belong to the corresponding divine nature and that human attributes must belong to the corresponding human nature, though the attributes of either the human or divine nature belong to the person of Christ. Because the attributes of either nature belong to Christ, Christ is theanthropic in person, but it is not accurate to refer to His natures as being theanthropic as there is no mixture of the divine and human to form a new third substance. The human nature always remains human, and the divine nature always remains divine. Christ is therefore both God and Man, no less God because of His humanity and no less human because of His deity.

Calvinistic theology generally holds that the two natures of Christ are united without any transfer of attributes. Just as any essence is composed of the sum of its attributes and their relationship, a change of any attribute would necessarily involve a change in essence. For instance, infinity cannot be transferred to finity; mind cannot be transferred to matter; God cannot be transferred to man, or vice versa. To rob the divine nature of God of a single attribute would destroy His deity, and to rob man of a single human attribute would result in destruction of a true humanity. It is for this reason that the two natures of Christ cannot lose or transfer a single attribute.

A significant variation, however, from this doctrine is the Lutheran teaching of the ubiquity of the human body of Christ. In connection with the Lutheran doctrine of the Lord's Supper, it is held that, although the elements are not transubstantiated into the body of Christ, they contain the body of Christ. This concept is considered to be supported by the teaching that the body of Christ is everywhere. In sustaining this doctrine, Lutheran theologians have felt that the doctrine of omnipresence as it relates to the divine nature is properly also an attribute of the human body of Christ. The Lutheran doctrine is challenged by Calvinists principally on the basis of the lack of biblical evidence for it and the contradiction involved in the concept of a body that is everywhere present. While it is normal for theology to consider Christ in His divine nature as omnipresent, the humanity of Christ always seems to have a local concept, and Christ is revealed to be seated now at the right hand of the Father in heaven.

In the incarnation no attribute of the divine nature was changed though there was a change in the manifestation. This is sometimes referred to as the kenosis doctrine or the self-emptying of Christ. It is clear that Christ, while on earth following His incarnation, did not manifest the glory of God except on rare occasions. But He surrendered no attributes. Christ was still all that God is even though He had sovereignly chosen to limit certain phases of His activity to the human sphere. Even during the period of humiliation, therefore, there is no need for qualifying the basic doctrine that both the human and the divine natures retain all their essential characteristics.

The two natures of Christ are not only united without affecting the respective attributes of the two natures, but they are combined in one Person. This union should not be defined as Deity possessing humanity as this would deny true humanity its rightful place. It is not, on the other hand, humanity merely indwelt by Deity. Christ did not differ from other men simply in degree of divine influence as sometimes advanced by modern liberals. In His unique personality He possessed two natures, one eternal and divine, the other human and generated in time. The union of these two natures was not one of sympathy alone nor merely a harmony of will and operation. Orthodox theology regards this union as personal and constitutional. As Charles Hodge put it: "The Son of God did not unite Himself with a human person, but with a human nature."[11]

One of the difficult aspects of the relationship of the two natures of Christ is that, while the attributes of one nature are never attributed to the other, the attributes of both natures are properly attributed to His person. Thus Christ at the same moment has seemingly contradictory qualities. He can be weak and omnipotent, increasing in knowledge and omniscient, finite and infinite.

[11]Hodge, II, 391.

These qualities can, of course, be traced to their corresponding nature but, as presented in Scripture, a variety of treatment can be observed. At least these seven classifications of this aspect of the truth can be observed in what is called the communion of attributes:

1. Some attributes are true of His whole person such as the titles Redeemer, Prophet, Priest and King. As Redeemer, Christ is both Man and God, both natures being essential to this function. It is therefore an attribute or characteristic true of His whole person.

2. Some attributes are true only of Deity, but the whole person is the subject. In some cases the person of Christ is related to an attribute peculiar to the divine nature. For instance, Christ said: "Before Abraham was, I am" (John 8:58). The whole person is the subject, but the attribute of eternity applies only to the divine nature. It is possible, however, to say of the person of the incarnate Christ that His person is eternal even though humanity was added in time.

3. Some attributes are true only of humanity, but the whole person is the subject. In contrast to John 8:58, in some cases attributes true only of His humanity are mentioned but the whole person is in view. On the cross Christ said: "I thirst" (John 19:28). The statement can be attributed only to the human nature, but the whole person is involved. This type of reference disappears after His resurrection and ascension and the resulting freedom from the limitations of His earthly life.

4. The person may be described according to divine nature but the predicate of the human nature. A seeming contradiction is sometimes found when the person of Christ is described according to His divine nature, but that which is predicated is an attribute of the human nature. An illustration is afforded in the revelation of Christ in glory in Revelation 1:12-18 where the deity of Christ is in evidence. Yet Christ is revealed as the One who "was dead" (v. 18), an attribute possible only for the humanity of Christ.

5. The person may be described according to human nature but the predicate of the divine nature. In John 6:62 (ASV) the significant statement occurs: "What then if ye should behold the Son of man ascending where he was before?" The title "Son of man" describes Christ according to His human nature, but the predicate

of ascending up where He was before could have reference only to the divine nature.

6. The person may be described according to the divine nature, but the predicate of both natures. According to John 5:25-27, Christ as the Son of God spoke to those who were spiritually dead, and those who heard lived. As the Son of man, however, Christ is said to execute judgment in the future. Hence, Christ is described as the Son of God, but the predicate of speaking can be attributed to both natures as demonstrated by the fact that the human nature is specifically mentioned as in view in the future judgment.

7. The person may be described according to human nature but the predicate of both natures. According to John 5:27 mentioned above, Christ will judge the world as One possessing both human and divine natures. Another example is found in Matthew 27:46 where Christ said: "My God, my God, why hast thou forsaken me?" Christ was speaking from the viewpoint of His human nature in His prophetic cry, addressing His Father as His God, but the pronoun "me" seems to refer to both natures or His whole person. Christ was being judicially forsaken because He was bearing the sin of the world. It was not simply the divine nature forsaking the human nature as some have held.

THE RELATION OF THE TWO NATURES TO THE SELF-CONSCIOUSNESS OF CHRIST

Much speculation has arisen over the problem of self-consciousness in such a unique Person as Christ. In His own self-consciousness was He aware of His deity and humanity at all times? Liberals have tended to postpone any recognition of divine self-consciousness until some point in His public ministry. The orthodox doctrine necessarily implies that Christ in His divine self-consciousness was aware of His deity at all times. There was no point in the life of Christ when He suddenly became aware of the fact that He was God. His divine self-consciousness was as fully operative when He was a Babe in Bethlehem as it was in His most mature experience. There is evidence, however, that the human nature developed and with it a human self-consciousness came into play. In view of the varied forms of manifestation of the divine and human natures, it seems possible to conclude that He had both a divine and a human self-consciousness, that these were never in conflict, and that Christ sometimes thought, spoke and acted from the divine self-consciousness and at other times from the human.

Vincent Taylor in a long discussion brings out the importance of the divine consciousness of Jesus.[12] He feels in the end that the divine consciousness is a natural corollary of His divine nature, but that the humanity of Christ must be taken into consideration as the humanity was not omniscient and therefore its self-consciousness was limited. Taylor, however, concludes,

> From the evidence as a whole we are entitled to conclude that His consciousness of divine Sonship is the key to the presentation of Jesus we find in all the Gospels. His divine consciousness is expressed in words and in deeds. It lies behind the high dignity of His role as the Son of Man, and is a presupposition of His death-grapple with evil. It accounts for the confidence with which He affirms, 'But I say unto you', His sovereign exercise of 'mighty works', His sense of being the bearer of the Spirit, and His acceptance of the vocation of the Suffering Servant of the Lord. All of these things are true of Him because He knows Himself to be the Son of God.[13]

Edward J. Young finds five important elements in the self-consciousness of Jesus Christ which he summarizes from Geerhardus Vos.[14] These are: (1) His consciousness that He was King, (2) His consciousness that He was the fulfillment of the eschatological hope of the Old Testament, (3) His consciousness of supernatural power, (4) His consciousness that He is the Saviour, (5) His consciousness of His deity.[15]

THE RELATION OF THE TWO NATURES TO THE WILL OF CHRIST

In view of the complete divine and human natures in Christ, the question has been raised whether each nature had its corresponding will. The problem is occasioned by ambiguity in the word "will." If by will is meant desire, it is clear that there could be conflicting desires in the divine and human natures of Christ. If by will, however, is meant that resulting moral decision, one person can have only one will. In the case of Christ, this will was

[12]Vincent Taylor, *The Person of Christ*, pp. 155-89.
[13]*Ibid.*, p. 169.
[14]Geerhardus Vos, *The Self-Disclosure of Jesus*, pp. 13-36.
[15]Edward J. Young, *The Study of Old Testament Theology Today*, pp. 90-92.

always the will of God. Hence, when Christ prayed in the garden of Gethsemane: "My Father, if it be possible, let this cup pass from me: nevertheless, not as I will, but as thou wilt" (Matt. 26:39, ASV), here, as in all other cases, the ultimate sovereign will of Christ was to do the Father's will. It was natural to the human nature to desire to avoid the cross even as it was in keeping with the divine nature to avoid the contact with sin involved in substitution. The will of God, however, was that Christ should die, and this Christ willingly did. It is therefore no more proper to speak of two sovereign wills in Christ than it is of two wills in an ordinary believer who has both a sin nature and a new nature. A conflict of desires should not be equated with a conflict of moral choice.

IMPORTANT RESULTS OF THE UNION OF THE TWO NATURES IN CHRIST

The incarnation of Christ plays such a large part in the doctrine of the person of Christ that it is obviously tremendous in its significance. At least these seven important results of the union of the two natures in Christ by the incarnation are revealed:

1. The union of the two natures in Christ is related vitally to His acts as an incarnate Person. Though the divine nature was immutable, the human nature could suffer and learn through experience with the result that the corporate person could be said to come into new experiences. Thus Christ learned by suffering (Heb. 5:8). In a similar way, the act of redemption in which Christ offered Himself a sacrifice for sin was an act of His whole person. It was traceable to both natures, not to the human nature alone nor to the divine. As Man Christ could die, but only as God could His death have infinite value sufficient to provide redemption for the sins of the whole world. Thus the human blood of Christ has eternal and infinite value because it was shed as part of the divine-human Person.

2. The eternal priesthood of Christ is also based on the hypostatic union. It was essential to His priesthood that He be both God and Man. By incarnation He became Man and hence could act as a human Priest. As God, His priesthood could be everlasting after the order of Melchizedek, and He properly could be a Mediator between God and man. Because of the human nature

His priesthood could evince a human sympathy (Heb. 4:15) and as the divine Son of God He was assured that God the Father would hear Him.

3. Though in ordinary cases a prophet does not need to have a divine nature, it is clear in examining the prophetic office of Christ that it is related to the act of incarnation. While God could speak from heaven as He did on many occasions in Scripture, it was the purpose of God to reveal Himself through a Man, and this required an incarnation. Hence, the eternal Logos, the Word of God, declared the nature of God by becoming Man (John 1:18).

4. The kingly office of Christ was dependent on both the divine and human natures, and would have been impossible apart from the incarnation. Though it is possible for God to rule as God, it was a function of Christ to rule not only in the divine sense but as the Son of David fulfilling the Davidic covenant and its purpose that the seed of David would sit upon the throne. According to the Davidic covenant, a Son of David would sit on the throne of Israel forever (II Sam. 7:16), and David's house, kingdom and throne were declared to be established forever (cf. Luke 1:31-33). To fulfill His kingly office, therefore, it was necessary to have a human birth which would link Him with David. And He had to have a divine nature that would assure Him the everlasting quality of His government and throne.

5. The incarnate person of Christ is worshiped as the sovereign God. In the period of His life on earth, He was worshiped even when His eternal glory was hidden, and it is now all the more fitting that He should be worshiped as the glorified God-Man. The recognition of His deity and sovereignty is related to His dominion as the second Adam. In the original creation dominion was given the first Adam, and it was God's declared purpose that man should rule creation. Though this prerogative was lost by Adam because of sin, it properly belongs to the incarnate Christ who will rule the earth, especially in the millennial kingdom.

6. In the ascension of the incarnate Christ to heaven, not only was the divine nature restored to its previous place of infinite glory, but the human nature was also exalted. It is now as the God-Man that He is at the right hand of God the Father. This demonstrates that infinite glory and humanity are compatible as illustrated in the person of Christ and assures the saint that

though he is a sinner saved by grace he may anticipate the glory of God in eternity.

7. The union of the two natures in Christ, while not affecting any essential attribute of either nature, did necessarily require certain unique features to be manifested such as the absence of the sin nature, freedom from any act of sin, and lack of a human father. This also of course was true of Adam before the fall and therefore is not a contradiction of the essential humanity of Christ. Though these elements find no parallel in the race after the fall of Adam, they do not constitute ground for denying the true humanity of our Lord.

Much necessarily remains inscrutable in the person of Christ. The problem of the theologian is not to understand completely, but to state the facts revealed in Scripture in such a way as to do full honor to the person of Christ. The portraits of Christ provided in the four Gospels as well as additional revelation provided in the rest of the New Testament fully support the orthodox theological statement of the person of Christ and the relation of the two natures. They justify the believer in Christ in worshiping the Son of God as possessing all the divine attributes and encourage the child of God to come to Him in full assurance of sympathy and understanding arising in His human nature and human experience.

8

THE LIFE OF CHRIST ON EARTH

THE HISTORICAL STUDY of the life of Christ provides much of the material contained in the New Testament on the person and work of Christ. Though a study of the Gospels is not the primary concern of systematic theology, the life of Christ on earth necessarily forms a background for the important doctrines which relate to His person and work. No other period of biblical history is given more minute revelation than the few years of Christ's public ministry.

BIOGRAPHICAL ACCOUNTS

Though each of the Gospels presents a full picture of the person of Christ, a particular emphasis can be observed in each. The gospel of Matthew is primarily directed to presenting Christ as the King, the Son of David who will reign over the house of Israel. Hence there is emphasis upon the genealogies, upon the credentials of the King, and extensive teaching on the subject of the kingdom itself in the Sermon on the Mount and the discourse in Matthew 13. The gospel of Mark is the gospel of action, presenting Christ and His works as the Servant of Jehovah. Little attention is paid to His background, and the emphasis is on the evidences that He is indeed the promised Deliverer of Israel. The gospel of Luke emphasizes the human aspect of Christ, dwelling upon the details of His birth, and presents Christ as the perfect Man born of the virgin Mary. The emphasis of the gospel of John is on the deity of Christ, and evidence is produced demonstrating that He is indeed the Son of God and that those who believe in Him receive eternal life.

The fact that there is a varied emphasis in the four Gospels does not imply that there is contradiction. It is rather that four different portraits are given of the same Person and, though there is variation, it is not a distorted presentation. The gospel of Luke, emphasizing the humanity, also presents full evidence that He is the Son of God. Hence, the four different biographies, when combined, give a perfect picture. Real problems are sometimes raised by the comparison of narratives in the four Gospels, but conservative scholarship has been united that there is no contradiction, that each record is authentic and inspired of the Holy Spirit.

Different principles have been used to analyze the life of Christ. The most common and beneficial is the combination of the chronological and geographical divisions which are related to His life. Using this method, this ninefold division is possible:

The Birth of Christ

The details of the birth of Christ are given in the gospel of Matthew and the gospel of Luke. In Matthew the central fact that Christ is the prophesied King of Israel and the promised Son of David is presented, and His genealogy is traced through Solomon and Jechoniah. As indicated in previous discussions, Matthew gives the legal genealogy while Luke seems to trace the lineage of Christ from David through Nathan and Mary His mother, and continues the line to Adam.

The gospel of Matthew presents Joseph's aspect of the story, the account of the visit of the Magi, and other details which confirm that Jesus Christ is the Son of David. The gospel of Luke traces some of the more human elements. The birth of John the Baptist and the related incidents, the experience of Mary and her Magnificat, the details of the birth in Bethlehem, and the visits of the shepherds and the words of Simeon and Anna with profound simplicity give the details of the birth of Christ.

The Thirty Years of Obscurity (Matt. 2; Luke 2)

Relatively few details are given concerning the life of Christ before His public ministry. Matthew's gospel records the flight into Egypt and the return to Nazareth, and immediately plunges into the ministry of John the Baptist which introduced Christ. The gospel of Luke alone presents the incident of Christ in the temple at the age of twelve. Here is early evidence of His Messianic consciousness and His divine omniscience. The Boy Jesus astonished the wise men of His day with His understanding and answers to their questions. After a brief glimpse of Christ in His youth, Luke also turns to the ministry of John the Baptist as it introduces Christ. It is evident from this brief narrative that the Spirit of God is not interested in satisfying the curiosity of those who would know the details of the early life of Christ. The glimpses given are sufficient to testify to His person and provide a background for His public ministry.

The Opening of Christ's Public Ministry (Matt. 3:1—4:11; Mark 1:1-3; Luke 3:1—4:13; John 1:19—2:12)

In the introduction to the ministry of Christ, the synoptic gospels as well as the gospel of John recount the ministry of John the Baptist, his message of repentance, and the baptism of Jesus Christ. All three of the synoptic gospels mention the temptation of Christ in the wilderness for forty days, though Mark's account is very short. The gospel of John emphasizes the early followers of Christ and the word of Christ to them. The details of the winning of Andrew, John, Peter, Philip and Nathanael are recited in rapid succession followed by the account of the opening miracle as recorded in the gospel of John, chapter 2, where Christ turned the water into wine at Cana and had a short ministry in Capernaum.

The Early Ministry of Christ in Judea (John 2:13—4:42)

Only the gospel of John records the early ministry of Christ in Judea. In John 2:13-25 the first cleansing of the temple is recorded on the occasion of Christ's visit to Jerusalem at the time of the first Passover. Here also is recorded the first prophecy of His coming death. The gospel of John then records the interview with Nicodemus and the contrasting account of the conversion of the woman of Samaria (John 3:1—4:42). Both of these incidents are in keeping with the theme of the gospel of John showing Christ as the Saviour.

The Ministry of Christ in Galilee (Matt. 4:12—18:35; Mark 1:14—9:50; Luke 4:14—9:50; John 4:43—8:59)

After leaving Jerusalem where He observed the first Passover, Christ began His extended ministry in Galilee, using Capernaum as His home after His rejection at Nazareth (Luke 4:16-30). The

Galilean ministry covered a period of a year and nine months and during this time Christ visited Jerusalem only on the occasion of healing the infirm man at the pool of Bethesda and possibly at the time of the second Passover mentioned in His public ministry. The close of His Galilean ministry was occasioned by His visit to Jerusalem at the time of the Feast of the Tabernacles mentioned in John 7:1-52 which was followed by a period of teaching ministry (John 7:53—8:59).

It is customary to recognize a threefold division of the Galilean ministry: (1) the period of ministry prior to the choosing of the twelve disciples (Matt. 4:12-23; 8:1-4; 9:1-17; 12:1-14; Mark 1:14—3:6; Luke 4:14—6:11) ; (2) the period of ministry from the choosing of the twelve disciples to the departure from Capernaum to northern Galilee (Matt. 4:23—8:1; 8:5-34; 9:18—11:30; 12:15—15:21; Mark 3:7—7:23; Luke 6:12—9:17; John 6:1-71) ; (3) the period from the withdrawal into northern Galilee to final departure from Galilee for Jerusalem (Matt. 15:22—18:35; Mark 7:24—9:50; Luke 9:18-50; John 7:1—8:59).

During the first period the disciples were given their first call to service, the great miracles at Capernaum and elsewhere were performed, and the early opposition to Christ appeared.

In the second period, the twelve disciples were formally chosen; the Sermon on the Mount giving the principles of the kingdom was delivered; the notable miracle of the raising of the son of the widow at Nain was performed; and in the face of the growing opposition Christ denounced the scribes and Pharisees and delivered the parables of Matthew 13. The opposition to Christ became more intense toward the close of this period. The miracle of the feeding of the five thousand was rejected, and the discourse on the bread of life occasioned much unbelief. The second period concluded with the rebuke of the scribes and Pharisees who came from Jerusalem to find fault with Christ for transgressing their traditions.

The third period included the tour of Tyre and Sidon and the first healing of a Gentile. In contrast to growing unbelief, Peter was the spokesman for the faith of the disciples in Christ. Christ foretold His death and resurrection repeatedly, and this dark shadow was in contrast to His transfiguration. During the third period, while withdrawn from Galilee and Capernaum, He returned for a brief visit to Galilee and later to Capernaum. The period closed with a visit to Jerusalem in the fall of the year, on which occasion the events and discourse of John 7:1—8:59 occurred.

The Perean Ministry (Matt. 19:1—20:34; 26:6-13; Mark 10:1-52; 14:3-9; Luke 9:51—19:28; John 9:1—12:11)

The Perean period of the ministry of our Lord receives its name from the fact that Christ upon His final departure from Galilee passed through Perea, ministering as He went; and after His arrival in Jerusalem He retired again to Perea until a few days before His passion. As Christ left Galilee He sent out the seventy disciples on their mission (Luke 10:1-24). The parable of the good Samaritan and the events of John chapters 9 and 10 occurred during the Perean ministry. After the feast of dedication in Jerusalem, some of the more important utterances of Christ were recorded. After the resurrection of Lazarus and the increased opposition to Christ which it aroused, Christ again withdrew into Ephraim. Until the time of His triumphal entry into Jerusalem at the beginning of the Passion Week, Christ was not inactive. The Scriptures record the cleansing of ten lepers, the interview with the rich young ruler, and Christ dining with Zacchaeus. While at Bethany He was anointed by Mary. The period of His Perean ministry extended from the fall until the following spring of Christ's last year.

The Passion Week (Matt. 21:1—26:5; 26:16—27:66; Mark 11:1—14:2; 14:10—15:47; Luke 19:29—23:56; John 12:12—19:42)

The exact order of the events of the Passion Week is disputed, depending on the date given His crucifixion. Three theories have been advanced: (1) that Christ was crucified on Wednesday,[1] (2) that Christ was crucified on Thursday,[2] (3) that Christ was crucified on Friday, the traditional view.[3] The reconstruction of the events of the week depends on the theory which is accepted. Gen-

[1]Cf. Eugene C. Callaway, *The Harmony of the Last Week.*
[2]Cf. James Gall, *Good Friday a Chronological Mistake.*
[3]Cf. A. T. Robertson, *A Harmony of the Gospels;* W. A. Stevens and E. D. Burton, *A Harmony of the Four Gospels.*

erally speaking, however, the order of events is sufficiently plain even if the day on which some of them occurred is not clear.

The Passion Week began with the triumphal entry of Christ into Jerusalem which occurred six days before the Passover—on Saturday if Christ was crucified on Wednesday and the Passover was on Tuesday,[4] on Sunday if Christ was crucified on either Thursday or Friday. In this dramatic entry into Jerusalem, Christ publicly fulfilled the prophecy of Zechariah 9:9. G. Campbell Morgan suggests that this may have been one of three entries into Jerusalem on successive days.[5] The day following the entry the second cleansing of the temple occurred. Tuesday probably marked the final messages of Christ to the people if the traditional chronology is assumed. On that day He warned them of the results of rejecting Him, answered the questions of His opponents and silenced them, pronounced woes on the Pharisees, and delivered the great Olivet Discourse. The traditional view holds that there is no record of events on Wednesday which, according to Callaway, was the day on which Christ died. The usual view is that on Thursday night Christ gathered His disciples for their last supper together. Some believe this to have been the Passover feast, others a preliminary supper which was held before the Passover, which was to be held two days later, after the death of Christ. Some believe two suppers were held on the same night, one following the other, the latter being the real Passover. While controversy exists as to the details, the beauty of these last moments of Christ with His disciples remains, with the important upper room discourse recorded in John 13-16 forming the main body of divine revelation.

The chronology of events following the arrest of Christ in Gethsemane indicates that these six separate trials were held, three before Jewish rulers and three before Roman rulers:

1. The trial before Annas, the father-in-law of Caiaphas (John 18:12-24), was held immediately after the arrest of Christ. In reply to questions, Christ told them to ask those who had heard Him teach. The trial was entirely illegal, being at night, contrary to Jewish law; no indictment was prepared; no witnesses were heard; and no counsel was provided for the Defendant—all required by the Jewish law.

[4]See Callaway.
[5]G. Campbell Morgan, *The Gospel According to John*, pp. 209-10.

2. The trial before Caiaphas immediately followed (Matt. 26:57-68; Mark 14:53-65). At this trial false witnesses were produced, but the uniformity of their testimony could not be attained. In answer to the direct question of whether He was the Christ, Jesus affirmed it, and was convicted on this confession.

3. The third trial was held the following morning (Matt. 27:1-2; Mark 15:1; Luke 22:66-71) probably because of the legal necessity of conforming to the Jewish law providing that trials must be held in daylight. Here Christ was asked if He was the Son of God. Upon His admission of His deity, Christ was convicted on the grounds of blasphemy and referred to the Roman rulers for sentence.

4. The fourth trial was held before Pilate (Matt. 27:11-14; Mark 15:1-5; Luke 23:1-7; John 18:28-38). Christ was here accused of forbidding tribute to Caesar, perverting the nation and claiming to be King of the Jews.

5. The trial before Herod is recorded only in one gospel (Luke 23:8-12). At this trial Christ was silent to all questions and after being mocked by the soldiers was returned to Pilate.

6. The final trial before Pilate resulted in a second acquittal and the offer to scourge and release Christ (Matt. 27:15-26; Mark 15:6-15; Luke 23:18-25; John 18:29—19:16). The alternative suggestion of Pilate that they accept the release of the wicked Barabbas and crucify Christ—made in the vain hope they would allow him to free Christ—was accepted by the Jews, and Pilate pronounced sentence on Christ according to the will of the Jews. In this travesty of justice, our Lord was condemned to death and led off to His crucifixion.

On the way to Calvary Christ carried His cross until, unable to bear it further, Simon of Cyrene was pressed into service. Upon reaching the scene of execution Christ was immediately crucified along with two thieves who were crucified on either side. Over His head was the inscription which in full was probably "This is Jesus of Nazareth, the King of the Jews."

The order of events of the crucifixion of Christ is as follows:

1. Upon arrival at Calvary Christ was offered wine mingled with gall which would dull His senses (Matt. 27:33-34; Mark 15:22-23; Luke 23:33; John 19:17).

2. After refusal of the drink, Christ was crucified along with

the two thieves (Matt. 27:35-38; Mark 15:24-28; Luke 23:33-38; John 19:18-24).

3. The first cry on the cross: "Father, forgive them; for they know not what they do" (Luke 23:34).

4. The soldiers divided the garments and cast lots for His coat, thus fulfilling Scripture (Matt. 27:35; Mark 15:24; Luke 23:34; John 19:23-24).

5. The chief priests and the scribes, as well as the people, mocked Jesus (Matt. 27:39-44; Mark 15:29-32; Luke 23:35-38).

6. One of the thieves believed on Him (Luke 23:39-43).

7. The second cry on the cross: "To day shalt thou be with me in paradise" (Luke 23:43).

8. The third cry: "Woman, behold thy son," and to John: "Behold thy mother" (John 19:26-27).

9. The three hours of darkness (Matt. 27:45; Mark 15:33; Luke 23:44).

10. The fourth cry: "My God, my God, why hast thou forsaken me?" (Matt. 27:46-47; Mark 15:34-36).

11. The fifth cry: "I thirst" (John 19:28).

12. The sixth cry: "It is finished" (John 19:30).

13. The seventh cry: "Father, into thy hands I commend my spirit" (Luke 23:46).

14. Jesus yielded up His spirit (Matt. 27:50; Mark 15:37; Luke 23:46; John 19:30).

This moving spectacle of our blessed Lord dying on the cross for the sins of the whole world is of inestimable theological significance. Christ lived as no other man has ever lived, and He died as no other man has ever died.

The Resurrection of Christ

The resurrection of Jesus Christ is one of the crucial events in His life on earth upon which the significance of His entire life and death hangs. It is the first step in a series in the exaltation of Christ, and is a fulfillment of the prophecy of Psalm 16:10 as well as Christ's own predictions of His resurrection (Matt. 16:21; 20:19; 26:32; Mark 9:9; 14:28; John 2:19).

The order of events as relating to the resurrection appearances of Christ is presented in Scripture as follows:

1. The guards witnessed the angel rolling away the stone (Matt. 28:2-4).

2. The arrival of the women, Mary Magdalene, Mary the mother of James, Salome and others (Matt. 28:1, 5-7; Mark 16:1-11; Luke 24:1-10; John 20:1).

3. Mary Magdalene ran to tell the apostles, the other women following more slowly (Matt. 28:8; Mark 16:8; Luke 24:8-10; John 20:2).

4. Mary Magdalene returned with Peter and John and saw the empty tomb (John 20:2-10).

5. The first appearance of Christ, Mary Magdalene remained after Peter and John left and saw Christ (John 20:11-17; cf. Mark 16:9-11).

6. Mary Magdalene returned to report the appearance of Christ (John 20:18).

7. The other women returned and saw Christ (Matt. 28:9-10). The best texts omit here the words "as they went to tell his disciples." They actually were on their way back to the garden.

8. The report of the guards watching the tomb (Matt. 28:11-15).

9. The third appearance of Christ, to Peter in the afternoon (Luke 24:34; I Cor. 15:5).

10. The fourth appearance of Christ, on the road to Emmaus (Mark 16:12-13; Luke 24:13-35).

11. The fifth appearance of Christ, to the ten disciples (Mark 16:14; Luke 24:36-43; John 20:19-23). Though Mark mentions eleven, there appeared to be only ten disciples here. The term "eleven" seems to be used loosely of the group.

12. The sixth appearance of Christ, to the eleven disciples (John 20:26-29).

13. The seventh appearance of Christ, to the seven disciples by the Sea of Galilee (John 21:1-23).

14. The eighth appearance of Christ, to the five hundred (I Cor. 15:6).

15. The ninth appearance of Christ, to James the Lord's brother (I Cor. 15:7). This explains apparently why James, not a believer before the resurrection (John 7:5), immediately after the resurrection is included as a believer (Acts 1:14; Gal. 1:19).

16. The tenth appearance of Christ, to the eleven on a mountain in Galilee (Matt. 28:16-20; Mark 16:15-18).

17. The eleventh appearance of Christ, at the time of the ascension (Luke 24:44-53).

All appearances of Christ after His ascension, while actual appearances, differ in character from those which precede the ascension in that they correspond more to a vision and had less corporeal reality. If the resurrection appearances of Christ after the ascension were the only appearances recorded, it might be argued that such appearances are not absolute proof of bodily resurrection. When they are coupled, however, with so many appearances before His ascension, they constitute evidence which is admissible. The argument of Paul in I Corinthians 15:4-8, where appearances before the ascension and His appearance to Paul after the ascension are cited, confirms the validity of this approach.

There were six appearances of Christ after His ascension:

1. The twelfth appearance of Christ, to Stephen (Acts 7:55-56).

2. The thirteenth appearance of Christ, to Paul on the road to Damascus (Acts 9:3-6; 22:6-11; 26:13-18).

3. The fourteenth appearance of Christ, to Paul in Arabia. This appearance is somewhat conjectural (Acts 20:24; 26:17; Gal. 1:12-17).

4. The fifteenth appearance of Christ, to Paul in the temple (Acts 9:26-30; 22:17-21).

5. The sixteenth appearance of Christ, to Paul in prison (Acts 23:11).

6. The seventeenth appearance of Christ, to the Apostle John (Rev. 1:12-20).

The fact of the resurrection of Christ, therefore, is one of the most well-attested events of ancient history and is given a prominent place in the scriptural presentation. The significance of His resurrection is subject to further discussion later.

The Ascension of Christ (Mark 16:19-20; Luke 24:49-53; Acts 1:8-11)

Though allusions in Scripture to the ascension of Christ are much fewer than to His resurrection, the accounts as given demonstrate the bodily departure of Christ from earth and His arrival in heaven. In addition to the accounts given in Mark, Luke and Acts, the Epistles refer to the ascension as a fact (Heb. 4:14; I Peter 3:22). The arrival of Christ in heaven is also repeatedly stated in Scripture in more than a score of passages (cf. Acts 2:33-36). It was a fitting climax for the life of Christ on earth and in fulfillment of His own declaration that He would return to the Father. The historical facts as they recount the birth, life, death and resurrection of Christ and culminate in His ascension to the right hand of the Father give a solid basis for theological consideration of the person and work of Christ. The historical narratives are fully in keeping with the theological implications which are drawn from them in the Epistles. Upon these facts rest our Christian faith and our hope of life to come.

MAJOR SPHERES OF THE EARTHLY LIFE OF CHRIST

Though the historical character of the Gospels makes them easy to understand, their theological interpretation is by no means uncomplicated. Few sections of Scripture require more careful analysis and precise interpretation. The reason does not lie in the complicated narrative, but rather in the fact that the incidents recorded are more than just history. They constitute a revelation of God and His purposes.

One of the reasons why the Gospels are difficult to interpret is that Christ lived in three major spheres and His teaching as well as His life are related to them. The right understanding of this fact is essential not only to a correct interpretation of the Gospels but gives the key to the entire New Testament.

The Sphere of Jewish Law

The law which was inaugurated for Israel through Moses was still in effect throughout the lifetime of Christ and in one sense did not terminate until His death (Gal. 3:23-25; 4:5). In much of His teaching, Christ affirmed the Mosaic law and declared it must be fulfilled (Matt. 5:17-19). As related to the life of Christ, it can be said that Christ lived under the law, that His teaching constituted a major interpretation of it, and that He kept it perfectly (II Cor. 5:21). Christ on numerous occasions contradicted the customary teaching of the law. He insisted, moreover, on its practical application to the spiritual issues of His day in contrast with the common evasion of the law by the scribes. As the Son of God, He also was free to interpret the law authoritatively and in some cases contrasted His own teaching with that of Moses.

Christ insisted that keeping the letter of the Mosaic law was not sufficient. The Mosaic law could be properly fulfilled only by those who attained its highest form of interpretation, centering in the love of God and love of one's neighbor. In some cases, Christ pointed out that the Mosaic law represented divine condescension in that God accommodated Himself to the weakness of the people, as in the case of the teaching on divorce. Frequently Christ appealed to the higher law of God of which the Mosaic law was a particular expression.

The Sphere of the Kingdom

Much of the teaching of Christ is directly related to the doctrine of the kingdom. The Gospels connect this line of truth specifically to the Old Testament revelation of the kingdom to be established on earth by the power of the Messiah. The gospel of Matthew in its opening portion especially related Christ to David as fulfilling the Davidic covenant. The gospel of Luke records the prophecy of the angelic messenger who promised Mary that her Son would reign on the throne of David and rule over the house of Israel forever.

In the opening section of Matthew the credentials of the King are presented and the predicted signs of His coming are recorded as fulfilled. In keeping with His relation to the kingdom, Christ revealed the spiritual principles which govern this kingdom in the Sermon on the Mount, giving present application of these principles to the particular situation, as well as speaking prophetically of the spiritual qualities which are to characterize His millennial kingdom. In the Olivet Discourse, specific prophecy is given concerning the great tribulation which will introduce His second coming and the establishment of His throne on the earth.

Though the New Testament doctrine of the kingdom is necessarily based on the Old, the tendency of scholars to limit the teaching of Christ to one phase of the kingdom or another is open to question. An examination of what Christ had to say about the kingdom should make plain that in some instances He spoke concerning the general government and authority of God over the universe. In other cases He dealt with the reign of God in the heart, or a spiritual kingdom. On yet other occasions He spoke specifically of the kingdom promise to David. It is,

therefore, an error to limit His teaching to making all His kingdom messages apply to the millennial period alone. On the
other hand, it is equally erroneous to limit His teaching to a
spiritual kingdom to be fulfilled before His second advent.

The kingdom teachings are found principally in the Old
Testament, and the kingdom partakes to some extent of the legal
character of this period. As presented in the teachings of Christ,
however, the millennial kingdom is a distinct sphere of rule
both in its content and in its application, and is to be contrasted
with the present age of the church or the past dispensation of
law.

The Sphere of the Church

In addition to the teachings of Christ relating to the Mosaic
law and the kingdom, prophecy is given of the church. The
first mention of this is found in Matthew 16:18, following the
rejection of Christ as King and the opposition to His message on
the spiritual principles of the kingdom. Earlier, in Matthew 13,
the entire interadvent age is revealed under the seven mysteries
of the kingdom of heaven. Chronologically the church coincides
with much of the development of this period revealed in Matthew 13.

The chief revelation concerning the church, however, is found
in the gospel of John in the upper room discourse. Here, apparently for the first time, the essential principles are revealed
which pertain to the purpose of God in the present interadvent
age. The basic spiritual principles are given in John 13. In
chapter 14 the fact that Christ will be in the Father's house during the present age and will send the Spirit to dwell in the
believer is unfolded. The vine and the branches in chapter 15
speak of the organic union of the believer with Christ, the new
intimacy of being friends of Christ, and the fact that believers
are chosen and ordained to bring forth fruit. The opposition
and persecution which will characterize the present age also are
revealed in chapter 15 in contrast with the protection of the
saints in the millennial kingdom. A major doctrine given in
John 16 is the work of the Holy Spirit in relation to the world
and the believer. The great purposes of God as they will be
fulfilled in the church are also implicit in the intercession of
Christ recorded in chapter 17. The fact that the believer will

be perfectly united to God and that he will be in Christ and Christ will be in him forms the center of the revelation.

A study of the four Gospels, therefore, will demonstrate three major spheres of revelation. It is a hasty generalization, however, to characterize the Gospels as law or as pertaining solely to the church or kingdom. Rather, Christ taught in all these spheres, and each utterance must be understood in its context and according to its content.

OFFICES OF CHRIST

Christ as Prophet

Without question, Christ is the greatest of the prophets. His teachings contained in the four Gospels demonstrate a greater variety of subjects, a broader scope of prophecy and a more comprehensive revelation than is found in any of the Old Testament records of the prophets. In almost every aspect of revelation, Christ made a distinct contribution.

Unlike all other prophets, Christ revealed God not only in His spoken ministry but in His life and person. As the Logos of John, Christ was eternally the source of knowledge, truth, wisdom and light. When He became incarnate, He became a declaration in human flesh of what God is (John 1:4-18). In His life, death and resurrection, Christ was a revelation of God far beyond that of any preceding prophet. Even after His resurrection Christ continued to exercise His prophetic office, teaching His disciples the things they needed to know to adjust themselves to the new age into which they were going. However, after His ascension, the Holy Spirit was sent to continue the prophetic work, revealing to the saints the truth that Christ would have them know (John 16:12-15).

The Office of Priest

Just as Christ fulfilled to the utmost the office of prophet so also He qualifies as the High Priest and is the embodiment of all that is anticipated in the Old Testament priesthood. As a Priest, He fulfilled the primary definition of what constitutes a priest: "a man duly appointed to act for other men in things pertaining to God."[6] Not only in His person but also in His work, Christ fulfilled the ministry of a Priest, offering gifts,

[6]Charles Hodge, *Systematic Theology*, II, 464.

sacrifices and intercession. He acted as a true Mediator between God and man. According to the epistle to the Hebrews, Christ fulfilled the five necessary requirements of the priesthood: (1) He was qualified for the office (Heb. 1:3; 3:1-6) ; (2) He was appointed of God (Heb. 5:1-10) ; (3) His priesthood was of a higher order than that of Aaron's—Christ's priesthood superseded Aaron's as Aaron's had superseded the patriarchal system (Heb. 5:6, 10; 7:1—8:6) ; (4) all functions of the priesthood were performed by Christ (Heb. 7:23-28; 9:11-28; 10:5-18) ; (5) His priesthood is eternal, indicating His superiority and finality (Heb. 7:25) . A detailed discussion of His priesthood is in a later section.

The Office of King

One of the fundamental purposes of the incarnation was the fulfillment of the earthly purpose of God in the Davidic covenant. The Old Testament had predicted the coming of a King who would fulfill the promse of God to David (II Sam. 7:16; Ps. 2; 45; 72; 110; Isa. 9:6-7; Dan. 7:13-14; Micah 5:2; Zech. 9:9) . When Christ came, He fulfilled the requirements of the prophesied King, though the full revelation of His work as King was reserved for His second coming.

The record in the New Testament is both historical and prophetic (Luke 1:31-33; John 1:49; 18:37; 19:12; I Cor. 15:25; I Tim. 6:15; Rev. 1:5; 17:14; 19:16) . The rejection of Christ as King by Israel (John 19:15) resulted in the postponement of the millennial kingdom, but it did not alter the certainty of complete fulfillment of His work as King, nor the fact that in His person He is the King of Israel.

Taken together, the three offices of Christ as Prophet, Priest and King are the key to the purpose of the incarnation. His prophetic office was concerned with the revelation of the truth of God; the priestly office was related to His work as Saviour and Mediator; His kingly office had in view His right to reign over Israel and over the entire earth. In Christ the supreme dignity of these offices is reached.

HUMILIATION OF CHRIST

One of the important considerations in the theological statement of the incarnation is the definition of what was involved in

the condescension and humiliation of Christ in becoming Man.
How could the eternal God take upon Himself human limitations
while retaining His eternal deity? Orthodox theologians have
answered the question by declaring that God in becoming Man
did not diminish His deity, but added a human nature to the
divine nature. How this actually affected the divine nature is
treated in the classic passage of Philippians 2:5-11. Some have
interpreted this statement as meaning that Christ in some sense
gave up part of His deity in order to become Man. As such a
conclusion would seriously affect the orthodox doctrine of the
deity of Christ, theologians have examined this passage minutely
to find an answer to the problem of what Christ actually did in
becoming Man.

In general, the act of the Son of God in the incarnation is
described first by the word "condescension," in that He, the
eternal God, condescended to become Man. As a Man He sub-
mitted to the death on the cross which is described by the term
"humiliation." After His passion, Christ rose from the dead and
later ascended into heaven where He was exalted to the right
hand of God the Father. The theological question is raised,
therefore, as to whether the process of condescension, humiliation and exaltation involved any change in the divine nature of
Christ.

The Exegesis of Philippians 2:5-11

The Philippians passage concerning the self-emptying or kenosis of the Son of God was introduced in connection with a practical exhortation to have the mind or attitude of Christ. The action of Christ in proceeding from glory to become Man and
suffer on the cross was cited as an illustration of the mind of
Christ. In the accompanying explanation, the apostle gave one
of the most concise theological statements of the incarnation to
be found anywhere in the Scriptures. Christ is described first of
all as "existing in the form of God" (v. 6, ASV). The word for
"existing" is not the usual Greek verb ōn (to be), but hyparchōn
which is found in a form used for both the present and the imperfect participle and carries the meaning of continued existence.
The thought is that Christ always has been in the form of God
with the implication that He still is. If the Greek form is taken
as the present tense instead of the imperfect, the word would

mean that Christ existed as God in the past, that is, before the incarnation, and is still existing in the form of God. This would be asserting that the deity of Christ continues unchanged by the act of the incarnation. If taken as a simple imperfect, it would refer to His state before the incarnation, without explicitly affirming continuity of the form of God though the implication of continuity would remain.

As stated by the apostle, Christ "existing in the form of God, counted not the being on an equality with God a thing to be grasped, but emptied himself, taking the form of a servant, being made in the likeness of men; and being found in fashion as a man, he humbled himself, becoming obedient even unto death, yea, the death of the cross" (vv. 6-8, ASV). The attitude of Christ which believers are exhorted to emulate is that He did not grasp at being on an equality with God as if it had to be retained by effort. Though having existed in the form of God from all eternity, He was willing to empty Himself, taking the form of a Servant, and ultimately He became obedient unto death.

The act of the incarnation is described by the strong word *ekenōsen* (English, kenosis), from *kenoō*, meaning "to empty" (cf. four other instances where used in the New Testament: Rom. 4:14; I Cor. 1:17; 9:15; II Cor. 9:3). Warfield considers the translation "emptied himself" (v. 7, ASV) as an error, apparently preferring the Authorized Version rendering "made himself of no reputation," that is, emptied Himself of the manifestations of Deity.[7] The crux of the exposition of this important passage hangs on the definition of the act of kenosis. Orthodox theologians have pointed out that the meaning of this word must be interpreted by the context itself. The passage does not state that Christ ceased to exist in the form of God, but rather that He added the form of a Servant. The word *morphēi*, translated "form," speaks of the outer appearance or manifestation. As it relates to the eternal deity of Christ, it refers to the fact that Christ in eternity past in outer appearance manifested His divine attributes. It was not mere form or appearance, but that which corresponded to what He was eternally. In becoming Man He took upon Himself the form of a Servant, that is, the outward appearance of a Servant and the human nature which corresponds to it. This is further defined as manifesting the likeness (Greek, *homoiōmati*) of man in that He

[7]B. B. Warfield, *Christology and Criticism*, p. 375.

looked and acted like a man. The passage declares in addition
that He was "found in fashion as a man" (v. 8), the word "fashion" (Greek, *schēmati*) indicating the more transient manifestations of humanity such as weariness, thirst and other human limitations. Taking the whole passage together, there is no
declaration here that there was any loss of deity, but rather a
limitation of its manifestation. It is certainly clear from other
declarations of Paul that he recognized that Jesus Christ in the
flesh was all that God is even though He appeared to be a Man.

The kenosis passage of Philippians 2, though it was probably
never intended to be a complete statement of the incarnation,
has been claimed as a scriptural basis for the idea that in the incarnation Christ in some sense emptied Himself of certain divine
attributes, especially the attributes of omniscience, omnipotence
and omnipresence. It is claimed that this passage justifies the
idea that a true incarnation involves surrender of certain qualities
of Deity and that therefore Christ was something less than God
while in the sphere of condescension and humiliation on earth.

A. B. Bruce in his work *The Humiliation of Christ* classifies the
kenotic views as falling into four types, all of which are denied
by orthodox theologians as constituting a rejection of the deity of
Christ. Bruce writes:

> Fortunately, however, we are not required by the history
> of opinion to be mathematically complete in our exposition,
> but may content ourselves with giving some account of four
> distinct kenotic types, which may for the present be intelli-
> gibly, if not felicitously, discriminated as, (1) the absolute
> dualistic type, (2) the absolute metamorphic, (3) the ab-
> solute semi-metamorphic, and (4) the real but relative. Of
> the first, Thomasius may conveniently be taken as the repre-
> sentative; of the second, Gess; of the third, Ebrard; and of
> the fourth Martensen.[8]

The first of these described as the absolute dualistic type as set
forth by Thomasius and others attempts to distinguish between
the ethical or immanent attributes of God and the relative or
physical.[9] According to this view, the relative and physical attributes, including omnipresence, omniscience and omnipotence,

---

[8]A. B. Bruce, *The Humiliation of Christ*, p. 179. For discussion of these
four types of kenotic theology, cf. Charles L. Feinberg, "The Hypostatic
Union," *Bibliotheca Sacra*, XCII (Oct.-Dec., 1935) 415-17; Louis Berkhof,
Systematic Theology, pp. 327-28.
[9]Bruce, pp. 179-87.

were surrendered by Christ in becoming Man. In opposition to this view, orthodox theologians have pointed out that God cannot change His nature by act of His will any more than any other being. Attributes inherent in a personal essence cannot be dismissed. This is contained in the divine attribute of immutability which is expressly affirmed of Christ (Heb. 13:8). Further, though there are problems stemming from certain scriptural statements concerning the human nature of Christ, there is considerable evidence that Christ retained omnipresence, omniscience and omnipotence even while on earth. Further, a loss in attributes would mean in effect that Christ was not God at all which is contradicted by innumerable scriptures and specifically by the gospel of John.

Bruce also points out a second view[10] known as the absolute metamorphic type supported by Gess. This position is even more radical and asserts that divine attributes were given up in the incarnation and Christ was entirely human though Gess asserts, according to Bruce, that Christ was not "simply an ordinary man," having a "superadamitic element."[11] The divine consciousness in Christ ceased entirely though it was later gradually reassumed, beginning with His experience in the temple at the age of twelve. This point of view is so extreme that it hardly requires refutation by those who accept the biblical testimony.

The third view, described by Bruce as the "absolute semi-metamorphic type," as espoused by Ebrard is another attempt at compromising the deity of Christ.[12] It held that the divine properties were disguised and appeared as a mode of human existence. The mode of existence of Christ was changed from that of the form of God to the form of a Man, from the eternal manner of being to a temporal manner of being. The difficulty with this view is that while it accommodates itself to the human appearance of Christ it in effect denies that He was actually God simultaneously with His human experience. It is not the picture of Christ which is afforded in the entire New Testament.

The fourth view known as the "real but relative"[13] is closer to the truth in that it affirms that Christ was God, but limits His experience to that of the human consciousness and remolds the

[10]*Ibid.*, pp. 187-97.
[11]*Ibid.*, p. 193.
[12]*Ibid.*, pp. 197-206.
[13]*Ibid.*, pp. 206-12.

divine attributes into properties of the human nature. Christ is limited in His experience of knowledge even though as God He was omniscient and limited in His experience of power. This, however, is contradicted by the fact that though Christ in His human nature is limited His divine consciousness is still omniscient and His divine will still omnipotent. The difficulties with all these views which fall short of ascribing to Christ a full deity is that they read into the passage in Philippians 2 more than it actually says and contradict many other scriptures which fully assert the deity of Christ during the period He was on earth.

The explanations of the so-called kenotic theologians are therefore judged inadequate either as an explanation of the incarnation itself or the revelation contained in Philippians 2. Objections which arise to their theories are far more serious than the problem which the false theory of kenosis attempts to solve.

First, it is impossible to surrender an attribute without changing the character of the essence to which it belongs. To rob sunlight of any of its various colors would change the character of the sunlight. To rob God of any attribute would destroy His deity. Hence, if Christ did not possess all the attributes of the Godhead, it could not be said that He possessed a true deity. As the attributes belong to the essence, it is impossible to subtract any attributes without changing the character of the essence of God. This is a far more serious problem than that occasioned by the humiliation of Christ.

Second, the attempt to distinguish between the importance of relative and absolute attributes is entirely unjustified as both are equally essential to Deity. The absolute attributes imply the necessity of the relative and, though there seems to be a justifiable theological distinction, one class of attributes is not more essential to Deity than the other.

Third, the false theory of kenosis is in direct conflict with scriptures which affirm the omniscience of Christ (John 2:24; 16:30), assert His omnipresence (John 1:48) and demonstrate His omnipotence as revealed in His many miracles. The purpose of the gospel of John was specifically to prove the deity of Christ during the period He was on earth and automatically excludes the idea that Christ was less than divine while in the sphere of humiliation.

The Proper Doctrine of Kenosis

If it is true that Christ did not give up any divine attribute or any essential quality of deity in becoming Man, how can the act of emptying Himself be defined?

First, it may be stated that the humiliation of Christ consisted in the veiling of His preincarnate glory. It was necessary to give up the outer appearance of God in order to take upon Himself the form of Man. In answer to the prayer of Christ to the Father (John 17:5) the manifestation of His glory was restored when His work on earth was finished. The glory was never surrendered in an absolute sense as is shown by the revelation of Himself as the glorified Lord on the Mount of Transfiguration. It may be implied that there was also a flash of glory when in the Garden of Gethsemane Christ said, "I am he" and those who beheld Him "went backward, and fell to the ground" (John 18:6). From these instances it would appear that the glory of Christ, though necessarily veiled in order to permit Him to walk among men, was not surrendered. The situation was the same in the Old Testament when He appeared in the form of the Angel of Jehovah and in some instances His glorious appearance was hidden from earthly eyes in order for Him to appear to men and converse with them. After the ascension Christ is never seen except in His glorified state.

Second, the union of Christ to an unglorified humanity unquestionably involved divine condescension and was a necessary factor in His ultimate humiliation on the cross. The humiliation was not the initial step of incarnation, but was involved in the whole program of God leading to His shameful death. The humanity to which Christ was united was not a glorified humanity, but one subject to temptation, distress, weakness, pain, sorrow and limitation. After His return to glory His humanity was glorified, but the original union with unglorified humanity is included in the kenosis.

Third, while it is not true that Christ in the incarnation surrendered the relative attributes of omnipresence, omnipotence and omniscience, He did embark upon a program where it was necessary to submit to a voluntary nonuse of these attributes in order to obtain His objectives. Christ does not seem to have ever exercised His divine attributes on His own behalf though they had abundant display in His miracles. This is qualified to some extent by the fact that His omniscience is revealed in His prophetic ministry, but He did not use His divine knowledge to make His own path easier. He suffered all the inconveniences of His day even though in His divine omniscience He had full knowledge of every human device ever conceived for human comfort. In His human nature there was growth in knowledge, but this must not be construed as a contradiction of His divine omniscience. Limitations in knowledge as well as limitations in power are related to the human nature and not to the divine. His omnipotence was manifested in many ways and specifically in the many miracles which He did, in some cases by the power of the Holy Spirit and in others on the basis of His own word of authority. Here again He did not use His omnipotence to make His way easy and He knew the fatigue of labor and traveling by walking. Though in His divine nature He was omnipresent, He did not use this attribute to avoid the long journeys on foot nor was He ever seen in His ministry in more than one place at a time. In a word, He restricted the benefits of His attributes as they pertained to His walk on earth and voluntarily chose not to use His powers to lift Himself above ordinary human limitations.

Fourth, on two specific occasions Christ is revealed to have performed His miracles in the power of the Holy Spirit (Matt. 12:28; Luke 4:14-18). In these instances Christ chose voluntarily to be dependent upon the power of the Father and the Holy Spirit to perform His miracles. In view of the fact that this is mentioned only twice and hundreds of miracles were performed, it would seem clear that Christ exercised His own power when He chose to do so as, for instance, when He commanded the waves to be still and caused Lazarus to come forth from the tomb at His command. The anointing of the Holy Spirit (cf. Luke 4:18) would support the conclusion that many of Christ's miracles were performed in the power of the Holy Spirit, but His deity still included omnipotence which was not surrendered in the kenosis.

The act of kenosis as stated in Philippians 2 may therefore be properly understood to mean that Christ surrendered no attribute of Deity, but that He did voluntarily restrict their independent use in keeping with His purpose of living among men and their limitations. The summary which is given by A. H.

Strong sets forth the true doctrine in comparison to the false in these words:

> Our doctrine of Christ's humiliation will be better under-
> stood if we put it midway between two pairs of erroneous
> views, making it the third of five. The list would be as fol-
> lows: (1) Gess: The Logos gave up all divine attributes;
> (2) Thomasius: The Logos gave up relative attributes only;
> (3) True View: The Logos gave up the independent exercise
> of divine attributes; (4) Old Orthodoxy: Christ gave up the
> use of divine attributes; (5) Anselm: Christ acted as if he
> did not possess divine attributes.[14]

THE IMPECCABILITY OF CHRIST

Orthodox theologians generally agree that Jesus Christ never committed any sin. This seems to be a natural corollary to His deity and an absolute prerequisite to His work of substitution on the cross. Any affirmation of moral failure on the part of Christ requires a doctrine of His person which would deny in some sense His absolute deity.

A question has been raised, however, by orthodox theologians whether the sinlessness of Christ was the same as that of Adam before the fall or whether it possessed a peculiar character be-cause of the presence of the divine nature. In a word, could the Son of God be tempted as Adam was tempted and could He have sinned as Adam sinned? While most orthodox theologians agree that Christ could be tempted because of the presence ot a human nature, a division occurs on the question as to whether being tempted He could sin.

Definition of Impeccability

The point of view that Christ could sin is designated by the term "peccability," and the doctrine that Christ could not sin is referred to as the impeccability of Christ. Adherents of both views agree that Christ did not sin, but those who affirm pec-cability hold that He could have sinned, whereas those who de-clare the impeccability of Christ believe that He could not sin due to the presence of the divine nature.

The doctrine of impeccability has been questioned especially on the point of whether an impeccable person can be tempted in any proper sense. If Christ had a human nature which was sub-

[14]A. H. Strong, *Systematic Theology*, p. 704.

ject to temptation, was this not in itself evidence that He could
have sinned? The point of view of those who believe that Christ
could have sinned is expressed by Charles Hodge who has summarized this teaching as follows:

> This sinlessness of our Lord, however, does not amount
> to absolute impeccability. It was not a *non potest peccare*.
> If He was a true man He must have been capable of sinning.
> That He did not sin under the greatest provocation; that
> when He was reviled He blessed; when He suffered He
> threatened not; that He was dumb, as a sheep before its
> shearers, is held up to us as an example. Temptation implies
> the possibility of sin. If from the constitution of his person
> it was impossible for Christ to sin, then his temptation was
> unreal and without effect, and He cannot sympathize with
> his people.[15]

The problem that Hodge raises is very real and, judging by
our own experience, temptation is always associated with peccability. Hodge, however, assumes certain points in his argument which are subject to question. In order to solve the problem as to whether Christ is peccable, it is necessary, first of all, to
examine the character of temptation itself to ascertain whether
peccability is inevitably involved in any real temptation and,
second, to determine the unique factor in Christ, that is, that He
had two natures, one a divine nature and the other a sinless human nature.

Can an impeccable person be tempted? It is generally agreed
by those who hold that Christ did not commit sin that He had no
sin nature. Whatever temptation could come to Him, then,
would be from without and not from within. Whatever may have
been the natural impulses of a sinless nature which might have
led to sin if not held in control, there was no sin nature to sug-
gest sin from within and form a favorable basis for temptation.
It must be admitted by Hodge, who denies impeccability, that in
any case the temptation of Christ is different from that of sinful
men.

Not only is there agreement on the fact that Christ had no sin
nature, but it is also agreed on the other hand that as to His
person He was tempted. This is plainly stated in Hebrews 4:15
(ASV) : "For we have not a high priest that cannot be touched

[15]Hodge, II, 457.

with the feeling of our infirmities; but one that hath been in all points tempted like as we are, yet without sin."

It is also clear that this temptation came to Christ in virtue of the fact that He possessed a human nature, as James states: "Let no man say when he is tempted, I am tempted of God; for God cannot be tempted with evil, and he himself tempteth no man" (1:13, ASV). On the one hand, Christ was tempted in all points except through that of a sin nature and, on the other hand, His divine nature could not be tempted because God cannot be tempted. While His human nature is temptable, His divine nature is not temptable. On these points all can agree. The question is, then, Can such a person as Christ is, possessing both human and divine natures, be tempted if He is impeccable?

The answer must be in the affirmative. The question is simply Is it possible to attempt the impossible? To this all would agree. It is possible for a rowboat to attack a battleship, even though it is conceivably impossible for the rowboat to conquer the battleship. The idea that temptability implies susceptibility is unsound. While the temptation may be real, there may be infinite power to resist that temptation and if this power is infinite, the person is impeccable. It will be observed that the same temptation which would be easily resisted by one of sound character may be embraced by one of weak character. The temptation of a drunken debauch would have little chance of causing one to fall who had developed an abhorrence of drink, while a habitual drunkard would be easily led astray. The temptation might be the same in both cases, but the ones tempted would have contrasting powers of resistance. It is thus demonstrated that there is no essential relation between temptability and peccability. Hodge's viewpoint that temptation must be unreal if the person tempted is impeccable is, therefore, not accurate.

As William G. T. Shedd points out, temptability depends upon a constitutional susceptibility to sin, whereas impeccability depends upon omnipotent will not to sin. Shedd writes:

> It is objected to the doctrine of Christ's impeccability that it is inconsistent with his temptability. A person who cannot sin, it is said, cannot be tempted to sin. This is not correct; any more than it would be correct to say that because an army cannot be conquered, it cannot be attacked. Temptability depends upon the constitutional *susceptibility*, while

impeccability depends upon the *will*. So far as his natural
susceptibility, both physical and mental, was concerned,
Jesus Christ was open to all forms of human temptation ex-
cepting those that spring out of lust, or corruption of nature.
But his peccability, or the possibility of being overcome by
those temptations, would depend upon the amount of voluntary resistance which he was able to bring to bear against
them. Those temptations were very strong, but if the self-de-
termination of his holy will was stronger than they, then they
could not induce him to sin, and he would be impeccable.
And yet plainly he would be temptable.[16]

The question of whether an impeccable person can be tempted
is illustrated by the example of the elect angels. This is brought
out by Shedd in his continued discussion on the matter of impeccability:

> That an impeccable being can be tempted, is proved by
> the instance of the elect angels. Having "kept their first es-
> tate," they are now impeccable, not by their own inherent
> power, but by the power of God bestowed upon them. But
> they might be tempted still, though we have reason to
> believe that they are not. Temptability is one of the neces-
> sary limitations of the finite spirit. No creature is beyond the
> possibility of temptation, though he may, by grace, be beyond
> the possibility of yielding to temptation. The only being who
> cannot be tempted is God: *ho gar theos apeirastos*, James
> 1:13. And this, from the nature of an Infinite Being. Am-
> bition of some sort is the motive at the bottom of all tempta-
> tion. When the creature is tempted, it is suggested to him
> to endeavor to "be as gods." He is incited to strive for a
> higher place in the grade of being than he now occupies.
> But this, of course, cannot apply to the Supreme Being. He
> is already God over all and blessed forever. He, therefore,
> is absolutely intemptable.[17]

Were the temptations of Christ real? If the temptation of an
impeccable person be considered possible, can it be said of Christ
that His temptations were real? If there were no corresponding
nature within to respond to sin, is it true that the temptation is
real?

This question must also be answered in the affirmative. In the
case of the human race, the reality of temptation can be easily
proved by the frequency of sin. While this is not true in the case
of Christ, it is nevertheless evident that Christ's temptations were

---

[16]William G. T. Shedd, *Dogmatic Theology*, II, 336.
[17]*Ibid.*, II, 336-37.

real. While Christ never experienced the inner struggle of two natures deadlocked as in Paul's case in Romans 7, there is abundant evidence of the reality of temptation. The forty days in the wilderness, at the close of which He was tempted, mark a trial to which no other human frame has ever been subjected. The temptation to turn stones into bread was all the more real because Christ had the power to do it. The temptation to make a public display of God's preservation of Christ by casting Himself from the temple was also most real. No other has ever been offered all the glory of the world by Satan, but Christ was so tempted and did not sin. While on the one hand it is true that Christ did not experience the temptations arising in a sin nature, on the other hand, He was tried as no other was ever tried. Added to the nature of the temptation itself was the greater sensitivity of Christ. His body being without sin was far more sensitive to hunger and abuse than that of other men. Yet, in full experience of these longings, Christ was completely in control of Himself.

The final test of the reality of His temptations is found in the revelation of His struggle in Gethsemane and His death on the cross. No other could know the temptation of a holy person to avoid becoming the judgment for the sin of the world. This was Christ's greatest temptation, as evidenced in the character of His struggle and submission. On the cross the same temptation is evident in the taunt of His enemies to come down from the cross. Christ willingly continued in suffering and of His own will dismissed His spirit when the proper time came. No greater realm of temptation could be imagined. While Christ's temptations, therefore, are not always exactly parallel to our own, He was tried in every part of His being even as we are tried. And we can come to Him as our High Priest with the assurance that He fully understands the power of temptation and sin, having met it in His life and death (Heb. 4:15). The temptations of Christ, therefore, possess a stark reality without for a moment detracting from His impeccability. A proper doctrine of the impeccability of Christ therefore affirms the reality of the temptations of Christ due to the fact that He had a human nature which was temptable. If the human nature had been unsustained as in the case of Adam by a divine nature, it is clear that the human nature of Christ might have sinned. This possibility, however, is completely removed by the presence of the divine nature.

The Proof of the Impeccability of Christ

The ultimate solution of the problem of the impeccability of Christ rests in the relationship of the divine and human natures. It is generally agreed that each of the natures, the divine and the human, had its own will in the sense of desire. The ultimate decision of the person, however, in the sense of sovereign will was always in harmony with the decision of the divine nature. The relation of this to the problem of impeccability is obvious. The human nature, because it is temptable, might desire to do that which is contrary to the will of God. In the person of Christ, however, the human will was always subservient to the divine will and could never act independently. Inasmuch as all agree that the divine will of God could not sin, this quality then becomes the quality of the person and Christ becomes impeccable.

Shedd has defined this point of view in these words:

> Again, the impeccability of Christ is proved by the relation of the two wills in his person to each other. Each nature, in order to be complete, entire, and wanting nothing, has its own will; but the finite will never antagonizes the infinite will, but obeys it invariably and perfectly. If this should for an instant cease to be the case, there would be a conflict in the self-consciousness of Jesus Christ similar to that in the self-consciousness of his apostle Paul. He too would say, "The good that I would, I do not; but the evil which I would not, that I do. It is no more I that do it, but sin that dwelleth in me. O wretched man that I am, who shall deliver me?" Rom. 7:19, 20, 24. But there is no such utterance as this from the lips of the God-man: On the contrary, there is the calm inquiry of Christ: "Which of you convinceth me of sin?" John 8:46; and the confident affirmation of St. John: "In him was no sin." I John 3:5. There is an utter absence of personal confession of sin, in any form whatever, either in the conversation or the prayers of Jesus Christ. There is no sense of indwelling sin. He could not describe his religious experience as his apostle does, and his people do: "The flesh lusteth against the spirit, and the spirit against the flesh," Gal. 5:17.[18]

Shedd like many of the early church Fathers does not clarify the distinction between desire and will. That the human and divine natures of Christ could have different desires is obvious, but in the nature of personality there cannot be two determina-

[18]*Ibid.*, II, 335-36.

tive wills. Decision may be a product of deciding between desires, but there cannot be two wills in the sense of sovereign wills in one person, even a unique Person like Christ. All orthodox theologians agree that the ultimate decision reached by Christ in all cases was an act of will of the person in which the divine nature dominated. The human will could never go beyond the stage of desire where this conflicted with the divine will.

The question of the impeccability of Christ therefore resolves itself into a question as to whether the attributes of God can be harmonized with a doctrine of peccability. The concept of peccability in the person of Christ is contradicted principally by the attributes of immutability, omnipotence and omniscience.

The fact of the immutability of Christ is the first determining factor of His impeccability. According to Hebrews 13:8 (ASV), Christ is "the same yesterday and to-day, yea and for ever," and earlier in the same epistle Psalm 102:27 is quoted, "Thou art the same, and thy years shall not fail" (Heb. 1:12). As Christ was holy in eternity past, it is essential that this attribute as well as all others be preserved unchanged eternally. Christ must be impeccable, therefore, because He is immutable. If it is unthinkable that God could sin in eternity past, it must also be true that it is impossible for God to sin in the person of Christ incarnate. The nature of His person forbids susceptibility to sin.

The omnipotence of Christ makes it impossible for Him to sin. Peccability always implies weakness on the part of the one tempted; he is weak to the extent that he can sin. On the part of Christ, this is clearly out of the question. While the human nature of Christ if left to itself would have been both peccable and temptable, because it was joined to the omnipotent divine nature, the person of Christ was thereby made impeccable. A careful distinction should be made between omnipotence, which has a quality of infinity and therefore would sustain impeccability, and the concept of sufficient power or grace. Impeccability is defined as being not able to sin, whereas a concept of sufficient power would be merely able not to sin. A moral creature of God sustained by the grace of God can achieve the moral experience of being able not to sin as is illustrated in every victory over temptation in the Christian life. All agree that Christ was able not to sin, even those who affirm His peccability. The contrast, however, is between the idea of sufficient power and omnipotence. The infinite quality of omnipotence justifies the affirmation that Christ is impeccable.

It is foolish speculation to attempt to decide what the human nature of Christ would have done if not joined to the divine nature. The fact remains that the human nature was joined to the divine nature and, while its own realm was entirely human, it could not involve the person of Christ in sin. On the ground of omnipotence, then, it may be concluded that Christ could not sin because He had infinite power to resist temptation.

The omniscience of Christ contributed a vital part to His impeccability. Sin frequently appeals to the ignorance of the one tempted. Thus Eve was deceived and sinned, though Adam was not deceived as to the nature of the transgression. In the case of Christ, the effects of sin were perfectly known, with all the contributing factors. It was impossible for Christ having omniscience to commit that which He knew could only bring eternal woe to Himself and to the race. Having at once infinite wisdom to see sin in its true light and at the same time infinite power to resist temptation, it is evident that Christ was impeccable.

It is rationally inconceivable that Christ could sin. It is clear that Christ is not peccable in heaven now even though He possesses a true humanity. If Christ is impeccable in heaven because of who He is, then it is also true that Christ was impeccable on earth because of who He was. While it was possible for Christ in the flesh to suffer limitations of an unmoral sort—such as weakness, suffering, fatigue, sorrow, hunger, anger and even death—none of these created any complication which affected His immutable holiness. God could have experienced through the human nature of Christ these things common to the race, but God could not sin even when joined to a human nature. If sin were possible in the life of Christ, the whole plan of the universe hinged on the outcome of His temptations. The doctrine of the sovereignty of God would forbid any such haphazard condition. It is therefore not sufficient to hold that Christ did not sin, but rather to attribute to His person all due adoration in that He could not sin. While the person of Christ could therefore be tempted, there was no possibility of sin entering the life of Him appointed from eternity to be the spotless Lamb of God.

9

CHRIST IN HIS SUFFERING
AND DEATH

No EVENT OF TIME OR ETERNITY compares with the transcending significance of the death of Christ on the cross. Other important undertakings of God such as the creation of the world, the incarnation of Christ, His resurrection, the second coming, and the creation of the new heavens and the new earth become meaningless if Christ did not die. A faithful student of Christology cannot escape, therefore, the responsibility of a careful study of this doctrine as it is not only the heart of gospel preaching, but without it other doctrines of Christology have no relevance.

In the study of Christ in His sufferings and death, one is in a holy of holies, a mercy seat sprinkled with blood, to which only the Spirit-taught mind has access. In His death Christ supremely revealed the holiness and righteousness of God as well as the love of God which prompted the sacrifice. In a similar way the infinite wisdom of God is revealed as no human mind would ever have devised such a way of salvation, and only an infinite God would be willing to sacrifice His Son.

Like other important doctrines, the death of Christ has been disputed by those who reject scriptural revelation. Some liberals affirm that Christ died, but did not literally rise from the dead. Some have held that Christ did not actually die and was merely revived. Both of these views, born of unbelief, question the validity of the death or resurrection of Christ and are equally destructive to Christian faith.

The biblical record of the death of Christ is a complete presentation both from the prophetic and the historical standpoints. Many passages in the Old Testament as well as in the Gospels predicted the death of Christ, such as Psalm 22, Isaiah 53, Mark 8:31, Luke 9:22 and similar references. If one accepts the biblical testimony, it is unavoidable that one also accepts the fact of the

death of Christ. All the Gospels and all of the Epistles either state
or assume the fact of His death (cf. Matt. 27:32-66; Mark 15:21-
47; Luke 23:26-56; John 19:16-42; Rom. 5:6; I Cor. 15:3; II Cor.
5:15; Rev. 5:9).

Historically, the biblical doctrine of the person and work of
Christ are essential to explain the existence of the church. Without the death of Christ there would be no sacrifice for sin, no
salvation, no resurrection and none of the other elements that
have formed the content of Christian faith from the beginning.
The fact that the Christian church was able to endure centuries
of persecution and to survive centuries of neglect and opposition
is difficult to explain apart from the system of theology stemming
from belief in Jesus Christ as the Son of God who actually died,
rose and ascended into heaven.

DEFINITION OF TERMS

Many important theological terms are involved in an accurate
presentation of the meaning of the death of Christ. Among these
important words are the following:

Atonement

In the Old Testament, atonement means "to cover," that is, to
put sin out of sight. It is not found in the New Testament except
in a mistranslation of Romans 5:11 where it should be translated
"reconciliation." Etymologically the word is a combination of
syllables "at-one-ment," meaning "to be made one" or "to reconcile." This meaning is not used in modern English. In current theology the word "atonement" is used to include all that
Christ accomplished by His death and in this technical meaning
includes far more than the Old Testament concept or its etymological derivation.

Expiation

Although not a biblical word, expiation may be defined as the
act of bearing a penalty for sin.

Forgiveness

In theological use forgiveness is an act of God in which charges
against a sinner are removed on the ground of proper satisfaction.
It has a judicial rather than an emotional basis.

Guilt

A general word, guilt represents any just charge against a sinner for any kind of sin or transgression, whether a breach of conduct, violation of law, a sinful state, a sinful nature, or sin that is imputed. Used in a popular sense, it is often considered merely a violation of moral law.

Justice

Derived from the Latin *justus*, justice means a strict rendering of what is due in the form of either merited reward or punishment.

Justification

In theology, justification is the judicial act of God declaring one to be righteous by imputation of righteousness to him. It is judicial not experiential, and all believers in Christ are equally justified.

Penalty

The word penalty represents the natural and judicial results of sin which end in suffering either in the form of retribution or chastening. In the case of Christ, His suffering was forensic, that is, representative and infinite in value and sufficient to pay the penalty for the sins of the whole world.

Propitiation

In its theological usage propitiation has in view the satisfaction of all God's righteous demands for judgment on the sinner by the redemptive act of the death of Christ.

Ransom

As used in theology, ransom represents the price paid by Christ to God in providing propitiation.

Reconciliation

The act of reconciliation in the salvation of a believer in Christ is the application of the death of Christ to the individual by the power of the Spirit changing his status from that of condemnation to complete acceptability to God. It reconciles man to God by elevating man to God's level morally and, therefore, is far deeper in meaning than reconciliation on the human plane where harmony between parties estranged is often accomplished by compromise.

Redemption

As used in reference to the death of Christ, redemption has in view the payment of the price demanded by a holy God for the deliverance of the believer from the bondage and burden of sin. This payment results in the sinner being set free from his condemnation and slavery to sin.

Remission

Coming from a Latin word meaning "to send back," remission means "a sending away" of sin in the sense of forgiveness, pardon and freedom from punishment due. It is practically synonymous with forgiveness.

Righteousness

The basic concept of righteousness is "conforming to a moral standard," especially the standard of God's own righteousness. Through the death of Christ, righteousness may be imputed to the believer, may be seen in a relative righteousness and human conduct and, in reference to moral acts, may be prompted by the Spirit of God.

Sanctification

In its broad sense, sanctification is the act of God setting apart someone or something to holy use. It may be positional, referring to the Christian's position in Christ; experiential, resulting from the power of the Holy Spirit in the life of a Christian; or ultimate, speaking of the complete perfection of the believer in heaven.

Satisfaction

This is a synonym for propitiation.

Substitution

Equivalent to the term "vicarious" as used of the death of Christ, substitution has reference to the death of Christ on behalf of the sinner (John 1:29). Christ died as a Substitute for sinners on the cross accomplishing salvation for those who put their trust in Him.

THEORIES OF THE ATONEMENT

In the history of the church a wide divergence of opinion has arisen concerning the meaning of the death of Christ. This divergence often stems from a point of view which regards the death of Christ as primarily being concerned with the sinner and his need for righteousness rather than contemplating the demands of God's justice which require punishment of sin in keeping with God's moral government of the universe. The principal theories are as follows:

Substitutional Atonement

This point of view, variously described as vicarious or penal, holds that the atonement is objectively directed toward God and the satisfaction of His holy character and demands upon the sinner. It is vicarious in the sense that Christ is the Substitute who bears the punishment rightly due sinners, their guilt being imputed to Him in such a way that He representatively bore their punishment. This is in keeping with the general idea of sacrifices in the Old Testament and is explicitly taught in the New Testament (see John 1:29; II Cor. 5:21; Gal. 3:13; Heb. 9:28; I Peter 2:24). It is further sustained by the use of such prepositions as *peri* (for), *huper* (in behalf of), and *anti* (in place of), which in numerous contexts support the idea of a divine Substitute for the sinner in the person of Christ on the cross. A. H. Strong's reference to "ethical atonement"[1] which satisfied God's holiness is similar to this point of view which is expounded at some length by Louis Berkhof.[2]

Payment-to-Satan Theory

One of the theories which was advanced in the early church by Origen and taught by Augustine and other early Fathers was that the death of Christ was paid to Satan in the form of a ransom to deliver man from any claims which Satan might have upon him.[3]

[1]A. H. Strong, *Systematic Theology*, pp. 750-71.
[2]Louis Berkhof, *Systematic Theology*, pp. 361-83.
[3]L. W. Grensted, *A Short History of the Doctrine of the Atonement*, pp. 32-55.

Though others besides Origen followed this teaching in the early church, in the course of the history of the church it faded from view and ceased to have any substantial adherents. In modern times it has been held only by certain sects.

Recapitulation Theory

This point of view championed by Irenaeus is based on the idea that Christ in His life and death recapitulates all phases of human life, including being made sin in His death on the cross. In so doing, He does properly what Adam failed to do. Irenaeus also regarded the suffering of Christ on the cross as satisfying the divine justice of God, but considered this only one phase of the total picture.

Commercial or Satisfaction Theory

One of the first well-organized theories of the atonement was offered by Anselm in the eleventh century in his classic work *Cur Deus Homo?* His teaching springs from the concept that the necessity of the atonement arises in the fact that God's honor has been injured by sin.[4] God could satisfy His honor by punishing the sinner or by accepting a suitable substitute. Being a God of love and mercy, God provided through His Son the satisfaction that was required. Christ in His life on earth perfectly kept the law of God but, as this was required of Him in any case, it did not constitute a satisfaction of the honor of God on behalf of sinners. Christ went further and died on the cross for sin which He did not need to do for Himself. As this was in the nature of a work of supererogation, the benefits of it were applied to sinners who had fallen short of attaining the righteousness of God. God's honor was thus vindicated and the sinner saved from the penalty of sin.

Objections to this view are principally that more than God's honor has been violated. While Anselm supports the substitutionary character of the death of Christ, he falls short of recognizing properly that a penalty was involved and his view is somewhat similar to the Roman Catholic doctrine of penance rather than a true biblical doctrine of propitiating a righteous God.

Moral Influence Theory

This point of view, which has had much support in modern

[4]Cf. George C. Foley, *Anselm's Theory of the Atonement.*

liberal theology, was first introduced by Abelard[5] in opposition to the commercial theory of Anselm. It proceeds on the premise that God does not necessarily require the death of Christ as an expiation for sin, but has rather chosen this means to manifest His love and to show His fellowship with them in their sufferings. The death of Christ therefore primarily demonstrates the love of God in such a way as to win sinners to Himself. The death of Christ does not constitute a satisfaction of divine law, but rather demonstrates the loving heart of God which will freely pardon sinners.

Liberal and neoorthodox theologians today adopt in one form or another the moral influence theory of Abelard. Actually no new view of the atonement has arisen in the twentieth century; existing opinions can be found in one or more of the classic theories which emerged in the nineteenth century or earlier. The general disposition outside of orthodoxy itself has been to consider the death of Christ as something less than penal and not vicarious in the strict sense of the term. Rather, Christ's death is, on the one hand, a demonstration of the love of God and, on the other, a revelation of God's hatred of sin. Right-wing liberals and neoorthodox scholars tend to support the moral influence theory while left-wing and extreme liberals regard the death of Christ as little more than an example or mystical influence.

Orthodox Christianity has always opposed this point of view as being quite insufficient to explain the many scriptures which present the point of view that the death of Christ is a propitiation of a righteous God and that His death is absolutely necessary to make it possible for God to justify a sinner. Though Christ's death is a demonstration of the love of God and should soften human hearts, it seldom does this apart from a saving work of God.

Theory of Thomas Aquinas

Among the various combinations of the views of Anselm and Abelard was that of Thomas Aquinas, often considered the norm for Roman Catholic theology. He countered the assertion of the necessity of the atonement by contending that God was under no necessity to offer atonement and could have allowed men to go unredeemed. He recognized, however, the historic fact that God

[5]Robert Macintosh, *Historic Theories of Atonement*, pp. 139-48.

had in Christ offered a satisfaction for sin and to some extent
went along with Anselm in holding this sacrifice sufficient and
applicable to those who were joined to Christ in the mystical
union of Christ and His church.

Theory of Duns Scotus

The contribution of Duns Scotus to theories of the atonement
lies principally in the contention that there is no absolute necessity for the atonement as far as the nature of God is concerned,
and that the demand for an atonement for sin proceeds entirely
from the will of God. He held that it was God's prerogative to
decide whether an atonement was necessary in the first place and,
having determined that it was, He could have chosen an angel
or any sinless man to have effected a sacrifice for sin. For Scotus
the main point was that God had accepted the sacrifice of Christ
as sufficient whether it was or not. The theory of Duns Scotus
has generally been considered quite inadequate by orthodox
theologians who prefer to find a necessity for the atonement in
the nature of God rather than the will of God. In modern theology there have been few if any adherents to this position.

Example Theory

As the title of this teaching indicates, this theory holds that
Christ in His death was merely our Example. Like the moral
influence theory, it denies that there is any principle of justice
which needs to be satisfied in God and that therefore the death
of Christ was not necessary as an atonement for sin, but is rather
a means of divine revelation which characterized the obedience
of Christ in dying on the cross. The origin of this point of view
is usually traced to the Socinians who are the forerunners of the
modern Unitarians. Like the moral influence theory, it is actually
a denial of many scriptures which teach to the contrary, and is
a restatement in variant form of a number of heresies which
plagued the early church. It was based upon Unitarian teachings
which affirm human ability and oppose the doctrine of human
depravity. In its Unitarian form it also denied the deity of Christ.
Though it is true that Christ in His death was our Example in
many ways, this did not constitute the efficacy of His death. It
provides no solid basis for the salvation of saints who died

before Christ, nor does it have in itself the power to redeem in the scriptural sense of the term. It assumes also that Christ is an Example to those who are still unsaved, whereas Scripture makes very plain that the example of Christ is for those who have already been redeemed by His death.

Mystical Experience Theory

As an outgrowth of the mysticism of Schleiermacher, Ritschl and others, the teaching was advanced that the death of Christ is to be understood best as exercising a mystical influence upon the sinner.[6] Though similar to some extent to the moral influence theory, this view considers the death of Christ as having more than an ethical influence. It involves the influence of Christ upon mankind for good in a general sense. Some of the advocates of this position did not question that Christ Himself had a sin nature, but they held that through the power of the Holy Spirit He gained victory over it and in His own experience of sanctification culminating in His death became a transforming power in mankind.

Like other false views of the atonement, the mystical experience theory bypasses many scriptures which plainly state man's hopelessly sinful estate and utter need of a supernatural work of God to deliver him of his just punishment for his sins. It does not provide the divine grace and enablement to lift him out of his present sinful state and bring him into right relationship to God. It involves a false view of the person of Christ and usually denies His sinless perfection. Like the moral influence theory, it does not provide for those who lived in Old Testament times.

Governmental Theory of Grotius

This point of view represented a compromise between the example theory and the orthodox view normally held by Protestant Reformers. Adherents trace the necessity of the death of Christ to the government of God rather than to an inexorable law of divine justice. They argue that inasmuch as God's divine government is the product of His will, He can alter it as He wishes, but must in the end uphold the principle of the divine government. Hence, the death of Christ was considered in the

[6]Grensted, pp. 329-38.

form of a nominal payment, a recognition of the principle of government which normally punishes sin, but it did not, according to this view, actually constitute a penal expiation. Christ deferred to the law by dying, but the actual penalty of this law is then set aside inasmuch as the principle of government has been recognized. This interpretation, which was considered to avoid some of the harsher doctrines contained in the concept of the penal and substitutionary atonement, had a natural attraction for those who did not want to go to the extreme of the Socinian position. It was adopted by the Calvinist Wardlaw[7] as well as the Arminian Miley,[8] and had quite a following in New England theology in the United States. The principal objection to this teaching is that it does not satisfy the scriptural representation of the death of Christ. It seems to make an unnecessary division between the government of God and the nature of God from which the government comes.

Theory of Vicarious Confession

This teaching is based upon the idea that God would forgive man if he could perfectly repent of his sins and confess them to God. Because man is unable to provide an adequate repentance, he is not able naturally to offer a true confession and Christ, on behalf of man by His death, demonstrated the awfulness of sin which is accepted by God as a completely adequate confession. This theory, like many others, falls short of a true and adequate explanation of scriptural revelation on the death of Christ. Confession of sin in itself is not vicarious. Like other views, it does not provide for a true penal satisfaction of the righteous demands of God. In any case, one man cannot confess or repent for another, though substitution in other cases may be valid. This view often attributed to John McLeod Campbell has not attracted many modern adherents and is actually without a true scriptural foundation.[9]

The only point of view which completely satisfies scriptures bearing on the death of Christ is the substitutional or penal concept of the atonement as embodied in numerous passages unfolding the doctrines of redemption, propitiation and reconciliation. Christ in His death fully satisfied the demands of a right-

[7]Ralph Wardlaw, *Systematic Theology*, pp. 358-72.
[8]John Miley, *The Atonement in Christ*.
[9]John McLeod Campbell, *The Nature of the Atonement*, pp. 124-25.

eous God for judgment upon sinners and, as their infinite sacrifice, provided a ground not only for the believer's forgiveness, but for his justification and sanctification. While certain aspects of other theories can be recognized as having merit, they fall short of establishing the true justice of God in exacting the penalty of the death of His Son. The substitutionary character of the death of Christ is further borne out in great doctrines which describe the substance of His work upon the cross such as justification, redemption, propitiation and reconciliation. An examination of the scriptural revelation concerning these doctrines will further substantiate the concept of substitutional atonement.

REDEMPTION

The doctrine of redemption both in Scripture and in theology is an important aspect of the work of God in salvation. Though it is difficult to find any one term which is comprehensive of the entire work of God on behalf of sinful men, if the term "salvation" be understood as the comprehensive term for the complete work of God for man in time and eternity, then redemption is particularly concerned with that aspect of salvation which was accomplished in the death of Christ.

Inasmuch as the historic concept of redemption has been subject to considerable criticism in modern theology, it is most important in the study of the death of Christ to determine the precise scriptural teaching on the act of redemption. A rich linguistic background is afforded in the Old Testament and upon this the New Testament builds its more complete doctrine. In general the study concerns itself with two major groups of words, namely *agorazō* and its derivatives and *lutroō* and its cognate forms. A third term *peripoieō* adds a confirming statement in Acts 20:28. From the study of these words and their use in the Scriptures a solid doctrine of redemption in Christ can be erected. The etymological study in this instance is prerequisite to the theological conclusions which follow.

The Idea of Purchase

This basic expression for redemption in Scripture is a verb *agorazō* derived from *agora*, a forum or a marketplace, and therefore means simply "to buy" or "to purchase."[10] Ordinarily it has reference to simple purchases of items in the marketplace, but in six instances in the Bible Christians are said to be redeemed or bought in reference to the death of Christ (I Cor. 6:20; 7:23; II Peter 2:1; Rev. 5:9; 14:3-4).

In the Septuagint and in general Greek usage the idea of purchase is the common concept of *agorazō*. It does not seem to be used in a theological sense in the Old Testament. Though *agorazō* is not found in connection with the purchase and freedom of slaves, Morris (after Deissmann) believes that this idea may be involved, because of the use of *timē*, meaning "price," with this verb in I Corinthians 6:20 and 7:23. *Timē* is a common word used in the purchase of slaves.[11]

Thus, a study of *agorazō* leads to the concept that Christians are bought by Christ and are therefore His slaves. Hence, the conclusion of Paul in I Corinthians 6:19-20 (ASV): "Or know ye not that your body is a temple of the Holy Spirit which is in you, which ye have from God? And ye are not your own; for ye were bought with a price: glorify God therefore in your body." The same thought is borne out in I Corinthians 7:23 (ASV): "Ye were bought with a price; become not bondservants of men." The teaching therefore is that Christ in the act of redemption purchased Christians and made them His slaves. They were therefore not to obey other masters in that they were bought at such a high cost with a view to accomplishing the will of God.

In II Peter 2:1 (ASV) the same expression is used in describing false prophets as those "who shall privily bring in destructive heresies, denying even the Master that bought them, bringing upon themselves swift destruction." The denial of the fact of the purchase of Christ is therefore described as a heresy of such proportion as to bring its teachers under the swift judgment of God. The blasphemy of their false doctrine is seen in the context of rejection of the loving redemption provided in Christ.

The fact that believers are in a special relationship to God as those purchased by the death of Christ is made the theme of the new song that is sung in heaven recorded in Revelation 5:9 (ASV): "Worthy art thou to take the book, and to open the seals thereof: for thou wast slain, and didst purchase unto God

[10]Cf. William F. Arndt and F. Wilbur Gingrich, *A Greek-English Lexicon of the New Testament*, p. 12.
[11]Leon Morris, *The Apostolic Preaching of the Cross*, p. 50.

with thy blood men of every tribe, and tongue, and people, and nation." Here specifically the death of Christ is the price that was paid. Offensive as is this truth to the false prophets mentioned in II Peter 2:1, it is the clear teaching of the Word of God and puts redeemed man in a special relationship as being purchased by that which is of infinite value.

In Revelation 14:3-4, the one hundred and forty-four thousand are twice declared to be "purchased" with special regard to their holy calling as those who will follow the Lamb and be "the firstfruits unto God and unto the Lamb" (Rev. 14:4, ASV). The emphasis in all of these passages therefore is on purchase through the death and shed blood of Christ with the resulting relationship that the believer is a bondslave to Jesus Christ and obligated to do His will.

Exagorazō

The verb *exagorazō*, found four times in the New Testament (Gal. 3:13; 4:5; Eph. 5:16; Col. 4:5), is obviously *agorazō* with the added prefix *ex*, meaning to buy back or to buy from, in which sense it is used in Galatians 3:13 and Galatians 4:5.[12] In Colossians 4:5 and Ephesians 5:16 it is used with the meaning of buying up the time, that is, making the most of it in view of the Lord's return.[13]

In Galatians 3 the statement is made that Christ has redeemed us from the curse of the law by being made a curse for us. In the context, in Galatians 3:10 the thought is brought out, based on a quotation from Deuteronomy 27:26, that everyone is cursed who does not perfectly keep the law. The argument is that the law's effect on man is that of cursing him because of incomplete obedience. No man is able to live up to the law perfectly. In addition to this argument, Paul points out that justification is by faith and not by the law in any event. As a curse rests upon everyone who does not comply fully with the law, it was necessary for Christ to die and take the curse upon Himself. This was fulfilled in keeping with Deuteronomy 21:23 that the curse is upon one who hangs upon a tree. The familiar concept of substitution is imbedded in the Hebraic understanding of a sacrifice, as is illustrated in the lambs which died on the altar

---

[12]Cf. Arndt and Gingrich, p. 271.
[13]*Ibid.*

and the scapegoat which was freed. Note should be taken of the fact that *huper* ("in behalf of" or "for") is used in the expression "a curse for us" in Galatians 3:13. The preposition seems in this context clearly to be used in a substitutionary sense. Morris cites Delitzsch, and even Bushnell and Manson, as agreeing that substitution is the inescapable meaning of this text.[14]

The curse, however, is not a curse of God, but the curse of the broken law. Moreover, in the ultimate administration it is God who judges Christ as *bearing the penalty of sin.* It is not sufficient to discover in this passage merely a satisfaction of the government of God as did Grotius. Even liberal theologians (e.g., Bushnell) have found it difficult to escape the idea that here the death of Christ is presented both as penal and substitutionary. Galatians 4:4 (ASV) gives added support in stating that Christ was "born of a woman, born under the law."

It is evident that if *agorazō* emphasizes the thought of purchase and resulting ownership as relating the believer to God, *exagorazō* is a more intensive form which has the idea of not only being bought, but being bought out of the market or bought back from a previous condition of obligation to the law. It is upon this platform that the resulting idea of being free from obligation is built. The purpose of God was that through the *exagorazō* Gentile believers might receive the blessing in Christ promised all nations through Abraham and might in addition be given the promise of the Spirit through faith (Gal. 3:14) .

The Use of Peripoieō

The word *peripoieō* is found three times in the New Testament (Luke 17:33; Acts 20:28; I Tim. 3:13) . Only one reference, namely, Acts 20:28, is used in reference to Christ. Generally speaking, the word means to save or to preserve one's self, that is, to preserve his own life (Luke 17:33) or to acquire, obtain or gain for oneself as in Acts 20:28 and I Timothy 3:13.[15] In Acts 20:28 (ASV) the exhortation is given: "Take heed unto yourselves, and to all the flock, in which the Holy Spirit hath made you bishops, to feed the church of the Lord which he purchased with his own blood." In contrast to the use of *agorazō*

[14]Morris, p. 54. Cf. Franz Delitzsch, *Commentary on the Epistle to the Hebrews,* II. 426; Horace Bushnell, *The Vicarious Sacrifice,* p. 121; Thomas W. Manson, *Jesus the Messiah,* p. 165.
[15]Cf. Arndt and Gingrich, p. 655.

which would emphasize the idea of purchase, the verb used here has more the thought of the result of the action, that the church has been "acquired." The idea is therefore one of possession rather than emphasis on the act of purchase. This is also true in I Timothy 3:13.

The additional expression "with his own blood" identifies the act of purchase as related to the death of Christ and therefore supports the idea of substitutionary atonement but also adds what is the main point of the apostle here, that the church of the Lord is especially precious because of the high price which was paid. The bishops are entrusted with that which cost God the death of His own Son. The combined force of *agorazō*, *exagorazō* and *peripoieō* is that of (1) purchase, (2) of being bought off the market, not subject to resale, and (3) of a possession regarded as precious in the sight of the Lord.

The Idea of Freedom from Bondage

One of the most important aspects of redemption is revealed in the Bible through the use of *lutroō* and its cognate forms which have the meaning of freed by paying a ransom, redeemed, set free, rescued.[16] The verb form is found three times in the New Testament (Luke 24:21; Titus 2:14; I Peter 1:18). The first of these references was a statement of the disciples on the road to Emmaus that they had hoped that Christ would "redeem Israel." The word here is used clearly in the thought of releasing them from their bondage to Rome and introducing the period of blessing of which the Old Testament prophets had spoken. To the disciples it therefore seemed impossible that these promises of deliverance should be fulfilled now that Christ had died on the cross. Leon Morris somewhat misses the point when he says: "The passage is not of first importance, for our purposes; for clearly a redemption rendered impossible by the cross can tell us little about the redemption effected by the cross."[17] The Scriptures here only record the thought of the disciples which as a matter of fact was wrong. The cross was going to be the stepping-stone to the ultimate deliverance of Israel, not only from their enemies but from the bondage of sin.

More specifically, however, in Titus 2:14 (ASV) the basic

16*Ibid.*, p. 484.
17Morris, p. 35.

idea of being set free by a ransom is revealed: "[Christ] gave himself for us, that he might redeem us from all iniquity, and purify unto himself a people for his own possession, zealous of good works." Here the ransom is that of Christ giving Himself for us (*huper hēmōn*). The believer is set free by the ransom paid by Christ on the cross. The expression "gave himself for us," though not speaking specifically of His death, is nevertheless a clear reference to it.

The final instance in the New Testament, I Peter 1:18 (ASV), is explicit on this matter: "Ye were redeemed, not with corruptible things, with silver or gold, from your vain manner of life handed down from your fathers; but with precious blood, as of a lamb without blemish and without spot, even the blood of Christ." Here clearly set forth is the concept of ransom by the death of Christ, something that was impossible by payment of silver and gold. By it the believer is set free from his former obligation and former vain life. Only an obvious prejudice against the idea of substitution can erase it from this passage, as it would be difficult to state the concept more explicitly than it is found here.

Twice in the New Testament the noun form *lutron* is used (Matt. 20:28; Mark 10:45). In both instances the word is properly translated "ransom" and refers to the death of Christ. According to Matthew 20:28 (ASV), "The Son of man came not to be ministered unto, but to minister, and to give his life a ransom for many." Mark 10:45 (ASV) is a parallel reference: "For the Son of man also came not to be ministered unto, but to minister, and to give his life a ransom for many." In both instances there is clear mention that the death of Christ constituted the ransom by which the sinner is set free. The New Testament usage is in entire harmony with the frequent use in Greek literature as a whole and in the Septuagint where it was a common term for the ransom money paid for the manumission of slaves.[18]

Mention should be made of *antilutron* occurring only in I Timothy 2:6 where Christ is said to be the One who "gave himself a ransom for all." The *anti* emphasizes the substitutionary character of the ransom.

---

[18]Cf. Arndt and Gingrich, pp. 483-84; Adolf Deissmann, *Light from the Ancient East*, p. 327; Morris, pp. 22-24.

One of the most common and definitive terms for redemption is the word *apolutrōsis* used ten times in the New Testament (Luke 21:28; Rom. 3:24; 8:23; I Cor. 1:30; Eph. 1:7, 14; 4:30; Col. 1:14; Heb. 9:15; 11:35, "deliverance"). The frequent use of this term in the New Testament is somewhat accentuated by the fact that outside of the Bible it is rarely used. The verb form *apolutroō* is not found in the Bible at all, and only eight times in other· literature.[19] It is obvious that *apolutrōsis* is a compound form somewhat more intensive than *lutroō* or *luō*. It may be defined as set free, released, pardoned, dismissed, sent away.[20] It is not difficult to establish that in all of its instances it has the concept of a ransom being paid with resultant deliverance of the one in difficulty.

Of the ten instances in which *apolutrōsis* is found in the New Testament, all but one are clear references to redemption in Christ and fully substantiate the idea of deliverance by payment of a price. Romans 3:24 states: "Being justified freely by his grace through the redemption that is in Christ Jesus." Here the great fact of justification without cost to the believer through the grace of God is made possible by the ransom price, that is, "the redemption that is in Christ Jesus." This is specified in verse 25 as being accomplished by the propitiation of Christ through faith in or by His blood. The payment of the ransom price is a declaration of the righteousness of God in forgiving sins in the Old Testament as well as in justifying the believer in the New Testament.

Almost identically the same thought is expressed in Ephesians 1:7 (ASV): "In whom we have redemption through his blood, the forgiveness of our trespasses, according to the riches of his grace." Here again the ransom price of His blood accomplishes the freedom and deliverance of the sinner in difficulty, though Abbott attempts to evade this.[21] In Hebrews 9:15 (ASV) Christ is declared to be "the mediator of a new covenant, that a death having taken place for the redemption of the transgressions that were under the first covenant, they that have been called may receive the promise of the eternal inheritance." As in the two former references, the ransom price has been paid in the death

[19]Morris, p. 26, cites Warfield's eight references.
[20]Arndt and Gingrich, p. 95.
[21]Cf. Morris, pp. 38-40.

of Christ and Christ Himself is constituted the Mediator of a new covenant thereby.

Though less explicit, other references confirm the same concept. First Corinthians 1:30 cites redemption as that which comes to us because we are in Christ, which is a corollary of righteousness and sanctification. Colossians 1:14 links redemption with our forgiveness of sins because we are in Christ. Several references may be construed eschatologically as a future deliverance stemming from the past redemption accomplished by Christ. Luke 21:28 refers to the fact that at the second coming "your redemption draweth nigh." Romans 8:23 (ASV) states that we are "waiting for our adoption, to wit, the redemption of our body." This seems to refer to resurrection of the body.

A similar reference to resurrection is found in Ephesians 4:30 where it mentions that we are sealed by the Holy Spirit "unto the day of redemption," that is, our deliverance from this world into the world to come through resurrection or translation. Ephesians 1:14 (ASV) may be construed in the same sense where the Holy Spirit is referred to as "an earnest of our inheritance, unto the redemption of God's own possession, unto the praise of his glory." Leon Morris[22] thinks this should be interpreted in the same light as Ephesians 1:7 which speaks of redemption through the blood of Christ. The context, however, would seem to point to the future aspect when God's own possession now sealed by the Holy Spirit of promise is fully delivered in the presence of the Lord. Only Hebrews 11:35, speaking of those who would not accept deliverance by denial of their faith, seems to have no direct connection with the death of Christ. All the other references with varied force refer either to the death of Christ or its result, in other words, the ransom paid with the resulting deliverance. The clear force of substitution involved in all of these instances gives added emphasis to previous revelation of this truth and should assure the believer of the great accomplishment wrought by Christ in His death.

Three remaining passages should be mentioned where the noun *lutrōsis* is used (Luke 1:68; 2:38; Heb. 9:12). Of these only Hebrews 9:12 (ASV) is of significance in the doctrine of redemption, for in a much discussed passage Christ is declared to have obtained redemption through His blood: "Nor yet through the

22*Ibid.*, p. 43.

blood of goats and calves, but through his own blood, entered in once for all into the holy place, having obtained eternal redemption." The emphasis here is on the cost of redemption which is declared to be eternal. Like the high priest of old who entered into the holy place after offering a sacrifice on the altar, so Christ, having offered His own blood and in virtue of His finished work, entered into the holy place. His entrance signifies that an eternal redemption has been wrought. The use of *lutrōsis* here instead of *apolutrōsis* is not especially significant, though it seems to imply more emphasis on the deliverance itself than the resulting state.

The study of redemption through Christ in the New Testament reveals clearly that Christ by an act of substitution in His death on the cross paid the ransom price and redeemed the enslaved sinner from his sinful and condemned position before God. Christ's death constituted an act of purchase in which the sinner is removed from his former bondage in sin by payment of the ransom price. The act of redemption takes the purchased possession out of the market and effects his release. Scholars may reject the New Testament teaching if they will, but the revelation of redemption is written clearly in the Scriptures.

PROPITIATION

As a biblical doctrine, propitiation embodies the concept that the death of Christ fully satisfied the demands of a righteous God in respect to judgment upon the sinner. The word "propitiation" appears only three times in the Authorized Version (Rom. 3:25; I John 2:2; 4:10) and an additional reference is found in the American Standard Version (Heb. 2:17). Other New Testament words related to this doctrine are from the same Greek root (cf. Luke 18:13; Heb. 2:17; Rom. 3:25 with Heb. 9:5; I John 2:2; 4:10; also see Matt. 16:22; Heb. 8:12).

The doctrine of propitiation has been complicated by contemporary theologians who deny that a loving God needs the death of Christ to satisfy His righteousness. Sometimes they argue that God's love does not require satisfaction, or that the word "propitiation" itself is improperly construed if it is defined as satisfaction.

Propitiation in the Old Testament

Although C. H. Dodd and others consider the concept of propitiating God as a crude prebiblical point of view derived from
pagan religions, Leon Morris has carefully demonstrated that
this is not the case. Citing George Smeaton, Morris declares concerning the word (Greek, *hilasmos:* "propitiation"), "The uniform
acceptation of the word in classical Greek, when applied to the
Deity, is the means of appeasing God, or averting His anger; and
not a single instance to the contrary occurs in the whole Greek
literature."[23] Morris goes on to demonstrate that the wrath of
God is an important doctrine in the Old Testament with over
580 occurrences of this concept. He summarizes the Old Testament doctrine of the wrath of God in these words:

> There is a consistency about the wrath of God in the Old
> Testament. It is no capricious passion, but the stern reaction
> of the divine nature to evil in man. It is aroused only and
> inevitably by sin, which may be thought of in general terms
> (Jb. 21:20; Je. 21:12; Ezk. 24:13), or may be categorized
> more exactly as the shedding of blood (Ezk. 16:38; 24:8),
> adultery (Ezk. 23:25), violence (Ezk. 8:18), covetousness
> (Je. 6:11), revenge (Ezek. 25:17), afflicting widows and or-
> phans (Ex. 22:23 f.), taking brethren captive (2 Ch. 28:11-
> 13), etc. Wrath comes upon Israel because of the evil of
> Jeroboam as repeated by Jehoahaz (2 Kings 13:3), and be-
> cause of the evil of Manasseh (2 Kings 23:26), while Moses
> feared that the desire of the two and a half tribes not to pass
> over Jordan would have a similar effect (Nu. 32:14). Pro-
> faning the sabbath arouses wrath (Ne. 13:18) which comes
> also upon men who 'have not told the truth about' God (Jb.
> 42:7, Moffatt), and Gideon feared that his repeated testing
> of the Lord would also cause God's anger (Jdg. 6:39).[24]

Morris further concludes, based on Old Testament usage:
"Where there is sin, the Old Testament teaches, there is wrath;
but this does not mean that all men are to be consumed, for that
wrath is the wrath of a loving father who yearns for His children
to come to Him."[25] The Old Testament concept of propitiation,
therefore, elevates it above the crude pagan idea of placating an
unreasonable deity and introduces a high concept of divine righteousness which is satisfied by a propitiation of a loving God who

[23]George Smeaton, *The Apostles' Doctrine of the Atonement,* p. 455, as
cited by Morris, p. 126.
[24]Morris, p. 131.
[25]*Ibid.,* p. 159.

desires to provide a proper basis by which the sinner can come to Himself. If this is the proper understanding of the Old Testament doctrine, it provides a broad platform upon which the New Testament concept can be understood.

Propitiation in the New Testament

The New Testament doctrine of propitiation like that of the Old Testament depends upon the concept of the wrath of God as requiring satisfaction. The wrath of God is expressly mentioned in Mark 3:5; Luke 21:23; Matthew 3:7; Luke 3:7; John 3:36; Romans 9:22; Ephesians 5:6; Colossians 3:6; Revelation 6:16; 11:18; 14:10; 16:19; and 19:15. These references to wrath using the Greek term *orgē* are also supported by another word *thumos*, meaning anger or wrath, mentioned frequently in the New Testament in such passages as Romans 2:5; 3:5; 4:15; 5:9; Ephesians 2:3; I Thessalonians 1:10; 2:16; 5:9; II Thessalonians 1:7-9; Hebrews 12:29, and Revelation 14:10, 19; 15:1, 7; 16:1, 19; and 19:15. The New Testament doctrine of propitiation is God's answer to the problem of His righteous judgment upon the sinner.

' One of the most important references to propitiation in the New Testament is found in Romans 3:25-26, "Whom God hath set forth to be a propitiation through faith in his blood, to declare his righteousness for the remission of sins that are past, through the forbearance of God; to declare, I say, at this time his righteousness: that he might be just, and the justifier of him which believeth in Jesus." The same Greek word (*hilasterion*) is found in Hebrews 9:5, the only other New Testament occurrence, where it is translated "mercyseat." Scholars have differed as to whether these two usages of the word are the same. Paul's argument in the Romans passage would seem to be that propitiation here is the act of satisfying the proper demands of a righteous God for judgment on sin as fulfilled in the death of Christ. This is supported by the references to the righteousness of God in I John 2:2 in the context of His forgiveness in I John 1:9.

Some, however, have preferred to consider the Romans passage as identical with that of Hebrews, namely, the place of propitiation rather than the act of propitiation. The ultimate meaning, however, is not too different as in either case it is a direct statement not only that God requires satisfaction for sin, but that such satisfaction was provided in the propitiation of Christ in His death. The opposition of modern authors such as C. H. Dodd who attempt to make this a pagan concept is not borne out by the text.

The two facts that place propitiation in the Bible above the pagan concepts in extrabiblical literature are first of all that it is not the question of satisfying a vengeful God, but satisfying a God who is just, righteous and holy in all of His dealing. Second, such a God, while on the one hand demanding complete satisfaction of His righteousness, is the same God who because of His love for lost mankind sent His Son to be that propitiation. Before such a revelation of grace, objections to the idea of propitiation fade and are refuted by the doctrine of sin and condemnation as well as by the necessity for the righteousness of God being satisfied before love is free to operate.

Other references to the concept of propitiation in the Scriptures bear this out. In Hebrews 2:17 it is stated of Christ, "Wherefore in all things it behoved him to be made like unto his brethren, that he might be a merciful and faithful high priest in things pertaining to God, to make reconciliation for the sins of the people." The Authorized Version's "reconciliation" is translated from the Greek *hilaskomai* which should have been rendered "to make propitiation for the sins of the people" (ASV). Although some scholars have felt this expression awkward, there is no good reason for avoiding the conclusions embodied in the translation of the American Standard Version that the expression "the sins" found in the accusative after the verb is an accusative of general respect. That is, propitiation is in respect to sin but actually directed toward God and His righteousness. This passage accordingly confirms what has been learned in other instances, namely, that Christ in His sacrifice is the answer to the problem of the sinner who is justly under the condemnation of God. Christ is His propitiation, that is, He satisfies the righteous demands of God completely.

The commonly quoted prayer of the publican in Luke 18:13 properly translated should read, "God, be thou propitiated to me, a sinner." Although the passage does not refer to the propitiation of Christ, it introduces the same concept. Other instances of words related to propitiation do not seem to throw any added light on the doctrine.

Taken as a whole, the doctrine of propitiation as revealed in the New Testament fully sustains the orthodox concept that Christ in His death on the cross through the shedding of His blood and the sacrifice of His life accomplished a satisfaction of divine justice which God accepts on behalf of the sinner. This propitiation makes possible the manifestation of His love toward men and bestowal of righteousness through justification by faith. The doctrine is supported by the necessity of propitiation occasioned by sin (Rom. 3:9, 23; 5:12), the righteousness of God (Ps. 119:137; 145:17; Rom. 3:25-26), and the historic fact that Christ actually died for sinful man (Isa. 53:5-7; I Cor. 15:3; Gal. 1:4; 3:13; Eph. 5:2; Heb. 9:22, 28; I Peter 1:18-19; 2:24; Rev. 1:5).

The Substitutional Character of Propitiation

In the Old Testament sacrifices the concept of substitution and temporary propitiation is constantly in view. All of the Old Testament offerings prefigure Christ in His substitutional sacrifice. The nonsweet-savor offerings, consisting principally of the sin offering and the trespass offering, represent Christ satisfying the demands of God by bearing the guilt and judgment of sin (John 1:29). The sweet-savor offering represents Christ satisfying the demands of God by presenting His merit for us (Eph. 5:2).

The New Testament doctrine is an advance on the Old in that the offering of Christ is once and for all (Heb. 9:28) and is a complete and eternal satisfaction for sin (Rom. 3:25; Heb. 10:4). In contrast to the Old Testament sacrifices which were animals unintelligent and involuntary in their substitution, Christ willingly dies and intelligently offers Himself as a sacrificial Substitute for sinners.

The objections of liberal scholars that a God of love does not need such propitiation and that forgiveness purchased is not true forgiveness has been often answered. Representing the liberal point of view, Henry Sloane Coffin argues:

> Certain widely used hymns still perpetuate the theory that God pardons sinners because Christ purchased that pardon by His obedience and suffering. But a forgiveness which is paid for is not forgiveness. The God of the prophets and psalmists, the God and Father of Jesus' own teaching, forgives graciously all who turn to Him in penitence. The cross

of Christ is not a means of procuring forgiveness: the Father waits to be gracious.[26]

Such objections of course are founded upon a concept of God which is not afforded in the Scriptures. It is true that God is a God of love and to this the Scriptures give abundant testimony. Contemporary thinkers are unwilling to face the fact that God is also revealed to be a God of righteousness as manifested in His many judgments in the Old Testament and in countless pronouncements that He must judge sin. The argument that God is a God of love and therefore not a God of righteousness is playing one attribute against another in a way that is contrary to biblical revelation.

The logic embodied in this point of view is faulty. Forgiveness by its very nature involves recompense. If the one sinned against forgives without recompense or justice, the one injured in effect bears the penalty himself. This is preeminently illustrated in the death of Christ who as God is the One sinned against, who as the sacrifice for sin bore the judgment which His own righteous nature demanded. Even in modern scholarship among liberals all do not follow the view of Coffin and tend to recognize that the death of Christ in some sense was accepted by God even if in less than a true substitutionary meaning.

Leon Morris has summarized the evidence for substitution in this way:

> In the last resort it seems that we are shut up to three possibilities: the moral view (that the effect of Christ's death is its effect on us), the view that Christ as our Substitute bore what we should have borne, and the view that Christ did not bear our suffering but something different which effects more or less the same thing. The first of these views is obviously inadequate. While it contains a truth, it is yet unable to meet the statements of scripture which persistently speak of something as being effected outside man, and that something as the most important part of the process. The third view has been rejected wherever it has been put forward and studied seriously. It is essentially Duns Scotus' view of *acceptilatio*, defined as 'the optional taking of something for nothing, or of a part for the whole.' It is Grotius' view that Christ did not bear our penalty, but such sufferings as would show the ill desert of sin. Always such views have been found inadequate, and, for all the earnestness with which

[26]Henry Sloane Coffin, *The Meaning of the Cross*, pp. 118, 121.

they are argued, the modern equivalents seem no more satisfying. Like Anselm's view, they find no *necessary* connection between Christ's sufferings and us. If we reject the
moral view as inadequate, there seem only two possibilities—
either Christ took my sins and bore their consequences, or
He did not take my sins, in which case they are still on me,
and I bear the consequences. Such views do not explain the
atonement. They reject it. We are left with the thought of
substitution.[27]

Results of Propitiation

At least three important results of propitiation can be derived
from the doctrine:

1. God is justified in forgiving sin. On the basis of the death
of Christ, God is fully justified in forgiving sin in that Christ has
paid the price in full.

2. God is justified in bestowing righteousness. In addition to
forgiving sin, propitiation permits God to impute the righteousness of Christ to the sinner as foreshadowed in the sweet-savor
offerings of the Old Testament. Hence, God can justify the
sinner and accept him in the merit of His Son.

3. God is justified in bestowing all grace on sinners. Having
been completely propitiated or satisfied by the death of Christ,
God is now free to pour out all blessings indicated by His loving
heart upon the objects of His grace. This may be manifested in
spiritual enablement, ministry for God, prayer, spiritual fruit,
spiritual sustenance, illumination of the Holy Spirit, sanctification
in all of its phases and ultimate glorification. On the basis of
being propitiated, God stands ready now to bless abundantly all
who come to Him.

RECONCILIATION

Few doctrines are more important in a total theology than the
doctrine of reconciliation. Though based on comparatively few
specific references, reconciliation has been hailed as a doctrine of
"vital concern both for doctrinal clarity and pulpit vitality."[28]
Vincent Taylor speaks of reconciliation as "the best New Testament word to describe the purpose of the Atonement."[29] Referring to Paul's discussion in II Corinthians 5, Taylor comments:

[27]Morris, *The Cross in the New Testament*, pp. 418-19.
[28]S. Lewis Johnson, Jr., "From Enmity to Amity," *Bibliotheca Sacra*, CXIX
(Apr., 1962) 139-49.
[29]Vincent Taylor, *The Atonement in New Testament Teaching*, p. 191.

"All through this section one cannot fail to be impressed with the immense importance St. Paul attaches to this message and to his sense of being divinely commissioned to declare it."[30] Leon Morris introduces the subject of reconciliation by quoting T. H. Hughes to the effect that "in the New Testament the basic idea of the atonement is that of reconciliation."[31] The importance attached to the doctrine of reconciliation not only justifies its discussion, but is also the occasion for major differences of opinion as to its meaning. A careful study of the scriptural presentation of the doctrine of reconciliation demonstrates that it is properly the work of God for man in which God undertakes to transform man and make possible and actual his eternal fellowship with a holy God. Provisionally, reconciliation was accomplished once and for all by Christ on the cross and the whole world was potentially reconciled to God. Reconciliation becomes actual and effective in the person of believers in Christ at the time of their salvation.

Reconciliation in the Old Testament

As most treatises on reconciliation recognize, the Old Testament doctrine of reconciliation adds little to the New Testament. Several words in the Old Testament are commonly translated "reconcile" such as *kaphar* (cf. Lev. 6:30; 8:15; 16:20; Ezek. 45:15, 17, 20; Dan. 9:24). It is a common word used of spreading pitch on the ark (Gen. 6:14), but translated, when in the *piel* form, to mean "to obtain forgiveness" and hence "to reconcile." Mention should also be made of *chata* translated "reconciliation" in II Chronicles 29:24 and *ratsah* found in I Samuel 29:4, translated "reconcile." These two words mean respectively "to bear the blame," in reference to the sin offering, and "to make oneself pleasing, to obtain favor." The Old Testament allusions actually add little either by way of background or definition to the New Testament doctrine. What is true of the Old Testament carries over into the Septuagint where only rarely the Greek words found in the New Testament for reconciliation are found and such instances as occur are not especially significant as Morris points out.[32] In the literature of Judaism, also discussed by Leon

[30]Taylor, *Forgiveness and Reconciliation*, p. 73.
[31]T. H. Hughes, *The Atonement*, p. 312, as cited by Morris, *The Apostolic Preaching* . . . , p. 186.
[32]Morris, *The Apostolic Preaching* . . . , p. 188.

Morris, little can be learned except that there was widespread understanding that man could not be reconciled to God unless something was done to appease the wrath of God. Such reconciliation seldom rose above an anthropomorphic concept of two people in disagreement resolving their difficulties. Though, as Morris states: "The best Rabbinic thought has risen to the concept of God Himself bringing about the reconciliation.[33] Taken as a whole, the doctrine of the reconciliation before the New Testament is not specific nor precise in its theology and to some extent confuses rather than clarifies the issues involved.

New Testament References

The most important reference to reconciliation is found in the Greek word *katallassō* (Rom. 5:10; I Cor. 7:11; II Cor. 5:18, 19, 20). The noun form (Greek, *katallagē*) occurs four times (Rom. 5:11; 11:15; II Cor. 5:18-19). Another form of the verb, *apokatallassō* (Eph. 2:16; Col. 1:20, 21), does not occur in any earlier Greek literature and Paul seems to have used this to express the completeness of reconciliation. It is properly translated "to reconcile completely."[34] Other variations of this verb do not relate properly to the doctrine. Taking the instances as a whole, there are eleven that specifically describe the relationship of God to man and in every instance man is said to be reconciled to God.

Four Interpretations of Reconciliation

In spite of the uniform usage of the Bible in presenting the doctrine of reconciliation, interpreters have differed concerning its precise meaning. William G. T. Shedd, for instance, is an advocate of the view that reconciliation has God as its object and holds that God is reconciled to man.[35] Charles Hodge takes a mediate position that reconciliation affects both parties.[36] This has attracted modern evangelical scholars such as Leon Morris. Still another view is held by A. H. Strong to the effect that man is changed, that is, reconciled to God. By reconciliation Strong means the total of man's salvation including election, calling, union with Christ, regeneration, conversion, justification, sanctification and perseverance.[37]

[33]*Ibid.*, p. 192.
[34]Arndt and Gingrich, p. 92.
[35]William G. T. Shedd, *Dogmatic Theology*, II, 395-97.
[36]Charles Hodge, *Systematic Theology*, II, 514.
[37]Strong, p. 886.

A fourth view typical of contemporary neoorthodoxy and Barthian theology teaches that reconciliation is accomplished by the incarnation of Christ rather than by His death.[38] Barth writes,

> In Jesus Christ there is no isolation of man from God or of God from man. Rather, in Him we encounter the history, the dialogue, in which God and man meet together and are together, the reality of the covenant *mutually* contracted, preserved, and fulfilled by them. Jesus Christ is in His one Person, as true *God, man's* loyal partner, and as true *man, God's.* He is the Lord humbled for communion with man and likewise the Servant exalted to communion with God. He is the Word spoken from the loftiest, most luminous transcendence and likewise the Word heard in the deepest, darkest immanence. He is both, without their being confused but also without their being divided; He is wholly the one and wholly the other. Thus in this oneness Jesus Christ is the Mediator, the Reconciler, between God and man. Thus He comes forward to *man* on behalf of *God* calling for and awakening faith, love, and hope, and to *God* on behalf of *man,* representing man, making satisfaction and interceding. Thus He attests and guarantees to man God's free *grace* and at the same time attests and guarantees to God man's free *gratitude.* Thus he establishes in His Person the justice of God vis-à-vis man and also the justice of man before God. Thus He is in His Person the covenant of its fullness, the Kingdom of heaven which is at hand, in which God speaks and man hears, God gives and man receives, God commands and man obeys, God's glory shines in the heights and thence into the depths, and peace on earth comes to pass among men in whom He is well pleased. Moreover, exactly in this way Jesus Christ, as this Mediator and Reconciler between God and man, is also the *Revealer* of them both.[39]

The first three interpretations of Shedd, Hodge and Strong are answered adequately by a study of the Scriptures themselves. The fourth view, that of Barth, characteristic of neoorthodox theology in general, is based on the false premise that reconciliation is revelatory rather than an act of God fundamentally changing man's relationship to Himself. Intrinsic to the Barthian position is the concept of history as it relates to Jesus Christ which make the incarnation God's redemptive act rather than the death of Christ. Orthodoxy continues to contend that the incarnation,

[38]Karl Barth, *The Humanity of God,* pp. 46-47.
[39]*Ibid.*

apart from the death and resurrection of Christ, would have reconciled no one.

Important Scripture Passages

The variety of opinions on the subject of reconciliation can only be resolved by a study of the Scriptures themselves. When these passages are allowed to speak, the evidence supports the concept that reconciliation effects a change in man which reconciles him to God.

II Corinthians 5:17-21. This central passage dealing with reconciliation introduces the concept that the believer reconciled to God is a new creation. The key phrase is found in verse 17 (ASV): "If any man is in Christ." The new creation is in contrast to the former position in Adam, in which man was doomed to die and under hopeless condemnation (Rom. 5:11-21). "The old things" are therefore said to be "passed away" in the sense that the believer in Christ has an entirely new position. He belongs to the new creation instead of the old, the last Adam instead of the first Adam.

This total change is indicated by the word "reconciliation" in that God has reconciled the believer "to himself through Christ." As Morris states:

> First of all let us notice that the process the apostle has in mind is one which is wrought by God. 'All things', he tells us, 'are of God, who reconciled us'; 'God was in Christ reconciling the world unto himself', 'him . . . he made to be sin on our behalf'. Though it is true that there is an aspect in which men may be exhorted to be reconciled to God, yet there is no question that Paul is thinking of something God has done for men, and not of some merely human activity.[40]

God is the subject, man is the object, Christ is the means.

Because man is given the new standing of being reconciled to God, he also has "the ministry of reconciliation" (II Cor. 5:18, ASV), as defined in II Corinthians 5:19 (ASV): "To wit, that God was in Christ reconciling the world unto himself, not reckoning unto them their trespasses." Here is the grand reason for man being reconciled to God, namely, that he is in Christ and in this position God has reconciled man unto Himself. By the act of imputation He does not impute their sins to them, but instead imputed sin to Christ.

[40]Morris, *The Apostolic Preaching* . . . , p. 202.

Of interest is the fact that "the world" (Greek, *kosmos*) is used, meaning something more than believers only. It is rather that Christ in His death made a forensic provision for the entire world and has provided reconciliation for all, not just the elect. It is this important point that makes emphatic the ministry of reconciliation as defined in the latter part of verses 19 and 20 (ASV) : ". . . having committed unto us the word of reconciliation. We are ambassadors therefore on behalf of Christ, as though God were entreating by us: we beseech you on behalf of Christ, be ye reconciled to God." God, having a provision in the death of Christ for all sinners, now can present a "whosoever" gospel. The appeal is that God has already provided reconciliation for all, but it is effective only when received by the personal faith of the individual. The contrast is between provision and application. The provision is for all, the application is to those who believe. Those who are already reconciled to God are the ambassadors through whom the message is delivered to those who have not yet availed themselves of the mercy of God.

The recipient of the message of reconciliation must receive the reconciliation. As Taylor expresses it:

> This passage is also of importance because it is complementary to the truth that it is God, and God alone, who can reconcile men to Himself. As we have already seen, although the verb, "to be reconciled," is passive, it denotes an active process of co-operation on man's part. Man cannot accomplish his reconciliation with God, but he can refuse it.[41]

Commentators have noted that up to II Corinthians 5:20 there is no direct connection of the doctrine of reconciliation with the death of Christ. Verse 21 (ASV) , however, makes plain that the act of reconciliation did not arise in a divine fiat, but in the work of Christ upon the cross: "Him who knew no sin he made to be sin on our behalf; that we might become the righteousness of God in him." It was the act of Christ in becoming sin by the imputation of the sins of the whole world to Him (cf. I John 2:2) that made possible reconciliation of a sinner to God.

Morris brings this out: "For although in these verses the apostle does not specifically mention the death of the Lord, there is not the slightest doubt that he has it in mind. For it is only through this death that man's trespasses are put away on Paul's view, and

[41]Taylor, *Forgiveness* . . . , p. 73.

thus the cross is vividly present to his mind in verses 19, 21."[42]
Forsyth concurs with this interpretation: "The New Testament
at least cannot sever Atonement from Reconciliation. The
greatest passage which says that God was in Christ reconciling
says in the same breath that it was by Christ being made sin for
us. The reconciliation is attached to Christ's death, and to that
as an expiation."[43]

The relationship of redemption, propitiation and reconciliation, therefore, becomes clear. Christ by His death redeemed or
paid the price for sin. This payment constituted a propitiation
or satisfaction of God's righteousness. This freed the love of God
to act in grace toward the sinner in reconciling the sinner to
Himself on the basis that Christ has died in his place. The believer who comes into the position of being in Christ through
faith and through the baptism of the Holy Spirit (I Cor. 12:13)
thus is reconciled to God because God sees him in Christ. The
whole act of reconciliation, therefore, is an act of God, a free gift
to man, provided for all men, effective to those who believe.
Those once estranged in Adam are now reconciled in Christ.

Romans 5:6-11. Considered by some to be just as important as
the passage in II Corinthians, the presentation of the doctrine of
reconciliation in Romans 5 is remarkable in many respects. It
expounds, first of all, the fourfold need of man for reconciliation,
presenting this in climactic order: (1) man's inability, or lack
of strength, in other words, "while we were yet weak" (v. 6,
ASV); (2) man's lack of merit: "ungodly" (v. 6, ASV); (3) man's
lack of righteousness, or his guilt before God: "sinners" (v. 8,
ASV); (4) man's lack of peace with God, being at enmity with
God: "enemies" (v. 10, ASV). From this fourfold indictment, it
is clear that man is without strength to accomplish his own reconciliation. He is without merit or righteousness. He has in fact
sinned against God and stands condemned for his disobedience.
Finally, his moral depravity has placed an insurmountable wall
between him and God, leaving him completely estranged from
God's love and mercy.

Certain theological conclusions also are presented forcibly in
Romans 5. First, it may be observed that the death of Christ is
mentioned in some way in each verse of the passage from verses

[42]Morris, *The Apostolic Preaching . . . ,* p. 203.
[43]Peter T. Forsyth, *The Cruciality of the Cross,* p. 138.

6 to 10. Here the emphasis is clearly on the means of reconciliation. Second, reconciliation is presented as something that man
desperately needs which he has no right to expect, but apart from
which he is utterly estranged from God.

Third, reconciliation is shown to be a work of God rather than
a work of man for God (cf. II Cor. 5:17-21). It is a work which
is objectively toward man, in contrast to propitiation which is
objectively toward God. This is stated in verse 10 (ASV): "For
if, while we were enemies, we were reconciled to God through
the death of his Son, much more, being reconciled, shall we be
saved by his life." The verb forms are passive, indicating that
God is the Actor and man is the recipient. This conclusion is
emphasized in verse 11 (ASV), where it is added, "And not only
so, but we also rejoice in God through our Lord Jesus Christ,
through whom we have now received the reconciliation."

Fourth, reconciliation is presented in this passage as a ground
for assurance. The logic is unanswerable. If Christ died for
sinners who at that time were estranged from God, unable to
reconcile themselves, and without any merit, if God by His
mercy has reconciled sinners to Himself, how much more will
He be merciful to those who are reconciled? In other words, if
God can save a sinner, then the one who is already reconciled
by the death of Christ shall certainly escape the wrath of God.
The child of God is saved "by [or, in] his life" (v. 10, ASV).
The life of Christ mentioned here is the life which was given on
Calvary and which in resurrection continued to provide the
basis for the believer's intercession and advocacy.

Some confusion has arisen because in verse 9 mention is made
of the wrath of God and of justification by the blood of Christ
resulting in salvation from divine judgment. Some, therefore,
have attempted to include this in the work of reconciliation.
Morris, for instance, writes: "There is an objective aspect to
reconciliation, and this may well be held to imply that there
is a sense in which God can be said to be reconciled to man."[44]
Morris ignores, however, that the Bible carefully avoids ever
saying this. It is more accurate to express it as God being
propitiated, and man being reconciled. All agree that there is
a Godward aspect of the atonement; the question is whether
the word "reconciliation" is properly used of this concept.

[44]Morris, *The Apostolic Preaching* . . . , p. 198.

Reconciliation necessarily depends upon other aspects of the work of God in salvation, namely, the redemption provided in respect to sin and the propitiation provided in respect to the righteous demands of God toward the sinner. These having been accomplished, however, God is now free to reconcile a sinner to Himself by declaring him to be in Christ and justified by faith. Technically, we are not saved because God has been propitiated, which is true of all men, nor because mankind as a whole has been provisionally reconciled. The act of salvation is a personal one by which the individual on the basis of all these works of God is placed in Christ, declared righteous, and therefore reconciled to a holy God. Taken as a whole, the Romans passage brings out in bold relief how tremendous is the scope of divine reconciliation, and how intrinsic is the work of Christ on our behalf as providing a basis by which reconciliation can be effected.

Ephesians 2:16. According to this passage, it was God's purpose to reconcile Jew and Gentile in the present age and form from them "one new man, so making peace" (Eph. 2:15, ASV). As Taylor expresses it: "St. Paul is not thinking only of the reconciliation of individuals to God, but also of the creation of a new divine community, the Church of God, in which His work of conciliation in Christ is to find its perfect embodiment."[45] The reconciliation which is afforded the believer in Christ not only reconciled Jew and Gentile in the body of Christ, but reconciled both unto God in the one body, referring to the church as a living organism. Reconciliation, therefore, is effective between men as well as between man and God. Hence it may be regarded as horizontal as well as perpendicular.

Colossians 1:20-22. This passage confirms and expands the universal extent of reconciliation, declaring that reconciliation extends to all things, but especially toward sinful man: "And through him to reconcile all things unto himself, having made peace through the blood of his cross; through him, I say, whether things upon the earth, or things in the heavens. And you, being in time past alienated and enemies in your mind in your evil works, yet now hath he reconciled in the body of his flesh through death, to present you holy and without blemish and unreprovable before him" (ASV).

[45]Taylor, *Forgiveness* . . . , p. 78.

The truth, as it is unfolded in this important passage, treats both the provision and application of reconciliation. All things are provisionally reconciled to God; this new relationship of peace has been made possible through the blood of the cross; it extends to all things, both in heaven and in earth provisionally; its application is specifically to sinners saved by grace who once were alienated and enemies through evil works, but now reconciled and presented holy, without blemish, and unreprovable before God. The act of reconciliation in the death of Christ does not in itself affect reconciliation for the individual, but rather it is provisional and makes possible the reconciliation of the individual. The natural state of the unsaved continues unchanged even after the death of Christ until such time that the reconciling work is made effective in him when he believes. Having believed, however, and coming into a new relationship in Christ, he is considered by God as holy and without blemish and unreprovable, even though his actual state may be far from perfection. This passage again indicates that it is the position of believer before God rather than his spiritual state which is in view. Even now the believer in this act of divine reckoning can be presented before a holy God.

Reconciliation Provided for All

Reconciliation in its provision is intended for all men, and theologians who differ on this subject usually do so by definition of terms. As Shedd writes in connection with his discussion of the vicarious atonement of Christ:

> In answering the question as to the "extent" of Christ's atonement, it must first be settled whether "extent" means its intended application, or its intrinsic value; whether the active or the passive signification of the word is in the mind of the inquirer. If the word means value, then the atonement is unlimited; if it means extending, that is, applying, then the atonement is limited.[46]

Properly understood then, the question of the extent of the atonement does not give basis for the universalist who would teach that all men are saved, for the Bible truly contradicts his concept. On the other hand, it does not support the adherent of limited atonement who would try to make the provision of reconcilia-

[46]Shedd, II, 466.

tion limited to the elect. A proper orthodox point of view is that reconciliation is provided for all, but applied only to the elect.

The main issue in the question of the extent of reconciliation is that of the design of the atonement. If the strict Calvinistic view is correct, God's essential purpose was to save the elect, and out of necessity the death of Christ was directed primarily to this end. A more tenable position, however, is reflected in moderate Calvinistic, Lutheran and Arminian theologians. They, in some cases, retain the essential features of Calvinism but hold that God's purpose in the death of Christ, while including the salvation of the elect, was a broader purpose to render the whole world savable or reconciled in the provisional sense.

The concept of reconciling the whole world has been given the term "unlimited atonement," whereas the more strict Calvinistic position is that of limited atonement. Many moderate Calvinists, while going along with the main tenets of Calvinism, nevertheless hold to unlimited atonement. The question is somewhat theoretical, as most theologians—even the strict Calvinists—agree that the death of Christ forensically was sufficient for all. The question is a technical one of God's purpose in the death of Christ. The best solution, however, is to be found in what Christ actually did. Here the broad statement of II Corinthians 5:19 where God is said to reconcile the "world," should be determinative. Just as redemption and propitiation were for all men (I John 2:2) but are applicable only to those who believe, so also is the work of reconciliation.

This concept of the universality of the provision of reconciliation is borne out in the context in which reconciliation is discussed. In II Corinthians 5:14, emphasis is given to the fact that all were dead spiritually. The three instances of "all" in II Corinthians 5:14-15 seem to be universal. This is followed by the limited application indicated in the phrase "they that live." Hence, the passage reads: "For the love of Christ constraineth us; because we thus judge, that one died for all [universal], therefore all [universal] died; and he died for all [universal], that they that live [restricted to elect] shall no longer live unto themselves, but unto him who for their sakes died and rose again" (II Cor. 5:14-15, ASV). The word "all" is used, then, in a universal sense in this passage, followed by the restricted application indicated in the phrase "they that live." This is reinforced by the use of the word "world," referring to all men, in verse 19.

Reconciliation Applied to the Elect When They Believe

The reconciling work of Christ for all men does not become effective even for the elect until that moment of faith in Christ in which they pass from death unto life. Ephesians 2:1 (ASV), referring to the Ephesian Christians, plainly indicates that even though they were elect prior to their salvation, they were "dead through . . . trespasses and sins." Because of this, they lived according to the pattern of the world and "were by nature children of wrath, even as the rest" (Eph. 2:3b, ASV). What is true of the Ephesian Christians is true today. Though the death of Christ occurred centuries ago, even the elect are not saved in any sense until reconciliation is applied. It is for this reason that the responsibility of carrying the message of reconciliation is pressed upon those who have already believed, and they are exhorted to carry the message to others.

Reconciliation in Relation to the Nonelect

The question may fairly be asked, What benefit is the death of Christ to those who have not received Him as Saviour? An unbeliever goes on to his eternal doom in much the same manner as if Christ had not died. If God has provisionally reconciled the whole world to Himself, how does this affect the unsaved, if at all?

The answer seems to be that the basis for his condemnation and judgment has been essentially changed. Apart from the death of Christ, a sinner would have been committed to his eternal punishment regardless of what he had done. Even if he had placed faith in God, he would still be in Adam, and there would be no provision of reconciliation or salvation for him. The provision having been made, however, the whole world is placed in an entirely different light. A person now proceeds to eternal punishment not because God has failed to provide, or because the love of God has been ineffective, but rather because he has rejected that which God has provided. This is set forth plainly in John 3:18 (ASV): "He that believeth on him is not judged: he that believeth not hath been judged already, because he hath not believed on the name of the only begotten Son of God." The condemnation of the sinner now is not simply because he is a sinner, but because he has rejected God's provision to care for his sin. Though he is still judged according to his works, his eternal punishment has a new character of being that which he chose in rejecting the love and grace in Christ.

Reconciliation in Relation to the Universe

One of the reasons why the death of Christ needed to extend to the entire world, not just to the elect, is the fact that the curse of sin inflicted on the universe by Adam had an effect far beyond the bounds of the human race. According to Romans 8:22 (ASV), "The whole creation groaneth and travaileth in pain together until now." The whole universe is laboring under the curse of God, which is manifested in many ways in nature as well as in man. It is for this reason that Colossians 1:20 (ASV) speaks of reconciling "all things unto himself," and specifically extends this reference to "things upon the earth, or things in the heavens." The question may be raised, however, as to what extent reconciliation actually extends to the earth. Grace, seemingly, is unknown to the angels, except as they observe it in the relationship of God to man. The fallen angels have no offer of salvation and, having once sinned, are doomed. The physical universe, however, having been cursed by the sin of Adam, is destined to have this curse relieved in the future millennial reign of Christ when the desert will once again blossom as a rose, and satanic power will be inactive. Ultimately God will destroy the present physical universe and replace it with a holy universe which stems from the reconciling work of Christ.

The Results of Reconciliation

In its broadest sense, the work of reconciliation extends to the total work of God on the behalf of the believer, while redemption is active toward the payment of the price for sin, and propitiation is directed to satisfaction of the righteousness of God. Reconciliation, then, deals with man's total need and total restoration. These certain aspects, however, should be mentioned specifically:

1. The baptism of the Spirit (I Cor. 12:13) is the work of God by which the believer is united to the body of Christ and comes

into his new position "in Christ." This, of course, is the key to the whole reconciling work of God.

2. In regeneration, the believer becomes a new creation, having received the very eternal life of God. Just as Adam became a natural man by having breathed into his body the breath of life, so the unregenerated man at the moment of salvation in Christ has breathed into his spiritually dead body the eternal life of God. As such, he is a new creature with a new nature and a new destiny.

3. By justification, the believer is declared righteous before God, because he is now in Christ. In this position there is imputed to him the righteousness of Christ and he is accepted as perfect in the presence of God.

4. The new position in Christ and His justification assures the believer's positional sanctification in which he is set apart as holy to God.

5. In his new position, as reconciled to God, the believer has the possibility of intimate fellowship with God assisted by the indwelling presence of the triune God and the transformation of his character through the new birth. Reconciliation, while essentially positional, has an experiential aspect as the believer walks in fellowship with God.

6. Ultimate sanctification is also assured the one who is thus reconciled to God, in which the believer's spiritual state is elevated to his high position.

7. The final state of reconciliation is that of glorification in the presence of God in which the last evidences of sin are destroyed and the believer stands perfect and complete, sharing the very glory of Christ in heaven.

10

CHRIST IN HIS RESURRECTION

The resurrection of Jesus Christ is one of the fundamental truths of Christian faith. The early disciples were impelled to bear their testimony for Christ because of their belief that Jesus Christ had actually died and risen bodily from the grave. James Orr has made the following comment:

> A first fact attested by all witnesses is that *Jesus died and was buried.* St. Paul sums up the unanimous belief of the early Church on this point in the words: "That Christ died for our sins according to the Scriptures, and that He was buried." The reality of Christ's death, as against the swoon theories, was touched on before, and need not be re-argued.[1]

The Old Testament forms an important background to the New Testament doctrine of the resurrection. J. Dwight Pentecost writes,

> From the Old Testament we learn these facts. First, there is resurrection from the dead. Second, resurrection is universal; it is for all men. Third, there are two kinds of resurrection: there is the resurrection to life and resurrection to death; there is resurrection for the righteous and resurrection for the wicked. We notice another fact from the Old Testament: not only would men rise to live again, but Jesus Christ, God's Messiah, God's Son, would be resurrected from the dead.[2]

From the standpoint of an apologetic for Christian theology, belief in Jesus Christ as the Son of God stands or falls with the question of His bodily resurrection. As Paul concluded in I Corinthians 15:17, "If Christ be not raised, your faith is vain; ye are yet in your sins." The resurrection, therefore, is properly considered a proof of the person of Christ, His deity, Messiahship, and His power to save from sin. Upon the resurrection

---

[1]James Orr, *The Resurrection of Jesus*, p. 92.
[2]J. Dwight Pentecost, *Things Which Become Sound Doctrine*, p. 145.

hangs the value and effectiveness of all His work in the past, present and future. The resurrection of Christ is also related to the proper fulfillment of prophecy concerning resurrection in both the Old and New Testaments, and is demanded by the concept of the infallibility of the Scriptures.

The doctrine of the resurrection of Christ is also strategic in that it is the first step in this series in the exaltation of Christ: (1) His resurrection; (2) His ascension to heaven and return to His preincarnate glory; (3) His exaltation in being seated at the right hand of the Father and the Father's throne; (4) His second coming to the earth in power and glory; (5) His occupying the throne of David as Ruler of the millennial earth; (6) His exaltation as Judge of all men at the great white throne; (7) His exaltation in the new heaven and the new earth.

From the standpoint of the ministry of Christ, the resurrection is the introduction to a new phase of His work on behalf of the saints. Resurrection was preparatory to His return to glory and to His present ministry as our Intercessor at the right hand of the Father. All His future work stems from His second coming and events related to the millennial kingdom. Few doctrines of the Christian faith are more necessary to the whole structure than the doctrine of resurrection. It is for this reason that the apostles and evangelical Christians through the centuries have placed such emphasis upon this doctrine.

EVIDENCES FOR THE RESURRECTION OF CHRIST

The resurrection is the cornerstone of any defense of the Christian faith. Upon it rests everything that is essential to Christian theology. Evidences for the resurrection are so abundant that they constitute one of the greatest apologetics for Christianity. These fall in various classifications.

The Resurrection Appearances: An Overwhelming Historic Proof

A careful study of the Scriptures will reveal the following order of events unfolded in the resurrection appearances of Christ:

1. According to Matthew 28:2-4, the guards saw an angel roll away the stone from the tomb, and because of this they were

terrified. The Scriptures in this way account for the illegal act of breaking the Roman seal placed on the door of the tomb and for the ineffectiveness of the guard to prevent removal of the body. The report of the soldiers suggested by the chief priest (Matt. 28:11-15), that someone stole the body while they slept, is false on the face of it. The probability is that Christ was raised from the tomb shortly after sundown the night before, and the opening of the tomb was not to allow Christ to come out but was a means of permitting others to enter and see the empty tomb.

2. Shortly after the stone was rolled away, Mary Magdalene, Mary the mother of James, Salome and others arrived at the tomb (Matt. 28:1, 5-7; Mark 16:1-11; Luke 24:1-10; John 20:1).

3. Upon learning that the stone was rolled away and hearing the announcement of the angel that Christ was raised from the dead, Mary Magdalene ran to tell the apostles, with the other women following more slowly (Matt. 28:8; Mark 16:8; Luke 24:8-10; John 20:2).

4. Upon informing the apostles, Mary Magdalene returned, preceded by Peter and John, and saw the empty tomb (John 20:2-10). She apparently did not understand at this time that Christ was actually raised from the dead, even though she had been told this by the angel.

5. The first appearance of Christ was to Mary Magdalene as she remained at the site of the tomb after Peter and John had left. Here she saw Christ and first mistook Him for the gardener but immediately recognized Him when He spoke to her (John 20:11-17; cf. Mark 16:9-11).

6. After she had seen the risen Lord, Mary Magdalene returned to report the appearance of Christ to her (Mark 16:10-11; John 20:18).

7. The second appearance of Christ was to the other women who were also returning to the tomb and saw Christ on the way (Matt. 28:9-10). The best texts seem to indicate that the phrase "as they went to tell his disciples" is an interpolation, and they were actually returning after telling the disciples.

8. The record of the guards concerning the angel's rolling away the stone is another testimony to the resurrection of Christ from unwilling witnesses (Matt. 28:11-15).

9. The third appearance was to Peter in the afternoon of the

resurrection day. Concerning this there are no details, but it is most significant that Christ first sought out Peter, the denier, of all the twelve (Luke 24:34; I Cor. 15:5).

10. The fourth appearance of Christ was to the disciples as they walked on the road to Emmaus. Due to supernatural withholding of recognition, Christ was able to expound to them the Old Testament scriptures concerning His death and resurrection, and was not known to them until He broke bread (Mark 16:12-13; Luke 24:13-35).

11. The fifth appearance of the resurrected Christ was to the ten disciples (Mark 16:14; Luke 24:36-43; John 20:19-23). Mark's account refers to them as the eleven, but it is obvious from the context that only ten were there, as Thomas was absent. After the departure of Judas, the remaining disciples were often referred to as the "eleven" even if all were not actually present. In a similar way, Paul refers to the "twelve" as witnesses of the resurrection (I Cor. 15:5), but actually Judas Iscariot was already dead.

12. The sixth appearance was to the eleven disciples a week after His resurrection. At this time Thomas was present (John 20:26-29).

13. The seventh appearance was to seven disciples by the Sea of Galilee (John 21:1-23). On this occasion He talked significantly to Simon Peter following the miraculous catch of fish.

14. The eighth appearance was to five hundred and is recited by Paul as an outstanding proof of His resurrection (I Cor. 15:6).

15. The ninth appearance was to James, the Lord's brother (I Cor. 15:7). There is some evidence that James was not a believer prior to the resurrection (John 7:3-5), but immediately after the resurrection he is numbered among the believers (Acts 1:14; Gal. 1:19). He later became one of the outstanding leaders in the apostolic church.

16. The tenth appearance was to eleven disciples on the mountain in Galilee. On that occasion He gave them the Great Commission to preach the gospel (Matt. 28:16-20). A similar commission is given in Mark 16:15-18 which may have been the same instance or an earlier appearance.

17. The eleventh appearance occurred at the time of His ascension from the Mount of Olives (Luke 24:44-53; Acts 1:3-9).

This is the last appearance of Christ to His disciples prior to His glorification in heaven.

18. The twelfth appearance of the resurrected Christ was to Stephen just prior to his martyrdom (Acts 7:55-56).

Subsequent appearances, while different in character, are confirmatory of the fact of His resurrection.

19. The thirteenth appearance of Christ was to Paul on the road to Damascus as he was about to continue his work of persecuting Christians (Acts 9:3-6; cf. Acts 22:6-11; 26:13-18). On this occasion Paul was converted.

20. The fourteenth appearance seems to have been to Paul in Arabia (Acts 20:24; 26:17; Gal. 1:12, 17). This appearance is not clearly stated but may be implied from Galatians 1:12. Some believe that the instructions to Paul, which he mentions in Acts 26:17, were given to him in Arabia, not at the original appearance on the road to Damascus. There is no record of the precise revelation given to Paul in Acts 9 or Acts 22. In Acts 22:10 he is promised a later revelation which would give him the necessary instruction.

21. The fifteenth appearance of Christ was to Paul in the temple when Paul was warned concerning the persecution which was to come (Acts 22:17-21; cf. 9:26-30; Gal. 1:18).

22. The sixteenth appearance of Christ was to Paul while in prison in Caesarea, when it is recorded that "the Lord stood by him," and told him that he would bear witness in Rome (Acts 23:11).

23. The final and seventeenth appearance of Christ was to the Apostle John at the beginning of the revelation given to him (Rev. 1:12-20).

Taken as a whole, the appearances are of such various character and to so many people under so many different circumstances that the proof of the resurrection of Christ is as solid as any historical fact that could be cited in the first century.

The Empty Tomb as a Witness to the Resurrection of Christ

All the evidence that exists concerning the tomb after the resurrection of Christ indicates that it was empty. This was the testimony of the disciples who carefully examined the tomb when they found the stone rolled away. The guard who was stationed at the tomb, according to Matthew's account, also reported that the tomb was empty. Only these three explanations are even possibilities:

1. It has been suggested that the disciples may have chanced upon the wrong tomb. This, however, is refuted not only by the presence of the angels, but by the Roman guard who certainly would not have been guarding the wrong tomb.

2. The soldiers themselves made the suggestion that someone had stolen the body while they slept. If this had been the case, the guard would have been summarily executed. Instead, according to Matthew's account, they were given money to spread the false story that someone had stolen the body. This was obviously an attempt at bribery to prevent the truth being told and was gladly accepted by the soldiers as it also assured them of intervention with the Roman authorities so that they would not be executed.

3. The complete lack of evidence for any alternative leaves the account of the resurrection of Christ the only plausible explanation. If it were not that this were supernatural and so intrinsic to the whole Christian faith, it would not even have been questioned. When the evidence of the empty tomb is added to the many other arguments for the bodily resurrection of Christ, it forms additional proof of the genuineness of the entire narrative. There would have been no motive on the part of the disciples to steal the body in the first place, and if the enemies of Christ had taken the body it would have been to their interest to have produced it when the accounts of the resurrection began to be circulated. There is no evidence, however, that the enemies of Christ made any effort to try to find the supposedly stolen body of Christ. The empty tomb remains a silent but eloquent witness to the fact of the resurrection.

The Character of the Human Witnesses to the Resurrection

It is clear from the accounts given in the Gospels that the witnesses to the resurrection of Christ were quite reluctant to believe their senses concerning this important event. Only when overwhelming proof was presented did they at long last accept the fact of His resurrection. The disciples certainly could not have been fooled in identifying Christ, as they knew Him well. They themselves, however, demanded tangible evidence such as Thomas required when he was not present at the first appearance of Christ to the eleven. There does not seem to have been any expectation on the part of the disciples that Christ would rise from the dead, even though He had told them plainly that this would be the case. Once the evidence was produced that Christ had actually been raised from the dead, no amount of persecution could make them waver in their testimony. They repeatedly showed willingness to die rather than give up their faith in Christ as their resurrected Lord. The reluctant testimony of the soldiers as well as the grudging admission of the leaders of the Jews add a touch of reality to the fact of Christ's resurrection.

The Dramatic Change in the Disciples After the Resurrection

One of the impressive arguments for the genuineness of the resurrection of Christ was the contrast in the disciples before and after the resurrection. Scripture indicates that the disciples before the resurrection were utterly disheartened, were meeting in fear in obscure places and were dismayed at the death of Christ. There is no indication in any of the narratives describing the disciples prior to the resurrection that they entertained any real hope that Christ would be restored to them in resurrection. On the day of resurrection itself, there is no evidence that they were credulous or accepted the testimony of the resurrection of Christ without requiring definite proof. It was evidently hard for them to believe their senses when they actually saw Christ risen. Once they were convinced, however, the disciples were joyous and fearless and, as illustrated in the case of Peter, bore a public testimony to the fact of the resurrection, challenging their hearers to consider the evidence. In their attitude before the resurrection of Christ as well as in their subsequent renewed hope and faith, their experiences followed a normal pattern, and there is no indication of accepting the fact of the resurrection apart from the solid proofs which were theirs in the postresurrectional appearances.

The Disciples' Experience of Divine Power in the Postresurrection Period

The book of Acts cites the evidence of the supernatural power of God in the ministry of the apostles. The book is, in a sense, the acts of the Holy Spirit rather than of the apostles themselves. The predicted power of the Spirit that would come upon them on the day of Pentecost was fulfilled in chapter 2 and in the subsequent experience of the church. Jews and Gentiles were transformed under the power of the gospel as they believed in a Christ who had died for them and arose again. The gospel was attested by supernatural acts of healing, by the divine judgment of Ananias and Sapphira, by the supernatural appearance of Christ to Saul, and numerous other events in which the supernatural power of God was evident. The book of Acts would have been meaningless and impossible if it had not been for an actual resurrection of Christ from the dead. The transforming power of Christ witnessed to by Christians through the ages is likewise without explanation if Christ did not actually rise. The book of Acts, therefore, can be considered a massive confirmation of the doctrine of resurrection.

The Evidence of the Day of Pentecost

Outstanding in the book of Acts is the support of the resurrection afforded in the events of the day of Pentecost. This event in itself is a demonstration of the power of God, but is attended by human phenomena which would be without proper explanation if Christ had not actually arisen from the dead. The day of Pentecost, occurring only fifty days after the death and resurrection of Christ, was the occasion for the sermon by Peter on the doctrine of resurrection as thousands gathered to hear. Those who listened to Peter had access to the garden where the tomb was located, and had undoubtedly investigated the reports of the resurrection of Christ which were commonly discussed in Jerusalem. As Peter declared the resurrection of Christ, there was no contradiction from the multitudes. The record indicates that instead of offering rebuttal to his assertion three thousand people, who were in a position to know the facts, believed that Jesus Christ had actually been raised from the dead. It is evident that Peter's confident assertion that Christ actually arose in fulfillment of the Old Testament prophecies of David, as recorded in Psalm 16:10-11, must have stemmed not only from his own personal conviction that these were the facts, but also from confidence that there was no one competent to contradict them. The events of Pentecost would be left without a reasonable explanation if Jesus Christ had not been raised from the dead.

The Evidence in the Custom of Observing the First Day of the Week

Early in the apostolic church, it was the custom of believers to gather on the first day of the week and observe it as a special day of worship and praise. On this day they observed the Lord's Supper and would bring their offerings (Acts 20:7; I Cor. 16:2). Orr states:

> It is the uncontradicted testimony of all the witnesses that it *was* the *Easter morning*, or, as the Evangelists call it, "the first day of the week," or *third day* after the Crucifixion, on which the event known as the Resurrection happened; in other words, that Jesus rose from the dead *on the third day*. The four Evangelists, whatever their other divergences, are agreed about this. The Apostle Paul, who had conversed with the original witnesses only eight or nine years after the event, confirms the statement, and declares it to be the general belief of the Church.[3]

From the first century, the great majority of Christians have continued to observe the first day of the week as a special day of religious significance. The only explanation that has a historic foundation of this change from the seventh day of rest to the first day of the week as a day of worship was that Christ rose from the dead on that day. The historic custom fully attested by the history of the church is therefore another compelling argument that Christ actually arose from the dead.

Milligan shows the convincing character of this change in custom:

> We have the institution of the Lord's day, of which there are traces within a week of the Resurrection, and which no one will dream of denying was expressly designed to commemorate that event. Surely there must have been a depth of conviction as well as an amount of power difficult to estimate, in a belief that could lead to such an institution. Nor

[3]Orr, pp. 114-15.

do we see the full force of this until we remember the totally different conceptions which the Sabbath and the Lord's day expressed,—the one the last day of the week, when man, weary of the work of the world, sought the joyful strength of God in which to face it; the one commemorating the close of the old creation, the other, the beginning of the new . . . it was believed that Jesus rose from the grave on that first morning of the week. It was this fact that made the difference, and a more powerful testimony to men's conviction of the truth of the event within a week after it is said to have happened, it would be impossible to produce.[4]

The Origin of the Christian Church

The historical existence of the Christian church from the first century is explained as stemming from the belief in the resurrection of Christ. Only such definite proof of the deity of Christ would have given the church the convincing power that it needed in the gospel witness. The dynamic which characterized the early church can be explained only on the basis that Christ actually arose from the dead. In the years since, millions of believers have been blessed and transformed by faith in Jesus Christ as their risen Saviour and Lord. If the resurrection is a myth, there is no adequate explanation for the power of the early church in its witness and for the willingness of its adherents even to die rather than renounce their Christian faith. The continuity of the church through the centuries, in spite of ignorance, unbelief and erosion of doctrine, would be difficult to explain if there were not a solid basis for its origination and continuation in the historic resurrection of Christ. Those who investigate the facts concerning the resurrection of Christ as contained in the Scripture certainly have abundant evidence on which to rest their faith in Jesus Christ as their Saviour and God.

THE RESURRECTION BODY

The facts concerning the resurrection body of Christ have been obscured by the modern rejection of the details of Christ's resurrection as recorded in the Scriptures. Liberals and neoorthodox scholars have summarily rejected the facts of the scriptural records, often with hardly any supporting argument. Common among such scholars is the view that Christ arose only in a

[4]William Milligan, *The Resurrection of Our Lord*, pp. 68-69.

spiritual sense—that He enjoyed continued existence after His death, but not a bodily resurrection.

Though no new evidence has been advanced in support of this rejection of Scripture, the technique has been to assume that the gospel narratives are in serious contradiction of each other, and that what actually happened is that Christ appeared to the disciples in visions or dreams. With no documentary proof whatever, they consider the accounts of the appearances of Christ on the resurrection day and immediately subsequent to it as later fabrications. Even Filson, who seems to accept the fact of the resurrection of Christ, in one sentence sweeps all the resurrection-day appearances into discard in his statement: "Most likely the first appearances to the apostles were in Galilee, and this led to a rallying of the believers in Jerusalem where such appearances continued."[5]

Though many liberal arguments have been so soundly refuted as to have fallen into discard even among liberals (such as the swoon theory, the imposture theory, the wrong-tomb theory, and the wishful credulity of the disciples), the modern mind still assumes that the resurrection is an impossibility and that early Christians were deceived either by their own senses or by other men. On the contrary, conservative scholarship has demonstrated for many generations that the scriptural accounts are self-sustaining, that they do not contain differences which cannot be reconciled, and in fact offer a web of interrelated facts which make the resurrection of Christ one of the best attested facts of the ancient world. If Scripture may be considered as reliable and infallible revelation, it is found to unfold a marvelous doctrine of resurrection as illustrated in the resurrection of Christ Himself.

The resurrection body of Christ is not only an important aspect of scriptural revelation unfolding the nature of Christ's resurrection, but is significant of the fact and character of the resurrection which believers in Christ may anticipate. The resurrection of Christ is at once an apologetic for His deity and His substitutionary death on the cross, and at the same time is substantiating evidence of the important place of the future resurrection of saints in the eschatological program of God. Although the doctrine of resurrection is discussed theologically in I Corinthians

[5]Floyd V. Filson, *Jesus Christ the Risen Lord*, p. 49.

15:12-50, the principal source of information is found in the accounts of Christ after His resurrection. Here, for the first time in history, occurs bodily resurrection which is more than restoration—the creation of a new body similar in some respects to the body laid in the tomb but in other important aspects dramatically different. Christ is given a new kind of body in contrast to those restored to life miraculously prior to the resurrection of Christ, such as Lazarus whose body was restored to what it was before he died.

The Resurrection Body of Christ Identified with the Body Laid in the Tomb

At least eight features identify the body of Christ raised from the dead as the same body which was laid in the tomb:

1. The nailprints in His hands and feet were retained in the resurrection body of Christ (Ps. 22:16; Zech. 12:10; John 20:25-29). The Scriptures both prophetically and historically record this important fact which would lead to the conclusion that the resurrection body is the old body transformed rather than the creation of a new body entirely different.

2. According to John 20:25-29, the resurrection body also retains the wound which was inflicted in His side on the cross. It was this identification which distinguished Christ from the others who died with Him and was one of the signs demanded by Thomas as proof of His bodily resurrection (John 20:25).

3. In His various appearances after His resurrection, Christ was readily recognized by His disciples as the same Person who died and rose again. Any hesitation in recognizing the resurrection of Christ is given special explanation in the Scriptures. Mary Magdalene, who because she was in tears did not immediately recognize Christ, identified Him as her Lord by His voice (John 20:16), even though she apparently had her back turned when He spoke to her. There seems to be no hesitation on the part of the women who met Him or in any of the other appearances except in the case of the disciples who met Him on the road to Emmaus (Luke 24:13-35). Here their delay in recognizing Him is attributed to the fact that they were supernaturally blinded (Luke 24:16, 31). The disciples were so certain of their identification of their risen Lord that they were willing to lay down their lives for this truth.

4. In Christ's appearance to His disciples in the upper room, He deliberately ate food to prove to them that He was not just a spirit and had actually risen from the grave (Luke 24:41-43).

5. The resurrection body of Christ had a material nature which could be felt. According to Matthew 28:9, the women held Him by the feet when they worshiped Him. In the appearance of Luke 24:39, He invites them to handle Him. In His first appearance to Mary Magdalene in John 20:17, it is implied that Mary clung to Him in a physical embrace, prompting Christ to say to her, "Touch me not" (literally, "Do not cling to me").

6. It is evident from these facts already itemized that the resurrection body of Christ was visible to the natural eye though it also had the capacity of disappearing in a miraculous way. This is illustrated in John 20:20 (ASV): "The disciples therefore were glad, when they saw the Lord."

7. According to John 20:22, the resurrection body of Christ had the ability of breathing and to this extent corresponded to a natural body.

8. Christ specifically states of His resurrection body that it possessed flesh and bone (Luke 24:39-40), thereby refuting the idea of the disciples that they were seeing merely a spirit when Christ appeared to them. Confirming these identifying features of the body of Christ raised from the dead is the fact of the empty tomb. Christ in His resurrection did not receive another body but the same body.

The Resurrection Body of Christ Changed

After His resurrection Christ manifested certain characteristics which were not seen before His death. Though there seems to be little question in the Bible of the identity of the resurrection body, these new qualities were added which distinguished it from the body laid in the tomb:

1. Christ in His resurrection body had a newness of life and a deliverance from the sufferings of His death to such an extent that on several occasions His recognition was somewhat delayed as in the case of Mary Magdalene who mistook Him for the gardener and the disciples on the road to Emmaus (Luke 24:31; John 20:16). The delay in recognition, however, is explained by other factors and is no greater than one would naturally

expect considering the tremendous transformation of resurrection.

2. The ordinary limitations of transportation and distance did not seem to restrict Christ after His resurrection. Though before His death He would become weary from long journeys, there is no evidence that His various appearances to His disciples required such ordinary means of transportation. He apparently was delivered from many of the limitations of time and space.

3. The resurrection body of Christ was characterized as having flesh and bones, but He did not seem to be restricted by physical barriers. This is evident in the fact that He could enter closed rooms without apparent difficulty (Luke 24:36; John 20:19).

4. Christ was able to appear and disappear at will after His resurrection (Luke 24:15; John 20:19).

5. No proof is offered in the Scriptures that the resurrection body of Christ required either rest or food to sustain it. Though He could eat, there is no evidence that He needed food to supply nourishment, and there is no mention of Christ sleeping after His resurrection. Insofar as Christ's resurrection body accommodated itself to the conditions of time and space, it was in keeping with the evident purpose of Christ to minister to His disciples prior to His ascension.

The Glory of the Resurrection Body

Although many of the features of the resurrection body of Christ were revealed in the Scriptures immediately after His resurrection, it is evident that some aspects were delayed in manifestation until after His ascension. During the forty days of His ministry between the resurrection and His ascension, there was no unusual outward appearance of glory such as had occurred on the Mount of Transfiguration prior to His death. It is evident that His ultimate glory was veiled in order to make possible a ministry to His disciples in scenes on earth. After His ascension into heaven, Christ never appeared again apart from His glory. In Acts 7:56, Stephen saw Christ standing at the right hand of the Father in the midst of the glory of God. In the appearance of Christ to Paul recorded in Acts 9:3-6, the glory of Christ was such that Paul was blinded. A similar experience befell the Apostle John in Revelation 1:12-20, where John fell at the feet of Christ as one dead when he beheld the glory of Christ in His resurrection.

From these indications, it is safe to conclude that the resurrection body of Christ possesses an intrinsic glory which mortal man cannot behold under ordinary circumstances. This glory was temporarily veiled until the time of Christ's ascension, but is now a permanent aspect of His resurrection body. The hope of believers for a resurrection body includes not only the features of the resurrection body manifested in Christ prior to the ascension, but also additional glorious features that will suit our bodies for the glorious presence of God. The resurrection body of believers not only includes the physical and visible aspects attributed to Christ's body but also involves the fact that our resurrection body will be similar to His in nature (Eph. 5:27; Phil. 3:21; I John 3:2).

WHO RAISED CHRIST FROM THE DEAD?

Like other important acts of God foundational to the Christian faith, the resurrection of Christ is related to each Member of the divine Trinity. God the Father is said to have raised Christ from the dead in numerous passages. This is implied in the Old Testament prophecy of the resurrection of Christ found in Psalm 16:10-11 where His deliverance from Sheol and corruption is attributed to God. Peter cites Psalm 16 in Acts 2:24-32 in relating the resurrection of Christ to God. A similar statement is made in Acts 13:30 where Paul states, "God raised him from the dead." The resurrection of Christ is specifically related to the Father in Romans 6:4 and Ephesians 1:19-20.

Without contradicting the participation of the Father in the resurrection of Christ, the Scriptures also reveal that Christ raised Himself from the dead. In John 2:19 Christ declared, "Destroy this temple, and in three days I will raise it up." A similar statement is made in John 10:17-18 where Christ claimed not only to have power to lay down His life but to take it up again. The work of the Holy Spirit in relation to the resurrection of Christ is less clear. The only reference to it in Romans 8:11 draws a parallel between the resurrection of Christ and the giving of life to the believers which, in both cases, is accomplished "through his Spirit that dwelleth in you." However, some have interpreted this passage to refer to the resurrection on the part of the Father in which the Holy Spirit somehow participated.

The relation of the resurrection of Christ to the three Persons of the Trinity is not, however, a contradiction. In other important works of God, such as the creation of the world and the incarnation of Christ, a similar participation of each Member of the Trinity can be observed. In revelation, however, the unity of the Trinity as well as Their distinction in persons is carefully supported, and no contradiction remains for one who accepts the doctrine of the Trinity. It is indeed the work of the triune God.

THE SIGNIFICANCE OF THE RESURRECTION OF CHRIST

All branches of systematic theology have tended to underestimate the significance of the resurrection of Christ. Orthodox scholars usually emphasize the apologetic significance of the resurrection as an attestation to the deity of Christ and the value of His substitutionary death. The resurrection of Christ is normally held to be a proof of the future resurrection of the saints. Often neglected, however, is the relation of the resurrection of Christ to His present work.

In liberal theology, the resurrection of Christ is rejected as a nonessential, and the conclusion is reached that Christ continues to exist after His death but not in a body. Scriptures relating to the subject are spiritualized or explained away. As James Orr noted a generation ago, the tendency now is to deny the resurrection as impossible, and therefore untrue.[6]

More important, however, than the liberal view in contemporary theology, is the neoorthodox concept of the resurrection of Christ. Though the more conservative of neoorthodox scholars tend to recognize the resurrection of Christ as a historic fact, they claim that in itself it does not have historic significance. Emphasis is placed upon the experience of Christ in the believer rather than in the fact of the empty tomb.

Richard R. Niebuhr has discussed at length the problems that the modern Protestant mind has in accepting the resurrection of Jesus Christ. In his introduction of the conflict between resurrection and the ideas of history Niebuhr writes,

[6]Orr, pp. 14 ff.

The intense analysis of the New Testament produced by the great age of historical investigation has emphasized, among other things, this fact that belief in Jesus as the risen Lord informs every part of the early church's thought. But the rise of historical criticism has also made it increasingly difficult for theologians and biblical scholars to accept the New Testament order of thought. They have felt obliged to remove the resurrection of Jesus from its central position and to place it on the periphery of Christian teaching and proclamation, because the primitive resurrection faith conflicts disastrously with modern canons of historicity.[7]

His subsequent discussion discloses the dilemma of modern scholars who on the one hand reject the actual event of the resurrection of Christ as a miracle, and yet have to account for its prominent place in the New Testament narrative.[8]

If accepted in the normal meaning of words, Scripture establishes the orthodox position concerning the resurrection as a proof of His person and His offices and at the same time demonstrates that the resurrection of Christ is the key to all of His present work as well as the consummation of the divine plan in the prophetic future. For the present discussion, only these major facets of the significance of the resurrection can be sketched.

The Resurrection Is a Proof of the Person of Christ

It is significant that the meaning of the three official names of Christ, namely, Lord Jesus Christ, is substantiated by His resurrection from the dead. The title Lord, usually regarded as a declaration of His deity and authority over all creation, is based on the assumption that Jesus Christ is the Son of God. Though in His life He offered many substantiating evidences, the supreme proof of His deity is the solid fact of His resurrection. It was this argument which Peter used in his Pentecostal sermon when he declared on the basis of the fact of His resurrection that Jesus is "both Lord and Christ" (Acts 2:36). Peter used the same argument of the resurrection of Christ in his presentation of the gospel to Cornelius (Acts 10:40). In the introduction to the epistle to the Romans, the Apostle Paul stated that Christ was

[7]Richard R. Niebuhr, *Resurrection and Historical Reason*, p. 1.
[8]Niebuhr cites Bultmann, Barth, C. H. Dodd, John Knox, Jacob Burkhardt, Strauss, Herrmann, Harnack, Schweitzer, William Adams Brown, John Baillie, Reman, H. N. Wieman, Lionel Phornton and Brunner as contributors to the discussion supporting denial of the resurrection as a miraculous event, although their treatment varies considerably (*Ibid.*, pp. 2-31).

"declared to be the Son of God with power, according to the spirit of holiness, by the resurrection from the dead." The early disciples considered the resurrection of Christ to be the final and convincing evidence that Jesus was all that He claimed to be, the very Son of God who existing from all eternity had become incarnate to fulfill the plan of God in His life, death and resurrection. The resurrection of Christ is, therefore, an important proof of His deity and has been so regarded by orthodox scholars from apostolic days to the present.

In the title Christ as attributed to the Lord Jesus is embodied the hope of Israel for a Messiah to deliver them from their sins. Though the death and resurrection of Christ were anticipated by Old Testament prophecies, Jewish leaders in the time of Christ did not realize their necessity for Him to fulfill His role of Messiah to Israel. It was only by His death that He could provide redemption and claim victory over Satan, and it was in His resurrection that He demonstrated the power of God which was to be ultimately manifested in the deliverance of Israel and the establishment of His righteous kingdom in the earth. The promise to David that He would have a Son who would reign forever is now made possible of fulfillment by Christ in His resurrection body and is in keeping with the claim of Christ that He was the Messiah of Israel (John 4:25-26). The specific relationship of resurrection to His Messianic character is also revealed in His conversation with Martha in John 11:25-27. In a word, it was necessary for Christ to die and to be raised from the dead in order to be what the prophet had anticipated, a Messiah who would be Israel's Deliverer and Saviour throughout all eternity. If Christ had not been raised from the dead, it is evident that His claim to Messiahship would have been thus destroyed. Conversely, the fact of His resurrection establishes His right to be Israel's Messiah in the past as well as in the future.

Jesus, the third title attributed to Christ, meaning "Jehovah saves," was His human name bestowed by the angel. He was given this name because He would "save his people from their sins" (Matt. 1:21). His work as Saviour, however, while inevitably related to His death on the cross, also demanded His resurrection. It was for this reason that Christ was commanded not only to die but to rise from the dead in John 10:17-18. According to John 12:27, where Christ prayed in regard to His death, "Father, save

CHRIST IN HIS RESURRECTION 209

me from this hour," He did not anticipate merely deliverance from death but prayed that if it were necessary to die, He would experience complete deliverance in His resurrection.

Milligan notes that the Greek is literally "save me *out of* this hour" (italics added). Milligan adds: "Our Lord prayed not merely that, if possible, He might escape suffering, but that, if it was impossible for Him to escape it, He would pass through it to a glorious deliverance,—that through death He might be conducted to that life beyond death in which the purpose of His coming was to be reached."[9] It is the uniform presentation of Scripture that His resurrection is a necessary counterpart to His work in death, and apart from His resurrection His death would have become meaningless (John 11:25; Rom. 5:10; 8:34; 10:9; Phil. 2:8-11; Heb. 5:7). The resurrection of Christ is, therefore, the proof of His person and of that which His person effected, namely, His work on the cross.

The Resurrection Is a Proof of His Offices

The three offices of Christ, those of Prophet, Priest and King, are each related to His resurrection. The offices of Christ are one of the major themes of the Old Testament as they relate to Christ. Moses anticipated Christ's office as a Prophet in Deuteronomy 18:18. The priestly office of Christ is prophesied in Psalm 110:4 and His kingly office is in fulfillment of the promise to David in II Samuel 7:16 (cf. Luke 1:31-33).

As a Prophet. The prophetic ministry of Christ, though largely fulfilled on earth prior to His death, needed the authentication of His resurrection to give authority to what He had already said as well as His continued ministry through the Spirit whom He would send (John 16:12-14). If Christ had not been raised from the dead, He would have been a false prophet and all of His ministry as recorded in the Gospels would have been subject to question. In like manner, His postresurrection ministry, bringing into climax much that He had taught before, would have been impossible apart from His bodily resurrection. The resurrection, therefore, constitutes a proof of the validity and authority of His prophetic office.

As a Priest. The resurrection of Christ is clearly related to the continuance of His priestly office. This was anticipated in Psalm

[9]Milligan, p. 125.

210 JESUS CHRIST OUR LORD

110 where Christ is declared to be a Priest eternal in character: "Jehovah hath sworn, and will not repent: Thou art a priest for ever after the order of Melchizedek" (v. 4, ASV). The concept of Christ as a Priest who continues to live forever is further substantiated in Hebrews 7:25 where it is said of Christ, "He ever liveth to make intercession for them." In contrast to ordinary priests, who have their priestly office terminated either by death or retirement as in the Levitical order, the resurrection of Christ made possible His continuance forever as our High Priest. This is the teaching of the New Testament as well as the anticipation of the Old. Hebrews 7:24 (ASV) states it explicitly: "But he, because he abideth for ever, hath his priesthood unchangeable." It is evident from the Scriptures that, apart from the resurrection, Christ's priestly office could not have been fulfilled.

As a King. The third office, that of King, fulfilled especially the anticipation of the Old Testament of a Son who would have the right to rule. Christ was not only to rule over Israel, fulfilling the promise to David of a Son who would reign forever, but over the entire world as the One to whom God has given the right to rule over the nations (Ps. 2:8-9). Christ's continuance on the throne forever after His death, in fulfillment of the plan of God that He should reign over all nations as well as the nation of Israel, would have been impossible if He had not been raised from the dead. His resurrection was essential to His unique fulfillment of each of His divine offices.

The Resurrection of Christ Is Essential to All His Work

Just as the bodily resurrection of Jesus Christ was a proof of His deity and lordship, so also was His resurrection an indispensable evidence of the efficacious value of His death on the cross. Here again, one is faced with the absolute question of whether Christ is all He claims to be. If He did not rise from the dead, then He is not the Son of God, and it follows that His death on the cross is the death of an ordinary man and of no value to others. If, on the other hand, Christ actually rose from the dead, He not only demonstrates by this means that He is indeed all He claims to be but that His work has the value set forth in the Scriptures, namely, a substitutionary sacrifice on behalf of the sins of the whole world.

It is for this reason that so frequently in Scripture the resurrection of Christ is linked with His work on the cross, as in Romans 4:25 (ASV) which states not only that Christ "was delivered up for our trespasses" but that He "was raised for [with a view to] our justification." In like manner, the resurrection of Christ is linked to real faith in Him as in Romans 10:9 (ASV) : "Because if thou shalt confess with thy mouth Jesus as Lord, and shalt believe in thy heart that God raised him from the dead, thou. shalt be saved." The resurrection of Christ and His substitutionary death are twin doctrines which stand or fall together.

As James Orr expressed it: "It seems evident that, if Christ died for men—in Atonement for their sins—it could not be that He should remain permanently in the state of death. That had it been possible, would have been the frustration of the very end of His dying, for if He remained Himself a prey to death, how could He redeem others?"[10] It is significant that those who deny the bodily resurrection of Christ always also deny His substitutionary sacrifice for the sins of the whole world.

The resurrection of Christ has not only a backward look toward the cross demonstrating the power of God in salvation, but it is also the doorway to His present work in heaven. One of the important reasons for the resurrection of Christ was the necessity of a victory such as His resurrection as a prelude to His work in heaven. Orr states, "The Resurrection of Jesus is everywhere viewed as the commencement of His Exaltation. Resurrection, Ascension, Exaltation to the throne in universal dominion go together as parts of the same transaction."[11] At least a dozen important aspects of His present ministry were contingent upon the fact of His resurrection:

Sending the Holy Spirit. The promise of Christ that He would send the Holy Spirit (John 14:26; 15:26; 16:7) was contingent upon His resurrection and His return to glory. The Holy Spirit was sent to continue the ministry of Christ which was, in a sense, suspended when He returned to heaven. As Christ expressed it in John 16:7 (ASV) , "Nevertheless I tell you the truth: It is expedient for you that I go away; for if I go not away, the Comforter will not come unto you; but if I go, I will send him unto you." The major feature of the present age, namely, the ministry of the Spirit, is therefore dependent upon the validity of Christ's

[10]Orr, p. 277.
[11]*Ibid.*, p. 278.

resurrection from the grave and His return to glory as the triumphant, resurrected Saviour.

Bestowing eternal life. Through the Spirit whom Christ sent
to the earth, He is able to bestow eternal life on all those who put
their trust in Him (John 11:25; 12:24-25). If Christ did not
literally rise from the dead, God's program of giving life for
spiritual death through faith in Jesus Christ would become in-
valid. He is able to bestow eternal life by virtue of who He is and
of what He has done in His death and resurrection.

Head of the church and the new creation. In His resurrection
from the dead, Christ also became Head of the new creation as
well as Head of the church. This is stated in Ephesians 1:20-23
(ASV), where the power of God is manifested:

> When he raised him from the dead, and made him to sit at
> his right hand in the heavenly places, far above all rule, and
> authority, and power, and dominion, and every name that
> is named, not only in this world, but also in that which is to
> come: and he put all things in subjection under his feet,
> and gave him to be head over all things to the church, which
> is his body, the fulness of him that filleth all in all.

As the Head of the new creation, He is able to form the church
as His body and give it eternal life. According to I Corinthians
15:45*b* (ASV), "The last Adam became a life-giving spirit." In
a similar manner, according to I Peter 2:4-5 (ASV), Christ comes
as "a living stone" with the result that believers "as living stones,
are built up a spiritual house, to be a holy priesthood, to offer
up spiritual sacrifices, acceptable to God through Jesus Christ."
This power to form the church is further amplified in I Peter 2:9
(ASV): "But ye are an elect race, a royal priesthood, a holy nation, a people for God's own possession, that ye may show forth
the excellencies of him who called you out of darkness into his
marvellous light."

This present undertaking of God like all other aspects of His
present work depends upon the validity of His resurrection and
is essential to His present exalted work. Milligan writes:

> Thus, then, it appears that the Resurrection of our Lord
> brings His work to its first stage of completion; for it per-
> fects the different offices by which the work is accomplished.
> It is an essential part of the work which He left the mansions
> of His Father's glory to perform. If He did not rise from the

dead and return to His Father, He is neither Priest, Prophet, nor King, in the full sense of any of these terms.[12]

The work of Christ as Advocate. The present ministry of Christ in heaven as the Advocate of the believer (I John 2:1, ASV) depends likewise upon His person and His work and is valid only because Christ is who He is and because He died on the cross for our sins and rose in triumph from the grave. It is because "we have an Advocate with the Father, Jesus Christ the righteous." His work as Advocate in turn depends on the fact that "he is the propitiation for our sins; and not for ours only, but also for the whole world" (I John 2:2, ASV) .

The work of Christ in intercession. The resurrection of Christ is specifically linked with His work in intercession in which Christ presents His petitions on behalf of weak and tempted Christians and intercedes for them before the throne of grace. According to Hebrews 7:25 (ASV) , this ministry is dependent on His resurrection: "Wherefore also he is able to save to the uttermost them that draw near unto God through him, seeing he ever liveth to make intercession for them." His resurrection is necessary to His perpetual intercession.

The bestowal of gifts. According to Ephesians 4:11-13, Christ gives gifted men to the church such as apostles, prophets, evangelists, pastors and teachers. His work in thus bestowing gifted men upon the church is, however, dependent on the fact revealed in the preceding verses that "when he ascended on high, he led captivity captive, and gave gifts unto men" (Eph. 4:8, ASV) . Now that He has "ascended far above all the heavens, that he might fill all things" (Eph. 4:10, ASV) , an act, of course, which depended upon His resurrection, He is able to be sovereign in His bestowal of gifts and gifted men.

Impartation of spiritual power. Just as the deliverance of Israel from Egypt was God's divine standard of power in the Old Testament, so the resurrection of Christ from the dead is a divine standard of power in the New Testament, especially in relationship to His work for the church. It was because of who He was and what He was able to do that He could say in Matthew 28:18 (ASV) , "All authority hath been given unto me in heaven and on earth." This standard of power is described especially in Ephesians 1:17-23 where the apostle expresses his prayer that the

12Milligan, pp. 151-52.

Ephesian Christians might "know what is . . . the exceeding greatness of his power to us-ward who believe, according to that working of the strength of his might which he wrought in Christ, when he raised him from the dead, and made him sit at his right hand in the heavenly places" (Eph. 1:18-20, ASV) . It was by virtue of His resurrection that He was able to send the Spirit who would be the channel through which the power would come according to Christ's own prediction in Acts 1:8 (ASV) : "But ye shall receive power, when the Holy Spirit is come upon you: and ye shall be my witnesses both in Jerusalem, and in all Judaea and Samaria, and unto the uttermost part of the earth." It is as the Christian enters into the reality that he has positionally in the risen Christ and becomes a partaker of Christ's victory over death that he is able to realize the power of God in daily living.

The raising of believers to a new position in Christ. It is in keeping with Christ's present work for believers that they be raised to a new position in Christ. According to Ephesians 2:5-6 (ASV) : "Even when we were dead through our trespasses, [God] made us alive together with Christ (by grace have ye been saved) , and raised us up with him, and made us to sit with him in the heavenly places, in Christ Jesus." By virtue of the resurrection of Christ the believer can now be triumphant in his new position, no longer being dead in trespasses and sins in Adam, but raised in newness of life in Christ Jesus.

Christ in His resurrection, the firstfruits from among the dead. In His resurrection from the dead, Christ fulfills the Old Testament anticipation in the Feast of the Firstfruits in that He is the first to be raised from the dead in anticipation of the future resurrection of all believers, as stated in I Corinthians 15:20-23 (ASV) : "But now hath Christ been raised from the dead, the firstfruits of them that are asleep. For since by man came death, by man came also the resurrection of the dead. For as in Adam all die, so also in Christ shall all be made alive. But each in his own order: Christ the firstfruits; then they that are Christ's at his coming." The resurrection of Christ, therefore, is the historical proof substantiating the hope of the believer that he too will be raised from the dead, in keeping with the prediction of Philippians 3:20-21.

Christ is now preparing a place. In the upper room, Christ told His disciples, "In my Father's house are many mansions; if it were not so, I would have told you; for I go to prepare a place for you. And if I go and prepare a place for you, I come again, and will receive you unto myself; that where I am, there ye may be also" (John 14:2-3, ASV). An important aspect of the present work of Christ stemming from His resurrection is that Christ is anticipating future rapture and resurrection of the church and is preparing a place for His bride in heaven. Here again, His present work would be meaningless unless it was supported by a literal resurrection from the dead.

His universal lordship over all creation. In Ephesians 1:20-23 it is brought out that Christ not only became Head over the church by virtue of His resurrection and ascension, but has resumed His position of Lord over all creation. Such would be impossible if He had not been literally raised from the dead as the One who had power to lay down His life and take it again.

Shepherd of the flock. In His death on the cross, Christ fulfilled the anticipation of Psalm 22 that He would die as the good Shepherd for His sheep. In His present ministry, however, Christ fulfilled what is anticipated in Psalm 23 as the great Shepherd who cares for His sheep. His present ministry is anticipated in a number of passages in the New Testament (John 10:14; Heb. 13:20; I Peter 2:25). Yet to be fulfilled after His second coming is the fulfillment of passages relating to His work as the chief Shepherd (I Peter 5:4).

The Future Work of Christ Is Also Dependent upon His Resurrection

In a number of particulars, the work of Christ yet to be fulfilled in keeping with the prophetic Scripture also depends upon His resurrection.

The resurrection of all men. It is anticipated in the prophetic Scriptures that Christ by the power of His own resurrection will raise the dead in a series of resurrections, probably in the following order:

1. the church at the time of the rapture (I Cor. 15:51-53; I Thess. 4:14-17)

2. Israel and the Old Testament saints at the time of His coming to the earth to establish His kingdom (Dan. 12:2, 13; Hosea 13:14; Matt. 22:30-31)

3. the tribulation saints at the time of His second coming (Rev. 20:4)

4. the probable resurrection of millennial saints at the end of the millennium, though this is not mentioned in the Scriptures specifically

5. the resurrection and judgment of the wicked dead at the end of the millennium (Rev. 20:12-14)

Regardless of time and character of resurrection, all resurrection is attributed to the power of Christ (John 5:28-29; I Cor. 15:12, 22) and depends upon the historical fact of His own resurrection.

The marriage of the Bridegroom and the bride. At the time Christ comes for His church at the rapture, He will be joined to the church in heaven in keeping with the figure of the Bridegroom coming for the bride. This figure in the Scriptures speaks of the eternal union and fellowship of Christ and His church and is an important aspect of His future work, logically depending upon the fact of His resurrection from the dead. The church in the present age is a bride waiting for the coming of her Husband (II Cor. 11:2; Rev. 19:7).

The judgment of all classes of moral creatures. In addition to His present work of administering chastening and disciplinary judgments in the life of the believer, Christ will also be the final Judge of all moral creatures, whether men or angels. These judgments can be itemized as referring (1) to the church (II Cor. 5:10-11); (2) to Israel nationally and individually (Matt. 24:27—25:30); (3) to the Gentiles at the time of His second coming to the earth (Matt. 25:31-46); (4) to angels, probably at the end of the millennium (I Cor. 6:3; II Peter 2:4; Jude 6); (5) to the wicked dead (Rev. 20:12-15). There also are general references to the fact of judgment as attributed to Christ in His power demonstrated in His resurrection (John 5:22; Acts 10:42; Rom. 14:10; II Tim. 4:1).

Reigning on David's throne. In the original prediction to David that his throne and seed would continue forever, it is implied that ultimately One would reign who would be a resurrected Person. In ordinary succession of kings who ultimately would die, it is unlikely that the throne would be actually established forever as stated in II Samuel 7:16. The prophecy given to David has its confirmation in the announcement of the angel to Mary, where it was stated of Christ, "He shall be great, and shall be called the Son of the Most High: and the Lord God shall give unto him the throne of his father David: and he shall reign over the house of Jacob for ever; and of his kingdom there shall be no end" (Luke 1:32-33, ASV). The specific promise given to David, therefore, is to be fulfilled in Christ and could not have been fulfilled if Christ had not been raised from the dead. This is confirmed in Peter's Pentecostal sermon in Acts 2:25-31 where the resurrection of Christ is tied in with the promise to David that God would set One of David's descendants upon His throne.

The final deliverance of the world to the Father. As a climax to the drama of history, Christ delivers a conquered world to the Father according to I Corinthians 15:24-28. The ultimate victory and the establishment of the sovereignty of Christ over all of His enemies could not have been accomplished apart from His resurrection. This is predicted in I Corinthians 15:26 (ASV), "The last enemy that shall be abolished is death." The ultimate resurrection of all men as well as the ultimate subjugation of the entire world to the sovereignty of Christ depends upon His resurrection. It is not too much to say that the resurrection of Jesus Christ is a link in the total chain of God's sovereign program without which the whole scheme would collapse.

Lewis S. Chafer has summarized the importance of the resurrection in these words:

> His resurrection is vitally related to the ages past, to the fulfillment of all prophecy, to the values of His death, to the Church, to Israel, to creation, to the purposes of God in grace which reach beyond to the ages to come, and to the eternal glory of God. Fulfillment of the eternal purposes related to all of these was dependent upon the coming forth of the Son of God from that tomb. He arose from the dead, and the greatness of that event is indicated by the importance of its place in Christian doctrine. Had not Christ arisen—He by whom all things were created, that are in heaven, and that are in earth, visible and invisible, whether they be thrones, or dominions, or principalities, or powers, He for whom things were created, who is before all things, and by whom all things consist (hold together)—every divine purpose and blessing would have failed, yea, the very universe and the throne of God would have dissolved and would have been dismissed forever. All life, light, and hope would have ceased. Death, darkness, and despair would have

reigned. Though the spiritual powers of darkness might have continued, the last hope for a ruined world would have been banished eternally. It is impossible for the mind to grasp the mighty issues which were at stake at the moment when Christ came forth from the tomb. At no moment of time, however, were these great issues in jeopardy. The consummation of His resurrection was sure, for omnipotent power was engaged to bring it to pass. Every feature of the Christian's salvation, position, and hope was dependent on the resurrection of his Lord.[13]

The Resurrection Is a Proof of the Inspiration of Scripture

Like other important prophecies which have been fulfilled, the resurrection of Christ is another confirmation of the accuracy and infallibility of the Scriptures and a testimony to its inspiration by the Holy Spirit. The resurrection of Christ fulfilled many prophecies both in the Old and New Testaments. Of importance in the Old Testament is Psalm 16:10 quoted by Peter in his Pentecostal sermon (Acts 2:27). As Peter points out, this promise could not have been fulfilled by David who died and whose tomb was known to them at the time of Peter's statements. It could only refer to Jesus Christ whose body did not see corruption.

In the New Testament narrative, Christ frequently referred to His coming death and resurrection, and these predictions again had their fulfillment when Christ rose from the dead (Matt. 16:21; 20:19; 26:61; Mark 9:9; 14:28; John 2:19). The Apostle Paul in giving his testimony before King Agrippa affirmed that the heart of his message was that which Moses and the prophets had predicted "how that Christ must suffer, and how that he first by the resurrection of the dead should proclaim light both to the people and to the Gentiles" (Acts 26:23, ASV). It is inevitable that anyone who denies the resurrection also denies the inspiration of Scripture and usually it is also true that those who deny the inspiration of Scripture deny the bodily resurrection of Christ. The two are linked as are many other important doctrines of biblical faith. The fact of the resurrection of Christ remains a pillar of the Christian faith without which the edifice soon totters and falls. The resurrection of Christ is, therefore, to be numbered among major undertakings of God which include His original decree, the creation of the physical world, the incarnation, the death of Christ, and His second coming to the earth.

[13]Lewis Sperry Chafer, *Grace*, pp. 272-73.

11

THE PRESENT WORK OF CHRIST

IN THE DOCTRINAL DELIBERATIONS of the church, the subject of the present work of Christ has been largely neglected and has been overshadowed by such important doctrines as the incarnation, death and resurrection of Christ. Part of this neglect has been caused by confusion concerning the nature of the present age arising from the varied concepts of the postmillennial, amillennial and premillennial interpretations. A proper understanding of the present work of Christ will do much to dispel this confusion.

Important distinctions must be observed if the present work of Christ is to be understood. The present lordship of Christ in heaven must be distinguished from His future lordship over the earth. The work of Christ in heaven must also be contrasted with the work of Christ indwelling the saints and both should be distinguished from the present ministry of the Spirit. As in other areas of theology, careful attention to the precise revelation of Scripture is the key to accurate understanding. The present work of Christ begins with the ascension and closes with His coming for His church.

THE ASCENSION OF CHRIST

The ascension of Christ is important in theology because, on the one hand, it is the second step in the exaltation of Christ beginning at His resurrection, and, on the other hand, because it begins His present work. Generally speaking, in orthodoxy the fact of the ascension of Christ has not been seriously disputed.

The Departure from Earth

Some difference of opinion has arisen in the doctrine of the ascension. The Lutheran church, following Martin Luther, has

219

generally maintained that the body of Christ is omnipresent in contrast to the Reformed theology which considers Christ as omnipresent only in His deity and local in respect to His resurrection body. Arguments in favor of the locality of the humanity of Christ have been stated at length by Charles Hodge who points out that locality is an essential attribute of a body and that an omnipresent body loses all the basic characteristics of a body. Reformed theologians accordingly have held that while Christ is spiritually present everywhere, He is bodily present in heaven during the present age and will return bodily in His second coming to the earth.[1]

The question has been raised whether Christ ascended into heaven prior to the event recorded in Acts 1. A number of expositors teach that Christ ascended to heaven on the day of His resurrection based on the implications of John 20:17 and Hebrews 9:6-20. They argue that just as the high priest in the Old Testament observed the Day of Atonement by taking blood into the holy of holies and sprinkling the mercy seat, so Christ, a new High Priest after a higher order, on the day of His resurrection applied the blood of His sacrifice to heaven itself.

This concept of an immediate ascension into heaven after His resurrection has been refuted, however, by able scholarship. Most conservative theologians hold that the work of Christ was finished on the cross and that the physical application of the blood never extended beyond the cross itself. Hebrews 9:12, which states that Christ entered into the holy place, properly translated by the American Standard Version indicates that it was "through his own blood" (dia with a genitive) rather than with His blood.

The statement to Mary in John 20:17 (ASV), "Touch me not; for I am not yet ascended unto the Father: but go unto my brethren, and say to them, I ascend unto my Father and your Father, and to my God and your God," actually is a prediction rather than a statement of immediate accomplishment. It is probable that the verb "I ascend" is a futuristic use of the present tense as A. T. Robertson points out.[2] In view of the fact that Christ appeared to others not long after His appearance to Mary Magdalene, it is unlikely that there would be a rapid ascension

[1]Cf. Charles Hodge, *Systematic Theology*, II, 630-34.
[2]A. T. Robertson, *A Grammar of the Greek New Testament in the Light of Historical Research*, p. 880.

into heaven and return in a comparative few minutes. Many, therefore, have concluded that it is improbable that Christ ascended in a formal way to heaven until the event of Acts 1. Scholars who have made a careful study of this particular problem such as W. H. Griffith Thomas,[3] A. T. Robertson,[4] B. F. Westcott,[5] Nathaniel Dimock,[6] and John Owen,[7] agree that Christ did not ascend to heaven to present His blood on the day of resurrection.

If Christ did not ascend on the day of His resurrection, it remains to be proved conclusively that He did ascend into heaven forty days later as recorded in Acts 1. This historic event is confirmed, first of all, by the anticipation of Christ, by the historic record of the ascension and by the allusions in the Epistles to the ascension as a fact.

In the Gospels there are numerous indications where Christ anticipates His return to glory, which He referred to as the return to the glory which He once had (Luke 9:51; John 6:62; 7:33; 14:12, 28; 16:5, 10, 16, 17, 28). The ascension, because of these many references, was undoubtedly an important event in the life of Christ marking the conclusion of His earthly ministry and bringing to culmination that series of events which had begun with His incarnation. The fact that it is singled out in the thinking and prophetic ministry of Christ makes clear that the ascension was important.

Three passages of Scripture are dedicated to recording this historic event: Mark 16:19-20; Luke 24:50-53; Acts 1:6-12. Though the Mark passage is sometimes questioned on textual grounds, Luke 24:51 (ASV) states, "And it came to pass, while he blessed them, he parted from them, and was carried up into heaven." As Kelly points out, there is no textual basis for contradicting Luke's statements,[8] although in the Luke passage the Greek word *anapherō*, translated "carried up," is omitted in some manuscripts. It is of interest that this is a different word from any of the words used in Acts 1.

The classic passage on the ascension is Acts 1:9-12 where these

---

[3]Cf. W. H. Griffith Thomas, "Ascension," *International Standard Bible Encyclopaedia*, I, 263-66.
[4]Robertson, *Word Pictures in the New Testament*, V, 312.
[5]B. F. Westcott, *The Epistle to the Hebrews*, p. 232.
[6]Nathaniel Dimock, *Our One Priest on High*, pp. 17-43.
[7]John Owen, *The Works of John Owen*, XV, 231-32.
[8]William Kelly, *Exposition of the Gospel of Luke*, p. 375.

four Greek words are used to describe various aspects of the ascension:

1. In verse 9 (ASV) it is stated, "As they were looking, he was taken up." The Greek for "taken up" is *epērthē*, from *epairō*. This verb is commonly used to indicate something which is lifted up, and the word is used, for instance, in relation to hoisting a sail in Acts 27:40.

2. In verse 9 (ASV) also, it is revealed that "a cloud received him out of their sight." The Greek word for "received up" is *hypelaben*. As A. T. Robertson points out, it is found in the "second aorist active indicative of *hupelambanō*, literally here 'took under him.' He seemed to be supported by the cloud."[9] There seems to be some significance in the fact that clouds are mentioned not only in connection with the ascension of Christ, but also in relation to His return in power and glory to the earth (Matt. 24:30; 26:64; Mark 13:26; 14:62; Luke 21:27; Rev. 1:7). The reference in I Thessalonians 4:17 in connection with the rapture is regarded by some as not a reference to literal clouds but to the saints being raptured as constituting themselves a cloud or large group of translated saints.

3. In Acts 1:10 a third word is used, *poreuomenou*, translated "as he went." It was a common word meaning to pursue a journey which would lead to the conclusion that the ascension is regarded as a departure from earth and also a journey to heaven.

4. A fourth Greek word *analēmphtheis* is used in Acts 1:11, translated "received up" (cf. Mark 16:19 and Luke 24:51 in ASV). This is, of course, a climactic concept, the resultant action springing from the preceding event. It is almost identical in meaning to *epērthē* in verse 9 and is used in Acts 20:13-14 of being taken aboard a ship.

Combining the concept of the four words, the entire picture of the ascension is given. The first word *epērthē* in Acts 1:9, in the passive form in which it is used, makes clear that the ascension is upward and that the Father is taking His Son to heaven. The second word *hypelaben* indicates that once Christ was in the atmospheric heaven He was received by clouds. A. C. Gaebelein believes it was a supernatural cloud similar to that on the Mount of Transfiguration and that which filled Solomon's tem-

⁹Robertson, *Word Pictures* . . . , III, 11.

ple.[10] There is no indication in the text that the cloud is other than a natural one. The third word connotes that the ascension was a journey, not merely a disappearance or a change of state, but an actual transmission from earth to heaven. The fourth word *analēmphtheis* concludes the picture by indicating that Christ was received into heaven as the destination of His journey.

Subsequent to Acts 1, it is constantly assumed in Scripture that Christ is in heaven. According to Hebrews 4:14 (ASV), we have "a great high priest, who hath passed through the heavens, Jesus the Son of God." In a similar manner in I Peter 3:22 (ASV) Jesus Christ is described as One "who is on the right hand of God, having gone into heaven; angels and authorities and powers being made subject unto him." The historic record of the ascension in Acts 1 is, therefore, confirmed by subsequent statements in the New Testament.

The Arrival of Christ in Heaven

In addition to the allusions in the Epistles to the ascension, there are many specific references where Christ is seen in heaven after His ascension. Obviously these confirm the statement of Mark 16:19 and Acts 1:11 that Christ arrived in heaven. Such an arrival is in keeping with the prophecies in which Christ anticipated this event (Luke 24:51; John 6:62; 7:33; 14:12, 28; 16:5, 10, 28).

In many passages in the New Testament, Christ is seen in heaven subsequent to His ascension (Acts 2:33-36; 3:21; 7:55-56; 9:3-6; 22:6-8; 26:13-15; Rom. 8:34; Eph. 1:20-22; 4:8-10; Phil. 2:6-11; 3:20; I Thess. 1:10; 4:16; I Tim. 3:16; Heb. 1:3, 13; 2:7; 4:14; 6:20; 7:26; 8:1; 9:24; 10:12-13; 12:2; I John 2:1; Rev. 1:7, 13-18; 5:5-12; 6:9-17; 7:9-17; 14:1-5; 19:11-16). This mass of scriptural evidence is one of the reasons why there has been so little question in orthodoxy concerning the reality of Christ's ascension. The ascent of Christ was (1) gradual, (2) visible, (3) bodily, and (4) received with clouds. It is of great significance to note these details because when Christ returns to the earth to establish His kingdom, His second advent will have all of these same characteristics.

The Significance of the Ascension

The fact that Christ ascended into heaven marked the end of

[10]A. C. Gaebelein, *The Annotated Bible*, I, 257.

His period of self-limitation. Even in His postresurrection ministry Christ to some extent limited the manifestation of His glory. The ascension also marked the end of His earthly ministry, including not only His sacrificial work on the cross but His prophetic ministry and miracles accomplished by His bodily presence.

Moreover, the ascension was important in that it anticipated His exaltation and glory in heaven. Upon His return to heaven, His preincarnate glory temporarily laid aside in earth was now to be fully manifested. He was to have the added glory now of victory over sin and death and is accordingly highly exalted (Eph. 1:20-23; cf. Phil. 2:9; Heb. 2:8).

In that Christ entered heaven bodily as the first resurrected Man to enter heaven, He is the Forerunner of all believers who will follow. It was more than simply a return to preincarnate glory of Deity, but also constituted a glorification of humanity. As Charles Hodge expressed it, "The subject of this exaltation was the Theanthropos; not the Logos especially or distinctively; not the human nature exclusively; but the Theanthropic person."[11] The ascension is the important link between His work on earth and His work in heaven which begins with the ascension.

THE PRESENT UNIVERSAL LORDSHIP OF CHRIST

The Present Position of Christ in Heaven

In addition to the great truth that Christ is the Head of the church, a truth which is considered subsequently, the Scriptures also emphasize the present position of Christ at the right hand of the Father (Ps. 110:1; Matt. 22:44; Mark 12:36; 16:19; Luke 20:42-43; 22:69; Rom. 8:34; Eph. 1:20; Col. 3:1; Heb. 1:3-13; 8:1; 10:12; 12:2; I Peter 3:22). This position is obviously one of highest possible honor and involves possession of the throne without dispossession of the Father. The implication is that all glory, authority and power is shared by the Father with the Son. The throne is definitely a heavenly throne, not the Davidic throne and not an earthly throne. It is over all the universe and its creatures.

One of the constant assumptions of the postmillennial and amillennial interpreters is that the throne which Christ is now occupying is the throne of David. An examination of the New Testament discloses that not a single instance can be found where

11Hodge, II, 635.

the present position of Christ is identified with David's throne. In view of the many references to the fact that Christ is now seated at the right hand of the Father, it is inconceivable that these two positions are identical, as none of the passages cited above use the expression "throne of David" as a proper representation of the present position of Christ. If Christ is now on the throne of David, it is without any scriptural support whatever.

The impossibility of David's throne and the Father's throne being identical is readily demonstrated by raising the simple question of whether David could sit on the Father's throne. The answer is obvious. David's throne pertained to the earth, to the land of Israel and to the people of Israel. It never contemplated any universality, and it never was anything more than an earthly throne.

The description of the throne of David in the Old Testament makes this clear. David's throne had to do with his rule over the people of Israel during his generation. That its continuity was promised was interpreted by the Jews as a promise of a future earthly kingdom. By contrast, every reference to the throne of the Father pictures it as in heaven. In point of time, the throne of the Father was eternal; it existed long before David was born or his kingdom or throne began. In all of these points, there is dissimilarity between the throne of David and the throne of God the Father which Christ now occupies.

The throne in heaven on which Christ is now seated is obviously also different from David's throne in that it is one of supreme honor, glory, victory, power and authority. The practical value to the believer of Christ's presence on this throne is demonstrated in that though the power of Satan and the temptations of the world are very real, Christ in this exalted position is able to sustain the believer in his hour of need. The church is positionally in Christ now, and the presence of Christ on the heavenly throne is our guarantee that we will be with Him in heaven ultimately. These important truths cannot be attributed to the throne of David as the church has no relationship to this throne nor was the throne of David one of infinite power and authority.

The Present Authority of Christ

Although Christ in some sense is awaiting the ultimate victory over the world anticipated in Psalm 110:1, He has extensive authority over the world as a whole even now. A major passage supporting this assertion is found in I Peter 3:22 where Jesus Christ is declared to have authority over angels, authorities and powers (cf. Heb. 1:4-13). According to Ephesians 1:21, Christ is in authority "far above all principality, and power, and might, and dominion, and every name that is named, not only in this world, but also in that which is to come." The passage continues with the declaration that "all things" are "under his feet" including the church (1:22).

The problem of evil in the world, often raised in philosophy as a contradiction of Christian faith, has its answer in this revelation. Christ now has all authority and ultimately will exercise it but, for divine purposes considered sufficient by God, He is waiting the future time of righteous judgment upon the world with its evil and sorrow. As Psalm 110:1 and Hebrews 10:13 point out, the day will come when His enemies are made His footstool. In keeping with the premillennial interpretation of Scripture, the subjugation of the earth is future rather than present and history will end with the triumph of Christ (I Cor. 15:24-28).

THE PRESENT WORK OF CHRIST IN HEAVEN

The major ministry of Christ in the present age relates to His church and is largely an expression of the work of Christ as our High Priest. Many aspects of His work, however, do not directly stem from the figure of the priesthood. These seven figures are used in Scripture to describe the varied ministry of Christ to His church in the present age:

The Last Adam and the New Creation

The term "last Adam" is found only once in the Bible (I Cor. 15:45) and is generally considered synonymous to the expression "second man," also found in this passage (I Cor. 15:47). The concept is expressed that Christ is the Head of the new creation composed of all those who are in Christ in comparison to Adam, the head of the old creation, which was composed of all those who are in Adam. Another term "new creation" is found twice in the Bible (II Cor. 5:17 and Gal. 6:15 in ASV marg.) and refers to individual persons who are in Christ as new creatures.

The concept of the new creation is that just as the old creation partakes of physical birth, the sin nature and spiritual death in

Adam, so one who is a new creature partakes of a new birth, a new nature, righteousness and sanctification, and inherits certain wonderful promises to be fulfilled in the future such as a spiritual body, ultimate incorruption and glory. Each individual in Christ is a new creation and the sum of all these individuals forms a theological concept known as the new creation.

Although some like Thomas C. Edwards believe Christ began His work as the last Adam on becoming incarnate[12] and others have suggested that His work began with His baptism and the bestowal of the Holy Spirit, probably the best view is that Christ entered His work as the last Adam in His resurrection from the dead. This is the inference of the mention of this doctrine in I Corinthians 15:45 (ASV) where Christ as the last Adam is said to have become "a life-giving spirit." Just as Adam was formed of the dust of the earth and was given physical life by God, so those spiritually dead when given new life in Christ become part of the new creation. The impartation of eternal life is mentioned frequently as the essential of salvation in Christ (John 1:4; 6:54; 10:28; 17:2). The contrast of those in the old creation and those in the new is brought out in many passages of Scripture such as Romans 5:12-21; I Corinthians 15:22 and Ephesians 2:1-10; related truths are found in other passages. The work of Christ as the last Adam is therefore one of forming a new creation out of individual believers in whom is placed eternal life. The very fact that it is compared to creation implies that God is the source of its power, execution and consummation and that the new creation is a supreme demonstration of grace and power.

Christ as the Head of the Body of Christ

A second important figure used in Scripture to describe the relationship between Christ and His church is the analogy of the human body in which Christ is revealed as the Head of the body which is the church.

The formation and growth of the church are compared to the formation and increase of a living body (Acts 2:47; I Cor. 6:15; 12:12-14; Eph. 2:16; 4:4-5, 16; 5:30-32; Col. 1:24; 2:19). The body is formed by the baptism of the Holy Spirit (I Cor. 12:13) and the Father is said also to participate in placing Christ as the Head

---

[12]Cf. Thomas C. Edwards, *A Commentary on the First Epistle to the Corinthians*, pp. 413-44.

of the body (Eph. 1:22). Christ is the life of the body and the One as its Head who directs its activity.

The body of Christ began with the advent of the Spirit in Acts 2 as can be demonstrated by comparison of Acts 1:5 with 11:15-16. The continued growth of the body is mentioned in Acts 2:47 as being derived from its inception on the day of Pentecost.

Believers joined to the body of Christ by baptism of the Spirit are members united by common life (Eph. 5:30) and are, therefore, disassociated from former relationships and urged to cleave to Christ as a wife cleaves to her husband (Eph. 5:31-32). The body of Christ is joined as the human body by joints and bands, being knit together and growing as a living organism (Col. 2:19).

Christ as Head of the Body Also Directs Its Activity

The concept of Christ as Head has various usages in the New Testament and a sixfold headship can be indicated:

1. *Dispensationally,* Christ is the Head of the corner to Israel at His second coming (Acts 4:11; I Peter 2:7).

2. *Racially,* Christ is the Head of every man (I Cor. 11:3).

3. *Ecclesiologically,* Christ is the Head of the church, His bride (Eph. 5:23; Rev. 19:6-8).

4. *Physiologically,* Christ is the Head of the body, the church (cf. all Scripture in this context).

5. *Cosmically,* Christ is the Head of principalities and powers and has the universal lordship (Col. 2:10).

6. *Representatively,* Christ is the Head of the new creation (Rom. 5:12-21), though the word "head" does not appear in the context.

Accordingly it should be observed that when Christ is referred to as the Head, it contextually should be classified according to its proper relationship.

Common to the concept of a headship, however, is the thought of being Lord or having the power to direct. As the Head of the corner, for instance, Christ will lead Israel. As the Head of every man, He is in authority over the race. As the Head of the church, His bride, He takes the place of lordship as a Husband. In relation to the universe, Christ is Head over all other powers. As the Head of the race, Christ again takes the place of leadership over humanity in the same way that Adam did.

The Scriptures frequently refer directly to the headship of

Christ over His church as His body (Eph. 1:22-23; 5:23-24; Col.
1:18; cf. I Cor. 11:3). The headship over the body in Ephesians
1:22-23 is revealed to be an important subdivision of His universal lordship. In Colossians 1:18 Christ is pictured as the Creator,
who in this capacity is Head over the church. In Ephesians 5:23-
24, the analogy of a husband's direction of a wife is carried over
to the direction of the body by Christ the Head. Just as a wife
should be in subjection to her husband, so the church is described
as being in subjection to Christ. The direction of the body by
Christ is, therefore, not an arbitrary and unreasonable lordship
over the church, but rather a loving direction of its members for
whom He died. The analogy to the human body, however, becomes dramatically evident in this relationship. Just as the human body is utterly dependent upon the human mind to direct
it into coherent action, not only to attain any desirable end but
also to minister to itself, so Christ is likewise revealed to direct
the members of His body, and the members in turn are utterly
dependent upon Him for coherent and intelligent action. An
effective member of the body of Christ, therefore, must submit
to the direction of Christ as Head of the body or the value of his
relationship to the body is lowered to that of being a paralyzed
member, that is, one who is alive but not obedient.

In keeping with the analogy of the human body in which there
is a constant process of nurture, there is a corresponding ministry
of Christ to His church embodied in three important passages:
Ephesians 5:29; Phil. 4:13; Colossians 2:19. The love of Christ for
His church, compared to the love of a husband for his wife, is
revealed in Ephesians 5:29 (ASV): "For no man ever hateth his
own flesh; but nourisheth it and cherisheth it, even as Christ also
the church." The Greek word for "nourish" (ektrephei) according to Arndt and Gingrich means to "nourish" or "rear" or "bring
up" as it is used in its only other New Testament occurrence in
Ephesians 6:4.[13] It therefore describes the general purpose of
God to bring the body to maturity in the development of its individual members and their relationship one to another.

The word "cherish" (thalpei) means literally to "keep warm"
and figuratively, "cherish, comfort."[14] The only other New Testament occurrence is in I Thessalonians 2:7 (ASV) in relation

[13]William F. Arndt and F. Wilbur Gingrich, A Greek-English Lexicon
of the New Testament, pp. 245-46.
[14]Ibid., p. 351.

to a mother cherishing her child. The thought here is that Christ not only provides that which will lead to maturity in the way of spiritual nourishment, but also provides the love, compassion and tender care such as a mother provides for her child. The figure is, therefore, rich in its spiritual connotation and reveals the heart of Christ for His own.

An added concept is given in Colossians 2:19 (ASV) where the ministry of the members to each other is also brought out: "The Head, from whom all the body, being supplied and knit together through the joints and bands, increaseth with the increase of God." As one member of the body of Christ is strengthened, it results in other members also being strengthened and also has the effect of increasing the body by adding new members. In Philippians 4:13 (ASV) it is indicated that the strength ultimately comes from Christ Himself, for Paul gives his testimony, "I can do all things in him that strengtheneth me."

Another important aspect of the ministry of Christ for His church relates to the sanctification of the body which is portrayed in Scripture in a threefold relationship: (1) positional sanctification; (2) progressive or experiential sanctification; (3) ultimate or final sanctification. The emphasis in the doctrine of sanctification in relation to the body is in the present tense, namely, the progressive aspect which is experiential. The work of sanctification is one of the great ministries of God to His own in which the three Members of the Trinity are severally involved. The principal passage dealing with the subject is Ephesians 5:25-27, which is supplemented by collateral references (Heb. 2:11; 9:12-14; 13:12). In Ephesians 5:26 (ASV) it is indicated that Christ gave Himself sacrificially on the cross with the purpose "that he might sanctify it [the church], having cleansed it by the washing of water with the word." This act of progressive sanctification has in view the ultimate presentation of "the church to himself a glorious church, not having spot or wrinkle or any such thing; but that it should be holy and without blemish" (Eph. 5:27, ASV).

A common view of expositors is that this passage refers to cleansing as revealed in the baptismal ordinance. The relation of this passage to water baptism, however, is entirely based on the use of the word "water." However, the frequent use of water as a figure in the Scriptures would make such a preliminary assumption hazardous. A careful examination of the passage does not support the interpretation that water baptism is in view here. The expression "washing" (*loutroi*) is commonly used for bathing or partial washing with no thought of a sacrament or ordinance (Acts 9:37; 16:33; Rev. 1:5). The washing here, however, seems to be a spiritual rather than a physical cleansing and water is used in a nonliteral sense as is frequently done in Scripture (cf. John 4:10-11, 14-15; 7:38; Heb. 10:22; Rev. 7:17; 21:6; 22:1, 17). In a similar way, the expression "washing of regeneration" (Titus 3:5) should be noted, where the washing is obviously not water but related to the Holy Spirit and His renewing as the passage itself states.

Because of these considerations, it is preferable to consider the phrase "with the word" not as a reference to the baptismal formula but rather to the Word of God itself. This is in keeping with other scriptures which indicate the sanctifying ministry of the Word of God. The thought of Ephesians 5:26 is, therefore, that Christ will sanctify His church through cleansing by application of the truth of the Word of God. It relates to the present work of sanctification rather than to the initial act of sanctification at the new birth or the ultimate sanctification which will be the believer's portion in heaven. The present cleansing of the body, however, has not only in view its present health, prosperity and usefulness in the hands of Christ, but also the ultimate state when the church, the body of Christ, will be purged of every taint of defilement or anything that would mar its perfect beauty.

Another major aspect of the ministry of Christ to His body is the bestowal of gifts on His church. Three major passages elucidate this ministry: Ephesians 4:7-16; I Corinthians 12:27-28; Romans 12:3-8. Although the Holy Spirit bestows gifts on men as individuals, it seems to be the work of Christ to bestow gifted men on the church. According to Ephesians 4:7-16 there are four types of gifted members, namely, apostles, prophets, evangelists, and pastors and teachers. The gift of being a pastor and teacher seems to be connected as one gift as indicated by the use of the Greek *kai*.

Five other gifts are mentioned in I Corinthians 12:28, namely, miracles, the gift of healing, the gift of helps, the gift of governments, and diversity of tongues. Still another list is provided in Romans 12:3-8.

The importance of bestowing gifts as well as gifted men on the church is indicated in Ephesians 4:12 as being designed "for the perfecting of the saints, for the work of the ministry, for the edifying of the body of Christ." The ultimate purpose is that believers may "come in the unity of the faith, and of the knowledge of the Son of God, unto a perfect man, unto the measure of the stature of the fulness of Christ" (Eph. 4:13). As a result of such maturity they no longer will be tossed about, but will speak the truth in love and edify the body of Christ (Eph. 4:14-16). Taken as a whole, the ministry of Christ to His body is one of the important vehicles of revelation of divine purpose and method.

The Work of Christ for His Sheep as the Great Shepherd

Another of the important figures used to depict the relationship between Christ and His church is that of the great Shepherd and the sheep. From the time of Abraham, Israel was known as a people who raised sheep. Therefore it was a part of their daily experience to know the characteristics of the relationship between a shepherd and his sheep. It was a natural development that the term "shepherd" should be used to represent a spiritual overseer who would care for his congregation in much the same way as a shepherd would care for his sheep. There are, accordingly, frequent allusions in the Bible to a shepherd with this significance (Ps. 23:1; 80:1; Eccles. 12:11; Isa. 40:11; 63:11-14; Jer. 31:10; Ezek. 34:23; 37:24; John 21:15-17; Eph. 4:11, pastors; I Peter 5:1-4).[15] Those who took places of leadership, even in nonspiritual contexts, were sometimes called shepherds (Isa. 44:28; 63:11). "Sheep without a shepherd" represented individuals or nations who had forgotten God (Num. 27:17; I Kings 22:17; II Chron. 18:16; Ezek. 34:5, 8; Zech. 10:2; Matt. 9:36; Mark 6:34). Even in modern times the term "shepherd" has been perpetuated in the term "pastor" as applied to a shepherd of a church. The word "sheep," in the sense of One who is offered as a sacrifice, is used of Christ, referred to as a Lamb (Isa. 53:7; John 1:29; Rev. 5:6, etc.).

In the Scriptures Christ is presented as a Shepherd in these three time relationships: (1) Christ as the good Shepherd giving His life for His sheep (Ps. 22; John 10); (2) Christ as the great

---

[15]Cf. James Patch, "Shepherd," *International Standard Bible Encyclopaedia*, IV, 2763-64.

Shepherd in His present work (Heb. 13:20); (3) Christ as the chief Shepherd who will be manifested as the King of glory caring for His own at His second coming (I Peter 5:4).[16] Of particular significance in the present discussion is the second time relationship, that of Christ as the great Shepherd.

In fulfillment of the figure as the great Shepherd Christ seeks and finds His sheep. Christ Himself used this concept in the parable of the lost sheep (Luke 15:3-7). A more extended revelation of the present work of Christ as Shepherd is given in John 10:1-28 where as the good Shepherd He lays down His life for His sheep and as the great Shepherd He has other sheep who are to be added to the flock (John 10:16). This is a reference to His present ministry in the church where both Jews and Gentiles form one flock under one Shepherd.[17]

In calling His sheep Christ uses the convicting work of the Holy Spirit (John 16:7-11), the proclamation of the gospel through God's appointed servants, as well as other means of bringing lost sheep to Himself.

Once the sheep are found, however, the great Shepherd leads His sheep. Few animals are more helpless than sheep in finding their own way and for this reason sheep are a natural illustration of man's complete inability to find God or to follow God in any self-directed way. Sheep have no ability to find food, water, shelter or protection and hence, are dependent upon a shepherd (John 10:4; Ps. 23:3). The present work of Christ, accordingly, is that of shepherding His sheep and providing for them. The true sheep are distinguished by their desire to follow the Shepherd and knowing His call (John 10:3-4, 14, 16, 27). One of the characteristics of sheep is that they know their own shepherd and hear his voice. Shepherds were accustomed to call their sheep by a peculiar guttural sound, which to human ears did not seem to be distinct in character. The sheep would, however, readily distinguish the call of their own shepherd.[18]

[16]Cf. Lewis S. Chafer, *Systematic Theology*, IV, 56-59.

[17]F. B. Meyer comments: "These other sheep must be the Gentiles—ourselves. Though He belonged by birth to the most exclusive race that has ever existed, our Lord's sympathies overflowed the narrow limits of national prejudice. He was the Son of Man; and in these words He not only showed that his heart was set on us, but He sketched the work which was to occupy Him through the ages" (*The Gospel of John*, p. 158).

[18]John Calvin comments on the expression "They know his voice" (John 10:4): "We must attend to the reason why it is said that *the sheep follow*;

Christ as the great Shepherd also provides for His sheep a more abundant and satisfying life (John 10:10). Just as Christ as the good Shepherd died that His sheep might have life, so the great Shepherd lives that the sheep might have life more abundantly. This is depicted beautifully in Psalm 23 in the green pastures and still waters which the Shepherd finds for His sheep. As a true Shepherd Christ also protects His sheep from wolves and other natural enemies, in contrast to the hireling who cares not for the sheep. Taken as a whole the figure of the great Shepherd is a beautiful picture of the faithful, loving Saviour and His relationship to those for whom He died. It depicts on the one hand the wonderful divine provision and, on the other, the utter need of the sheep for that which God alone can supply.

Christ as the True Vine in Relation to the Branches

In the upper room discourse on the night before His crucifixion, the Lord Jesus used the figure of the vine and the branches to describe His relationship to His disciples. This revelation of the ministry of Christ to and through His disciples portrays the conditions for fruit-bearing as well as the ministry of the Father, the privilege of the branches in relationship to the vine, and the danger of superficial connection. As in other figures that are used to describe spiritual truth, it is an illustration which should not be pressed beyond proper bounds.[19] Seen within the limitation described in the Scriptures themselves, the figure provides another important means of revealing the relationship between Christ and His own.

In its New Testament usage, the word for "vine" (Greek, *ampelos*) is always associated with fruit-bearing (Matt. 26:29; Mark 14:25; Luke 22:18; James 3:12). Christ is the true vine. The word for "true" (Greek, *alēthinē*) has the connotation of that which is ultimate, perfect or infinite. It refers to that which not only bears the name or resemblance but corresponds in its real nature to that which it is called. Christ as the true vine is in

it is, because *they know* how to distinguish *shepherds* from wolves *by the voice*. This is the spirit of discernment, by which the elect discriminate between the truth of God and the false inventions of men" (*Commentary on the Gospel According to John*, I, 396-97).

[19]Hugh MacMillan, for instance, in his work *The True Vine* is rich in his presentation of the spiritual truth in this figure, but falls short of a satisfactory doctrinal exposition. For a better exposition of this passage, see Gaebelein, *The Gospel of John*, pp. 292-300, and Kelly, *Exposition of the Gospel of John*, pp. 303-17.

contrast to Israel, which has proved to be a false vine not bearing proper fruit for God (Judges 9:7-15; Ps. 80:8; Isa. 5:1-7; Ezek. 15:2; Hosea 10:1). Christ is the true vine in the same sense that He is the true life and the true bread. Those who are properly related to Christ, therefore, have a true fruitfulness and an abundant life.

Expositors of the figure of the vine and the branches, as given in John 15, have often erred by attempting to pursue the figure too far. It is obvious that every figure of speech or illustration is designed to teach a particular truth, and the figure cannot in all its particulars be made to agree with its corresponding spiritual counterpart. Accordingly, those who press this figure beyond reasonable bounds end with explanations of details contradicted by other portions of Scripture.

In any attempt at exposition of this passage it is necessary first to state clearly the purpose of the figure. The theme of the passage is indicated in the eightfold repetition of the word "fruit." The major concept, therefore, is fruitfulness, such as normally would be expected of a branch properly related to the vine. Inasmuch as fruitfulness is in view, it is, therefore, an error to attempt to make this an illustration of salvation, condemnation or imputation, as these great doctrines are not in view. The central thought is that fruitfulness depends on the kind of branch in the vine. A fruitful branch must have a counterpart in regenerated souls who are supernaturally united to Christ and thus qualified to bring forth fruit.

The major problem in exegesis of this figure is to determine the character of the unfruitful branches. These branches, of course, do not reveal any true ministry of Christ, as they do not in any real sense partake of the ministry of the vine but are described as being cast into a fire where they are burned. Various explanations have been advanced to account for their character.

Some have attempted to describe the unfruitful branches as genuinely saved Christians who, because of fruitlessness, are taken from this life because they have committed the sin unto death (I John 5:16). This point of view regards their ministry as being useless to the extent that God takes them out of this world.

A second view is advanced by A. C. Gaebelein[20] who considers the fruitless branches as professing Christians joined to the pro-

[20]Gaebelein, *The Gospel* . . . , pp. 296-97.

fessing church. These outwardly appear to be in union with Christ but actually are not joined to the true vine. This lack of vital connection is revealed in the fact that they are cut off and in the end reveal that they are fitted for destruction instead of fruitfulness.

R. H. Lightfoot states that point of view in another way: "Since true discipleship is bound to show itself in fruit-bearing (15:8), any unfruitful branch is removed (in 15:2, 6 there is perhaps an indirect reference to the defection of Judas, as being typical of all faithless discipleship), and fruitful branches are pruned, to increase their capacity to bear fruit."[21]

A third view, probably the least satisfactory, is that the unfruitful branches have reference to Israel, and Judas in particular, who are cut off to make way for fruitful believers in Christ. A parallel is cited in Romans 11:17 where the unfruitful branches are broken off the olive tree and new branches are grafted in which will bear fruit. Undoubtedly the major problem in the exposition of this passage is the attempt to make explicit that which is only implied. The practice of pruning the vine and cutting out unfruitful branches was common in the care of natural vines. The major point is that true fruitfulness is derived from proper connection to the true vine. It apparently was not the intent of the passage to develop at length the precise relationship of the unfruitful branches. In John 15:6 the appeal is made to human customs rather than to divine activity in this regard.

The ministry of the true vine to the true branches has as its main thought the truth that Christ is the source of life and fruitfulness for all who are related to Him. The branches have both their existence and life because they are joined to Christ. Apart from Christ they can do nothing.

In the figure the thought of sanctification is obviously indicated because the branches are purged by a work of the Father as well as by the word of Christ (John 15:2-3). As vines are seldom fruitful unless properly pruned, so the work of Christ through His word is designed to make the fruitful branches bear more fruit. The main condition for fruitfulness is embodied in the words "Abide in me" (John 15:4). Abiding describes the relationship in which a believer has the full benefit of union with Christ. This involves obedience to the Lord as stated in the com-

[21]R. H. Lightfoot, *St. John's Gospel, A Commentary*, p. 282.

mand "If ye keep my commandments, ye shall abide in my love; even as I have kept my Father's commandments, and abide in his love" (John 15:10). The fruitful branch is both yielded to Christ and in complete dependence upon Him.[22] Answered prayer is assured the believer who is abiding in Christ and praying according to His will.

The passage emphasizes degrees of fruitfulness which are stated as (1) fruit, (2) more fruit, and (3) much fruit. Attending fruitfulness is the wonderful joy of serving the Lord as indicated in John 15:11 (ASV) : "These things have I spoken unto you, that my joy may be in you, and that your joy may be made full." The joy of the Christian is in sharp contrast to the pleasure of the world. True Christian joy is the by-product of fruitfulness and is wrought in the heart by the Spirit who produced His own fruit of love, joy and peace.

It is most significant that the branches of the vine are useless for anything other than bearing fruit (Ezek. 15:2-5). The character of branches of the vine makes it impossible to use them for building, they are of no use as firewood, and their beauty as branches is negligible. Only in fruitfulness can a branch related to the vine fulfill its divine purpose and function. In a similar way in Christian experience, the secret of an effective service does not lie in natural endowments or in advancement of self-interests but is rather expressed fully in permitting the life of fruitfulness of Christ to be manifested through the believer. The result of abiding in Christ as symbolized in the vine and the branches has been summarized in the triad "Fruit perpetual; joy celestial; prayer effectual." The joy mentioned is given special character by Christ as being "my joy" (John 15:11), that is, the joy that was in the heart of Christ in fulfilling the will of God in His life.

When understood in their proper significance, the vine and the branches teach the basic lessons of proper relationship to Christ, dependence, faith and fruitfulness together with the wonderful spiritual by-products of joy and answered prayer which are realized by the true branches.

[22]Lewis S. Chafer summarizes the meaning of this figure: "The contribution which the figure of the Vine and its branches makes to the doctrine of the Church is particularly that, by the unbroken communion of the believer with His Lord, the enabling power of God rests upon him both for his own priceless experience of joyous fellowship and for fruitfulness by prayer and testimony unto the completion of the Body of Christ" (Chafer, IV, 61).

Christ as the Chief Cornerstone in Relation to the Stones of the Building

Frequently in Scripture a stone or rock is used to portray spiritual truths and is usually used in relationship to Christ. Christ is symbolized in the smitten rock from which flow rivers of living water (Exodus 17:6; cf. I Cor. 10:4; John 4:13-14; 7:37-39). In relation to His first coming to the earth, He was a "stumbling-stone" to the Jews (Rom. 9:32-33; cf. I Cor. 1:23; I Peter 2:8). At His second coming He will be the headstone of the corner in His relationship to Israel (Zech. 4:7; cf. I Peter 2:7), while in the present age He is the foundation and chief cornerstone for the church (Eph. 2:20; cf. I Peter 2:6). Christ is also the stone of destruction to unbelievers (Matt. 21:44). In some contexts, the idea of a stone is used of other spiritual truths; for instance, it symbolizes the kingdom of God which is to fill the whole earth (Dan. 2:35),[23] and which is introduced by the reference to the "stone . . . cut out without hands" (Dan. 2:34). The latter depicts the second coming of Christ in judgment, much as in Matthew 21:44. From these many allusions to Christ as a stone and related revelations, it is clear that the concept of the stone has many connotations of spiritual significance.

In describing the necessity of Christ as the foundation of the Christian life, the figure of a building is used in I Corinthians 3:11-15, where it is stated that all must be based upon the foundation which is Christ: "For other foundation can no man lay than that which is laid, which is Jesus Christ" (v. 11, ASV). This thought is used in an introductory way as the only proper preparation for the kind of life which will count for eternity. Christian life must be based upon the foundation which is supplied, namely, Christ, and only after this is appropriated can the Christian life be erected upon the foundation. The word "stone" does not occur in this context but the thought is similar to that of other passages such as Isaiah 28:16 (ASV), where the prophecy was given: "Therefore thus saith the Lord Jehovah, Behold, I lay in Zion for a foundation a stone, a tried stone, a precious cornerstone of sure foundation: he that believeth shall not be in haste." In the Isaiah passage, the concept of foundation and stone is one and the same, the terms "foundation" and "corner" indicating use, and the term "stone" indicating character. In the entire

[23]Cf. H. A. Ironside, *Lectures on Daniel the Prophet*, pp. 38-39.

figure, Christ is portrayed as indispensable, with all the building depending upon Him. He is indeed the only foundation stone for Christian life and faith in time or eternity.

In Ephesians 2:20 (ASV), a further revelation is given describing Christ as the cornerstone: "Being built upon the foundation of the apostles and prophets, Christ Jesus himself being the chief corner stone." Here as in I Corinthians 3:11-15 the word "stone" is not in the original but is properly supplied by the translator. The thought of Christ as the foundation is repeated in this passage, but with the added idea that He is also a cornerstone. Although the complete connotation of this expression is not entirely clear it at least reveals Christ as essential to the structure of the building and to its symmetry, indicates the degree of the corner and gives significance to the whole building. In modern times, the cornerstone is often employed to state the essential facts relating to the purpose of the building and is accordingly the most prominent and significant portion of the building. Christ as the chief cornerstone reveals the purpose of the building which is His church, and apostles and New Testament prophets form the foundation along with Christ, although Christ is the most important stone. This may be a part of the explanation of Matthew 16:18 where the symbolism of a rock is related to Peter's testimony. The resultant interpretation, then, would be: "You are Peter [a little stone or sliver of rock], and on this rock [consisting of many flaked pieces—the totality of apostles and prophets, Eph. 2:20] I will build my church" (RSV).

Probably the most important passage in the New Testament on Christ as the stone is found in I Peter 2:4-8, where most of the factors mentioned in earlier revelation are repeated and Isaiah 28:16 is quoted. An additional thought is provided in this passage in the concept that Christ is a *living* stone. When Christ was in the tomb, His body was lifeless and in this respect was similar to an inanimate stone. In His resurrection, however, Christ became the living stone, a supernatural figure of speech embodying the natural qualities such as permanence and value of precious stones but also the supernatural in the sense that the stone is alive and has a living character.[24]

[24]William Kelly comments: "In nature no object lies more obviously void of life than a stone. But this only makes the power of grace the more impressive. Even John the Baptist could tell the haughty Pharisees and Sadducees, who pleaded their descent from Abraham, that God was able of the stones to raise up children to Abraham" (*First Epistle of Peter*, p. 127).

The living character of Christ as stone is carried over into the description of the stones of the building which represent individual Christians. Some take Ephesians 2:21 as an individual believer and others as the whole church corporately. In the Petrine passage, however, clearly the whole church is in view. The stones of the building are like Christ in the tomb, without life. Now in resurrection life, like Christ, they become living stones which not only have the quality of life but, fitted together, form as a corporate group a living unit, the church, the body of Christ which is one with Christ in life and structure. The figure, therefore, implies that our relationship to Christ includes eternal life, oneness, the security of being on a sure foundation, and the privilege of being a spiritual house (I Peter 2:5). Christ is also evidently present within the building as well as its chief cornerstone. The building has the quality of growth which continues throughout the present age, not only in the fact that additional stones are being added as the lost are won to Christ, but also that individual Christians grow in their capacity and usefulness.

As depicting the present work of Chirst, the figure of Christ as the foundation and cornerstone related to the stones of the building as believers is rich with spiritual significance. It makes clear that the only important aspects of life are those that are related to Christ. Only as life is founded upon Him can a true building be erected for time and eternity.

Christ as the High Priest and the Royal Priesthood

The scriptural revelation of the work of Christ as our great High Priest is one of the most important aspects of His present work. Actually His priesthood is something more than a mere figure or symbol of truth, because Christ is a Priest in a more literal sense than He is a vine or a Shepherd. The truth concerning His priesthood may be considered in four divisions: the nature of His priesthood, His sacrifice as High Priest, His intercession as High Priest, and the royal priesthood of the believer as related to Christ the High Priest.

The nature of His priesthood. In considering the nature of His high priesthood, it is important to understand the essentials of priesthood. W. G. Moorehead defines a priest in this way: "One who is duly qualified to minister in sacred things, particularly to offer sacrifices at the altar, and to act as mediator between men and God."[25] According to Scripture, Christ fulfilled all of the essential qualities of a Priest. He ministered in sacred things (Heb. 5:1), and His life and ministry were concerned with "things pertaining to God." Christ was made a Priest by God Himself (Heb. 5:4-10) in contrast to contemporary high priests who were elected under authority of the Roman government in a manner unrecognized by the Scriptures. According to I Timothy 2:5, Christ was a true Mediator. He offered sacrifice to God (Heb. 9:26) and, on the basis of His sacrifice, offered intercession to God (Heb. 7:25). In all of these respects it is evident that the priesthood of Christ unquestionably is established as valid and that Christ fulfilled the full-orbed ministry of a Priest.

One of the important aspects of the priesthood of Christ is His fulfillment of what was anticipated in Melchizedek, the priest, to whom Abraham gave tithes.[26] Christ as the fulfillment of the Melchizedek type is declared to be superior and replacing the Aaronic priesthood. Christ in His priesthood is supreme over all other priesthoods both in His person and work. Christ as a High Priest fulfilled much that was anticipated in the Aaronic priesthood and in His *person* and *order* fulfilled that which was anticipated by Melchizedek. The supremacy of Christ's priesthood is supported by its more important characteristics, namely, that His priesthood is eternal, untransmissible and based on supernatural resurrection. In contrast to the Aaronic priesthood, Christ was eternal and fulfilled the description given of Melchizedek, who was "without father, without mother, without descent, having neither beginning of days, nor end of life; but made like unto the Son of God; abideth a priest continually" (Heb. 7:3). This description means that Christ like Melchizedek as far as the record is concerned has no priestly lineage either before Him or after Him and serves by direct appointment of God.

The eternal priesthood of Christ as represented in Melchizedek is brought out in Hebrews 5:5-6, 9 which states that Christ fulfilled Psalm 110:4: "The LORD hath sworn, and will not repent: Thou art a priest for ever after the order of Melchizedek." For this reason Christ can be "the author of eternal salvation" (Heb. 5:9) and have "the power of an endless life" (Heb. 7:16). Like-

[25]W. G. Moorehead, "Priest," *International Standard Bible Encyclopaedia*, IV, 2439-41.
[26]Charles C. Ryrie summarizes the particulars of the Melchizedek priesthood as being fourfold: (1) royal, (2) individual, (3) timeless, (4) inclusive (*Biblical Theology of the New Testament*, p. 246).

wise, the exercise of Christ's priestly office is eternal as is His work
of intercession (Heb. 7:23-26).

One of the problems raised concerning the eternal priesthood
of Christ is the question of the point in time when Christ assumed His priestly office. Probably the most common tendency
has been to assume that His priestly work began with the cross
and the glorification that followed His resurrection. As William
Milligan points out:

> Such writers as Tholuck, Riehm, Hofmann, Delitzsch,
> Davidson, and Westcott admit with more or less distinctness
> that the High-priesthood of our Lord began with His Glorifi-
> cation; but they cannot allow that the death upon the cross
> was "an essential part of His High-priest's work, performed
> in the outer court, that is, in this world," and they are thus
> driven to the expedient of saying that, High-priestly as that
> act was, the Priesthood of Christ only attained its complete-
> ness after His Resurrection. This distinction, however, be-
> tween incompleteness and completeness cannot be main-
> tained; and the true solution appears to be suggested by our
> Lord's own words. It began upon the cross, and the cross
> was the beginning of His glory.[27]

It is clear from Scripture, however, that Christ long before His
dying on the cross served as a Priest in the sense of interceding
for man and acting as a Mediator. On occasion He prayed all
night, and specifically, according to Luke 22:32 (ASV), Christ
declared of Peter, "I made supplication for thee, that thy faith
fail not." Inasmuch as intercession is a priestly function, Christ
was doing the work of a Priest.

Other suggestions have included the idea that He began His
priestly work when He was inducted to it by the baptism of John
or at the incarnation itself. It is better, however, to hold that
Christ's priesthood was eternal as to its office even though some
functions of His priesthood may not always have been performed.
Christ is a Priest eternally in the same sense that He is the Saviour
eternally (Ps. 110:4, quoted in Heb. 7:20-21, which indicates that
Christ was a Priest at the time the psalm was written a thousand
years before the birth of Christ, even though His incarnation and
subsequent events were necessary for the exercise of this priesthood).

[27]William Milligan, *The Ascension and Heavenly Priesthood of Our Lord*,
p. 81.

Another very important point in the priesthood of Christ is that it was not only eternal but untransmissible, that is, it was not passed on to another. This is the thought of Hebrews 7:24, "But this man, because he continueth ever, hath an unchangeable priesthood." Although some like Westcott have argued that the word "unchangeable" (Greek, *aparabaton*) means only "inviolable,"[28] the context seems to indicate that "unchangeable" is a better meaning and even Westcott concedes that, as a matter of fact, the priesthood of Christ is unchangeable. It follows, therefore, that earthly priests do not succeed Christ in any sense of the term, that only Christ is High Priest. The continued priesthood of Christ is based on His resurrection, the symbols of which were used by Melchizedek when he brought forth bread and wine in Genesis 14:18-19. The everlasting efficacy of the sacrifice of Christ symbolized in the bread and wine and confirmed by His resurrection makes possible His continuous priesthood.

In addition to fulfilling the Melchizedek type, Christ also fulfilled certain aspects of the Aaronic priesthood especially in its sacrificial system. Like Aaron Christ met all the requirements of a Priest and was superior to Aaron in the duration of His priesthood, in the method of His induction into the office of Priest by God, and by the fact that He possessed an untransmissible priesthood.

Christ is the fulfillment of the Aaronic priesthood in that He fulfills all that was anticipated in the functioning of the Aaronic priesthood. Hence Christ is said (1) to minister in the heavenly sphere as did Aaron (Heb. 8:1-5) ; (2) Christ served the realities rather than the shadows (Heb. 8:5) ; (3) Christ administered a new and better covenant than the Mosaic covenant (Heb. 8:6) ; (4) Christ offered a final and complete sacrifice for sin rather than the daily offerings of Aaron (Heb. 7:27) . In a word, Christ fulfilled all that Aaron was and did. It should be borne in mind that the principal concept here is not that Christ's priesthood was designed to fulfill Aaron's, but rather that the Aaronic priesthood was designed by God in the first place to point to Christ and to require the sacrifice and work of Christ as Priest to fulfill it completely. Hence, the work of Christ as a Priest does away with the former Aaronic system completely and replaces it. This is important to the argument of Hebrews, which demonstrates that

[28]Westcott, p. 192.

Christ is superior to all others, be they angels, Moses or Aaron. Although Christ like Aaron was truly Man and knew temptations, except those rising from a sin nature (Heb. 4:15), He did not sin although, being human, He knew agonizing prayer and suffering (Heb. 5:7-8).

His sacrifice as High Priest. The second aspect of the work of Christ as our great High Priest was in His sacrifice. He was both the Sacrificer and the sacrifice as He was both the Lamb and the Priest. In His death He fulfilled the three major works represented in the sacrifice, namely, (1) the redemption which God demanded, (2) the propitiation which met all the righteous demands of a holy God in relation to human sin, and (3) reconciliation in the sense that He provided reconciliation for the entire world.

One of the unfortunate misunderstandings of the sacrifice of Christ is the doctrine of perpetual offering as taught in Roman Catholic theology and represented in the doctrine of the mass. In its early history the Roman Church held that the mass represented the sacrifice of Christ as a continual offering. They did this on the ground that sacrifice was unsuited for heaven and that only earthly priests could offer such a sacrifice. Their position shifted later to the view that Christ offered a perpetual offering in heaven and hence an earthly representation of the sacrifice in the mass is permissible and in fact required. The whole theory of a perpetual offering, however, depends upon the premise that this is essential to a perpetual priesthood. Although certain Protestant scholars, such as Milligan[29] and Henry B. Swete,[30] have been sympathetic to this idea of a perpetual sacrifice in some sense in heaven, this whole teaching has been refuted effectively by Arthur J. Tait[31] and Nathaniel Dimock.[32]

A number of important arguments refute the Roman Catholic position:

1. The Roman Catholic doctrine of perpetual offering is based on a wrong premise because it is not true that a perpetual offering is essential to perpetual priesthood. If God could forgive sins in the Old Testament prior to the act of Christ upon the cross, it is

---

[29]Milligan, pp. 133-34.
[30]Henry B. Swete, *The Ascended Christ,* p. 50.
[31]Arthur J. Tait, *The Heavenly Ascension of Our Lord.*
[32]Dimock, *The Sacerdotium of Christ* and *Our One Priest* . . . ; cf. Westcott, who also supports the concept of a finished offering.

also possible for Him to forgive sins after the cross without a continuous sacrifice (Rom. 3:25-26).

2. In the Roman Catholic view there is confusion of the offering or sacrifice with the intercession which follows. While both are essential to priesthood, both are not necessarily continuous.

3. In a similar way the Roman theory confuses the offering with the offerer. The presence of Christ in heaven is not the same as the presence of the offering in heaven.

4. The Roman Catholic theory confuses typology by making the Priest and the sacrificial Lamb the same. The Lamb died, but the Priest did not.

5. The theory of perpetual offering is refuted by direct statements of the Bible which indicate that Christ offered Himself as a sacrifice once for all (I Cor. 15:3-4; Heb. 1:3; 7:27; 8:3; 10:10-14). In the Hebrews 8:3 passage the copula "it is" is omitted in the Greek. Probably the past tense is intended instead of the present as found in the ancient Peshitta Syriac Version.[33] John Owen also holds that the past tense is intended, citing Beza as well as the Syriac Version as proof.[34]

6. The support of the typology of Hebrews 9:7 upon close examination does not support the idea of perpetual offering. The word used for offered (Greek, *prospherei*) in Hebrews 9:7 does not mean offering in the sense of a sacrifice, but rather of "bringing near." Likewise, Christ did not enter with His blood into the holy place, but *through* His blood. The uniform manner of reference in the epistle to the Hebrews is that Christ entered *through* His blood, rather than *with* His blood. In Hebrews 9:12 and 13:12 the use of *dia* with the genitive is found. A similar expression can be noted in the use of *en* with the locative (Heb. 9:25; 10:19; 13:20). The thought is that Christ entered not as one bringing blood to complete a sacrifice, but as One who is clothed in blood, entering on the basis of the sacrifice. Dimock concluded accordingly: "Is it too much to say—and to say with confidence—that, in full view of the teaching of this truth, the idea of anything like a sacrificial oblation, or offering for sin by the Saviour in Heaven is quite inadmissible—is, to the soul fully enlightened by this truth, utterly inconceivable?"[35]

[33]Dimock, *Our One Priest* . . . , p. 9.
[34]Owen, XV, 28.
[35]Dimock, *Our One Priest* . . . , p. 49.

From these arguments and the precise use of prepositions in the New Testament, it may be concluded that the sacrifice of Christ was completed on the cross once and for all, that Christ did not present literal blood in heaven any more than His literal blood is applied to the believer now (cf. I John 1:7), that all cleansing in earth and heaven is on the basis of the blood shed on Calvary, and that the work of Christ in sacrifice was finished when He died.

Some Protestants have attempted to adopt a variation of the Roman view in declaring that Christ's presence in heaven constitutes a perpetual offering. Such a heavenly sacrifice would destroy the objective reality of Christ's one act of dying on the cross. His work on the cross has to do with the guilt of our sin whereas His work in heaven is entirely different. The orthodox view that the offering of Christ as a sacrifice for sin was accomplished once for all on the cross is far better than the other view. On the basis of this accomplished sacrifice, Christ can forever intercede for those who trust in Him and in this way fulfill His complete work as Priest. This view is the only one which fully satisfies all the related scriptures, gives the proper place to His work of sacrifice, and provides a suitable distinction between the sacrifice and the intercession which follows.

His intercession as High Priest. The third major aspect of the priesthood of Christ is His intercession as our High Priest in heaven. Some difference of opinion has existed as to the nature of this intercession, centering in the question as to whether this intercession was both vocal and real as some Lutheran theologians hold. The opposite extreme held by some Protestants is that it is neither vocal nor real, but merely His presence in heaven. The proper biblical definition seems to be between these two extremes, in that the intercession of Christ need not be vocal as there are other methods of communication to the Father, but that it is in the end a real intercession just as vocal intercession would be. A further complication is the confusion of intercession with propitiation as if the present ministry of Christ in heaven is a part of the propitiatory work which was accomplished once for all on the cross.

Both Milligan and Swete hold that the intercession of Christ consists in a continuous presentation of the glorified life of Christ and does not involve the element of vocal prayer. Swete writes,

> For the intercession of the Ascended Christ is not a prayer,
> but a life. The New Testament does not represent Him as an
> *orante*, standing ever before the Father, and with outstretched
> arms, like the figures in the mosaics of the catacombs, and
> with strong crying and tears pleading our cause in the pres-
> ence of a reluctant God; but as the throned Priest-King, ask-
> ing what He will from a Father who always hears and grants
> His request. Our Lord's life in heaven is His prayer.[36]

In other words, Swete holds that the presence of Christ in heaven
in itself constitutes intercession and, therefore, he denies that intercession as such is either real, that is, actual prayer, or vocal,
that is, expressed in words.

In contrast to the view of Swete and Milligan is the Lutheran
position that the intercession of Christ is real and vocal as expressed in the Latin phrase *vocalis et realis*. The Lutheran view
is that Christ in heaven offers real intercession and that this is
characterized by the same qualities found in all prayer. Reformed
theologians other than Lutherans took a middle view between the
two extremes, affirming on the one hand that intercession is not
necessarily vocal, as the presence of Christ in heaven is sufficient,
but holding on the other hand that such intercession is real and
effective. They also separated propitiation from intercession,
supporting the idea that propitiation was finished on the cross,
but that intercession is continuous. Those who follow closely
biblical usage will probably agree with the Reformed theologians
as against the Lutheran view.

Only two direct references to intercession of Christ are found
in the New Testament (Rom. 8:34; Heb. 7:25). These passages
simply state that Christ ever lives and therefore is able to intercede continually. The Greek word used (*entugchanō,* in its noun
form *enteuxis,* I Tim. 2:1; 4:5) is translated "intercession" and
"prayer" and hence is similar to the prayers of men. The inference that intercession is also prayer and hence real is confirmed by the intercession of the Holy Spirit in Romans 8:26-27
where the Holy Spirit is engaged in real intercession. It would
imply that the intercession of Christ is equally real.

Although problems remain, the fact that Christ on earth prayed
with all characteristic human factors as illustrated in Hebrews
5:7 would seem to lead to the conclusion that in heaven also His
intercession is real even though it may not necessarily take the

[36]Swete, pp. 95-96.

form of words. His intercession is therefore more than mere presence in heaven; it is real and may be vocal but not necessarily so.

The wonderful results of intercession give assurance to the believer of security in Christ, hope for eternal salvation, protection from spiritual and physical dangers in life and a pledge of ultimate sanctification. Spiritual triumph for the believer is inevitably linked to the heavenly Intercessor.

Intercession is also related to the believer's fellowship with God both by preventing sin and providing advocacy when the believer does sin against God. On the divine side the adjustment is immediate, on the human side it is dependent on confession (I John 1:5—2:2).

The royal priesthood of the believer as related to Christ the High Priest. The fourth and final major aspect of the priesthood of Christ is the royal priesthood of the believer as related to Christ the High Priest. As an important corollary of Christ in His office and work as Priest, the priesthood of individual believers is revealed in Scripture. Frequent mention is found in the Bible of the believer's work as a priest under Christ the High Priest (Rom. 12:1; Heb. 13:15-16; I Peter 2:5; Rev. 1:6; 5:10; 20:6). Other passages may be added to these basic texts which relate to exhortations to pray and similar doctrines. The priesthood of the believer is one of the important areas of spiritual life presented in the Bible and one of the great truths reclaimed in the Protestant Reformation. The work of the believer-priest, like the work of Christ, is divided into two areas: the believer's sacrifices and the believer's intercession.

At least four sacrifices are mentioned as belonging properly to the believer-priest. The first of these, which is the foundation for others to follow, is the sacrifice of our body (Rom. 12:1). In contrast to animals of sacrifice in the Old Testament who gave their lives in death in their sacrifice on the altar, the believer is exhorted to give his body a living sacrifice. Such a sacrifice is regarded as holy and acceptable to God because of the fact that the believer has been cleansed by the blood of Christ. It is also a reasonable sacrifice, that is, one which can be properly expected, in view of all that God has done on behalf of the believer. This foundational exhortation obviously enters into any true exercise of priestly function on the part of the believer in Christ. Until the individual has surrendered his heart, mind and body to the

Lord as a living sacrifice, there can be no proper exercise of his priestly prerogatives. From this experience of yieldedness flow all the possibilities of usefulness and joyous experience of the Christian life.

A second sacrifice which the believer-priest can offer to the Lord is the sacrifice of praise (I Peter 2:5, 9; Heb. 13:15). Just as the altar of incense lent its fragrance to the air of the tabernacle and later the temple and gave itself wholly to the recognition of the perfections of God, so the believer as a priest should be constantly offering a sacrifice of praise to God. Such praise involves recognition of the nature of God and His wonderful works and especially His grace manifested to those who have trusted Him. Such a sacrifice is of course possible only for a believer who has offered himself to God first and who has experienced a life of yieldedness in which he has come to know the joy of the Holy Spirit and to possess spiritual understanding of the gracious dealings of God. The sacrifice of praise has depth and meaning only as the believer-priest recognizes the perfections of God and devotes his heart and mind to worship, adoration and praise. This work of the believer-priest on earth will undoubtedly be continued in heaven and constitutes a major aspect of his experience in eternity.

A third sacrifice is a sacrifice of good works or doing good (Heb. 13:16). This comprehends all the service rendered to God in the path of His divine will. The whole Christian life in a sense is a sacrifice of good works. In a similar way the Levites performed their function in the Old Testament as they assisted the priests. Though not specifically offering sacrifice and doing priestly works, nevertheless, they offered in a sense a sacrifice of good works to God. Likewise now a believer-priest, though not always engaged specifically in intercession or sacrifices of a priestly character, is nevertheless offering a sacrifice to God whenever he is accomplishing God's will in his life. Such a point of view contemplates the Christian life as one fundamentally fulfilling the will of God rather than self-satisfaction and adds dignity to even the humble tasks which may not seem to resemble a priestly ministry.

The fourth sacrifice mentioned in Hebrews 13:16 is that of the sacrifice of substance which has in view the fact that all earthly goods are a solemn trust which should be used to the glory of God. The New Testament saint, while not obligated to keep the

details of the Mosaic law in which God required Israelites to give
a specific portion of their worldly goods, should nevertheless according to the Bible offer his sacrifice of substance (1) systemat-
ically; (2) regularly (I Cor. 16:2) ; (3) proportionately (I Cor.
16:2) ; (4) sacrificially (II Cor. 8:2) ; (5) liberally (II Cor. 9:6,
13) ; (6) cheerfully (II Cor. 9:7) ; (7) trusting God to supply his
own needs (II Cor. 9:8) .

In addition to offering the four sacrifices outlined in the Scriptures, the believer-priest should offer intercession to God. This
aspect of his priestly work involves all his work in prayer, regardless of its particular character. In view of the individual's position in Christ which has constituted him a member of a royal
priesthood, he may pray in Christ's name (John 14:13-14) . He
also has the right to bring his own personal needs to God and expect God to supply (Phil. 4:6-7, 19) . The believer-priest, however, should not be occupied only with his own needs, but also
with the needs of others (Eph. 6:18) . His prayer should be characterized as being continual, that is, uninterrupted (I Thess.
5:17). As priests, believers have the right to enter into the heavenly
holy of holies (Heb. 10:19-22) and there may plead their case
and intercede before a mercy seat made gracious by the shed
blood of Christ. In offering his sacrifices and intercession, the
believer-priest is fulfilling in large measure his total effective ministry for God in this world. The fulfillment of his priestly re-
sponsibilities is integral in any vital Christian experience and
effective witness for God.

Christ the Bridegroom and His Bride

Of the seven figures relating Christ to the church, the Bridegroom is more eschatological than any of the others, depicting as
it does the ultimate in Christ's work for His bride. The figure of
marriage is often used in Scripture to depict spiritual truth and
is not limited to believers in the present age. In the Old Testament Israel was related to God in the figure of marriage. The
disobedience of Israel to the law and the worship of idols was
regarded as being spiritually unfaithful to her husband and a
violation of her marriage vows (Isa. 54:1-17; Jer. 3:1, 14, 20;
Hosea 2:1-23) . By contrast the church in the New Testament is
referred to as a bride not yet joined to her Husband (II Cor. 11:2;
Eph. 5:25-27; Rev. 19:6-8) . The viewpoint of Bullinger and Sir

Robert Anderson, who limit the term "bride" to Israelite Christians in the first part of the present age, has not met with general acceptance of the church.[37] The bride seems to include both Jews and Gentiles in the entire present age related to Christ by faith and anticipating a future relationship of which marriage is an illustration. The bride and the body of Christ are one, as clearly taught in Ephesians 5:23-32.

In the present age Christ is preparing a place for His bride (John 14:2). Although this is not defined, whatever heavenly preparation is necessary is being made that the bride may be brought to the Father's house in due time. Some have taken this as a reference to the New Jerusalem which may be in preparation as the eternal place of the dwelling of the saints.

More important is the present work of Christ in preparing the bride for her future place. As A. C. Gaebelein writes, "Heaven . . . is a prepared place for a prepared people."[38] The bride in her natural beauty and endowment could never hope to be admitted to the courts of heaven and the immediate presence of God unless a dramatic transformation was effected. Even if admitted to heaven, the bride in her present condition would be very uncomfortable and unsuited for a heavenly situation. It is accordingly indicated in the Scriptures that Christ has undertaken in this present age to prepare the bride for her future role and to give her the beauty and spiritual character required to be in the presence of a holy God.

This work is anticipated in Ephesians 5:25-33 where the bride of Christ, which is also His body, is pictured as being prepared for this future marriage. This work is based, first of all, upon the work of Christ on the cross, indicated in Ephesians 5:25 (ASV) in the expression that "Christ also loved the church, and gave himself up for it." It is obvious that apart from the death of Christ on the cross the whole work of grace and transformation of the bride would have been impossible. Having accomplished this on the cross once and for all, Christ is presently engaged in a work of sanctification described in Ephesians 5:26 (ASV), where the purpose of Christ is stated to be "that he might sanctify it, having cleansed it by the washing of water with the word." This present work of sanctification should not

[37]E. W. Bullinger, *How to Enjoy the Bible*, pp. 94-96; Bullinger, *The Companion Bible*, Part VI, pp. 1769, 1912.
[38]Gaebelein, *The Gospel* . . . , p. 266.

be confused with water baptism, as many expositors have done, as the work of sanctification and cleansing by the washing of water with the Word is a continuous action, not an ordinance or sacrament. The "word" used in sanctification does not refer to baptism but the Word of God as a whole as it is applied to the bride. In brief, this embraces the total ministry of the Word of God to Christians in the present age and is the scriptural support for preaching the Word not only as a means of winning the lost but as providing progressive sanctification for those who are already saved.

The present work of sanctification described in verse 26 will culminate in a future work revealed in Ephesians 5:27 (ASV) where it is said that Christ has the goal "that he might present the church to himself a glorious church, not having spot or wrinkle or any such thing; but that it should be holy and without blemish." When the work of Christ for His church has been consummated, the church will be in heaven without any evidence of sin which spoiled its testimony in this world. There will be no spot, that is, visible defilement; no wrinkle, that is, no evidence of age or corruption, or anything of a similar nature such as a blemish. Instead, the whole church will be completely holy and adapted to the environment of heaven.

A further thought is introduced in the description of the bride as the wife of Christ in Revelation 19 (ASV). After the announcement of the coming marriage feast and the declaration in verse 7, "His wife hath made herself ready," the passage continues in verse 8, "And it was given unto her that she should array herself in fine linen, bright and pure: for the fine linen is the righteous acts of the saints." Here the result of the present work of Christ is defined as clothing the bride in fine linen, namely, the righteous acts which stemmed from the present work of the sanctifying application of the Word of God.

The work of Christ for the church in this present age therefore partakes of the character of the loving ministry anticipating that future joyous occasion when the bride will stand complete in heaven with every beauty and grace. The marriage relationship is viewed in three phases: (1) The bride is already joined to Christ in legal marriage as a result of the price that was paid at Calvary and the acceptance of the offer of salvation. (2) The bride is now awaiting the coming of her Bridegroom, which will occur at the rapture of the church. (3) Subsequent to the rapture, the marriage feast will be observed (Rev. 19:7-9). The present work of Christ will therefore have its consummation in these future events and ultimately the church, which is now incomplete and plagued with many deficiencies, will stand perfect in heaven in every beauty and grace. The figure of the Bridegroom and the bride is a proper conclusion to all the other figures which depict the relationship of Christ to His church and especially emphasizes that which is yet ahead.

THE PRESENT WORK OF CHRIST ON EARTH

While the heavenly work of Christ views Him as the glorified One located in heaven, the present earthly work of Christ sees Him as present and active in His church on earth. Three major aspects of this ministry must be considered: (1) the presence of Christ in the church; (2) the work of Christ in the church; (3) the relation of the present work of Christ to the present work of the Holy Spirit.

The Presence of Christ in the Church

The Scriptures reveal that not only is the Holy Spirit indwelling the church, but that Christ also is present. This is in keeping with the doctrine of omnipresence but implies also a special sense in which Christ is ministering to the church. As far as His human nature and body is concerned, Christ is in heaven. In His divine nature, however, He is present in the world and especially indwelling those who are His own.

The concept of the presence of Christ in the earth has undoubtedly suffered from confusion with the doctrine of the presence of the Holy Spirit which in turn has been caused by a faulty understanding of the relationship of the Persons of the Trinity. While orthodox theology has fully recognized the doctrine of the Trinity, the exposition of that doctrine has not always been clear in describing how the activity of one Member of the Godhead relates to the activity of Another. The proper point of view is that while the three Persons of the Trinity are one God they are nevertheless three Persons, and it is not proper or scriptural to confuse Their persons or Their activity even though the two are interrelated.

The danger involved in confusing the Persons of the Trinity

is illustrated in the erroneous view that the coming of the Holy
Spirit at Pentecost fulfilled the promises that Christ would come
again. This view, of course, is unmindful of the fact that all of
the New Testament was written after Pentecost, and it considers
the coming of Christ as yet future even though Pentecost had
already taken place. In spite of the untenable character of this
point of view, Hugh Thompson Kerr expresses this view: "The
Holy Spirit is the living Christ. Pentecost is the fulfillment of
the promise that He would come again."[39] Confusion of the
Persons of the Trinity in this manner is never justified and reveals
a faulty understanding of what constitutes the distinction of the
Persons of the Trinity.

The confusion of the person of Christ with that of the Holy
Spirit is a very common one, however. Milligan writes: "The
Spirit bestowed by our Lord in His glorified condition is not
really the Spirit but the Spirit in which He Himself is filled; or,
in other words, His own spirit."[40] Such a view of the Holy Spirit
of course tends toward a Unitarian point of view which in essence
denies that there are distinct Persons in the Trinity. The proper
view is that the three Persons are identified in essence in that
They are one God, but in Their persons They are triune. Frederic Platt also confuses this concept when he writes: "As Christ
being God is identical with God, so the Holy Spirit being God
is identical with God. . . . The indwelling Spirit therefore, is
the indwelling of God-in-Christ."[41] Such confusion of the Persons
of the Trinity is not justified by the scriptural revelation and is
a variation from what is normally considered orthodox.

The problem is not one of easy solution, however, as it may
be conceded that in some scriptures it is not always clear which
Person of the Trinity is in view. The term "Spirit of Christ"
grammatically permits the thought of Spirit of Christ in the sense
of being the Spirit *of* the second Person (genitive), or in the
sense of being the Spirit *from* Christ (ablative) that is, the third
Person. The form is the same in either case (*Christou*). The
occasions where this expression is found in Scripture (Rom.
8:2-3; II Cor. 3:17; Gal. 4:6; Phil. 1:19; I Peter 1:11) must be
interpreted by their context, but in every case it is either One

---

[39]Hugh Thompson Kerr, *After He Had Risen*, p. 93; cf. review by R. T.
Chafer, *Bibliotheca Sacra*, XCI (Oct., 1934), 488.
[40]Milligan, p. 179.
[41]Frederic Platt, *Immanence and Christian Thought*, p. 452.

or the Other, that is, either Christ or the Holy Spirit, not Both or a combination of Both. W. H. Griffith Thomas states the proper point of view in these words: "It is essential to preserve with care both sides of this truth. Christ and the Spirit are different yet the same, the same yet different. Perhaps the best expression we can give is that while their Personalities are never identical, their presence always is."[42] The presence of Christ must therefore be distinguished from the presence of the Holy Spirit and likewise Their respective indwellings of the believer. In a similar way, the indwelling of the Father must not be made identical with the indwelling of Christ or of the Holy Spirit (John 14:23; Eph. 4:6; II John 9). The fact is that all three Persons of the Trinity indwell the believer and, as Griffith Thomas states, if One is present the Other is also present although Their persons can be distinguished and in some cases Their ministries. It may be concluded that Christ is present in the world, not because the Holy Spirit is present in the world, but because Both are present.

The doctrine of the presence of Christ in the earth in the present age is related somewhat to the interpretation of the Lord's Supper. The Roman Catholic Church, holding to the doctrine of transubstantiation which involves the identity of the elements of the Lord's Supper with the body of Christ, obviously teaches that Christ is present in the earth bodily and specifically in the elements of the Lord's Supper. The Lutheran Church has held a similar doctrine which has been called consubstantiation for want of a better title, which has viewed the body of Christ as present in the elements, but without change in their substance. This has been in keeping with their doctrine of the omnipresence of the body of Christ. The Zwinglian view of the Lord's Supper holds that Christ is not bodily present in the elements and in fact is absent, being in heaven bodily. For this reason the elements represent His presence though not constituting His presence in the earthly scene. The Zwinglian view does not deny the spiritual presence of Christ in the earth, but denies that His presence is in any special sense in the elements of the Lord's Supper. Calvin seems to have held a position somewhat between the Zwinglian and the Lutheran views in that he believed that

[42]Griffith Thomas, *The Holy Spirit of God*, p. 144.

the elements held the spiritual presence of Christ, but not the bodily presence of Christ.

All views of the Lord's Supper, however, take for granted that Christ is in the world in some sense. They differ in defining the precise sense in which Christ is related to the Lord's Supper. Both the Zwinglian and the Calvinistic points of view seem to be in harmony with the complete revelation of the presence of Christ as afforded in the New Testament.

The doctrine that Christ is present in the world in keeping with His omnipresence is not quite the same concept as the thought of Christ indwelling the church. The Scriptures seem to teach that Christ's presence in the church is presence in a special sense and involves a special association, union and activity. The doctrine of the indwelling presence of Christ is easily established as a doctrine of the Scripture, as there are many scriptural references (Matt. 28:20; John 14:18, 20, 23; 15:4-5; 17:23, 26; Gal. 2:20; Col. 1:26-27; I John 3:24). The key passage is Colossians 1:26-27 where the indwelling of Christ is declared to be a mystery (cf. Rom. 16:25-26), that is, a New Testament truth not revealed in the Old Testament. The idea of Christ indwelling the saints is not found in the Old Testament. The teaching of these passages is sufficiently plain to demonstrate beyond doubt that Christ does indeed indwell His church corporately as well as indwelling the individuals who are members of the church. The very fact of Christ's presence is the believer's assurance that he belongs to Him and is the object of divine love and ministry.

The Work of Christ in the Church

The fact that Christ is indwelling the church is related to the imparted divine life received by the believer when he is born again at the moment of saving faith by the act of regeneration. Although regeneration is a work of the Holy Spirit, the eternal life which is imparted is inseparably related to Christ Himself as "the life" (John 1:4; cf. John 10:10; 11:25; 14:6; Col. 3:4; I John 5:12).

A parallel can be found in the conception of Christ in connection with His incarnation. Although Christ was conceived by the Holy Spirit, yet the life which was imparted was that of the second Person of the Trinity and the first Person is spoken of as His Father. Likewise the believer is born again through the immediate agency of the Holy Spirit. The first Person is his Father, but the eternal life which is imparted is related to the second Person. The concept of life is also found in other figures relating Christ to the church such as the vine and the branches, the head and the body, and the last Adam and the new creation.

The indwelling Christ is also the source of our strength (Phil. 4:13) and power is provided through His presence as indicated in Matthew 28:18-20.

Moreover, the indwelling Christ is the ground of the believer's hope according to Colossians 1:27, "Christ in you, the hope of glory." Because Christ is in us now we have hope of being like Him (I John 3:2) and of having ultimate deliverance from our present mortal body (Rom. 8:20-23). The day of our redemption, that is, the redemption of our bodies, is assured (Eph. 4:30). Therefore, the indwelling presence of Christ is a vital Christian truth related to victorious Christian experience and providing evidence for faith and hope.

The Relation of the Present Work of Christ to the Present Work of the Holy Spirit

Although the present work of Christ and the present work of the Holy Spirit are interrelated, they must also be kept in their proper distinction. The Holy Spirit is sent by Christ to His church to minister on His behalf (Luke 24:49; John 14:16-17, 26; 15:26; 16:7-15; Acts 1:8; 2:38). Christ could not send Himself and in the fact that He sent the Holy Spirit, the distinction in Their persons is made evident. The Holy Spirit is the Agent of Christ and in some sense what the Holy Spirit does, Christ does also, but this should not contradict the distinction of Their persons and ministry otherwise. It is also true that there is a relationship between the work of the Holy Spirit and the work of Christ in that Both participate in common things such as regeneration, providing sources of strength for the believer and in giving hope (Rom. 15:13; Col. 1:27). Accordingly, the present work of Christ as a whole includes a great undertaking in the earthly sphere. In many respects it is the extension of that which Christ undertook when on earth Himself. It is as a whole anticipatory of that ultimate work when the believer will be presented faultless in the presence of God in glory.

12

THE FUTURE WORK OF CHRIST

THE COMING OF CHRIST FOR HIS CHURCH

MANY SCRIPTURES TESTIFY to the fact that the present age will culminate in the coming of the Lord for His church. According to I Thessalonians 4:13-18, this event will close the age with the resurrection of the dead in Christ, and living saints will be "caught up" to meet the Lord in the air and thereafter "be with the Lord." In view of the extensive consideration of biblical truth relating to this subject in a previous publication by the author,[1] the present discussion is limited to three important aspects of the doctrine of the coming of the Lord for His church: (1) the rapture of the church, that is, the coming of Christ for His church; (2) Christ in relation to the church in heaven; and (3) the second coming of Christ to the earth.

Four Views of the Rapture

Four major interpretations have been advanced by those accepting the inspiration and infallibility of the Scriptures. These views are concerned not only with the character and events related to the second coming, but primarily deal with the question of the relation of these events to the predicted time of tribulation or trouble which will sweep all the world and especially the nation Israel. The four views relate the coming of Christ for His church and His second coming to the earth to this time of tribulation as follows:

1. The posttribulation view, that Christ will come for His church as a phase of His return to earth after the tribulation.

2. The midtribulation view, that Christ will come in the middle of the seven-year period predicted by Daniel, but before the great tribulation of the last three and a half years.

[1]Cf. John F. Walvoord, *The Rapture Question.*

3. The partial-rapture view, that Christ will catch out of the world those who are spiritually qualified before the tribulation and, as others become qualified, will catch them up to Himself throughout the tribulation period.

4. The pretribulation view, which holds that Christ will come for His church before the seventieth week of Daniel, the seven-year period preceding Christ's coming to the earth to establish His millennial kingdom.

Of the four views it may be said that an insignificant fraction of expositors follow the partial-rapture view, and it has never attained the status of orthodoxy within Evangelicalism. The midtribulation view has experienced some popularity in the present generation, but has practically no literature and is held by no specific group or denomination. The great body of students of Scripture who are premillennial hold either the pretribulational or posttribulational view.[2]

Posttribulationism. Unquestionably the majority view as far as the rapture is concerned is the posttribulational view, namely, that Christ will come for His church in connection with His second coming to the earth. This is the view advocated by the amillenarians and postmillenarians and by some premillenarians. They contend that to divide the rapture from the second coming to the earth by a period of at least seven years is to bifurcate what the Scriptures intend to be a single event.

Posttribulationists who have written on this subject usually attack the pretribulational view, rather than support their own position. Arguments gleaned from their writings in favor of the posttribulational position may be itemized as follows:

1. The argument from history. Posttribulationists appeal to the fact that the early church Fathers were posttribulational and conclude that, therefore, the pretribulation position is new and novel. Pretribulationists reply by noting that modern posttribulationism with its doctrine of tribulation first and then the rapture is not what the early church Fathers believed at all, for the early church held the any-moment view of the Lord's return, thinking erroneously that they were already in the great tribulation. The modern form of posttribulationism which places the

[2]See *ibid.* for discussion of these four views and their supporters: partial-rapture theory, pp. 105-25; posttribulationism, pp. 127-70; midtribulationism, pp. 171-89. Only a summary of this material is presented here.

tribulation still future and to be followed by the rapture is in some respects more recent than pretribulationism as it is taught today. Pretribulationists hold with the early church to the doctrine of imminency, but disagree that we are already in the great tribulation. Posttribulationists disagree with the early church doctrine of imminency but, like the early church, place the rapture after the tribulation.

2. The church will be preserved through the tribulation. This posttribulational argument attempts to play down the scriptures that teach that the time of tribulation will be unprecedented in its severity and to advance the position that the wrath of God in this period will be poured out only on unsaved people, while the church will go through the period without experiencing the wrath of God. Pretribulationists observe that this is not what the Bible teaches inasmuch as evidence seems to point to the martyrdom of most of those who do come to Christ in the period and that the nature of the judgment, such as earthquakes, pestilence, war, famine, etc., would affect believers as well as unbelievers. Pretribulationists also point out that posttribulationists adopt an extensive spiritualization of prophecies which should be taken literally in order to avoid contradiction of their viewpoint.

3. There are saints in the tribulation. Posttribulationists have seized upon the fact that there are saints in the tribulation as proving that the church is there as well. Pretribulationists reply by admitting that there will be people saved during the tribulation period. However, it is noted that none of the technical terms relating them to the saints of the present age, such as the phrase "in Christ," or "the baptism of the Spirit" or similar terms are to be found. The word "church" is never used in any passage dealing with the great tribulation.

4. The Bible predicts events occurring before the rapture; therefore, it cannot be imminent. This posttribulational argument is an admission that the early church Fathers were wrong in believing in imminency because of events which must occur before the rapture according to posttribulation interpretation. The events usually cited, however, such as the predicted death of Peter, the destruction of Jerusalem, and implications that the period will be a long time, actually do not stand in the way of current belief in the imminent return of Christ and did not

even hinder this in the first century. Even the few years from Pentecost to the time of Paul's conversion and later revelation of rapture truth in its details could be considered a long time. The destruction of Jerusalem is nowhere stated to be either before or after the rapture. The death of Peter could, of course, have taken place any day. This posttribulation argument certainly does not militate against the doctrine of imminency today.

5. The prophecy of a resurrection occurring at the beginning of the millennium is cited as supporting posttribulationism. Pretribulationists, of course, agree with posttribulationists that there will be a resurrection before the millennium in connection with Christ's second coming to the earth and this is explicitly taught in Revelation 20:4-6. Pretribulationists hold, however, that this resurrection relates to tribulation saints and possibly Old Testament saints, but does not include specifically the dead in Christ of the present age. All premillennial interpretations of Scripture agree that there is more than one resurrection, as the Scriptures indicate as a minimum the resurrection of Christ, the resurrection of the righteous related to the second coming and the resurrection of the wicked after the millennium. The further division of the resurrection of the church before the tribulation and the resurrection of other saints after the tribulation would be an additional refinement.

6. The same expressions are used for the Lord's return for His church as are used for His second coming to the earth. Pretribulationists agree that the word "coming" (Greek, *parousia*) and other similar words may be used of both events, but find nothing strange in such usage. These are general words and must be invested by the context with their particular meaning as these same words are used of other events in the Bible and are not technical words.

7. The tares are gathered out "first" in the parable of wheat and tares in Matthew 13. Pretribulationists reply that in the first place the order is not important here as even posttribulationists admit that the separation of the wheat and the tares occurs simultaneously as illustrated in the judgment of the sheep and the goats in Matthew 25:31-46. The reference to the wheat and tares, however, relates to the second coming and not to the rapture, as the entire interadvent age from the first coming to the earth to the second coming to the earth is in view in this passage.

Significantly, in the same chapter in the parable of the dragnet, the order is reversed and the good fish are gathered into the vessels and subsequently the bad are "cast away" (Matt. 13:48-50, ASV). The rapture, however, is not in view in either parable.

8. Expressions like "the day" and "the day of the Lord" are technical terms which could not refer to more than one event. Pretribulationists observe that the expression "the day of the Lord" actually is a long period of time, including the entire millennium. In the nature of the case, an expression like "day" is a general term and has to be given meaning in the context. It is not true that this word is always used in the same sense in the Bible and, as a matter of fact, it would be impossible to make this expression always a technical term.

9. The chronology of II Thessalonians 2:1-12 requires two signs preceding the Lord's return, namely, the apostasy and the revelation of the man of sin. Pretribulationists observe that this passage is given as a correction of an error which had been taught the Thessalonians, namely, that they were already in the day of the Lord and in the period of trouble which this would bring upon the earth. These signs relate to the day of the Lord, not the rapture. This passage is actually an argument for pretribulationism rather than posttribulationism as the restrainer apparently is to be identified with the restraint of sin in the present age. This must be removed before the tribulation can come. Whether or not the restrainer is the Holy Spirit as many believe, it would be natural for an event like the rapture to cause such a lifting of restraint, and the subsequent revelation of the man of sin. If there is any evidence in this passage relating to this question, it is for the pretribulational view rather than the posttribulational view.

10. The term "the end" is a technical expression always referring to the end of the interadvent age. Pretribulationists note that passages where this expression occurs (I Cor. 1:7-8; Heb. 3:6, 14; 6:11; Rev. 2:26) refer to a time which must necessarily be defined by the context. Significantly, not one of the five texts used as proof are linked with the posttribulational coming of the Lord and only one instance (I Cor. 1:7-8) even mentions it. Like other terms such as "the day" and "coming," the expression "the end" is not technical in itself; therefore, it could conceivably

be used of the end of the church period as well as the end of the tribulation.

11. Certain passages, such as Matthew 24:31, relate the rapture to the end of the tribulation and lead naturally to posttribulationism. Pretribulationists point out that a rapture is not mentioned in Matthew 24:31, and in the passage neither translation nor resurrection is specified. As in many other instances, posttribulationists are assuming what they are trying to prove.

These brief answers to the principal posttribulational arguments could be greatly expanded. The basic problem, however, is that posttribulationism has been occupied with refuting the pretribulational arguments, but seldom if ever offers solid proof that the rapture occurs after the tribulation. As a matter of fact, not a single passage in the New Testament relating to the rapture contextually can be proved to refer to the close of the tribulation period. Posttribulationists therefore are driven completely to inference.

It is most significant that in all of the passages dealing specifically with the second coming of Christ to the earth not one word can be found concerning translation of living saints. Pretribulationists concede that there will be a resurrection of certain saints at this time, but in none of these resurrections is the church specifically mentioned. In fact, passages such as Revelation 20:4-6 specifically refer to the tribulation saints. It is significant that the great majority of educational institutions which are premillennial are also pretribulational, especially the Bible institute movement which has specialized in the premillennial interpretation of the Scripture.

The midtribulation rapture. In the current dispute between pretribulationists and posttribulationists it is natural that some should be attracted to a mediate position. Although comparatively little literature has been created and no specific school of thought has emerged in support of the midtribulation view, it has been adopted by some contemporary evangelical scholars.[3] Their position is that the church will be raptured at the end of the first three and a half years of the seven years of Israel's covenant (Dan. 9:27) and therefore will be caught out of the world

[3]Norman B. Harrison, *The End*; J. O. Buswell, *A Systematic Theology of the Christian Religion*, II, 450 ff.

before the time of the great tribulation which is the last three and a half years.

The principal argument in favor of midtribulationism is the identification of the trump which will be sounded at the rapture with the seventh trump of Revelation 11. This identification, however, is completely faulty as the series of trumpets culminating in the seventh trumpet are trumps of angels having to do with the pouring out of wrath upon the earth and have no relation to the rapture or translation of living saints or to the resurrection of the dead in Christ. The seventh trumpet of Revelation is near the end of the great tribulation, not at its beginning, as the day of wrath has begun much earlier (Rev. 6:17). This seventh trumpet is not the last, in any event, as there is a further trumpet mentioned in Matthew 24:31. The midtribulation theory renders impossible the imminency of the coming of the Lord as the events of the first half of Daniel's seventieth week would have to occur first.

Partial-rapture theory. This point of view, which arose a hundred years ago in the works of Robert Govett, has been principally expounded by G. H. Lang in the twentieth century.[4] The concept of a partial rapture is derived from Scripture passages in which believers are urged to be prepared for the return of the Lord. Major passages cited by partial rapturists are Matthew 24:40-51; 25:13; Mark 13:33-37; Luke 20:34-36; 21:36; Philippians 3:10-12; I Thessalonians 5:6; II Timothy 4:8; Titus 2:13; Hebrews 9:24-28; Revelation 3:3; 12:1-6. Adherents to this point of view hold that believers must have good works in order to qualify for the rapture. Even in its simplest presentation, it is obvious that this is founded on a misapprehension of grace, the basis of salvation and the nature of the body of Christ. If the question is raised, How many works are required to qualify? it becomes immediately apparent that this teaching rests on a questionable foundation. According to I Corinthians 15:51, "all" Christians will be included in the translation and resurrection at the rapture. It is because of these objections that most evangelical scholars have considered the partial-rapture view unworthy of serious consideration.

Pretribulation rapture. This point of view is adopted in the discussion which follows and holds that Christ will come for

[4]Cf. Robert Govett, *Entrance into the Kingdom*; G. H. Lang, *The Revelation of Jesus Christ: Firstborn Sons, Their Rights and Risks.*

His own before the seventieth week of Daniel is fulfilled and therefore before the great tribulation. This interpretation has been generally followed in most advanced study of prophecy among premillenarians in the twentieth century and is in harmony with the doctrine of the imminency of the rapture held by the early church Fathers. A thorough study of the doctrine in the last century has brought to light many details which formerly were obscure, and this study has tended to harmonize the premillennial interpretation of the Scripture and solve problems which in former generations were only partially answered. Generally speaking, this view is held by most premillenarians today, especially those who distinguish the program of God for Israel and the church and who tend to interpret prophecy in a normal, literal way.

In the author's work *The Rapture Question* some fifty arguments for pretribulationism are set forth in the conclusion.[5] Without attempting to restate all of these it may be observed here that pretribulationism depends upon two important premises. First, the church is regarded as a body of saints distinct from those of other ages, either before or after. Second, the tribulation is viewed as a future period of unprecedented trouble which will occur in the last half of Daniel's seventieth week, a seven-year period which is future and subsequent to the rapture. Generally speaking, opponents of pretribulationism have begged the question by assuming that the word "church" includes saints of all ages, often with no proof whatever, and have tended to neglect the specifics given in the prophetic Word concerning the tribulation itself.

The supporting evidence for pretribulationism falls into these six categories:

1. Pretribulationism is an outgrowth of the same type of hermeneutics which lead to premillennialism, namely, a literal interpretation of prophecy as opposed to the amillennial, spiritualized or allegorical interpretation of prophecy. Consistent premillennial hermeneutics lead to pretribulationism. This is evidenced by the fact that many who have abandoned pretribulationism often abandon premillennialism also.

2. No positive evidence can be produced that the church is in the tribulation. No specific term such as "in Christ," the word

[5]Walvoord, pp. 191-99.

"church" itself, or reference to the body of Christ, distinguishing the saints of the present age from other ages, is ever used in connection with those in the tribulation itself.

3. According to the accounts of the tribulation in the Scripture, the events are related to Israel and the Gentiles and not to the church. In fact, the church is promised deliverance from the period according to I Thessalonians 5:9 (cf. I Thess. 1:9-10; Rev. 3:10; 6:17). Whenever the truth of the rapture of the church is presented in the Bible, it is always in the form of predicting it as an imminent event. It is therefore offered as a hope to believers and a basis for comfort and exhortation with no events indicated as necessarily occurring first (I Thess. 4:18; 5:6; Titus 2:13; I John 3:1-3).

4. The period in which sin is permitted to manifest itself without restraint seemingly is impossible until the restrainer (probably to be identified as the Holy Spirit) is removed (II Thess. 2:7). This would seem to require the rapture first before the tribulation can begin.

5. A number of events are described in prophecy as occurring in heaven between the rapture and Christ's coming to the earth, such as the judgment seat of Christ (II Cor. 5:10) and the consummation of the marriage union (Eph. 5:27). On earth a period of time is needed between the rapture and the second coming to provide a group of saints who will remain in their natural bodies and populate the earth in the millennium (Isa. 65:20-25). If a rapture occurred at the end of the tribulation, it would leave no saints in their natural bodies to populate the millennial earth. The necessity of this interval is brought out in the divine judgments related to the second coming, namely, the judgment of the Gentiles (Matt. 25:31-46) and the judgment of Israel (Ezek. 20:34-38). Both of these judgments presume that there has been no separation of the saved from the unsaved such as a rapture would have effected at the time of the second coming.

6. Many contrasts exist between the rapture of the church and the second coming of Christ to the earth which tend to prove that they are distinct events and separated by a time period. The rapture pictures the saints meeting Christ in the air while at the second coming Christ meets the saints on earth. At the rapture the saints go to heaven; at the second coming the saints

come to the earth. At the rapture there is no indication that sin is judged in the earth as it occurs before the day of wrath; at the second coming Christ establishes His kingdom, returning to the Mount of Olives, remaining on earth where He reigns as King. At that time sin will be brought into judgment, and righteousness and peace will fill the earth. The second coming clearly follows the great tribulation which is given as a definite sign of the Lord's return. The rapture is constantly viewed as a signless event which is imminent.

The arguments for pretribulationism offered at length in the author's *The Rapture Question* as well as other important contributions to this field of study, such as J. Dwight Pentecost's *Things to Come* and Gerald Stanton's *Kept from the Hour*, demonstrate that pretribulationism is not wishful thinking, but is based upon a solid principle of interpretation and many passages of Scripture, and is supported by innumerable collateral proofs. The pretribulation point of view welcomes thorough investigation.

The Doctrine of the Rapture in Scripture

The fact that Christ would return to take His own out of the world is first introduced in the upper room discourse in John 14:1-3. The disciples, already alarmed by predictions that Christ was going to leave them and that they would not be able to follow Him (John 13:33-36), are now informed that Christ is going to come for them and take them to the Father's house. This was an obvious contradiction of their previous hope that Christ was going to reign on earth and quite different in its general character. It indicated that their hope was heavenly rather than earthly and that they were going to be taken out of the earth to heaven rather than for Christ to come to the earth to be with them.

In the first of Paul's epistles to the Thessalonians, further exposition is given the doctrine of the rapture as it was held by the early church. The Apostle Paul accompanied by Timothy and Silas had visited Thessalonica and, in the course of their ministry extending over three Sabbath days, had led a small number to the Lord. After being forced to leave because of persecution, Paul sent Timothy back to Thessalonica to ascertain their condition. Upon his return to Paul, Timothy reported on their progress and also brought back certain theological questions he was unable to answer. Among them was the question of the relationship between the translation of living Christians and the resurrection of the dead.

This rather mature question coming from young Christians indicates the extensive character of the teaching ministry of Paul to them subsequent to their conversion. They apparently already believed in the doctrine of the resurrection of the dead, and they also believed that Christ would come at any moment to catch the living to be with Himself. The relationship of these two events was the matter in point. In answer to their questions, the apostle states in I Thessalonians 4:15-17 (ASV):

> For this we say unto you by the word of the Lord, that we that are alive, that are left unto the coming of the Lord, shall in no wise precede them that are fallen asleep. For the Lord himself shall descend from heaven, with a shout, with the voice of the archangel, and with the trump of God: and the dead in Christ shall rise first; then we that are alive, that are left, shall together with them be caught up in the clouds, to meet the Lord in the air: and so shall we ever be with the Lord.

From the Thessalonian passage it will be observed: (1) The same Lord who ascended from the Mount of Olives to heaven would descend bodily from heaven to the realm of the atmospheric heavens. (2) His coming would be signaled by a shout, the voice of the archangel and the trump of God. (3) At these signals the dead in Christ would be raised to rejoin their souls and spirits, which would come with Christ from heaven when He came (I Thess. 4:14). (4) Living saints instantly transformed would meet the Lord in the air and without dying would be introduced to their heavenly existence. (5) Having thus met the Lord in the air, saints translated and resurrected would be forever with the Lord (I Thess. 4:17). This doctrine was introduced to them as a comfort in the loss of their loved ones as well as an encouragement to them in their time of persecution. It is noteworthy that no intimation is given of any intervening time of tribulation such as is discussed in I Thessalonians 5.

A major contribution to the doctrine of the rapture was given later to the Corinthian church as recorded in I Corinthians 15:51-58. This important theological passage is introduced by a restatement of the gospel that Christ died for our sins, and that He rose from the dead, thus supporting the doctrine of the resurrection of all men. At the conclusion of this discussion, the truth of the rapture is described as a mystery, a truth unrevealed in the Old Testament.

The Corinthian passage makes more explicit what is implied in Thessalonians, namely, that believers will receive a new body in contrast to our present corruptible, mortal and sinful body. This heavenly body will be like the body of our Lord and suited for the heavenly sphere. The resurrection body will be incorruptible, that is, will not be subject to the decay and deterioration of age. It will be immortal in that it will be deathless. While it is not expressly stated in this passage, it is implied in I John 3:2 that our resurrection bodies will be sinless, a conclusion confirmed in Philippians 3:21 (ASV) where our bodies are said to be "conformed to the body of his glory." This resurrection and translation is said to take place "in a moment, in the twinkling of an eye, at the last trump" (I Cor. 15:52).

Although there are other allusions to the coming of the Lord for His church in Scripture, these major passages bring out the central doctrine, namely, that when Christ comes living Christians will be translated and the dead in Christ will be raised from the dead. After meeting Christ in the air they will go to the Father's house as promised in John 14:1-3 and in the heavenly sphere will fulfill predicted events which will take place in heaven prior to Christ's second coming to the earth.

CHRIST AND THE CHURCH IN HEAVEN

The Judgment of the Church in Heaven

After meeting Christ in the air at the time of the rapture, the church will proceed to heaven. There, according to many New Testament passages, the church will be judged for reward. If the rapture concerns only Christians, it is evident that only Christians will be involved in this judgment as only such will be eligible for the rapture itself. If Israel and other Old Testament saints are raised at the time of the rapture, they also may be judged or their judgment may be reserved to a later time, namely, the time of Christ's second coming to the earth when their rewards will be distributed in the form of privileged places of service in the millennial kingdom. As the judgment of the church does not concern the matter of salvation, it is primarily a question of rewards for service.

The central passage on the judgment of the church is II Corinthians 5:8-10 (ASV):

> We are of good courage, I say, and are willing rather to be absent from the body, and to be at home with the Lord. Wherefore also we make it our aim, whether at home or absent, to be well-pleasing unto him. For we must all be made manifest before the judgment-seat of Christ; that each one may receive the things done in the body, according to what he hath done, whether it be good or bad.

Paul declares that it is his fundamental purpose to live in such a way that his life will be well spent in the Master's service. When he is judged at this judgment seat, it will be determined what is good and what is bad.

Although some have attempted to make this a Protestant purgatory, that is, a time of punishment for unconfessed sin, it seems clear from the general doctrine of justification by faith that no condemnation is possible for one who is in Christ. Discipline such as is administered in this life will be of no value to those already made perfect in heaven. The bad works are discarded as unworthy of reward but good works are rewarded. The penalty is the loss of reward. It is obvious that with imperfections which beset every Christian, no one will be able to claim perfection in that day. All will have a measure of failure, and it may be that all will have some reward. The judgment will be a general evaluation of a summary kind, but it is gracious rather than retributive.

The judgment seat of Christ, however, is a real issue with Paul. He speaks of "knowing therefore the fear of the Lord" (II Cor. 5:11, ASV). This fear is fear of regret that his life will be revealed as one wasted and spent in selfishness rather than in devotion and complete obedience to Christ. Christians contemplating the rapture of the church, therefore, must also face the fact that their lives will then be brought in review before God and that they will be rewarded according to what they have done.

Three figures are used in the New Testament to illustrate the principles involved in the judgment seat of Christ. The first of these is found in Romans 14:10-12 (ASV): "But thou, . . . why dost thou set at nought thy brother? For we shall all stand before the judgment-seat of God. For it is written, As I live, saith the Lord, to me every knee shall bow, and every tongue shall confess to God. So then each one of us shall give account of himself to God." In this passage life is viewed as a stewardship with every Christian having to give an account of his stewardship at the judgment seat of Christ. An application is made of this truth that we should not judge each other, but rather should give our principal attention to fulfilling our own stewardship in such a way that we will have a good report when we must render account.

In I Corinthians 3:11-15 the figure of a building is used to illustrate the principle of judgment. In verse 11 the foundation of the building is revealed to be Christ who as Saviour provides a foundation for every Christian life. On this foundation every man must build his building. Ultimately the building is to be tested by fire which "shall prove each man's work of what sort it is" (I Cor. 3:13, ASV). When tested in this way, reward is promised for that which abides, and loss is assured for that which is burned: "If any man's work shall abide which he built thereon, he shall receive a reward. If any man's work shall be burned, he shall suffer loss: but he himself shall be saved; yet so as through fire" (I Cor. 3:14-15, ASV). In view of the fact that the building is to be tested by fire, Christians are urged to build their house of gold, silver and precious stones, which are incombustible, in contrast to wood, hay and stubble which are easily consumed by fire (cf. I Cor. 3:12).

No meaning is assigned to the particular materials mentioned from scriptural background. However, gold is often used to represent the glory of Deity; silver is the metal of redemption, and precious stones reflect wealth of other kinds. The use of these materials undoubtedly reflects Christian life and witness which, as gold, manifest the glory of God, as silver, the extension of the gospel and, as precious stones, accomplish many things which are of value in God's sight. By contrast, wood, hay and stubble represent three degrees of worthlessness. Stubble is fit for nothing. Hay is suitable only for beasts. Wood, while being a useful tool of man, can also be destroyed by fire. The final test of all man's work is what evaluation is placed upon it at the judgment seat of Christ. Christians, accordingly, are urged to build a life which embodies eternal values.

A third figure is found in I Corinthians 9:24-27 (ASV) where life is compared to an athletic contest:

> Know ye not that they that run in a race run all, but one receiveth the prize? Even so run; that ye may attain. And every man that striveth in the games exerciseth self-control in all things. Now they do it to receive a corruptible crown; but we an incorruptible. I therefore so run, as not uncertainly; so fight I, as not beating the air: but I buffet my body, and bring it into bondage: lest by any means, after that I have preached to others, I myself should be rejected.

The objective in a race is to win the prize and to this end all minor considerations must be put aside.

In like manner the Christian's goal is to receive reward at the judgment seat of Christ, and therefore he must accomplish the will of God. The Apostle Paul not only likens life to a race, but also to a boxing match where he beats his own body in order to bring it under subjection. The figure speaks of self-discipline and self-control. The reward promised is an incorruptible crown in contrast to the corruptible crown of laurel, pine or parsley leaves which soon fade away, so often given athletes in Greek contests. Paul wanted to live and preach in such a way that he himself might not be considered worthless at the judgment seat of Christ. The term "rejected'" refers to his rewards and life rather than to his personal salvation, and Paul had in mind that an athlete who did not conform to the rules would have his victory disallowed.

In addition to these figures of speech, Christ in the seven messages to the churches of Asia in Revelation 2-3 challenges those in each church to live in the will of God that they might receive their proper reward at the judgment seat of Christ. No more searching analysis can be made of any human work than the question of Christ's evaluation at that future tribunal.

The Marriage Union of Christ and the Church

As indicated in some earlier discussion, the present work of Christ and the church is set forth in the figure of Christ as the Bridegroom and the church as the bride. The future aspect of this figure includes the consummation of the marriage union between Christ and His church. In keeping with the Oriental symbolism, the church in its relation to Christ will follow the pattern of the customary marriage in Christ's day. The first step in such a marriage was the legal union consummated when the parents of the bridegroom and the bride agreed on the marriage and entered into formal contract in which the dowry was paid. As fulfilled in the symbolism of Christ in the church, this occurs at the moment an individual believes in Christ as his Saviour and accepts the payment of his redemption which Christ Himself paid on the cross. The bride accepts this situation and acknowledges Christ as her loved One as well as her Redeemer. Throughout the present age, Christ is preparing His bride for the future consummation as indicated in Ephesians 5:26. The church as a pure virgin is awaiting the coming of her Bridegroom as indicated in II Corinthians 11:2. The first phase of the marriage is an indication of the grace of God, for while the Bridegroom is altogether lovely, the bride has little to commend herself in natural or spiritual beauty. The transformation into a lovely bride is made possible by the grace of God.

The second phase of the Oriental wedding was marked by a procession of the bridegroom to the home of the bride accompanied by his friends, often at a late hour at night, as illustrated in the parable of the ten virgins (Matt. 25:1-13). In the case of Christ, this will be fulfilled at the rapture of the church when Christ the Bridegroom comes from the Father's house to the earth to receive His bride and take her back to the place that He has prepared for her (John 14:1-3). When this event takes place, the church will be forever with the Lord, and the marriage union is consummated.

A third aspect of an Oriental wedding was the marriage feast held for the benefit of guests. The ten virgins of Matthew 25 were such guests as well as others. There has been some difference of opinion as to whether the symbolism of the marriage feast is fulfilled in heaven following the rapture or whether it will be on earth in connection with the second coming of Christ. According to Revelation 19:7-9 the wedding feast is announced at the close of the tribulation and is related to the second coming of Christ to the earth. For this reason, the wedding feast may have its fulfillment spiritually in the millennium itself when saints of all ages will be present to join the festivities with Christ the Bridegroom and the church as the bride. The fact that the wedding feast is announced in Revelation 19 prior to the second coming of Christ is another indication that the rapture itself must have already occurred as the Bridegroom goes for His bride before the wedding feast. The two illustrations in Matthew (22:1-14; 25:1-13) both picture the wedding feast on earth and lead to the conclusion that the wedding feast is related to Christ's second coming to the earth and the millennial kingdom which will follow. In both of these instances in Matthew, the bride is not mentioned. According to Oriental custom the bride did not necessarily attend the wedding feast although, as a matter of fact, the church as the bride will be present in the millennial scene.

The figure of marriage wonderfully illustrates the love of Christ for His church which prompted Him to give Himself for it (Eph. 5:25), which explains His present work for His church (Eph. 5:26) which will be brought to consummation at the rapture when the church, perfect in every way, is presented to the Bridegroom (Eph. 5:27).

THE COMING OF CHRIST TO REIGN

The Second Advent Defined

The second coming of Christ to the earth is the theme of many passages in both Testaments, the more important passages being as follows: Deuteronomy 30:3; Psalm 2; Isaiah 63:1-6; Daniel 2:44-45; 7:13-14; Matthew 24-25; Mark 13; Luke 21; Acts 1:11; Romans 11:26; I Thessalonians 3:13; 5:1-4; II Thessalonians 1:7— 2:12; II Peter 2:1—3:17; Jude 14-15; Revelation 1:7; 19:11-21.

The first reference to the second coming of Christ in the Scriptures is found in connection with the prediction of the regathering of Israel in Deuteronomy 30:1-5. The promise is given in connection with the invitation to Israel to repent and return to the Lord, which repentance is predicted as taking place just before the second coming of Christ in Zechariah 12:10-14. This theme is amplified in many other scriptures and reveals that the second coming of Christ has the immediate object of delivering Israel from her persecutors and restoring those who were dispersed to their land.

In Daniel 2:44-45 and 7:13-14 it is revealed that the second coming of Christ will end the times of the Gentiles and bring in the millennial kingdom of Christ. Daniel 7:13-14 (ASV) describes it in these words:

> I saw in the night-visions, and, behold, there came with the
> clouds of heaven one like unto a son of man, and he came
> even to the ancient of days, and they brought him near before
> him. And there was given him dominion, and glory, and a
> kingdom, that all the peoples, nations, and languages should
> serve him: his dominion is an everlasting dominion, which
> shall not pass away, and his kingdom that which shall not
> be destroyed.

The coming of Christ as portrayed in Isaiah 63:1-6 reveals that there will be a terrible judgment upon unbelievers in the day of Christ's return and that it will be a day of vengeance. This of course is confirmed by many later passages.

One of the most comprehensive passages in the New Testament is found in Matthew 24:27-30. Here, in answer to the question of the disciples concerning the signs of His coming and the end of the age, Christ reveals a comprehensive order of events which will precede and follow His second coming. In the early portion of Matthew 24 a general description of tribulation which characterizes the present age and especially the end of the age is described. There will be wars, famines, pestilences and earthquakes as well as persecution of those who confess the Lord. There will be many false prophets and much iniquity, and the love of many professing Christians will grow cold. As the age comes to its end the gospel of the kingdom will be preached to all the world.

Matthew 24 also indicates the specific character of the period just preceding the second coming as fulfilling the time of great tribulation anticipated in the prediction of the time of Jacob's trouble (Jer. 30:7) and the great tribulation of Daniel 12:1. Christ predicts that this time of great tribulation will be a spectacular event which will result in immediate persecution of the people of Israel who are in Judea. They are accordingly exhorted to flee immediately (Matt. 24:15-20). This time is designated as the "great tribulation," unprecedented in its severity, which will end in the destruction of all flesh if it were not cut short by the second coming of Christ. During this period there will be many false reports of a secret coming of Christ and an abundance of false christs and false prophets (Matt. 24:21-26).

The second coming of Christ itself is described in graphic terms in Matthew 24:27-30 (ASV):

For as the lightning cometh forth from the east, and is seen
even unto the west; so shall be the coming of the Son of man.
Wheresoever the carcase is, there will the eagles be gathered
together. But immediately after the tribulation of those days
the sun shall be darkened, and the moon shall not give her
light, and the stars shall fall from heaven, and the powers of
the heavens shall be shaken: and then shall appear the sign of
the Son of man in heaven: and then shall all the tribes of the
earth mourn, and they shall see the Son of man coming on
the clouds of heaven with power and great glory.

In demonstration of the fact that the second coming of Christ
will not be a secret event, it is described as lightning spreading
across the heavens from the east to the west as the glory of Christ
becomes manifest to the entire world. It will occur after the
tribulation and be immediately preceded by darkening of the
sun and the moon, and by stars falling from heaven. The sign
of the Son of man predicted in Matthew 24:30 is apparently the
glory of the Lord which will appear in the heavens as Christ
returns. All the earth will see this event, and it may extend
over an entire twenty-four-hour period which in the earth's rota-
tion would permit the entire earth to see it. According to Matthew, Christ will come back accompanied by clouds and with
great power and glory.

According to Matthew 25:31-46, after the second coming to the
earth Christ will establish His throne and then judge the nations,
separating the sheep from the goats, that is, separating the saved
from the unsaved. The sheep and the goats, although they must
be saved by faith and by grace as are the saints of all ages, are
manifested in that time by their works which demonstrate their
true character. The goats, representing the unsaved, are cast into
everlasting fire. The sheep, the tribulation saints among the
Gentiles who have survived the persecutions, will be ushered into
the millennial kingdom. A similar judgment related to the second coming may be observed in Ezekiel 20:34-38 where the rebels,
that is, unsaved Israelites, are purged out and believing Israel is
ushered into their promised land. Passages parallel to Matthew
24-25, such as Mark 13 and Luke 21, confirm these major facts
and add detail. The gospel of John, while introducing the subject of the rapture of the church (14:1-3), does not deal at length
with the subject of the second coming to the earth. It is probable,
however, that the Acts 1:11 reference has to do with the second

coming of Christ to the earth. According to this passage He will come to the earth as He went to heaven, that is, gradually, bodily, visibly and accompanied by clouds.

The second coming of Christ referred to in Romans 11:26 confirms the Old Testament predictions that Christ in His second coming will deliver Israel from her persecutors and bring great spiritual revival to His ancient people. In general the Pauline letters are more concerned with the rapture than they are with the second coming to the earth. Some have taken I Thessalonians 3:13 as a picture of Christ coming to the earth with His saints from heaven. Others have referred to it as the arrival in heaven in connection with the rapture because the coming is stated to be "before God" and related to the church.

The day of the Lord in I Thessalonians 5:1-4 has to do with the period immediately preceding Christ's coming to the earth, which is a time of tribulation and speaks of the wrath of God which will be poured out in the great tribulation as well as the second coming of Christ itself. This time of judgment is in contrast to the prospect of the church for the coming of Christ for them when they will be caught up to be with the Lord as revealed in the preceding chapter.

Another important factor relative to the second advent is revealed in II Thessalonians 1:7—2:12. The fact that Christ will be revealed in glory in the heavens and will take vengeance on unbelievers is repeated, as in other passages. Detail given concerning the period preceding the second coming reveals that it will be a time of apostasy, that in it the "lawless one" will be revealed who will oppose God and exalt himself to be god and as such will be worshiped in the temple of God. Revealed here is the fact that this evil character cannot take his place in the world until the restraint which now characterizes the present age is removed. Many have understood this to be a reference to the Holy Spirit in His restraining work which will be removed in large measure when the rapture of the church takes place. The wicked person of whom this passage speaks will support his work by satanic miracles which will deceive those who do not believe the truth. This will come to an end at the second coming of Christ when he will be destroyed as indicated in II Thessalonians 2:8 and confirmed by Revelation 19:20.

An extensive revelation is given in II Peter 2:1—3:17 relative to the apostasy which will characterize the present age and which will have its culmination in the period preceding the Lord's return. However, the passage especially emphasizes the destruction of the heavens and the earth which will follow the millennial kingdom (II Peter 3:10). Second Peter in general describes the broad context of the second coming, that is, the events which precede and events which will ultimately follow, but it does not describe the second coming specifically.

Jude quotes Enoch as predicting the second coming of Christ (Jude 14-15). Here are gathered many of the elements found in preceding passages such as the fact that the Lord will be accompanied by myriads of His saints and at His second coming will execute judgment upon the wicked. In Jude as in II Peter the second coming of Christ is presented as a judgment of God upon apostasy.

The last book of the Bible, the book of Revelation, is in many respects the capstone of the doctrine of the second coming of Christ. This truth is introduced in chapter 1 with the pronouncement "Behold, he cometh with the clouds; and every eye shall see him, and they that pierced him; and all the tribes of the earth shall mourn over him. Even so, Amen" (Rev. 1:7, ASV). Most of the book of Revelation consists in exhortations and predictions in view of the Lord's return and unfolds in more detail than any other portion of Scripture the great tribulation which will precede the second advent.

The great tribulation is climaxed by the vision which John records in Revelation 19:11-21. In this, Christ is pictured as coming from heaven on a white horse accompanied by the armies of heaven to claim His right as King of kings and Lord of lords to judge the wicked earth. The resultant description gives in graphic detail the destruction of the armies which had been previously gathered in a final gigantic world war. All of these armies oppose Christ at His second coming. Not only the armies, but the world ruler and the false prophet are destroyed, and the beast and the false prophet are cast alive into the lake of fire.

This glorious event is the prelude to the establishment of the millennial kingdom of Christ. The early verses of Revelation 20 indicate that Satan will be bound and cast into the bottomless pit to remain inactive for the entire thousand years of Christ's reign on earth. The vision which John sees is given specific interpretation, namely, that Satan is so bound that he will not deceive the nations. He will remain bound for a thousand years and after this will be loosed. This interpretation makes impossible the spiritualization of this passage as many have done in an attempt to eliminate the millennial reign of Christ. In the verses which follow, the millennial kingdom is established.

The Second Advent in Relation to the Program of God

The second advent is not only an important event, in itself of tremendous significance, but its relationships extend to every important undertaking of God related to the end time.

Relation to Israel. As previously indicated the second coming of Christ has a most important relation to Israel as a nation. At this coming of Christ, Israel is delivered from her enemies and persecutions which characterized the time of Jacob's trouble just prior to the second advent. It also is the time in which Israel is brought into the millennial reign, which is a time of deliverance, glory and blessing for the nation. This deliverance is indicated in many passages such as Joel 2, Matthew 24-25, Romans 11:26 and Revelation 19:17-21. Zechariah 14:1-3 indicates that Jerusalem itself in the midst of military conflict will be rescued by the return of the Lord.

The second coming of Christ also will be the occasion for Israel's judgment. Those who survive the tribulation will be judged concerning their relationship to Christ and those who are worthy to enter the kingdom will be brought into the promised land while others will be purged out (Ezek. 20:34-38; Matt. 24:9—25:30). It is probable that the judgment of Israel raised from the dead also will take place at this time and Israel will be rewarded (Dan. 12:2-3).

Those Israelites living on earth who qualify for entrance into the kingdom are brought into the land promised to their fathers and fulfill extended passages of prophecy relating to the regathering, revival and restoration of the nation Israel (Isa. 25:9-10; 27:12-13; 61:3—62:12; 65:18—66:24; Jer. 23:1-40; 31:1-40; 33:1-26; Ezek. 33:21—37:28; 40:1—48:25; Dan. 2:44-45; 7:9-27; Zech. 13:8-9; Rom. 11:26; Rev. 20:4).

Relation of the second advent to Gentiles. As previously indicated, the second coming marks the important transition from the times of the Gentiles to the millennial kingdom of Christ and ends the period beginning with the captivity of Israel in the seventh century B.C. As Daniel's prophecies indicate, four great world empires run their course, culminating in the final world empire which will rule the world at the time of the great tribulation. This empire of the end times constitutes the final portion of the fourth empire.

The second coming of Christ is the occasion for the judgment of the Gentiles, both nationally and individually (Ezek. 38:1–39:29; Dan. 2:44-45; Matt. 25:31-46; Rev. 19:15). This judgment is specifically directed to Gentiles living at the second coming. Gentiles who have put their faith in Christ are ushered into the blessings of the millennial kingdom and all others are put to death.

Relation of the second advent to the creation as a whole. When Christ returns to the earth there is also a dramatic change in creation as a whole. A curse which fell upon the physical world as a result of Adam's sin is now at least partially relieved and the natural world is restored to the fruitfulness and Edenic beauty it had before the fall (Isa. 11:6-8; 35:1-10; 65:18-25; Rom. 8:21-22). As a result of the removal of the curse the desert will be reclaimed, water will be found in the wilderness, and prosperity will characterize the earth. The fact that the earth is abundant in its fruitfulness contributes immeasurably to the prosperity and blessing which characterize Christ's reign on the earth.

Relation of the second coming to Satan and sin. As plainly stated in Revelation 20:1-3 Satan is bound and rendered inoperative at the beginning of the millennial reign of Christ. It may be assumed that at the same time all demonic activity will cease. As Christ will be reigning with absolute authority over the world, no open wickedness will be permitted and any sin or rebellion against Christ will be immediately judged and put down (Isa. 11:3-5). While human beings in their natural bodies on earth will still have a sin nature capable of falling short of the perfect will of God, there will be no stimulus of this by Satan or evil spirits, and whatever sin eventuates will be due solely to the evil heart of man. This situation makes possible a world in which all people at least outwardly profess to follow the Saviour, and civilization as a whole attains an unusually high standard of morality and spirituality. Only at the end of the millennium when Satan is again loosed is there rebellion against Christ resulting in judgment upon those who join hands with Satan (Rev. 20:7-10).

Relation of the second advent to the tribulation period. The second coming clearly marks the end of the tribulation. All millennial views agree that this is the case, although the postmillennial theory associates the coming of Christ with the closing period of trouble in the millennium rather than a period of tribulation before the millennium. At the second coming of Christ the tribulation comes to an abrupt close and sin is judged.

Relation of the second advent to the rapture. As indicated in a previous discussion, the pretribulational concept of the rapture places the translation of the saints more than seven years before the second advent. While both are "comings" of the Lord, at the rapture Christ comes only to the air to remove the saints from earth and take them back to heaven; while at the second advent Christ comes to the earth, His feet touch the Mount of Olives (Zech. 14:4), and He assumes His proper role as King over the whole world (Zech. 14:9). As indicated in previous discussion, the rapture of the church and the second advent to the earth are different events distinguished by many important characteristics.

The second advent in relation to the millennium. As indicated plainly in Revelation 19-20 the millennium immediately follows the second advent according to the premillennial interpretation. The postmillennial view places the second advent after the millennium, and the amillennial view denies that the millennium follows. If the many passages cited concerning the second coming and the kingdom on earth are understood in their normal meaning, it teaches unmistakably a kingdom on earth following the second advent, the duration of which is stated in Revelation 20 to be a thousand years. Just as the first coming of Christ was literal, personal and bodily and was followed by the present age, so the second coming of Christ will be followed by the millennium kingdom. The analogy of this first coming as well as the description of His second coming demands a personal and literal return of Christ. The various judgments, His manifested glory, the resurrections related to the second advent and many other factors combine to require such an interpretation. Few events of the Scripture are given more accurate presentation and are more clearly described by preceding and succeeding events than the second coming of Christ. In view of this obvious fact, it is unnecessary that any form of interpretation should be adopted which would explain away that which is so plainly taught in the prophetic Word.

THE MILLENNIAL KINGDOM AND THE ETERNAL STATE

An Earthly Kingdom

The premillennial interpretation of the reign of Christ holds that He will reign on earth for a thousand years after His second advent.[6] This is in contrast to the amillennial view which identifies the millennium with the present church age or the intermediate state, and the postmillennial view which views the kingdom as partially concurrent with the present age and climaxing with the second advent. If the premillennial interpretation is correct and we can understand the scriptures relating to this kingdom in their normal literal sense, a panorama is unfolded in both the Old and New Testaments which provides many details of this reign of Christ on earth. Its general characteristics are unfolded in such passages as Isaiah 2:1-4; 11:1-16; Psalm 72; Jeremiah 23:5-8; 31:31-40; Ezekiel 37; Daniel 2:44-45; 7:13-14; Micah 4:1-8; 5:2-5; Zechariah 14. The outstanding New Testament passage is Revelation 20.

Christ as Supreme Ruler of the Millennial Kingdom

According to Psalm 2:6 (ASV), God will fulfill His purpose of setting His Son on the throne over the earth, "Yet I have set my king upon my holy hill of Zion." As King over all the earth, Christ will fulfill hundreds of prophecies that anticipate such a situation.

The Scriptures present Christ in His first coming as a King (Matt. 1:1; 21:1-11; Luke 1:32-33). It was in His offer to Israel as their King that He was rejected (Mark 15:12-13; Luke 19:14). Even His cross bore the inscription that He was "the King of the Jews" (Matt. 27:37). When He returns to the earth in His second coming, He obviously will be coming as King (Rev. 19:16) and will fulfill the promise given to David that of his

[6]This discussion is abbreviated in view of the author's extended volume, Walvoord, *The Millennial Kingdom*.

seed One would come to reign on the throne forever (II Sam. 7:16; Ps. 89:20-37; Isa. 11:1-9; Jer. 23:5-6; 33:14-26).

The evidence in support of the concept that Christ will reign on earth is so abundant that only by wholesale spiritualization can these passages be construed to mean anything other than their ordinary meaning. The characteristics of the reign of Christ are plainly set forth in many passages, such as Isaiah 11, and the New Testament confirms the literal interpretation. The announcement to Mary, for instance, concerning the birth of Christ plainly interprets these prophecies in their literal sense. In Luke 1:32-33 (ASV) the angel announced the birth to Mary in these words: "He shall be great, and shall be called the Son of the Most High: and the Lord God shall give unto him the throne of his father David: and he shall reign over the house of Jacob for ever; and of his kingdom there shall be no end." All of the references previously cited in support of the earthly rule of Christ likewise are proof texts for the fact that Christ will reign over the earth. Associated with Him in His reign will be resurrected saints of all ages, some of whom, like David, will have a particular rule (Isa. 55:3-4; Jer. 30:9; 33:15-17; Ezek. 34:23-24; 37:24-25; Hosea 3:5; Amos 9:11). The church likewise will reign with Christ as will also all the tribulation saints who have been martyred (II Tim. 2:12; Rev. 20:4-6). Numerous other passages confirm this concept of Christ's reigning assisted by other rulers, some of whom may be resurrected saints (Isa. 32:1; Ezek. 45:8-9; Matt. 19:28; Luke 19:12-27).

Principal Features of the Political Government of the Millennium

It was God's original intent in creating Adam that he should rule the earth. Due to the fall, this responsibility was transferred to Christ who as the last Adam will accomplish that in which Adam failed.

The rule of Christ on earth will be an absolute one characterized as a rule of a rod of iron with immediate judgment on any who oppose Him (Ps. 2:9; 72:9-11; Isa. 11:4; Rev. 19:15). A prominent feature of the government will be perfect justice in contrast to the inequities often suffered at the hands of modern governments. The meek and the poor will enjoy equity in that day (Isa. 11:3-5) and the wicked are warned of immediate judgment (Ps. 2:10-12).

The political judgment of Christ will be principally directed to those who survive the tribulation and enter the millennium in their natural bodies, both of Israel and of the Gentiles. The sheep of Matthew 25:31-46 and the godly remnant of Israel left after the rebels are purged out (Ezek. 20:33-38) will comprise the earthly citizens of the millennium. There is evidence that they will rapidly multiply and before the end of the thousand years will be able to fill the earth with renewed population. These who enter the millennium also are anticipated in the wheat of the parable of the wheat and the tares (Matt. 13:24-30) and the good fish of the parable in Matthew 13:47-50. In this political government Israel will have a prominent place, and numerous passages relate to this in Scripture (Isa. 9:6-7; 12:1-6; Jer. 23:5; Micah 4:1-8).[7] Many passages likewise refer to Christ's rule over the entire earth of which Zechariah 14:9 may be taken as representative. Gentiles, although in a subordinate role in relation to Israel, will nevertheless be greatly blessed in the millennium and share in the prosperity of the period.

Spiritual Characteristics of the Millennium

While the millennial kingdom is primarily a political rule, there is much to foster and promote spiritual life during this period because of the unusual characteristics of the kingdom. The amillennial objection to a literal kingdom on the ground that it is primarily moral and spiritual is beside the point. Premillenarians agree that there is much evidence of spiritual blessing and righteousness in this period, and this is derived from the fact that the kingdom is governed by Christ.

The fact that the glorified Christ is in the earthly scene and is visible to those in the millennium is unquestionably an important factor in the spiritual life of the period. As is anticipated in Jeremiah 31:34, everyone will have the evidence before him that Christ is indeed the Son of God and all that the Scriptures claim of Him. Missionary effort will be unnecessary for the knowledge of the Lord will be universal as Isaiah says, "For the earth shall be full of the knowledge of Jehovah, as the waters cover the sea" (Isa. 11:9b, ASV). Christ as the world Ruler of the millennial

[7]Cf. *ibid.*, pp. 303-4.

kingdom will be the object of worship, and the universal instruction in biblical truth as well as the many demonstrations of divine power and the abundant ministry of the Holy Spirit will foster a spiritual life on a worldwide scale unprecedented in the history of the world.

The millennium will be a period which will feature personal righteousness as well as national righteousness in keeping with Solomon's prediction "In his days shall the righteous flourish, and abundance of peace, till the moon be no more" (Ps. 72:7, ASV). The righteous rule of Christ Himself is described in specific terms in Isaiah 11:3-5. The absence of war and universal peace (Ps. 72:7; Isa. 2:4) will provide the context in which spiritual life will flourish. The praise of the Lord and the joy which will attend the blessings of that period are described in Isaiah 12:3-4 and 61:3-7. In addition to the presence of Christ the power of the Spirit will tend to foster and promote a deep spiritual life (Isa. 32:15; 44:3; Ezek. 39:29; Joel 2:28-29).

A broad difference of opinion has existed concerning the exposition of Ezekiel 40:1—46:24, which describes temple worship and sacrifices in the millennial scene. Whether this passage should be interpreted literally, as many premillenarians do, or symbolically, in either case it supports the concept of a deep spiritual life in the millennial kingdom.[8] Taken as a whole the millennial kingdom will be characterized by righteousness, joy and peace on a worldwide scale similar to that which was enjoyed by the early church.

Economic, Social and Physical Aspects of the Millennium

Many prophecies combine to give other aspects of the millennial kingdom. Because of the righteous rule of Christ and the efficient political government, there will be justice for individuals and peace among nations. Physical and financial prosperity will characterize the period as the curse laid upon the earth because of Adam's sin seems to be lifted (Isa. 35:1-2; cf. 30:23-24; 35:7). Poverty and lack of necessary physical things will be reduced to a minimum in an era of prosperity such as the world has never known (Jer. 31:12; Ezek. 34:25-27; Joel 2:21-27; Amos 9:13-14).

The blessings of the millennium will even extend to the hu-

[8]For further discussion see *ibid.*, pp. 309-15.

man body. Indications are that disease will be at a minimum and physical health the normal situation (Isa. 29:18; 33:24; 35:5-6; 61:1-3; 65:20). The world population which will be small at the beginning of the millennium due to devastating judgments of the tribulation and purging judgments of the second coming of Christ will be supplanted by a rapidly growing population. Multiplied births will characterize both Israel and the Gentiles (Jer. 30:19-20; Ezek. 47:22).

Important changes also will occur on the face of the earth at the beginning of the millennium such as the division of the Mount of Olives (Zech. 14:3-8). Jerusalem is seemingly elevated to a high plateau (Zech. 14:10) and the rest of the land will be depressed.[9] These changes in topography are related also to the division of the land pictured in Ezekiel 45:4-19; 48:1-27.[10]

The multiplied details of every aspect of life relating to the millennium make untenable the efforts to spiritualize all these scriptures and require them to conform to the present age. The description of this period is so graphically different in all of its aspects that it demands a literal fulfillment in the period following the second coming of Christ. The millennial kingdom will be the crowning work of Christ prior to the eternal state.

The Close of the Millennium

The thousand-year reign of Christ will close, according to Revelation 20:7-9, with a rebellion against Christ as God and King. This will be occasioned by the loosing of Satan who has been bound throughout the millennial kingdom and who upon his release immediately prompts many on earth to rebel against Christ. Those who are deceived in this way have been born during the millennium and, while forced by circumstance to make an outward profession of faith in Christ, nevertheless reveal their true state of unbelief as soon as opportunity arises. Those who rebel, led by Satan, encompass the city of Jerusalem in an attempt to take it by force and, according to Revelation 20:7-9, are destroyed by fire which comes from heaven. With the destruction of the army, Satan himself is cast into the lake of fire (Rev. 20:10) where the beast and the false prophet were cast a thousand years before. The millennial kingdom, the most ideal state imaginable

[9]Charles L. Feinberg, *God Remembers*, pp. 257-58.
[10]Merrill F. Unger, "The Temple Vision of Ezekiel," *Bibliotheca Sacra*, CV (Oct., 1948), 427-28.

for man apart from the eternal state itself, thus closes with another graphic demonstration of the wickedness of the human heart, even under such ideal circumstances, and forever shuts the mouths of any who would question God's justice in judging the world. *

The Judgment of the Great White Throne

The vivid description of the final judgment of the dead follows in Revelation 20:11-15. The implication of this passage is that the judgment concerns itself only with the wicked dead although this is not stated explicitly. The great white throne is pictured as being in space, and both earth and heaven flee away and apparently are dissolved. Before this throne, the dead are brought, raised from the dead, and then are judged by their works. Whoever was not found in the book of life was cast into the lake of fire. While there has been some debate as to the exact character of the book of life, there can be little question that at this point the absence of their names in the book of life is a clear indication that they are not saved. On this basis they are cast into the lake of fire to join Satan and the beast and the false prophet. The tragic fact of this judgment is that none of these cast into the lake of fire needed to have this destiny. Christ had died for every one of them, and their passage into this place of unending torment is a judgment which God Himself, although unwilling that any should perish, is forced to exact by His own justice and their failure to appropriate the grace of God.

The New Heaven and the New Earth

Revelation 21-22 present the glorious picture of the eternal state following the millennial kingdom. In Revelation 21:1-8, the introductory passage states the main features of this period. The old heaven and earth have been dissolved and a new heaven and a new earth created in which circumstances are radically different from our present earth as indicated by the cryptic statement "the sea is no more" (v. 1, ASV). The new heaven and the new earth are seen as the resting place of the holy city, the New Jerusalem, which comes down out of heaven and is described as a bride adorned for her Husband. In this new blessed estate God will be in fellowship with His people and present in the

world, sorrow will be no more, evil and unbelief will be excluded,
and all will be able to partake freely of the blessings which God
will shower upon them.

The Heavenly Jerusalem

The principal feature of the new heaven and the new earth
is the heavenly Jerusalem described as coming down from God
in Revelation 21:2. Details are furnished concerning this city,
beginning in Revelation 21:9. Difference of opinion has existed
as to whether the New Jerusalem thus described refers to the
millennial period or the eternal state. Many considerations seem
to indicate that the city is described here as it will appear in
the eternal state.

It is not impossible, however, that the heavenly Jerusalem
was in existence before this period, as it is not said to be created
at this time. The new heavens and new earth are said to be
created, but the New Jerusalem comes down from heaven. Some
believe, therefore, that the heavenly Jerusalem will be a satellite
city throughout the millennial reign of Christ, and in this city
resurrected and translated saints will dwell. By contrast, those in
their natural bodies will live on the millennial earth itself. While
there is no clear scripture which supports this concept and it
must be held merely as an inference, it would solve a number
of problems incident to the relationship of resurrected and translated beings to those still in their natural bodies who will conduct themselves in a normal way on the earth. Undoubtedly if
this is the case, those in the heavenly Jerusalem will be able to
commute to the millennial earth throughout the thousand-year
reign of Christ and participate in its activities.

As presented in Revelation 21:9–22:5, the New Jerusalem is
in its place on the new earth in the eternal state. It seems clear
from several scriptures that the New Jerusalem will be the home
of the saints of all ages and will include not only the church, but
also saved Israelites as well as saved Gentiles of the Old Testament period, tribulation saints and millennial saints. This may
be inferred from the hope of Old Testament saints such as Abraham's anticipation of an eternal city (Heb. 11:10-16) and a few
references to the new heaven and the new earth in other Old
Testament passages (Isa. 65:17-18; 66:22).

One of the clearest references concerning the saints who will

be in the heavenly Jerusalem is found in Hebrews 12:22-24
(ASV) :

> But ye are come unto mount Zion, and unto the city of the
> living God, the heavenly Jerusalem, and to innumerable hosts
> of angels, to the general assembly and church of the firstborn
> who are enrolled in heaven, and to God the Judge of all, and
> to the spirits of just men made perfect, and to Jesus the
> mediator of a new covenant, and to the blood of sprinkling
> that speaketh better than that of Abel.

In the heavenly city according to this passage are the angels, the
church, Jesus Christ as the Mediator, and the spirits of just men
made perfect, a reference to other saints. It should be noted that
while saints of all ages will be in the heavenly Jerusalem, which
city will be the principal feature of the new heavens and the new
earth, saints nevertheless retain their corporate identity, that is,
Israelites remain Israelites, Gentiles remain Gentiles, the church
remains the church, and angels remain angels.

The New Jerusalem described in detail beginning in Revelation 21:9 is revealed to be a city of indescribable beauty. Commentators differ as to the extent to which this description should
be taken literally. However, there does not seem to be any real
reason why the specifications of this city should not be taken in
their ordinary sense. Nothing would be more natural than for the
saints of the future to live in a place of such beauty as is described here.

In general the city is described as being square surrounded by
a wall with three gates on each of its four sides. The gates are
inscribed with the names of the twelve tribes of Israel, confirming the concept that Israel is included in this city. The foundations of the wall have the names of the twelve apostles which
would relate the church to this city. Angels guarding the gates
make clear that the holy angels will also participate in the city.

Most graphic dimension is that of the size of the city which
measures 1,342 miles in each of its four sides and is a like dimension in height. Some understand that the city is in the form
of a cube, others in the form of a pyramid, with other variations
which combine these various concepts. The foundations of the
city are revealed to be garnished with precious stones reflecting
every color of the rainbow, with the streets of the city being
transparent gold and the gates of the wall being pearls.

The most important feature of the city is the fact that there is no temple in it, for God Himself dwells in the city. Likewise there is no darkness and no need of artificial light, for the glory of the Lamb will illuminate the whole city, and eternity will be one continuous day. In chapter 22 a major feature is a pure river which comes from the throne of God. Also described is the tree of life whose fruit ministers to those who live in the eternal state. The leaves of the tree will be for the health of the Gentiles. This does not imply sickness, but rather the well-being of those who partake of it. The servants of the Lord are pictured serving God in these glorious surroundings and continuing forever to enjoy the presence of the Lord.

It is in this eternal state that the promise of I Corinthians 15:24 is fulfilled, when a conquered world is presented to the Godhead by Christ. This must not be construed as ending the role of Christ as King, but rather ending its temporal phase and beginning its eternal characteristics. With the introduction of the eternal state the revelation of Scripture comes to its close and the unending day of the glorious eternal state begins.

With the close of the prophetic narrative, the biblical revelation of Jesus Christ also comes to its conclusion. All that was anticipated in the beginning of eternity related to the first and second comings of Christ has now been fulfilled, and Christ is honored as King of kings and Lord of lords. The eternity which stretches beyond the horizon of scriptural revelation is one of unspeakable bliss for the saints and unending joy in the presence of God. In the center of the service and worship of the saints will be Jesus Christ, "the same yesterday, and to day, and for ever." To this eternal destiny every believing heart turns in anticipation and joyous expectation.

BIBLIOGRAPHY

Alford, Henry. *The Greek Testament.* Rev. Everett F. Harrison. 4 vols. Chicago: Moody, 1958.

Arndt, William F. and Gingrich, F. Wilbur. *A Greek-English Lexicon of the New Testament.* Chicago: U. Chicago, 1957. Pp. 909.

Baillie, D. M. *God Was in Christ.* New York: Scribner, 1948. Pp. 213.

Baillie, John. *The Place of Jesus Christ in Modern Christianity.* New York: Scribner, 1929. Pp. 219.

Barth, Karl. *Dogmatics in Outline.* Trans. G. T. Thomson. London: SCM, 1949. Pp. 155.

———. *The Epistle to the Romans.* Trans. Edwyn C. Hoskyns from 6th ed. London: Oxford U., 1933. Pp. 547.

———. *The Humanity of God.* Richmond: Knox, 1960. Pp. 96.

Berkhof, Louis. *Systematic Theology.* Rev. and enlarged. 2d ed.; Grand Rapids: Eerdmans, 1941. Pp. 759.

Berkouwer, G. C. *The Person of Christ.* Grand Rapids: Eerdmans, 1954. Pp. 368.

———. *The Providence of God.* Grand Rapids: Eerdmans, 1952. Pp. 294.

Boettner, Loraine. *The Person of Christ.* Grand Rapids: Eerdmans, 1943. Pp. 215.

Bowman, John Wick. *The Intention of Jesus.* Philadelphia: Westminster, 1943. Pp. 263.

Braaten, Carl E. *History and Hermeneutics.* Philadelphia: Westminster, 1966. Pp. 205.

Bruce, Alexander Balmain. *The Humiliation of Christ.* Edinburgh: T. & T. Clark, 1899. Pp. 455.

———. 'The Synoptic Gospels" in W. R. Nicoll (ed.), *The Expositor's Greek Testament.*

Brunner, H. Emil. *Revelation and Reason.* Trans. Olive Wyon. Philadelphia: Westminster, 1946. Pp. 440.

Bullinger, Ethelbert William. *How to Enjoy the Bible.* London: Eyre & Spottiswoode, 1907. Pp. 436.

———. *The Companion Bible.* Grand Rapids: Kregel, 1964.

Bultmann, Rudolf Karl. *Jesus Christ and Mythology.* New York: Scribner, 1958. Pp. 96.

———. *Theology of the New Testament.* 2 vols. New York: Scribner, 1951, 1955.

291

Burrows, Millar. *An Outline of Biblical Theology*. Philadelphia: Westminster, 1946. Pp. 380.

Bushnell, Horace. *The Vicarious Sacrifice*. London: Dickinson, 1892. Pp. 476.

Buswell, J. Oliver. *A Systematic Theology of the Christian Religion*. 2 vols. Grand Rapids: Zondervan, 1962, 1963.

Callaway, Eugene Charles. *The Harmony of the Last Week*. Atlanta: Ponce de Leon Ave. Baptist Church, 1923. Pp. 115.

Calvin, John. *Commentary on the Gospel According to John*. 2 vols. Trans. William Pringle from original Latin. Grand Rapids: Eerdmans, 1949.

Campbell, John McLeod. *The Nature of the Atonement*. 3d ed.; London: Macmillan, 1869. Pp. 412.

Chafer, Lewis Sperry. *Grace*. Philadelphia: Sunday School Times, 1922. Pp. 373.

———. *Systematic Theology*. 8 vols. Dallas: Dallas Theological Seminary, 1948.

Chafer, R. T. Review of Hugh Thompson Kerr, *After He Had Risen*. *Bibliotheca Sacra*, XCI (Oct., 1934), 488.

Coffin, Henry Sloane. *The Meaning of the Cross*. New York: Scribner, 1959. Pp. 164.

Come, Arnold B. *An Introduction to Barth's "Dogmatics" for Preachers*. Philadelphia: Westminster, 1963. Pp. 251.

Constitution of the Presbyterian Church in the U.S.A. Philadelphia: Bd. of Chr. Educ. of the Presb. Church in the U.S.A., 1955.

Cullmann, Oscar. *Christ and Time*. Philadelphia: Westminster, 1950. Pp. 253.

———. *The Christology of the New Testament*. Philadelphia: Westminster, 1959. Pp. 342.

Dabney, Robert L. *Christ Our Penal Substitute*. Richmond: Presb. Committee of Pubn., 1897. Pp. 115.

Davidson, Andrew Bruce. *An Introductory Hebrew Grammar*. Edinburgh: T. & T. Clark, 1946. Pp. 236.

Deissmann, G. Adolf. *Light from the Ancient East*. Trans. Lionel R. M. Strachan. London: Hodder & Stoughton, 1910. Pp. 514; 68 illus.

Delitzsch, Franz. *Commentary on the Epistle to the Hebrews*. 2 vols. Grand Rapids: Eerdmans, 1952.

Dibelius, Martin. *Jesus*. Philadelphia: Westminster, 1959. Pp. 160.

Dimock, Nathaniel. *Our One Priest on High*. Memorial ed. with Introd. by H. C. G. Moule. London: Longmans, Green, 1910. Pp. 88.

———. *The Sacerdotium of Christ* and *Our One Priest on High*. Memorial ed. with Introd. by H. C. G. Moule. London: Longmans, Green, 1910. Pp. 151.

Dods, Marcus. "The Gospel of St. John" in W. Robertson Nicoll (ed.), *The Expositor's Greek Testament*, Vol. I.

Dorner, I. A. *History of the Development of the Doctrine of the Person of Christ.* 5 vols. New York: Scribner, n.d.

Edwards, Thomas Charles. *A Commentary on the First Epistle to the Corinthians.* 3d ed.; New York: Hodder & Stoughton, 1897. Pp. 491.

Fairbairn, Andrew Martin. *The Place of Christ in Modern Theology.* New York: Scribner, 1893. Pp. 556.

Fairbairn, Patrick. *The Typology of Scripture.* Philadelphia: Daniels & Smith, 1852. Pp. 324.

Feinberg, Charles Lee. *God Remembers.* Wheaton: Van Kampen, 1951. Pp. 283.

———. "The Hypostatic Union," *Bibliotheca Sacra.* XCII (July-Sept., 1935), 412-26.

Filson, Floyd V. *Jesus Christ the Risen Lord.* Nashville: Abingdon, 1956. Pp. 288.

Foley, George Cadwalader. *Anselm's Theory of the Atonement.* Bohlen Lectures, 1908. New York: Longmans, Green, 1909. Pp. 319.

Forsyth, Peter Taylor. *The Cruciality of the Cross.* London: Hodder & Stoughton, 1909. Pp. 218.

———. *The Person and Place of Jesus Christ.* Boston: Pilgrim Press, 1909. Pp. 357.

Gaebelein, Arno C. *The Angels of God.* New York: Our Hope, 1924. Pp. 116.

———. *The Annotated Bible.* 9 vols. New York: Our Hope, 1913-21.

———. *The Gospel of John.* New York: Our Hope, 1925. Pp. 414.

Gall, James. *Good Friday a Chronological Mistake.* Edinburgh: Gall & Inglis, n.d. Pp. 94.

Govett, Robert. *Entrance into the Kingdom.* Part 1, 2d ed.; London: Thynne, 1922. Pp. 222.

Green, Edward M. B. *The Meaning of Salvation.* Philadelphia: Westminster, 1966. Pp. 256.

Grensted, Laurence William. *A Short History of the Doctrine of the Atonement.* New York: Longmans, Green, 1920. Pp. 376.

Guille, George E. *Isaac and Rebekah.* Chicago: Bible Inst. Colportage Assn., 1914. Pp. 31.

Harrison, Norman B. *The End.* Minneapolis: Harrison, 1941. Pp. 239.

Hengstenberg, E. W. *Christology of the Old Testament.* 4 vols. Edinburgh: T. & T. Clark, 1875-78.

Henry, Carl F. H. (ed.). *Jesus of Nazareth: Saviour and Lord.* Grand Rapids: Eerdmans, 1966. Pp. 277.

Hodge, Charles. *Systematic Theology.* 3 vols. New York: Scribner, 1877.

Hofmann, Hans. *The Theology of Reinhold Niebuhr.* Trans. Louise Pettibone Smith. New York: Scribner, 1956. Pp. 269.

Irenaeus. "Against Heresies," *Ante-Nicene Christian Library,* Vol. IX. Eds. Alexander Roberts and James Donaldson. Edinburgh: T. & T. Clark, 1871.

Ironside, Henry Allan. *Lectures on Daniel the Prophet.* New York: Loizeaux, 1920. Pp. 253.

Jamieson, Robert; Fausset, A. R.; and Brown, David. *A Commentary, Critical, Experimental and Practical on the Old and New Testaments.* 6 vols. Grand Rapids: Eerdmans, 1945.

Johnson, S. Lewis. "From Enmity to Amity," *Bibliotheca Sacra*, CXIX (April, 1962), 139-49.

Josephus. "Antiquities."

Justin Martyr. "Dialogue with Trypho," *Ante-Nicene Christian Library*, Vol. II. Eds. Alexander Roberts and James Donaldson. Edinburgh: T. & T. Clark, 1867.

Keil, C. F. and Delitzsch, Franz. *Biblical Commentary on the Old Testament: The Twelve Minor Prophets.* 2 vols. Grand Rapids: Eerdmans, 1954.

Kelly, William. *Exposition of the Gospel of John.* London: Race, 1923. Pp. 452.

———. *Exposition of the Gospel of Luke.* London: Pickering & Inglis, n.d. Pp. 513.

———. *The First Epistle of Peter.* London: Weston, 1904. Pp. 266.

———. *Lectures on the Book of Daniel.* 2d ed.; London: Morrish, 1881. Pp. 240.

Kerr, Hugh Thompson. *After He Had Risen.* New York: Revell, 1934. Pp. 95.

Kerswill, William D. *The Old Testament Doctrine of Salvation.* Philadelphia: Presb. Bd. of Pubn., 1904. Pp. 215.

Klausner, Joseph. *The Messianic Idea in Israel.* Trans. W. F. Stinespring. New York: Macmillan, 1955. Pp. 543.

Kligerman, Aaron J. *Messianic Prophecy in the Old Testament.* Grand Rapids: Zondervan, 1957. Pp. 155.

Koontz, John V. "Mary's Magnificat," *Bibliotheca Sacra.* CXVI (Oct.-Dec., 1959), 336-49.

Lang, George Henry. *The Revelation of Jesus Christ: Firstborn Sons, Their Rights and Risks.* London: Oliphants, 1945. Pp. 420.

Latouche, E. D. *The Person of Christ in Modern Thought.* London: Clarke, 1912. Pp. 419.

Lawson, John. *Comprehensive Handbook of Christian Doctrine.* Englewood Cliffs, N.J.: Prentice-Hall, 1967. Pp. 287.

Lawton, John Stewart. *Conflict in Christology.* London: Soc. for Promoting Chr. Knowledge, 1947. Pp. 331.

Lightfoot, Robert Henry. *St. John's Gospel, A Commentary.* Ed. C. F. Evans. Oxford: Clarendon, 1956. Pp. 368.

Machen, J. Gresham. *The Virgin Birth of Christ.* New York: Harper, 1930. Pp. 415.

Macintosh, Douglas Clyde. *Personal Religion.* New York: Scribner, 1942. Pp. 411.

Macintosh, Robert. *Historic Theories of Atonement.* London: Hodder & Stoughton, 1920. Pp. 319.

Mackintosh, H. R. *The Doctrine of the Person of Christ.* Edinburgh: T. & T. Clark, 1927. Pp. 540.

MacMillan, Hugh. *The True Vine.* 6th ed.; London: Macmillan, 1890.
Pp. 328.
Manson, Thomas Walter. *The Teaching of Jesus.* Cambridge: U. Press,
1959. Pp. 352.
————. *Jesus the Messiah.* Philadelphia: Westminster, 1946. Pp. 267.
Meyer, Frederick Brotherton. *The Gospel of John.* London: Marshall,
Morgan & Scott, 1950. Pp. 384.
Michaeli, F. "Salvation, O.T." in J. J. Von Allmen (ed.), *A Companion
to the Bible.* New York: Oxford, 1958. Pp. 382-84.
Miley, John. *The Atonement in Christ.* Boston: Hunt, 1879. Pp. 351.
Milligan, William. *The Ascension and Heavenly Priesthood of Our
Lord.* London: Macmillan, 1892. Pp. 374.
————. *The Resurrection of Our Lord.* New York: Macmillan, 1905.
Pp. 318.
Moorehead, W. G. "Priest," *International Standard Bible Encyclopae-
dia,* Ed. James Orr. Grand Rapids: Eerdmans, n.d. Pp. 2439-41.
Morgan, G. Campbell. *The Gospel According to John.* New York:
Revell, n.d. Pp. 333.
————. *The Teaching of Christ.* New York: Revell, 1913. Pp. 333.
Morris, Leon. *The Apostolic Preaching of the Cross.* 1st ed.; Grand
Rapids: Eerdmans, 1955. Pp. 296.
————. *The Cross in the New Testament.* Grand Rapids: Eerdmans,
1965. Pp. 454.
Mueller, John Theodore. *Christian Dogmatics.* St. Louis: Concordia,
1934. Pp. 665.
Murray, Andrew. *The Power of the Blood of Jesus.* London: Marshall,
Morgan & Scott, 1936. Pp. 128.
Nicoll, W. Robertson (ed.). *The Expositor's Greek Testament.* 5 vols.
Grand Rapids: Eerdmans, n.d.
Niebuhr, Richard R. *Resurrection and Historical Reason.* New York:
Scribner, 1957. Pp. 184.
Oehler, Gustav Friedrich. *Theology of the Old Testament.* New York:
Funk & Wagnalls, 1883. Pp. 593.
Orr, James. *The Resurrection of Jesus.* London: Hodder & Stoughton,
1908. Pp. 288.
Owen, John. *The Works of John Owen.* Ed. William H. Goold. 24
vols. London: Johnstone, 1850.
Patch, James. "Shepherd," *International Standard Bible Encyclo-
paedia.* Ed. James Orr. Grand Rapids: Eerdmans, n.d. IV, 2763-64.
Payne, J. Barton. *The Theology of the Older Testament.* Grand Rap-
ids: Zondervan, 1962. Pp. 554.
Peake, A. S. "The Epistle to the Colossians" in W. Robertson Nicoll
(ed.), *The Expositor's Greek Testament,* Vol. III.
Pentecost, J. Dwight. *Things Which Become Sound Doctrine.* Westwood, N.J.: Revell, 1965. Pp. 159.
————. *Things to Come.* Findlay, Ohio: Dunham, 1958. Pp. 633.
Platt, Frederic. *Immanence and Christian Thought.* London: Kelly,
1915. Pp. 541.

Reese, Alexander. *The Approaching Advent of Christ*. London: Marshall, Morgan & Scott, n.d. Pp. 328.

Ritschl, Albrecht. *A Critical History of the Christian Doctrine of Justification and Reconciliation*. Edinburgh: Edmonston & Douglas, 1872. Pp. 605.

Robertson, Archibald Thomas. *A Grammar of the Greek New Testament in the Light of Historical Research*. 5th ed.; New York: Richard R. Smith, 1923. Pp. 1,454.

——. *A Harmony of the Gospels*. New York: Harper, 1922. Pp. 305.

——. *Word Pictures in the New Testament*. 6 vols. Nashville: Broadman, 1930-33.

Ryrie, Charles C. *Biblical Theology of the New Testament*. Chicago: Moody, 1959. Pp. 384.

Sanday, William. *Christologies Ancient and Modern*. Oxford: Clarendon, 1910. Pp. 244.

Saphir, Adolph. *Christ Crucified*. 5th ed.; London: James Nisbet, 1889. Pp. 181.

Scofield, C. I. (ed.). *New Scofield Reference Bible*. New York: Oxford U., 1967. Pp. 1,377.

Shedd, William Greenough Thayer. *Dogmatic Theology*. 3 vols. 3d ed.; New York: Scribner, 1891.

Smeaton, George. *The Apostles' Doctrine of the Atonement*. Edinburgh: T. & T. Clark, 1870. Pp. 548.

Spurrier, William A. *Guide to the Christian Faith*. New York: Scribner, 1952. Pp. 242.

Stalker, James. *The Christology of Jesus*. London: Hodder & Stoughton, 1899. Pp. 298.

Stanton, Gerald B. *Kept from the Hour*. Grand Rapids: Zondervan, 1956. Pp. 320.

Stauffer, Ethelbert. *Jesus and His Story*. New York: Knopf, 1960. Pp. 243.

Stevens, William Arnold and Burton, Ernest DeWitt. *A Harmony of the Four Gospels*. New York: Scribner, 1904. Pp. 283.

Strong, Augustus Hopkins. *Systematic Theology*. New York: Armstrong, 1902. Pp. 600.

Suetonius. "Cladius," XXV.

Swete, Henry Barclay. *The Ascended Christ*. London: Macmillan, 1910. Pp. 168.

Tait, Arthur J. *The Heavenly Ascension of Our Lord*. London: Scott, 1912. Pp. 247.

Taylor, Vincent. *The Atonement in New Testament Teaching*. London: Epworth, 1941. Pp. 319.

——. *Forgiveness and Reconciliation*. London: Macmillan, 1952. Pp. 242.

——. *The Person of Christ*. New York: St. Martin, 1959. Pp. 321.

Tertullian. "Against Marcion," *Ante-Nicene Christian Library*, Vol. XV. Eds. Alexander Roberts and James Donaldson. Edinburgh: T. & T. Clark, 1870.

——. "Against Praxes," *Ante-Nicene Christian Library*, Vol. XV. Eds. Alexander Roberts and James Donaldson. Edinburgh: T. & T. Clark, 1870.

Thielicke, Helmut. *Between Heaven and Earth*. Trans. John W. Doberstein. New York: Harper & Row, 1965. Pp. 192.

Thomas, W. H. Griffith. "Ascension," *International Standard Bible Encyclopaedia*. Ed. James Orr. Grand Rapids: Eerdmans, 1952. Pp. 263-66.

——. *The Holy Spirit of God*. 3d ed.; Grand Rapids: Eerdmans, 1955. Pp. 303.

Thomson, William H. *Christ in the Old Testament*. New York: Harper, 1888. Pp. 477.

Unger, Merrill F. "The Temple Vision of Ezekiel," *Bibliotheca Sacra*. CV (Oct.-Dec., 1948), 418-31.

Vos, Geerhardus. *The Self-Disclosure of Jesus*. Grand Rapids: Eerdmans, 1954. Pp. 311.

Walvoord, John F. *The Millennial Kingdom*. Findlay, Ohio: Dunham, 1959. Pp. 373.

——. *The Rapture Question*. Findlay, Ohio: Dunham, 1957. Pp. 204.

——. *The Revelation of Jesus Christ*. Chicago: Moody, 1966. Pp. 347.

Wardlaw, Ralph. *Systematic Theology*. Ed. James R. Campbell. 3 vols. Edinburgh: Black, 1857.

Warfield, Benjamin Breckenridge. *Christology and Criticism*. New York: Oxford U., 1929. Pp. 459.

——. *The Person and Work of Christ*. Ed. Samuel G. Graig. Philadelphia: Presb. & Ref., 1950. Pp. 575.

Watson, Richard. *Theological Institutes*. 2 vols. 29th ed.; New York: Nelson & Philipps, 1850.

Webster's New International Dictionary of the English Language. 2d ed.

Westcott, Brooke Foss. *The Epistle to the Hebrews*. 2d ed.; London: Macmillan, 1892. Pp. 504.

Young, Edward J. *The Study of Old Testament Theology Today*. Westwood, N.J.: Revell, 1959. Pp. 112.

SUBJECT INDEX

A

Adam, in relation to universal sin and condemnation, 56-57
Adonai, in relation to Christ, 38
Alexandrian theology, 12
Angel of Jehovah, 44-46
   as a theophany of Christ, 52-54
Arianism, 12, 22
Ascension, 132-33, 219-24
   departure of Christ from the earth, 219-23
   nature of the event, 220-21
   preliminary to His arrival in heaven, 223
   question of time of, 220-21
   related to union of two natures, 121-22
   significance, 223-24
Atonement, definition, 154
Attributes of Christ
   as Creator, 47-48
   eternity, 22-25, 27
   eternity, importance of, 22-23
   eternity, proof in Scripture, 23-24
   eternity, as proof of other attributes, 23
   eternity, in relation to deity of Christ, 23
   eternity, in relation to preexistence, 22-23
   fullness of the Godhead in Him, 30
   immutability, 29-30
   miscellaneous qualities of deity, 31
   omnipotence, 29
   omnipresence, 28
   omniscience, 28-29
   preexistence, 24-26, 27
   preexistence, collateral proofs, 26
   preexistence, support in the Scriptures, 25-26
   the same as the Father and the Son, 27
   self-existence, 28
   sovereignty, 30
Authority of Christ, 225-26

B

Baillie, belief in eternity of Christ, 23-24
Barth, belief in eternity of Christ, 23-24
   opposition to liberalism, 19
   on reconciliation, 180
   view of Scripture, 20
Barthianism, 13-15
Berkhof, on covenant idea, 34
Berkouwer, on liberal view of Christ, 111
Birth of Christ, 100-101
   critical problems concerning, 102-5
Body of Christ, Christ as the Head, 227-32
Bridegroom, representing Christ, 250-53
Bruce, on types of kenosis of Christ, 140-41
Brunner, 15
   view of Scripture, 20
Bultmann, view of history, 112
   view of Scripture, 20
Bultmannism, 15-16

C

Calvin, in relation to eternal covenant, 33-34
Calvinism
   moderate doctrine of reconciliation, 187
   on relation of the two natures of Christ, 115
   view of Christ's presence in the Lord's Supper, 256
Chafer, on Christ as the vine, 237
   on importance of resurrection, 217-18
Chief cornerstone, Christ as, 238-40
   summary of significance, 240
Christ
   incarnation of, 96-105
   incarnation of, reference to in ancient literature, 96-97

298

person of, according to Cullmann, 17
as Priest, His sacrifice, 244-48
teaching of, according to Bultmann, 15-16
Christology, principles governing
  interpretation, 20-21
Christomonism, 14
Church, in relation to Christ, 135-
  36
Coffin, on propitiation, 175-76
Commercial or satisfaction theory
  of the atonement, 158
Covenant, of grace, 33-35
  of redemption, 33-35
Creator, Christ as, 47-48
Crucifixion of Christ, 129-30
Cullmann, in support of preexistence of Christ, 26-27
  view of Christ, 17

D

Death of Christ, 153-90
  prophecies of, 91-92
Decree of God, 34-35
Deity of Christ, 107-9
  Berkhof on, 108-9
  Burrows on, 108
  in early church, 107
  evidence for, 108-9
  linked to His eternity and to the
    infallibility of Scripture, 27
  opposed by liberals, 107-8
  in relation to doctrine of scrip-
    tural infallibility, 109
  Spurrier on, 108
Dimock, on perpetual sacrifice,
  244-45
Divine nature of Christ, union with
  human, 112-14
Dods, on eternity of Christ, 24
  on propitiation in Old Testa-
    ment, 172
Duns Scotus, theory of the atonement, 160

E

Earthly life of Christ, nature's
  spheres of, 133-36
Elohim, in relation to Christ, 37-38
Evolution, 13
Example theory of the atonement,
  160-61
Expiation, definition, 154

F

Faith, in relation to salvation, 58-
  59
First Begotten, 42-44
Forgiveness, definition, 154

G

Gaebelein, on theophanies of
  Christ, 53-54
Genealogy of Christ, problems of,
  103-5
Glory of Christ, in prophecy, 94-95
Gospels, problems of in relation to
  Christology, 20-21
Great Shepherd, Christ as, 232-34
  Christ's work as, 232-34
Great white throne judgment, 287
Grotius, governmental theory of
  atonement, 161-62
Guilt, definition, 155

H

Heavenly Jerusalem, 288-90
  inhabitants of, 288-89
Heavenly work of Christ
  as Bridegroom, 250-53
  as Head of the body, 227-32
  as chief cornerstone, 238-40
  as the great Shepherd, 232-34
  as the vine, 234-37
Hegel, philosophy of, 12
Heilsgeschichte
  in relation to Christ, 26-27
  school of interpretation, 19-20
Henry, view of Christ and the
  Scriptures, 19-20
Hermeneutics, in relation to Christology, 17-18
High Priest
  Christ as, theory of perpetual
    sacrifice, 244-46
  as representing Christ, 240-50
Hodge, on divine attributes of
  Christ, 31
  on impeccability, 146-47
Human nature of Christ, united
  with divine nature, 112-14
Humanity of Christ, 109-22
  in contemporary theology, 111-
    12
  evidence for, 110-12
  fundamental to orthodoxy, 109-
    10
Humiliation of Christ, 137-45
Hunter, belief in eternity of Christ,
  23

I

Impeccability of Christ, 145-52
  defined, 145-49
  proof of, 150-52
  proper doctrine, 149
  in relation to immutability, 151
  in relation to omnipotence, 151-
    52
  in relation to omniscience, 152

in relation to reality of temptation, 148-49
in relation to temptability, 145-
49
in relation to the will of Christ,
150-51
Indwelling of Christ in the church,
253-56
Infancy of Christ, 101-2
Inspiration of the Bible, in relation
to Christology, 17-18
Intercession of Christ, 246-48
Lutheran view, 247
Irenaeus, on theophanies of Christ,
55
Ironside, on theophanies of Christ,
54

J

Jehovah, in relation to Christ, 37
Jewish law, in relation to Christ,
133-34
John the Baptist, as forerunner of
Christ, 98
Joseph, annunciation to, 99-100
Judgment of the church in heaven,
269-72
Judgment seat of Christ, 270-72
Justice, definition, 155
Justification by faith, 60
definition, 155
Justin Martyr, on theophanies of
Christ, 54-55

K

Kelly, on theophanies of Christ, 54
Kenosis of Christ, 27, 138-45
arguments for, 142
proper doctrine, 143-45
Kingdom doctrine, in relation to
Christ, 134-35
Kingly office of Christ, 137
related to union of two natures,
121

L

Last Adam and new creation, 226-
27
related to Christ, 226-27
Liberalism, in relation to Christology, 19-20
rise of, 13
Life of Christ, 123-33
Lightfoot, belief in eternity of
Christ, 23
Lord's Supper, related to Christ's
presence in the church, 256
Lordship of Christ, present in
heaven, 224-26

Luther, in relation to eternal cove-
nant, 33-34
Lutheranism, on the natures of
Christ, 115-16

M

Machen, on virgin birth of Christ,
104
Marriage of Christ to the church,
272-74
Mary, annunciation to, 98-99
Messianic prophecies, 79-95
birth of Christ, 86-87
concerning Christ's glory, 94-95
concerning death of Christ, 91-
92
concerning life of Christ, 88-91
concerning offices of Christ, 88-
89
concerning person of Christ, 87-
88
concerning resurrection of Christ,
92-94
general characteristics of, 81-83
lineage of Christ, 83-86
neglect of in 20th century, 79
principal types of, 81
related to coming kingdom, 89-
90
related to the Servant of Jehovah, 90-91
summary of, 91
Millennial kingdom
close of, 286-87
an earthly kingdom, 282
economic, social and physical aspects, 285-86
eternal state, 282-90
principal features of, political
government, 282-84
reigned over by Christ, 282-83
spiritual characteristics of, 284-
86
Moral influence theory of the atonement, 158-59
Morris, on propitiation in the Old
Testament, 172-73
on reconciliation, 181, 182-84
on redemption, 164-67
on substitutional character of
propitiation, 176-77
Mystical experience theory of the
atonement, 161

N

Natures of Christ
related to communion of attributes, 117-18
related to His self-consciousness,
118-19

relation of human to divine, 114-
18
results of union of, 120-22
Neoorthodoxy, 13-15
New heaven and new earth, 287-
88
New Jerusalem, 288-90
described in detail, 289
Nicaean Council, in relation to
Christ, 22
Niebuhr, on resurrection of Christ,
206-7
view of Scriptures, 20

O

Offices of Christ, 136-37
Old Testament history
major lines of divine revelation
relating to Christ, 36
in relation to Christ, 36-61
theophanies, 51-55
Only Begotten, 44
Orr, on resurrection of Christ, 191
Orthodoxy vs. liberalism, 13

P

Passion week, 127-30
Payment-to-Satan theory of the
atonement, 157-58
Penalty, definition, 155
Perpetual offering of Christ, Roman
Catholic theory, 244-45
Person of Christ
Barthian view of, 14-15
communion of attributes, 117-18
defined in early church, 12
important results of the union of
two natures, 120-22
impossibility of complete definition, 7-9
as incarnate, 106-23
as preincarnate, 106-7
prophecies of, 87-88
related to the will of Christ, 119-
20
relation of two natures, 114-18
union of the divine and human
natures, 112-14
view of Baillie, 18-19
view of Reinhold Niebuhr, 15
view of Ritschl, 111
view of Schleiermacher, 111
Posttribulationism. See Rapture
Preexistence of Christ. See Attributes of Christ, preexistence
Presence of Christ in the church,
253-56
indwelling, related to the Holy
Spirit, 253-56
related to the Lord's Supper, 256

Present work of Christ, 219-57
related to present work of the
Spirit, 257
Preservation, related to Christ, 48-
51
Pretribulationism. See Rapture
Priesthood of the believer, 248-50
sacrifices of, 248-50
Priesthood of Christ
His intercession, 246-48
nature of, 240-44
related to royal priesthood of the
believer, 248-50
related to union of two natures,
120-21
Priestly office of Christ, 136-37
Prophetic office of Christ, 136
related to union of two natures,
121
Propitiation, 171-77
definition, 155
in the New Testament, 173-75
in the Old Testament, 172-73
results of, 177
substitutional character of, 175-
77
summary, 175
Providence, evidence for, 49-51
related to Christ, 48-51
related to preincarnate work of
Christ, 51

R

Ransom, definition, 155
Rapture
arguments for, 264-65
arguments for posttribulationism,
259-63
arguments for pretribulationism,
265-67
of the church, four views, 258-67
exposition of doctrine of, 267-69
midtribulation view, 258
partial-rapture theory defined,
259
posttribulation, 259-64
pretribulation view defined, 259
Recapitulation theory of the atonement, 158
Reconciliation, 12, 177-90
applied to the elect when they
believe, 188
Barth on, 180
conclusions from Romans 5, 183-
84
definition, 155-56
four interpretations of, 179-81
major Scripture passages, 181-
86

302

in New Testament, 179
in Old Testament, 178-79
in relation to the nonelect, 188-89
in relation to the universe, 189
Redemption, 12, 163-71
concept of freedom, 165-66
definition, 156
idea of freedom from bondage, 167-71
idea of purchase, 163-65
Resurrection of Christ, 12, 130-32, 191-218
as an apologetic for Christian theology, 191-92
appearances of Christ, 192-95
appearances of Christ after resurrection, 131-32
Chafer on importance of, 217-18
character of human witnesses to, 196-97
empty tomb as a witness to, 195-96;
essential to all His work, 210-15;
evidences, 192-200
fulfills Feast of Firstfruits, 214
glory of His resurrection body, 204-5
His resurrection body, 200-205
His resurrection body changed, 203-4
Old Testament background, 191
Old Testament prophecies, 92-94
order of events, 130-32
Orr on proofs, 211
proof of His offices, 209-10
proof of His person, 207-9
proof of the inspiration of Scripture, 218
related to bestowing eternal life, 212
related to Christ as Head of the church and the new creation, 212
related to Christ reigning on David's throne, 216-17
related to exultation of Christ, 192
related to the final deliverance of the world to the Father, 217
related to His being Shepherd of the flock, 215
related to His bestowal of gifts, 213
related to His future work, 215-18

related to His impartation of spiritual power, 213-14
related to His now preparing a place, 214-15
related to His resurrection of all men, 215-16
related to His universal lordship over all creation, 215
related to His work as Advocate, 213
related to judgment of moral creatures, 216
related to the marriage of the Bridegroom and the bride, 216
related to raising believers to new position in Christ, 214
related to sending the Holy Spirit, 211-12
significance, 206-18
supported by custom of observing the first day of the week, 199-200
supported by disciples' experience of divine power, 198
supported by dramatic change in the disciples, 197
supported by evidence of the day of Pentecost, 198-99
supported by origin of the Christian church, 200
who raised Christ from the dead? 205-6
Righteousness, definition, 156
Ritschl, 12-13
on person of Christ, 111

S

Sacrifices of believer-priest, 248-50
Salvation, condition of in the Old Testament, 58-59
in Old Testament, Abraham's, 60
in Old Testament based on cross of Christ, 58-59
in Old Testament as deliverance, 60
in Old Testament, Moses', 60
in Old Testament related to Christ, 55-61
in Old Testament related to evolution, 56
in Old Testament related to universal sin and condemnation, 58-60
in Old Testament revelation of a coming Saviour, 57
in Old Testament revelation of the way of salvation, 57-59
in Old Testament summary, 61
way of, 58-59

Sanctification, definition, 156
Satisfaction, definition, 156
Schleiermacher, 12-13
  on person of Christ, 111
Scriptures, view of determines
  Christology, 20-21
Second coming of Christ, 12
  definition, 274
  description, 274-79
  relation to creation as a whole,
  280
  in relation to divine program,
  279-82
  in relation to Gentiles, 279-80
  relation to millennium, 281-82
  in relation to Satan and sin, 280-
  81
  in relation to tribulation period,
  281
Self-consciousness of Christ, 118-
  19
Servant of Jehovah, 90-91
Shedd on impeccability of Christ,
  147-48
  on proof of impeccability of
  Christ, 150
Shepherd and sheep, related to
  Christ, 232-34
Smith, on neglect of Messianic
  prophecy, 79
Son of God, 38-42
  theories of, 38-42
Spiritual gifts, bestowed upon the
  church by Christ, 231-32
Stewart, on belief in eternity of
  Christ, 23
Substitution, definition, 156-57
Substitutional atonement, theory
  of, 157

T

Taylor, on reconciliation, 182
Tertullian, on theophanies of
  Christ, 55
Thielicke, on virgin birth of Christ,
  105
Theophanies, miscellaneous,
  of Christ, proof of, 52-55
  in relation to Christ, 54-55
Theories of the atonement, 157-63
Theory of the atonement by vicari-
  ous confession, 162-63
Thomas Aquinas' theory of the
  atonement, 159-60
Throne of Christ, in heaven, 224-
  25
Titles of Christ
  Adonai, 38
  the angel of Jehovah, 44-46

Elohim, 37-38
  first Begotten, 42-44
  Jehovah, 37
  in the Old Testament, 36-46
  the only Begotten, 44
  Son of God, 38-42
Trends in Christology, 18-21
Trial of Christ, 128-29
Trinitarianism, in relation to Christ,
  32
Trinity, doctrine of in relation to
  Christ, 11
True vine, representing Christ,
  234-37
Types of Christ
  Aaron, 64
  Abel, 64
  Adam, 64-65
  Benjamin, 65
  David, 65
  feasts of Jehovah, 75-77
  Isaac, 65-66
  Joseph, 66-67
  Joshua, 67
  kinsman-redeemer, 67
  Melchizedek, 67-68
  Moses, 68-69
  Old Testament priesthoods, 74-
  75
  Old Testament sacrifices, 71-73,
  74
  the tabernacle, 73
  typical events, 69-71
  typical institutions and ceremo-
  nies, 74-78
  typical persons, 64-69
  typical things, 71-73
Typology of Christ, 62-78
  defined, 62-63
  extremes of interpretation, 63
  kinds of, 63
  see also Types of Christ
Two natures of Christ, related to
  the will of Christ, 119-20

U

Unlimited atonement, 186-88

V

Vine and the branches
  a figure of Christ and the church,
  234-37
  summary of significance, 237
Virgin birth, of Christ, 104-5
  New Testament evidence, 105
Vos, on self-consciousness of
  Christ, 119

304

W

Westcott, belief in eternity of Christ, 23
Will of Christ, related to two natures, 119-20
Work of Christ
in the church in present age, 256-57
on earth in present age, 253-58
in eternity past, 32-35
in future, 258-90
in heaven, 226-53

in relation to covenant of redemption and covenant of grace, 33-35

Y

Young, on self-consciousness of Christ, 119

Z

Zwingli, view of Christ's presence in the Lord's Supper, 256

SELECTIVE SCRIPTURE INDEX

GENESIS

1:1	38
1:2	47
3	56
3:6	83
3:15	8, 57, 83, 84, 87, 90
3.21	69
4:4	58, 71
4:7	58
4:8	83
4:25	83
6	83, 84
6:14	178
9	83, 84
11:12	103
12:1-3	83, 84
14	67
14:18-19	243
15:6	60
15:9	72
16:7-13	44, 52
17:19	83, 84
18:1-33	54
21:17	52
21:17-19	52
22	66
22:7	71
22:11-18	52
22:15-18	44
24	66
24:7	45, 52
24:40	45, 52
28:14	83, 84
28:16	49
30:22-24	66
31:11	52, 53
31:11-13	45
32:24-32	52, 54
37:3	66
37:4	66
37:8	66
37:18	66
37:23	66
37:24	66
37:28	66
39:4	66
39:11-20	66
41:1-45	67
41:38	67
45:1-15	67
45:5	45
45:16-18	67
48:15-16	45, 52, 53
49:10	83, 84, 86, 89
49:24	49, 90

EXODUS

2:11-15	68
2:16-21	68
3:1	45
3:2	52, 53
3:7-10	68
3:14	24
4:19-31	69
12:5	72
13:21	45, 52, 53
14:1	53
14:19	45, 52
14:29-31	49
16:4	70
17:1-6	69
17:5-7	73
17:6	70, 238
22:8-9	38
22:23	172
23:20	45
23:20-23	52, 53
24:9-11	54
32:31-35	69
32:34	45, 52, 53
33:2	52, 53
33:9-23	54
40:38	54

LEVITICUS

1:5	72
1:10	72
1:14	72
4:3	72, 80
4:5	80
4:14	72
4:16	80
4:24	72
5:7	72
6:22	80
6:30	178
8:15	178
12:6	72, 101
12:8	72
14:4-7	72

14:22-23	72	**RUTH**
14:30-31	72	3:12-13 67
15:13-14	72	4:4-6 67
15:29-30	72	
16:5-10	72	**I SAMUEL**
16:15	76	2:35 89
16:20	178	24:6 81
16:24	77	24:10 81
17:11	71	29:4 178
23	75	
23:11	76	**II SAMUEL**
25:27	67	7:12-13 83
25:48-49	67	7:12-16 85, 89
		7:16 121, 137, 209, 216, 283
NUMBERS		14:4-20 53
7:17	72	14:17-20 52
7:87-88	72	19:21 81
15:27	72	19:27 52, 53
17	73	23:1 81
19:17	72	24:14-17 52, 53
20:16	45, 52, 53	24:22 72
21:5-9	73	
22:22-35	52, 53	**I KINGS**
24:17	89	7:10-11 90
27:17	232	19:5-7 52, 53
32:14	172	19:35 52
34:1-2	69	22:17 232
35	77	
		II KINGS
DEUTERONOMY		1:1-16 53
1:30-31	49	1:3 52
4:39	28	1:15 52
7:14	94	13:3 172
18:15-18	88	19:35 45, 53
18:15-19	68	23:26 172
18:18	209	
19:1-13	77	**I CHRONICLES**
21:23	165	3:11-12 103
27:26	165	21:11-30 52, 53
30:1-5	274	21:15-18 45
30:3	274	
33:4-5	69	**II CHRONICLES**
		5:6 72
JOSHUA		7:5 72
5:13-15	54	18:16 49
7:5-9	67	20:17 49
13	67	28:11-13 172
20	77	29:24 178
JUDGES		**EZRA**
2:1-4	52, 53	7:1-5 103
2:1-5	45	
5:23	52	**NEHEMIAH**
6:11-23	45	13:18 172
6:11-24	52, 53	
6:39	172	**JOB**
9:7-15	235	19:25 56, 90
13:3-23	52, 53	21:20 172
13:9-20	45	26:13 47

29:14	69
33:4	47
42:7	172

PSALMS
2	89, 274
2:6	282
2:7	40, 41, 42
2:8-9	210
2:9	283
2:10-12	284
2:12	60
2:45	137
16:10	93, 130, 218
16:10-11	199, 205
22	49, 91, 153, 215, 232
22:1	92
22:6-8	92
22:14-16	92
22:16	202
22:18	92
22:22	93
23	215, 234
23:1	49, 61, 232
23:3	233
23:6	61
24	94
31:1-3	49
31:20-21	49
34:7	52
34:8	60
34:20	92
35:5-6	52
35:11	92
36:7	60
37:39-40	60
41:9	92
46:1	77
68:18	37
72	94, 137, 282
72:7	285
72:8	51
72:9-11	283
72:11	51
80:1	49, 232
80:8	235
82:6	38
89:20-37	283
90:2	23
102:12	37
102:25-27	30, 37
102:27	151
104:30	47
110	89, 137
110:1	38, 224, 225, 226
110:4	68, 89, 209, 210, 241, 242
118:22	90
118:22-24	93
119:137	175

132:9	69
139:7-10	28
142:5	77
145:17	175

PROVERBS
8:22-23	23
15:3	28

ECCLESIASTES
5:6	52
12:11	232

ISAIAH
2:1-4	89, 282
2:4	285
4:1-6	89
4.2	94
4:6	77
5:1-7	235
6:5	37
7:13-14	87
7:14	57, 81, 86, 88, 99, 105
8:14	90
9:6	24, 41, 105, 108
9:6-7	37, 88, 89, 137, 284
11	90
11:1	82
11:1-9	283
11:1-16	282
11:2-3	91
11:3-5	280, 284, 285
11:4	283
11:6-8	280
11:9	284
12:1-6	284
12:3-4	285
25:9-10	279
27:12-13	279
28:14-18	90
28:16	238, 239
29:18	286
30:23-24	285
32:1	283
32:15	285
33:24	286
35:1-2	285
35:1-10	280
35:5-6	91, 286
35:7	285
37:35	91
37:36	52, 53
40:3	37, 88, 108
40:11	49, 232
40:12-13	47
42:1-7	90
44:3	285
44:28	232
49:1-7	90

49:7	89
50:6	92
52:13—53:12	90
52:14	91
52:15	89
53	82, 90, 153
53:5	91
53:5-7	175
53:7	92, 232
53:9	66, 92
53:10	92, 93
54:1-17	250
55:3-4	283
61:1-2	83
61:1-3	286
61:3-7	285
61:3—62:12	279
61:10	69
63:1	94
63:1-6	274, 275
63:9	45, 49, 52, 53
63:11-14	232
64:6	69
65:17-18	288
65:17-25	67
65:18-25	280
65:18—66:24	279
65:20	286
65:20-25	266
66:1	28
66:22	288

JEREMIAH

6:11	172
21:12	172
22:30	85, 104
23:1-40	279
23:5	284
23:5-6	31, 37, 90, 108, 283
23:5-8	282
23:24	28
30:7	275
30:9	283
30:19-20	286
31:1-40	279
31:10	49, 232
31:12	285
31:31-40	282
31:34	284
33:1-26	279
33:14-26	283
33:15-17	283
36:30	104
36:30-31	85

LAMENTATIONS

4:20	81

EZEKIEL

1:1-28	54
8:18	172
15:2	235
15:2-5	237
16:38	172
20:33-38	284
20:34-38	266, 276, 279
23:25	172
24:8	172
24:13	172
25:17	172
33:21—37:28	279
34:5	232
34:8	232
34:11-12	49
34:23	49, 232
34:23-24	283
34:25-27	285
37	282
37:24	49, 232
37:24-25	283
38:1—39:29	280
39:29	285
40:1—46:24	285
40:1—48:25	279
45:4-19	286
45:8-9	283
45:15	178
45:17	178
45:20	178
47:22	286
48:1-27	286

DANIEL

2:34-35	238
2:44-45	274, 279, 280, 282
3:25-28	45
3:28	52, 53
6:22	52, 53
7:9-27	279
7:13-14	137, 274, 282
9:24	178
9:25	86
9:25-26	81
9:27	263
10:1-21	54
12:1	275
12:2	215
12:2-3	279
12:13	215

HOSEA

2:1-23	250
3:5	283
10:1	235
11:1	102
12:4	52, 54
13:14	215

JOEL
2   279
2:21-27   285
2:28-29   285
2:32   108

AMOS
9:11   283
9:13-14   285

MICAH
4:1-8   282, 284
5:2   23, 27, 86, 88, 137
5:2-5   282

ZECHARIAH
1:9   53
1:9-21   52
1:12-13   45
2:3   52
3:1-10   52
4:1-7   52
4:7   90, 238
5:5-10   52
6:4-5   52
6:13   89
9:9   90, 128, 137
10:2   232
12:8   52
12:10   37, 202
12:10-14   274
13:8-9   279
14   282
14:1-3   279
14:3-8   286
14:4   281
14:9   281, 284
14:10   286
14:16-19   77

MALACHI
3:1   37, 88

MATTHEW
1:1   282
1:2-16   83
1:13-15   103
1:16   108
1:20-21   99
1:21   101, 208
1:21-22   57
1:25   43
2   124
2:1-12   101
2:9   102
3:1—4:11   125
3:3   88
3:7   173
3:17   39, 66
4:12—18:35   125

4:12-23   126
4:23—8:1   126
5:17-19   133
8:1-4   126
8:5-34   126
8:17   91
9:1-17   126
9:2-7   109
9:6   29
9:18—11:30   126
9:36   232
11:10   88
12:1-14   126
12:6   37
12:8   37
12:15—15:21   126
12:17-21   91
12:28   144
12:38-40   93
12:38-42   92
13   13, 123, 126, 135, 261
13:24-30   284
13:47-50   284
13:48-50   262
13:57   69
15:22—18:35   126
16:13-16   42
16:18   135, 239
16:21   92, 93, 130, 218
16:22   171
17:9   93
17:22-23   92
17:23   93
18:20   108
19:1—20:34   127
19:28   283
20:18-19   92
20:19   93, 130, 218
20:28   168
21:1-11   282
21:1—26:5   127
21:4-9   90
21:11   69
21:12-13   37
21:37-39   66
21:44   238
22:1-14   274
22:24   40
22:30-31   215
22:44   38, 224
24   274, 276, 279
24:9—25:30   279
24:15-20   275
24:21-30   275
24:27—25:30   275
24:30   222, 276
24:31   263, 264
24:37-38   73
24:40-51   264
25   274, 276, 279

25:1-13	273, 274
25:13	264
25:31-32	109
25:31-46	216, 261, 266, 276, 280, 284
26:3-4	66
26:6-13	127
26:14-15	66
26:16—27:66	127
26:29	234
26:31	92
26:32	93, 130
26:38	111
26:39	120
26:57-68	129
26:61	218
26:63-64	42
26:64	95, 113, 222
27:1-2	129
27:11-14	129
27:15-26	129
27:19	66
27:24	66
27:32-66	154
27:33-34	129
27:35	66, 130
27:35-37	66
27:35-38	130
27:37	282
27:39-44	130
27:45	130
27:46	118
27:46-47	130
27:63	93
27:50	130
28:1	131, 193
28:2-4	130, 192
28:5-7	131, 193
28:8	131, 193
28:9	114, 203
28:9-10	131, 193
28:11-15	131, 193
28:16-20	131, 194
28:18	29, 30, 213
28:18-20	257
28:19	109
28:20	28, 108, 256

MARK

1:1-3	125
1:2	88
1:14—3:6	126
1:14—9:50	125
1:29-34	29
2:7-10	109
3:5	173
3:7—7:23	126
6:34	232
7:24—9:50	126
8:31	92, 93, 153

9:9	93, 130, 218
9:31	92, 93
10:1-52	127
10:32-34	92
10:33-34	93
10:45	168
11:1—14:2	127
11:9-10	90
12:36	38, 224
13	274, 276
13:26	222
13:33-37	264
14:3-9	127
14:10—15:47	127
14:25	234
14:28	130, 218
14:53-65	129
14:58	93
14:62	113, 222
15:1	129
15:1-5	129
15:6-15	129
15:12-13	282
15:21-47	154
15:22-23	129
15:24	130
15:24-28	130
15:29-32	130
15:33	130
15:34-36	130
15:37	130
16:1-11	131, 193
16:8	131, 193
16:9-11	131, 193
16:12-13	131, 194
16:14	131, 194
16:15-18	131, 194
16:19	28, 95, 113, 222, 223, 224
16:19-20	132, 221

LUKE

1	98
1:31-33	89, 121, 137, 209 217, 282
1:32-33	217, 282
1:35	31, 66, 98
1:38	99
1:46-55	99
1:68	170
2	124
2:1-2	100
2:6-7	100
2:7	43
2:9	100
2:10-12	101
2:11	42
2:14	101
2:21	101
2:24	72
2:26	42

2:29-32	101
2:34-35	101
2:35	65
2:38	42, 170
2:52	110
3:1—4:13	125
3:4	37
3:7	173
3:23-28	103
3:23-38	83
3:36	103
4:14-18	144
4:14—6:11	126
4:14—9:50	125
4:16-30	125
4:18	144
4:18-19	83
6:12—9:17	126
7:12	44
7:27	88
8:25	29
8:42	44
9:18-50	126
9:22	92, 93, 153
9:44	92
9:51	221
9:51—19:28	127
10:1-24	127
10:22	109
15:3-7	233
17:26-27	73
17:33	166
18:13	171, 174
18:31-33	92
18:33	93
19:12-27	283
19:14	282
19:29—23:56	127
19:37-38	90
20:34-36	264
20:42-43	224
20:43	38
21	274, 276
21:23	173
21:27	95, 222
21:28	169, 170
21:36	264
22:18	234
22:32	67, 242
22:37	91
22:66-71	129
22:69	224
22:69-70	113
23:1-7	129
23:8-12	129
23:18-25	129
23:26-56	154
23:33	129
23:33-38	130
23:39-43	130

23:43-44	130
23:46	130
24:1-10	131, 193
24:13-35	131, 194, 202
24:15	204
24:21	167
24:30-31	113
24:31	203
24:34	131, 194
24:36	204
24:36-43	131, 194
24:39-40	203
24:41-43	203
24:44-53	132, 194
24:49	257
24:49-53	132
24:50-53	113, 221
24:51	95, 221, 222, 223

JOHN

1:1	23, 24
1:1-2	108
1:1-3	28
1:1-14	112
1:3	8, 47, 109
1:4	227, 256
1:4-18	136
1:10	109
1:11	68
1:14	44
1:15	26
1:17	31, 67
1:18	26, 44, 46, 121
1:19—2:12	125
1:21	88
1:29	71, 156, 157, 175, 232
1:30	26
1:41	81
1:48	28, 142
1:49	42, 69, 137
2:13-25	125
2:13—4:42	125
2:19	130, 218
2:19-21	93
2:24	142
2:24-25	108
2:25	28
3:1	250
3:1—4:42	125
3:13	26, 28, 108
3:14	250
3:14-16	73
3:16	26, 42, 44, 66
3:16-17	41
3:17	26
3:18	42, 188
3:20	250
3:31	26
3:35	66, 109
3:35-36	42

Reference	Page
3:36	173
4:10-11	231
4:13-14	238
4:14-15	231
4:25	81
4:25-26	208
4:29	88
4:43—8:59	125
5:19-29	109
5:22	216
5:22-23	109
5:25-27	118
5:27	30
5:28-29	216
5:36	91
5:46	88
6:1-71	126
6:14	88
6:33	26
6:38	26
6:42	26
6:50-51	26
6:54	227
6:58	26
6:62	26, 117, 221, 223
6:64	29
7:1-52	126
7:1—8:59	126
7:3-5	194
7:5	131
7:29	26
7:33	221, 223
7:37-39	238
7:38	231
7:53—8:59	126
8:12	22
8:23	26
8:28	88
8:42	26
8:46	150
8:58	22, 24, 27, 117
9:1—12:11	127
9:39	26
10	232
10:3-4	233
10:4	233
10:10	234, 256
10:11	67
10:14	215, 233
10:16	233
10:17-18	205, 208
10:18	29, 67
10:27	233
10:28	227
10:32-36	38
11:25	209, 212, 256
11:25-27	208
11:27	42
12:12—19:42	127
12:24-25	212
12:27	208
12:29	69
12:32-33	92
12:38	91
12:41	37
13-16	128
13:1	29
13:11	29
13:15	63
13:21	111
13:33-36	267
14	135
14:1	109
14:1-3	95, 267, 269, 273, 276
14:2	251
14:2-3	215
14:6	31, 257
14:12	221, 223
14:13-14	250
14:16-17	257
14:18	28, 256
14:20	28, 256
14:23	28, 255, 256
14:24	88
14:26	211, 257
14:28	221, 223
15	135, 235
15:2-3	236
15:4	236
15:4-5	256
15:6	236
15:8	236
15:10	237
15:11	237
15:24-25	66
15:26	211, 257
16	135
16:5	221, 223
16:7	211
16:7-11	233
16:7-15	257
16:10	221, 223
16:12-14	209
16:12-15	136
16:16-17	221
16:28	221, 223
16:30	29, 142
17	135
17:2	29, 109, 227
17:5	26, 31, 143
17:23	256
17:24	26
17:26	256
18:4	29
18:6	143
18:12-24	128
18:28-38	129
18:29—19:16	129
18:37	137
19:12	137

19:15	137
19:16-42	154
19:17	129
19:18-24	130
19:26-28	130
19:28	29, 117
19:30	130
20:1-2	131, 193
20:2-10	131, 193
20:11-17	131, 193
20:16	202, 203
20:17	42, 113, 203, 220
20:18	131, 193
20:19	204
20:19-23	131, 194
20:20	203
20:22	113, 203
20:25	63
20:25-29	202
20:26-29	131, 194
20:27-28	113
20:28	108
21:1-23	131, 194
21:15-17	232
21:17	29, 108
21:25	8

ACTS
1	220, 221
1:1-11	113
1:3-9	194
1:5	228
1:6-12	221
1:8	214, 257
1:8-11	132
1:9	222
1:9-12	221
1:10-11	222
1:11	95, 223, 274, 276
1:14	131, 194
1:24	29
2	198
2:21	108
2:24-32	205
2:25-31	93, 217
2:27	218
2:33-36	133, 223
2:34-35	38
2:36	30, 37, 207
2:38	257
2:47	227, 228
3:13	91
3:20-23	88
3:21	223
3:22-23	69
3:26	91
4:11	90, 228
4:27	91
4:30	91
7:18	40

7:23-28	68
7:25	68
7:30-35	45, 52
7:43	63
7:55-56	132, 195, 223
7:56	113, 204
8:32	72, 91
9:3-6	132, 195, 204, 223
9:20	42
9:26-30	132, 195
9:37	231
10:40	207
10:42	109, 216
11:15-16	228
13:23	100
13:30	205
13:32-33	40
13:33	42
13:34	40
13:34-37	93
15:14	67, 69
15:17	69
16:33	231
17:27	28
17:31	109
18:5-6	68
20:7	199
20:13-14	222
20:24	132, 195
20:28	163, 166
20:30	40
22:6-8	223
22:6-11	132, 195
22:17-21	132, 195
23:11	132, 195
26:13-15	223
26:13-18	132, 195
26:17	132, 195
26:23	218
27:40	222

ROMANS
1:2-4	58
1:2-5	112
1:3	100
1:4	39
2:5	173
2:14	114
3:5	173
3:9	175
3:22	69
3:23	175
3:24-25	169
3:24-26	67
3:25	77, 171, 175
3:25-26	173, 175, 245
4	59
4:14	139
4:15	173
4:25	211

5:6	154
5:6-10	184
5:6-11	183
5:9	173
5:10	209
5:10-11	179
5:11	154, 184
5:11-21	181
5:12	175
5:12-21	65, 227
5:14	63, 64
6:4	205
7	149
7:19-20	150
7:24	150
8:2-3	254
8:2-4	67
8:11	205
8:21-22	280
8:22	189
8:23	169, 170
8:26-27	247
8:28-30	34
8:29	43
8:33-34	77
8:34	209, 223, 224, 257
9:5	108, 112
9:22	173
9:32-33	238
9:33	90
10:9	209, 211
10:13	91
11:1-27	67
11:11	90
11:11-12	67
11:15	179
11:7	236
11:24-26	69
11:26	274, 277, 279
12:1	248
12:3-8	231
14:10	216
14:10-12	270
15:6	38
15:13	257
15:21	91
16:25-26	256

I CORINTHIANS

1:7-8	262
1:17	139
1:23	238
1:30	29, 37, 169, 170
3:11-15	238, 239, 271
3:12-15	95
5:7	75
6:3	216
6:15	227
6:19-20	164
6:20	164

7:11	179
7:23	164
8:6	47
9:15	139
9:16-27	95
9:24-27	272
10:4	73, 238
10:11	63
11:3	228, 229
12:3	30
12:12-14	227
12:13	183, 189
12:27-28	231
15:3	154, 175
15:3-4	245
15:4-8	132
15:5-7	194
15:6-7	131
15:12	216
15:12-50	202
15:17	191
15:19	109
15:20	76
15:20-23	214
15:22	216, 227
15:23	76
15:24	290
15:24-28	95, 217, 226
15:25	137
15:25-28	113
15:26	217
15:45	212, 226, 227
15:45-47	65
15:47	226
15:51	264
15:51-52	95
15:51-53	215
15:51-58	268
15:52	269
16:2	199, 250

II CORINTHIANS

3:17	254
5	177
5:8-10	95
5:8-11	270
5:10	266
5:10-11	216
5:14-15	187
5:15	154
5:17	226
5:17-21	181, 184
5:18-20	179
5:19	183
5:19-21	182
5:21	133, 157, 183
8:2	250
8:9	72
9:3	139
9:6-8	250

9:13	250
11:2	68, 216, 250, 273
13:13	109

Galatians

1:4	175
1:12	195
1:12-17	132
1:17	195
1:18	195
1:19	131, 194
2:15	114
2:20	256
3:10	165
3:13	67, 157, 165, 166, 175
3:14	166
3:23-25	67, 133
4:4	41, 57, 100, 105, 166
4:5	133, 165
4:6	255
4:8	114
4:22-31	63
4:28	65
4:29	65
5:17	150
6:15	226

Ephesians

1:3	38
1:3-5	26
1:4	25
1:4-11	34
1:7	169, 170
1:11	34
1:14	169, 170
1:17-23	213
1:18-20	214
1:19-20	205
1:20	224
1:20-22	223
1:20-23	212, 215, 224
1:21-22	226
1:22	109, 228
1:22-23	229
2:1	188
2:1-10	227
2:3	114, 173, 188
2:5-6	214
2:14	76
2:15-16	185
2:16	179, 227
2:20	90, 238, 239
2:21	240
3:11	34
4:4-5	227
4:6	255
4:7-16	231
4:8	213
4:8-10	37, 223
4:10	213

4:11-16	232
4:16	227
4:30	169, 170, 257
5:2	175
5:5	38
5:6	173
5:16	165
5:20	38
5:23	228
5:23-24	229
5:23-33	251
5:25	274
5:25-27	230, 250
5:25-32	67, 68
5:26	231, 273, 274
5:26-27	252
5:27	29, 205, 266, 274
5:29	229
5:30-32	227, 228
6:4	229
6:18	250

Philippians

1:19	254
2	140, 142, 144
2:5-11	138
2:6	108, 138
2:6-7	100
2:6-8	139
2:6-11	112, 223
2:7	66, 139
2:8	140
2:8-11	209
2:9	41, 224
2:9-10	30
2:9-11	51
2:10	113
3:10-12	264
3:17	63
3:20	223
3:20-21	214
3:21	29, 108, 109, 205, 269
4:6-7	250
4:13	229, 230, 257
4:19	250

Colossians

1:14	169, 170
1:15	43
1:15-17	47
1:16	48, 50, 109
1:16-17	24, 27, 28
1:17	48, 50, 109
1:18	30, 43, 229
1:20	189
1:20-21	179
1:20-22	185
1:24	227
1:26-27	256
1:27	257

2:9   27, 30, 108
2:10   228
2:19   227, 228, 229, 230
3:1   224
3:4   256
3:6   173
3:13   109
4:5   165

I THESSALONIANS
1:9-10   266
1:10   173, 223
2:7   229
2:16   173
3:13   274, 277
4:13-18   95, 258
4:14-17   215, 268
4:16   223
4:17   222
4:18   266
5   268
5:1-4   274, 277
5:6   264, 266
5:9   173, 266
5:17   250

II THESSALONIANS
1:7-9   173
1:7—2:12   274, 277
2:1-12   262
2:7   266
2:13   34
3:9   63

I TIMOTHY
1:15   100
2:1   247
2:5   75, 113, 241
2:6   168
3:13   166, 167
3:16   108, 112, 223
4:5   247
4:12   63
6:15   137

II TIMOTHY
1:9   34
1:12   29
2:12   283
4:1   109, 216
4:8   264
4:18   70

TITUS
2:7   63
2:13   108, 264, 266
2:14   167
3:5   231

HEBREWS
1:2   42, 109
1:3   40, 50, 109, 137, 223, 245
1:3-13   224
1:4-13   226
1:5   42
1:5-14   26
1:6   43, 109
1:8   42
1:10   109
1:10-12   30, 37, 108, 109
1:12   151
1:13   38, 223
2:7   223
2:8   224
2:11   230
2:12   93
2:14   111, 112
2:14-15   67
2:17   171, 174
3:1-6   137
3:6   262
3:14   262
4:11   63
4:14   95, 132, 223
4:15   120, 146, 149, 244
5:1   75, 241
5:1-10   137
5:4   64
5:4-10   75, 241
5:5   42
5:5-6   64
5:6   68, 89, 137
5:7   209, 247
5:7-8   244
5:8   120
5:10   68, 137
6:11   262
6:20   68, 223
7:1—8:6   137
7:3   241
7:17   68
7:18-19   67
7:20-21   242
7:21   68
7:23-26   242
7:23-28   137
7:24   74, 210, 243
7:25   29, 69, 75, 137, 210, 213, 241, 247
7:26   223
7:27   64, 75, 243, 245
8:1   223, 224
8:1-5   64, 243
8:1-6   75
8:3   245
8:5   63
8:6   64, 243
8:12   171
9:4   73

9:5   171, 173
9:6-20   220
9:7   245
9:7-8   77
9:11-28   137
9:12   170, 220, 245
9:12-14   230
9:15   169
9:22   175
9:23   63
9:23-28   77
9:24   95, 223
9:24-28   264
9:25   245
9:26   241
9:28   157, 175
10:4   175
10:5-18   137
10:10-14   245
10:12   223, 224
10:13   38, 223, 226
10:19   245
10:19-22   250
10:22   231
11:4   64
11:7   73
11:10-16   288
11:11   60
11:17   44, 66
11:26   60
11:28   43
11:35   169, 170
12:2   223, 224
12:22-24   289
12:23   43
12:29   173
13:8   29, 106, 108, 141, 151
13:11-13   77
13:12   230, 245
13:15   248, 249
13:16   248, 249
13:20   49, 215, 233, 245
16:18-19   77

JAMES
1:13   147, 148
2:5   34
2:17   59
3:12   234
5:10   63

I PETER
1:1-2   34
1:10-11   94
1:11   254
1:15-19   75
1:18   67, 167, 168
1:18-19   67, 175
1:18-20   26
1:19   71

2:4-5   212
2:4-8   239
2:5   240, 248, 249
2:6-8   90, 238
2:7   228
2:9   212, 249
2:21-23   72
2:22-24   91
2:24   157, 175
2:25   215
3:20   73
3:22   28, 30, 95, 132, 223, 224,
                                226
5:1-4   232
5:3   63
5:4   49, 215, 233

II PETER
1:1   38
1:4   114
2:1   164, 165
2:1—3:17   274, 277
2:4   216
2:5   70
2:5-9   73
2:7   70
2:9   70
3:10   278

I JOHN
1:1-3   112
1:5—2:2   248
1:7   246
1:9   173
2:1   67, 213, 223
2:1-2   69
2:2   171, 173, 182, 187, 213
2:19   205
2:23   42
3:1-3   266
3:2   206, 257, 269
3:5   150
3:24   256
4:2-3   111
4:9   44
4:10   171
5:9-12   42
5:12   256
5:16   235
5:20   108

II JOHN
9   255

JUDE
6   216
14-15   274, 278
24   29
25   29

REVELATION

1:5	43, 137, 175, 231
1:6	248
1:7	37, 222, 223, 274, 278
1:8	108
1:11	25, 27
1:12-16	54
1:12-18	31, 117
1:12-20	132, 195, 204
1:13	113
1:13-18	223
2	272
2:23	108
2:26	262
3	272
3:3	264
3:10	50, 266
3:11	95
5	232
5:5-12	223
5:9	154, 164
5:10	248
5:12-21	228
6	232
6:9-17	223
6:16	173
6:17	264, 266
7:9-17	223
7:17	231
11	264
11:18	173
12:1-2	105
12:1-6	264
14:1-5	223
14:3-4	164, 165
14:10	173
14:14	113
14:19	173
15:1	173
15:7	173
16:1	173
16:19	173
17:14	137
19	281
19:6-8	228, 250
19:7	216, 252
19:7-9	253, 273
19:8	69, 252
19:11-16	223
19:11-21	274, 278
19:15	173, 280, 283
19:16	30, 137, 282
19:17-21	279
19:20	277
20	278, 281, 282
20:1-3	280
20:4	216, 279
20:4-6	261, 263, 283
20:6	248
20:7-10	281, 286
20:11-15	287
20:12-15	216
21:1-8	287
21:2	288
21:5	109
21:6	231
21:9	288, 289
21:9—22:5	288
22:1	231
22:13	108
22:17	231

Moody Press, a ministry of the Moody Bible Institute, is
designed for education, evangelization and edification.
If we may assist you in knowing more about Christ and
the Christian life, please write us without obligation to:
Moody Press, c/o MLM, Chicago, Illinois 60610.